User-Driven Applications for Research and Science

Building Programs for Fields with Open Scenarios and Unpredictable User Actions

Sergey Andreyev

Apress®

User-Driven Applications for Research and Science: Building Programs for Fields with Open Scenarios and Unpredictable User Actions

Sergey Andreyev
Moscow, Russia

ISBN-13 (pbk): 978-1-4842-6487-4
https://doi.org/10.1007/978-1-4842-6488-1

ISBN-13 (electronic): 978-1-4842-6488-1

Managing Director, Apress Media LLC: Welmoed Spahr
Acquisitions Editor: Joan Murray
Development Editor: Laura Berendson
Coordinating Editor: Jill Balzano

Cover image designed by Freepik (www.freepik.com)

Distributed to the book trade worldwide by Springer Science+Business Media LLC, 1 New York Plaza, Suite 4600, New York, NY 10004. Phone 1-800-SPRINGER, fax (201) 348-4505, e-mail orders-ny@springer-sbm.com, or visit www.springeronline.com. Apress Media, LLC is a California LLC and the sole member (owner) is Springer Science + Business Media Finance Inc (SSBM Finance Inc). SSBM Finance Inc is a **Delaware** corporation.

For information on translations, please e-mail booktranslations@springernature.com; for reprint, paperback, or audio rights, please e-mail bookpermissions@springernature.com.

Apress titles may be purchased in bulk for academic, corporate, or promotional use. eBook versions and licenses are also available for most titles. For more information, reference our Print and eBook Bulk Sales web page at www.apress.com/bulk-sales.

Any source code or other supplementary material referenced by the author in this book is available to readers on GitHub via the book's product page, located at www.apress.com/9781484264874. For more detailed information, please visit www.apress.com/source-code.

Printed on acid-free paper

To my parents

Table of Contents

About the Author

Sergey Andreyev worked at the Computer Center of the Russian Academy of Sciences. He started on the systems for applied optimization, and then he found that he was fascinated by sonogram images. He received a PhD for the design of new algorithms and programming systems for speech analysis. He likes to implement new ideas in new areas, and he has designed complicated systems for telecommunications, thermodynamics, and analysis of big electricity networks. He has also worked on applications for foreign language studies and for organizing photo archives. Photography is one of his hobbies.

About the Technical Reviewer

Carsten Thomsen is a back-end developer primarily but works with smaller front-end bits as well. He has authored and reviewed a number of books and created numerous Microsoft Learning courses, all to do with software development. He works as a freelancer/contractor in various countries in Europe, using Azure, Visual Studio, Azure DevOps, and GitHub. He is an exceptional troubleshooter and asks the right questions, including the less logical ones. He enjoys working on architecture, research, analysis, development, testing, and bug fixing. Carsten is a good communicator with great mentoring and team-lead skills, as well as excellent skills researching and presenting new material.

Preface

For decades, the world of applications has been based on a simple rule: programmers know better than anyone else what users need. If we follow this trajectory, when developers provide users with new programs or updated versions of existing programs, users have to work with whatever they are given. As a result, millions of users struggle with features they don't need and implement their own workarounds to jump hurdles and cobble in order to make the programs meet their needs. How did it come to be that developers have to keep an iron grip on their products? History shows that the removal of this obstacle benefits both sides.

The golden age of the automobile started when manufacturers like Ford began to provide customers with cars they could drive wherever and whenever they wanted. Auto makers provided an instrument, but ultimately it was up to the customer to decide when and how to use the instrument. It works perfectly this way, even to this day.

Science and engineering (both research and practice) received a huge boost when Newton and Leibniz independently invented calculus. The creators didn't instruct scientists on how the new method had to be used in order to solve a problem. Each scientist or engineer had to decide for himself or herself whether it was worth investing time to acquire a deep understand of calculus. Scientists had to think about ways to apply this new math instrument to their particular research work. And it has worked this way for 300 years.

Decades ago, one of my colleagues perfectly formulated a motto of big programming companies: "Users have to deal with what they are given." The time of trade beads in the land of programs is over. Users have become much more exacting and demand products that help them solve their particular tasks.

Users know their areas of expertise much better than any developer. Nowhere is this more apparent than in areas of science and engineering; in these areas, users suffer more than anywhere else from the "one size fits all" programs. Users must be granted complete control over the programs in order to make them useful. This book explains the design of such programs and demonstrates the work of programs of the new type–user-driven applications.

Fifty years ago, a software crisis happened when big efficient programs could not be developed within the required time. The number of programs at that time was relatively small; the biggest and the most important of them were used in crucial sectors of industry and defense, so the disaster with any such program was very loud. Edsger Dijkstra played the pivotal role in tackling the problem[1]. That crisis was purely technical, and the solution was in applying the new programming technique. Since then, structured programming and new languages made it possible to write programs of any level of complexity nearly error free. Decades ago, the most important part of any program was some algorithm of calculations around which everything else was constructed while interface played no role at all. At that time, the numbers of developers and users were small and comparable. If there were questions about the results of a program, it meant there were questions about the algorithm that was used. Those questions were discussed between the program developers and the users. As a result of the discussion, after some time, users got the new version. Developers had absolute control over programs, and such control was never questioned.

The introduction of personal computers had a dramatic impact on the world of computing and programs. No longer was it unusual for the number of developers and users for a given application to differ by three or four (occasionally, five or six) orders of magnitude. A program of any complexity was supposed to work without problems; error-free work aligned with the objectives of an application was expected and not even discussed. Interface, not calculations, became the crucial part of a program. Problems with error-free programs emerged from an absolutely unexpected side. With a huge number of users, it was unrealistic to expect that all of them would be satisfied with a single interface design, even an excellent one. More likely, there would be a wide range of requests. In an attempt to answer users' demands, developers turned to adaptive interface. It was declared as a way to adapt a program to users' requirements; each user had to adapt the task to whatever was provided by developer. More than 30 years of using the innumerable variants of adaptive interface neither solved nor softened the problem. Millions of people around the world struggle with programs in an attempt to get the programs to do what they want them to do. As a rule, users lose but continue to fight. With the number of people affected by this problem, it is not so much a technical issue, but a philosophical crisis, and such a crisis cannot be solved by technical adjustments.

---

[1]Dijkstra, Edsger W. *A Case against the GO TO Statement,* published as *Go-to statement considered harmful* in Communications of ACM 11, 1968, 3: 147-148

The crisis is rooted in the developers' control over applications and can only be solved by giving full control of applications over to users. Developers are still responsible for the default view and error-free work of a program, but the user must be allowed to do whatever is needed. The idea of giving full control of our applications might sound crazy to the majority of developers, but consider that we as developers are also users of many different programs. Start using a new tool or platform and before long you will let go of older programs in which others dictate your use. With the full control of applications in your hands, everything now depends only on your abilities.

What has to change in order to give control of applications to users? There is a single necessary and sufficient condition: each and every screen object must become movable and resizable by users. If a user can easily perform these operations over any object at any moment, then the full control of the application is automatically passed on to the user. Thus, we need an easy-to-use algorithm of movability which can be applied to objects of arbitrary shape and complexity. Globally, there are unlimited screen objects being produced by skilled and imaginative developers. Users will not read huge manuals to begin using a new program, so the algorithm of movability must provide an easy way of dealing with an arbitrary object. At the same time, this algorithm must be easy to implement, otherwise it will be not useful.

This book describes an algorithm of total movability and demonstrates its implementation in many different situations—from the simplest examples to real-world and highly sophisticated applications. The proposed algorithm is only an instrument to develop user-driven applications. If, instead of this algorithm, you decide to use your own, you will arrive at exactly the same results. Programs can be based on any algorithm of movability, but all will obey the same rules of user-driven applications.

Sergey Andreyev
November 2020

Introduction

We live among solid objects, and each of them is used for one or another purpose. Clothes, cars, and houses have sizes, and we use all these things considering their sizes. Some clothes (for example, sweaters) possess a bit of elasticity, and it is easy enough to use such things for years, while the body inside might change throughout this period. Houses and their parts are usually fixed, but even they have movable parts, which can be useful (sliding panels, movable partitions, changeable tables).

Half a century ago, computers played the role of big and powerful calculators, so nearly everything in the computer programs was fixed. With the introduction of the first programming languages, the classical idea of math functions with parameters was transformed into programs and made computers much more useful. Yet, there was no interface in the modern understanding; all the flexibility was limited to entering different input numbers and receiving the results calculated by the fixed program code.

- Computers were big and costly, so they could be used only by corporations, universities, or state agencies. Thus, the number of computers was small.

- Computers were used to solve a limited number of tasks that were exclusively engineering and scientific or were required by country defense.

- The core of each program was some math instrument either well known for years or designed to solve a particular task. The number of people who understood each math problem was limited.

- The math equations that helped to solve the problem had to be translated into machine code or a bit later into the sentences of computer languages; at that time, FORTRAN was the most popular language. The number of people who could write programs was also limited. Because it is much harder to become a good mathematician than to learn a programming language, a significant number of those who worked with equations and wanted to get results from computers also turned into programmers.

Even when those who worked with equations and waited for the results of calculations (those were the first users) and those who turned those equations into code (first programmers) were different people, the numbers of those people were comparable and small, so all problems were usually discussed and solved through a personal conversation. This chain—equations, coding, discussion of results, and changes in equations and code—was organized as an endless loop. The program input and output were in numbers; coding of equations was the main part of the whole process, and there was no interface at all in its modern meaning. The crucial part of the process was the coding, so programmers had control over the whole process.

Things began to change quickly after the introduction of personal computers and especially after they switched into the graphical mode. (At the beginning they worked in text mode, but that was not for long, and few people remember it now.) Now the world of computers and programs differs in nearly every aspect from the one described several lines earlier.

- Computers became personal; they are cheap and plenty.

- Computers are used to solve a vast variety of tasks. Engineering and scientific programs are still used, and they are exceptionally important, but they are far outnumbered by other applications. What is more important is the number of users for engineering and scientific programs. This number is insignificant in comparison with the users of other applications, so the vector of programming development is set by other more numerous applications.

- Each program is based on the ideas that are coded, but those hidden algorithms and equations stopped being the most important part. Now the main thing is the interface.

- A huge number of different programs require a huge number of programmers who differ a lot by the level of professionalism, skills, and results.

Only one thing is still the same—programmers' control over the results of their work. All mentioned changes were forced by achievements in technology and the science of programming, while the control over applications is based more on philosophy and psychology. You can read about the new ideas, and they may sound attractive, but if they are against your practice of many years, then it is difficult to accept them. I'll write about this psychological aspect of new ideas a couple of pages ahead.

The most useful and popular programs are developed by few people for thousands or millions of users. It became obvious decades ago that when there is such a developers-to-user ratio, the fixed interface causes the disappointment of many users, so numerous solutions were proposed throughout the last 30+ years; the whole area of such ideas is known as *adaptive interface*. Some of these solutions were interesting and perfectly implemented, but all of them were purely technical and missed the main thing: the problem is philosophical, and it is impossible to solve such types of problems simply by more accurate tuning of the currently used instrument. Problems of such type require more global changes.

Many years ago, I developed complex systems for my own research work in the area of speech analysis. Those programs were also used by other researchers and practitioners in the area of voice recognition. Later I used the developed programming technique to design applications for specialists in thermodynamics, telecommunication, and analysis of big electricity networks. Engineering and scientific programs even from faraway areas have a lot of common features, so the best solutions from one area can be easily used in others. I worked in different areas, I was familiar with the best programs for all those areas, and I began to feel more and more that there was stagnation in the development of the best applications. Stagnation was not in one or another particular area, but there was stagnation in the whole area of engineering and scientific programs, so there had to be the same cause of stagnation for the whole wide area of important programs.

Finally, I got to the core of the problem and knew what had to be done. It took me some time to think out an algorithm and to produce the first results; this happened in 2006. Because my main interest was in the area of engineering and scientific programs, my first experiments on movability of the screen objects were also in this area. I want to underscore from the beginning that movability is not the change of the object location according to some coded scenario. Movability means that a user can grab any screen object at any moment and do with it whatever he wants. After the first movable/resizable plotting areas were developed, further improvements succeeded quickly as it turned out that *user-driven applications* contain strict, and I would say iron, logic. Shortly thereafter I formulated several simple rules of new applications.

> *Rule 1*: All elements are movable.

> *Rule 2*: All parameters of visibility must be easily controlled by users.

Rule 3: Users' commands on moving and resizing of objects or on changing the parameters of visualization must be implemented exactly as they are; no additions or expanded interpretation by the developer are allowed.

Rule 4: All parameters must be saved and restored.

Rule 5: The previously mentioned rules must be implemented at all levels beginning from the main form of an application and up to its furthest corners.

These rules were formulated when I worked mostly on different scientific programs. Since then I developed user-driven applications for other absolutely different areas, but these rules work in all of them without any change at all. The rules are absolutely independent of the area in which they are applied, and these rules do not depend on the underlying programming technique. If you want, you can develop your own algorithm of movability and use it in your programs. Regardless of the underlying algorithm, an attempt to design anything with movable elements will require the implementation of the same rules and will produce user-driven applications.

Movability does not change a view of a program. The purpose of any particular program is the same regardless of movability of its elements. If the older (unmovable) version of any application has a good view, then exactly the same view can be used as a default one for an analogous user-driven application.[2] Movability changes the code but much more important is that it changes the way we deal with applications. Decades ago, at the time of the big computers, the programs were never given to users. Users formulated the task and were given the results, but the whole process of design and even getting the results from the computer was done by developer. Later personal computers turned out to be a profitable product, and in parallel the programs were also turned into products. Though programs are sold as other products, users have limited control over them. Users have exactly that level of control over programs that developers agree

---

[2]Only throughout years of my work with user-driven applications did the same amazing thing happen again and again. I took a good-looking program and turned this program into a user-driven one. The initial view was the same that I liked. With all the involved elements now movable and resizable, I start to change the view. At first these are minor changes such as some proportions or colors or use of different fonts, but somewhere along the way I have an idea of cardinal change, and the result is much better than the original one. Without total movability, I would never think about such a change of the view that, at the beginning, I considered to be perfect.

to give them. For programs that are used on PCs this level is miserable. This remnant of the old times is based on two related things: on the old philosophy of the developer–user relation and on the lack of instrument (algorithm) that would allow to change this philosophy.

User-driven applications are not ruled by developers but by users! This means that users are not restricted by the developers' ideas of what can be or cannot be done. Users can do whatever they want with all the elements. Developers have to provide a good-looking default view (as good as they can) and prevent a program from crashes regardless of whatever users are doing with the program elements.

I understand that after decades of developers' absolute ruling over the programs on PCs, my idea of giving full control to users sounds a bit strange (to say the least), but look at the main ideas under which the programs on phones and smartphones work now. Only three simple actions (click, move, and squeeze) are available, but there are no limitations on these actions. Whatever you get on the screen depends only on your skills and ability to use these commands.

Programs on our computers can do a lot of amazing things, but the commands are mostly the same: press, move, squeeze, and maybe reconfigure. The screen objects can be different in size and shape; some objects require accurate work with their parts, so I use mouse as an element of control. The keyboard is never used to control my programs except when a user needs to type something.

I want to emphasize from the beginning that the proposed change of the developer–user relation doesn't change the task of any application. Neither has it changed the default view of an application if this default view is good. If user doesn't like the proposed view but likes the application, then the user quickly changes the view to whatever is preferred and continues to use this application. What is more important: the view of a program or the needed and received results? To demonstrate that the switch to user control doesn't destroy the application, I took one very well-known program—Calculator from the Windows system—and made its exact copy but working under full user control. You are going to estimate the difference yourself because this program is included as one of the examples in the book.

Suppose that you work with some database. You need to get data and maybe change it. From time to time everyone has to deal with some data, so this task is familiar to everyone. You look at the data through some program; this program is developed by the people who thought a lot about the best way to search for the needed data, to demonstrate it, and to change. The program shows the data through some fields on the screen. These fields are positioned on the screen in such a way that, from a developer's point of view, would be the best. Maybe there are some variants to change this view, but those variants are still the views that developers consider as being good for users. The interface with all its variants is entirely controlled by developers.

Working with the data in the way you prefer is not a purely theoretical example. I designed such a program called Personal Data years ago, and you will find it among the examples in this book. This example demonstrates the interface adaptation not only to a variety of tasks, but also, which is more important, to an unlimited variety of unpredictable tasks. From my point of view, it is an interesting but not the most impressive example. User-driven applications give users much more, especially in such applications where the outcome is unpredictable or the number of possible variants is infinitive. Such programs are of high demand in the areas where users, as a rule, are much better specialists in their particular area than the developers of applications they have to work with. This statement is correct for all branches of science and engineering, so researchers from all areas can get the highest benefits if their old-type programs are turned into user-driven.

This is not the first book about my ideas, and there is some inheritance between my previously written books and this one. The first version of my main book, *World of Movable Objects* [2], was written in 2010; throughout the following years it was changed many times. Each new version included new results and got new examples, so the volume was constantly growing; the last version has nearly 1,000 pages and contains 200 examples from many different areas. In 2016 the much smaller book *Elements of Total Movability* was written. While working on this book, I understood that the main book had to be rewritten again, but I also understood that it would require too much effort. Instead, I decided to write a new book, the one you are reading now. I use some examples from both mentioned books, but nearly all of them have been changed. In 2019 I wrote the book *Illustration for Geometric Optics* [3]. Several examples from that book are useful in the current one, so they appear closer to the end.

User-driven applications cannot be developed without total movability of all the screen elements. The main purpose of this book is to explain the work of new applications, but this is impossible without the explanation of movability for the most often used elementary objects, so the book starts with the discussion of the construction elements for new design, while real applications are discussed in the second half of the book.

Chapter 1: Foundation

This chapter contains the main definitions and makes you acquainted with the basic classes that are used to implement movability of the screen elements.

Chapter 2: Simple Objects

This chapter explains the movability for graphical objects of the most popular shapes: line, rectangle, regular and arbitrary polygon, circle, ring, etc.

Chapter 3: Complex Objects

This chapter explains the movability of objects that consist of different elements involved in synchronous, related, and individual movements.

Chapter 4: Groups

This chapter demonstrates the union of the screen elements when they are used together for some subtask. Groups can be based on different principles, and this increases their variety. Such variety is demonstrated in my book [2] where the chapter about groups is nearly the biggest one. In the current book, only my favorite class of groups is discussed, so this is the shortest chapter of the book.

Chapter 5: Graphical Analogs of Ordinary Controls

This chapter demonstrates the substitution of popular ordinary controls with graphical elements that have the same functionality but that eliminate the ruling of operating system over an important group of screen objects.

Chapter 6: Elements of Data Visualization

Data can be visualized in many different ways, and an application designer cannot predict the best view of a program for each particular user. Understanding of the data and its analysis highly depend on the possibilities of the data visualization, which is available to the users. Objects of data visualization were discussed in my book [2], while in the current book only variants of the bar charts and pie charts are demonstrated.

Chapter 7: Examples

When all the screen elements are movable, then programs can be developed as user-driven applications, so the emphasis in the discussion has now switched from the details of movability algorithm to the overall design. There are only a few examples in this chapter, and they are purposely selected to differ as much as possible from each other.

Calculator is a version of a well-known program.

Family Tree got high interest from all round the world because it is one of those tasks in which a developer cannot predict all possible users' requirements. It is just a task in which a user must be provided not with a set of choices but with an instrument to do whatever he needs.

Function Viewer is another example of the task with unlimited and unpredictable users' requests. This example demonstrates that an application can be designed not as a set of predetermined variants but as an instrument for solving sophisticated tasks. *Function Viewer* is not a real scientific application, but it is as close to this type as possible for a demonstration example, which has to be understandable by any reader.

Several examples on the theme of geometric optics demonstrate that user-driven applications allow its users to deal with the situations that program developers could not predict. These programs are not used as specialized scientific calculators but rather like instruments of research and analysis of the unknown.

Appendix A: Ordinary Controls

I try to minimize the use of ordinary controls in the programs. When years ago I only started my work on movability of the screen objects, it was impossible to imagine the design of sophisticated programs without using controls at all. It is impossible to design programs on a mix of movable and unmovable objects (even a single unmovable element makes a total mess), so the movability of controls was an important part of the developed algorithm.

Later I substituted the most popular controls with graphical analogs, and now ordinary controls are rare elements in my programs. Examples in this part demonstrate the movability of solitary controls, of controls with different types of comments, and of special groups with inner elements based on controls.

Usually the first opened form of any program illustrates the general idea of this application by showing the element(s) to be used. It is not a problem to do when an application deals with one or another specific object. This book will demonstrate many different objects; an attempt to show them all in one form would make it too crowded, so I picked only some of them.

When you start the program accompanying this book and see these objects for the first time (Figure I-1), you don't know anything about their special features. What you have to know is the fact that everything is movable. Later each class is discussed in detail, and the same objects are changed in all possible ways.

Several pages back I promised to write more about the psychological effect of the new programs; the opening form of the accompanying application is a good example of such an effect. I want to demonstrate the new ideas in the best possible way, and the first impression is important, so when I prepare the opening form of the accompanying program, I think a lot about the elements to be demonstrated, about their shapes, colors, sizes, and positions.

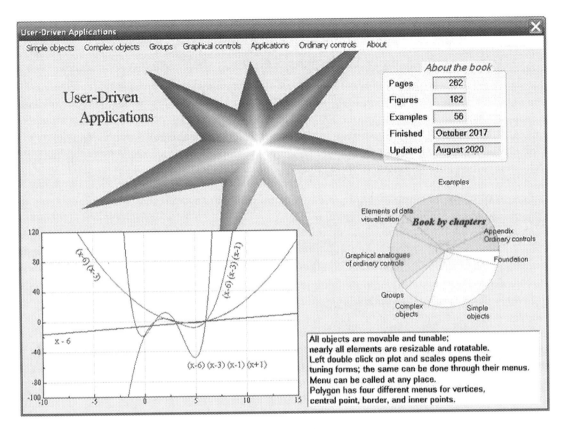

Figure I-1. *The main form of the accompanying program*

I was doing the same thing 20 years ago when I was a developer of sophisticated programs and designed those applications according to the rules of adaptive interfaces. Those older programs were mostly based on ordinary controls. Each computer has a font provided by an operation system. Some users change this font, but not all controls use this font. Some controls ignore the changes made by users; others make adjustments. The whole system was simply a mess. I would spend days trying to provide the best possible placement of all the screen elements. I would make the view better and better; I would be proud of the result. Then I would try the prepared program on another computer with different default fonts and look in astonishment at the result. The damage to the prepared excellent view would be unbelievable. And there would be no way to get anything else because it was the result of the adaptive interface. The user couldn't do anything; everything was predetermined by the best wishes of the developer and by those system settings that are out of the users' control.

In user-driven applications, there is a chance to get a bad view instead of a good one, but the probability of such a situation is low. First, throughout the main part of the book there are hardly any ordinary controls at all. The appendix is devoted to such elements, but until then there are only a few ordinary controls. Second, and this is the most important, no damage to the view is fatal because the user can change everything.

Can the unrestricted actions by user damage the view of an application? Surely. It can be done accidentally or on purpose. If user organizes a real mess with some element or the whole view, then the default view of the particular element or of the whole form can be reinstalled through a menu command. As a programmer, I provide an easy-to-use instrument for changes and restoration, but it is for user to decide about the use of this instrument.

Nearly everything is allowed. There are no restrictions from the point of "This is good, so it is allowed; this is bad, so it is prohibited." As a developer, I do not estimate the changes introduced by the user from the point of good versus bad. My only concern is about the existence of elements, so all of them have limitations on the minimal size that prevent their disappearance through squeezing. Otherwise, the user can do whatever is desired. As I said, there are menu commands to reinstall the default view(s), so no limitations on a user's doings are needed. From the beginning, I demonstrate that the total control over application is given to users, and I am not going to take it back. From time to time, I mention in the short information the elements without menus. If there is no such information, then a menu can be called anywhere, and a menu at empty places always includes a command to reinstall the default view. Don't be afraid to do whatever you want!

For whom is this book? For developers, for users, and for managers.

Throughout the bigger part of the book I discuss all the sides of organizing movability for all the involved elements and the main ideas of writing user-driven applications. There is always something to discuss from the point of programming. All code is available, but for better understanding of the described ideas, the important parts of the code are included in the text to give additional comments.

The opening part of the book is mostly for developers because this part is written with the emphasis on the algorithm and the code. Further on, I write more about overall design and the change it brings to users.

The second part of the book is also for users. They need to know that there are things that can be installed into all the programs, and such additions benefit users. The only way for users to estimate these new features is to try the programs in which these features work. I tried to do my best while preparing the demonstration program for this book.

Users are not going to read manuals for all new programs, but if there is something that makes the new programs different, then users have to be informed about this new feature. When somebody talks about the natural way of controlling a program, it is nonsense. Hunger and thirst are natural, but not the movement of a screen window (now it is called a *form*) by its title bar. It is easy to do when it is known, but whenever anyone is introduced to Windows or a similar operating system, this somebody has to be told about such a possibility; it's even better if such a possibility is demonstrated. It is easy to move icons around the screen and place them at the needed positions, but nobody is born with such knowledge. The same thing happens with the squeezing of information on smartphones: there is nothing natural in resizing by moving two fingers, but it is easy to do **after it is demonstrated**.

All objects in my programs are movable and resizable (except those that are purposely declared unmovable and/or nonresizable). Any border point of an object can be used for resizing. In some cases, not the resizing (zooming) of an object is needed but its reconfiguring. Usually it is done by some border points, and it is up to developer to organize reconfiguring exactly by those points that users would think the most likely to start such change. Forward movement of an object is done by any inner point. These three movements—forward movement, resizing, and reconfiguring—are started by the left mouse button. Rotation of an object is started at any inner point by the right button. The use of left and right buttons is not fixed anywhere in the algorithm, but it is a widely used practice. Whenever the same types of movement are organized in other programs, they are started with the same buttons, so I simply use the same commands that many users expect to be used for mentioned movements.

Movability in user-driven applications is universal. It is a default feature of each and all. However, the rules of new applications declare that everything is controlled by the user, so the user can also regulate the movability. (For example, the user organizes the preferable view and wants to avoid an accidental change of all or some elements. In such a case, the user can declare everything unmovable until the moment when he decides to change it back.) Such regulation is needed and often used in densely populated applications like sophisticated scientific programs.

By default, in user-driven applications, everything is movable. If any object is declared unmovable, there is no visual indication of such a change, but there can be two types of reaction when an unmovable object is pressed.

- The mouse with the pressed button can be freely moved around the screen while there is no reaction from an object.

- The mouse is fixed at the pressed point and cannot be moved anywhere until it is released.

For years I used the first scenario, and many examples of my big book [2], especially those examples that were written years ago, work according to this scenario. Later I began to think that the second scenario with the fixed cursor is much better from the point of informing users about the possibilities and limits. In the examples of the current book, I use the second scenario. Mostly the selection of a scenario based on movement restriction depends on your personal view on the problem: if you think that some discrepancy between the cursor movement and object movement in those special situations is OK, then you can use the first scenario.

There is one thing that users have to know: *everything is movable, resizable, and tunable.*

Any object is moved by inner points and resized by border. Tuning starts through the menu command, so to start the tuning of an object, you call a menu on this object. Usually the same menu can be called at any point of an object, but in those rare situations when different parts of an object have different functionality, menus for those parts can be different. Usually one or another menu can be called at any point. If there are some elements without menus, then it is mentioned in the information.

This book is accompanied by a demonstration program. The source code for this program is available on GitHub via the book's product page, located at `www.apress.com/9781484264874`. All source files are written in C#. My algorithm of movability uses some basic classes from `MoveGraphLibrary.dll`, which is included in the project. All classes of this library are described in the file `MoveGraphLibrary_Classes.doc` (and PDF), which is placed at `https://sourceforge.net/projects/movegraph/files/`.

Several examples of the accompanying program use the JPG files that are placed in the `Resources` subdirectory of the project.

CHAPTER 1

Foundation

This chapter defines the terms and introduces the basic classes that are used to implement movability. It also explains the main (mandatory) methods and their parameters.

There was a time when computers were not known yet, but there were plenty of fairies. There is some evidence that at that time some people understood the importance of turning an unmovable object into a movable one, so, for example, the transformation of a big pumpkin into a grand coach was done with the help of a magic wand [4]. When I came to the conclusion that all screen objects had to be movable, I quickly found two things. First, those magic wands were not available anymore. Second, there were no public algorithms of movability that any programmer could use, so I had to rely on thinking and programming—two processes I am more familiar with than magic. I started by formulating the basic principles on which such algorithms must be invented and used:

- Every screen object has to be movable, so the proposed algorithm must work with the elements of an arbitrary shape.

- I don't need an algorithm exclusively for my own use. The movability of the screen objects greatly improves the programs to the benefit of all users, so an algorithm must be easy in use by any programmer.

- Users are not going to read instructions to understand the rules of movability for each new object in every program. These rules must be universal and extremely easy in use.

From time to time (too often, I think), you can see a declaration that an interface is organized in a natural way. I strongly oppose such declarations because there is absolutely nothing natural in the world of computers and programs. There are a lot of complicated things that are born by the cleverness of skillful people after many hours, months, or years of thinking and experimenting. If at the end of this process some sophisticated things look simple, then that is even more credit to their authors.

S. Andreyev, *User-Driven Applications for Research and Science*, https://doi.org/10.1007/978-1-4842-6488-1_1

Users are not going to read instructions, but they must be informed that in the new programs **all objects are moved by inner points and resized by borders**. I would like to limit the instructions to this single statement, but a short addition is also needed (though it's the same for old and new programs). Screen objects might have a lot of tunable parameters, so if user needs to regulate some object, then the menu on this object is called, while the menu at any empty place allows the user to deal with general parameters.

From the beginning I worked on an algorithm not only for myself but that could be used by any programmer. Movability has to be implemented by designers. In one way or another, it has to be incorporated into the code of a program, so an algorithm of movability has to be easy to understand and use for any developer. I did my best, and whenever I see a chance to simplify an existing algorithm, I make the needed changes, release the new library version, and write the necessary comments about the new or changed features. Whether I am successful in thinking of a powerful and easy-to-use algorithm is for developers to decide. There can be different opinions on some proposals, so whenever I have any doubts about the advantages of a new idea, I try to make changes in such a way that the new alternatives do not block the use of the older versions.

Screen objects are the products of developers' skills and imagination, and I don't want to interfere with the results of others' work. Programmers think a lot about the view of the screen objects, so movability is added as an invisible feature and has no visual marks. It is possible to demonstrate visually the existence of this new feature; in some cases, this demonstration can be even helpful, but such cases are rare. In my big book [2], there are several examples that demonstrate different ways of informing users about movability, but in the current book and its examples, I am going to minimize such demonstrations.

The main idea of my algorithm of movability is simple. An object is covered by an invisible layer; when an object is pressed with a mouse, then this layer is used to decide about the pressed object, about the pressed part of an object, and about the consequences of the press. Some parts of an object can be used for forward movement of the whole object, while other parts can be used for resizing or reconfiguring, so this invisible layer contains the information about the movement to be started at each point of the mouse press.

The only instrument that is used by my algorithm is an ordinary mouse. It is easy in use and precise, so it can deal even with a single screen point. (Such accuracy is not always required, but it is available.) All movements are organized in a press-move-release way.

We have lots of objects on the screen. These objects can overlap, and the parts of objects can be used to start different movements, so it would be helpful to give users some tip about the movement that can be started at the current cursor position. Such information is also stored in the mentioned invisible layer, and the change of cursor shape is used as a prompt.

Four types of movements can be organized for screen objects and their parts, as shown here:

Forward movement	The size of an object is not changed, and an object is moved without any change of relative positions of its parts and without rotation.
Resizing	All parts of an object are increased or decreased with the same coefficient, but the general shape is not changed.
Reconfiguring	Only some part of an object is moved, thus changing its relative position with other parts and the general view of an object.
Rotation	The general shape and the size of an object are not changed, but the whole object is turned from its original position around some point that is used as a center of rotation.

A mouse, which is an instrument for all these movements, allows us to use its left and right buttons and also to start some actions either with a single click or with a double-click. These things are not specified in the algorithm itself, but in my applications I try to use the commands that are already used for similar actions in other programs. When in the following text you read that "such movement is started with the press of the left button," you have to understand that it is not a demand by the algorithm to start it only this way but rather the description of how it is organized in my programs.

Three movements—forward movement, resizing, and reconfiguring—are started with the left button press; the choice between these three movements is decided by the pressed point. Usually all border points are used for resizing, but some of them (and occasionally some inner points) can be used for reconfiguring. It would be too difficult for users to start the resizing exactly on the border point and nowhere else, so a sensitive strip is organized along the border. The strip is narrow in comparison with the object size but wide enough (six pixels by default, but it can be changed) to make the start of resizing easy. The same idea is used for reconfiguring: each special point is surrounded by a sensitive circle in which the reconfiguring can be started. The default radius of such circle is three pixels, but it can be changed; to make the reconfiguring easier, I often increase radius to four or five pixels.

The start of rotation is distinguished from three other movements by using the different mouse button: the right one. The rotation of an object usually starts at any inner point.

There can be lots of objects on the screen. These objects and their parts can be involved in different individual, synchronous, and related movements, so somebody has to organize and supervise all these movements. I call this somebody a *mover*; this is an object of the `Mover` class.

Two sides participate in the process of moving: a movable object and a mover. It is impossible to explain their interrelation separately for one side and then for another. Regardless of which side I start, there is a moment in explanation when I have to switch from one side to another, and this will happen several times. Let's start with the mover.

The mover keeps a queue of objects that it has to supervise. Regardless of the number of objects involved in movements, it is enough to have a single mover for each form and for each page of `TabControl`. (If you want to organize the movement of objects on a `panel`, then a mover is provided for this panel. Such an example is demonstrated in my book [2].)

Moving is organized as a press-move-release process that is started by pressing the needed object at the needed point. Objects can overlap, and if the user presses the mouse at some point of overlapping, then the user expects the upper object at this point to be grabbed and moved. The mover does not know anything about the order of objects on the screen and their painting, but the mover knows everything about the objects in its queue, analyzes them strictly according to their order in this queue, and grabs for moving the first available object at the pressed point. Thus, if you want to grab for moving the upper object at the place where they overlap, then the screen objects must be painted in the reverse order than in the mover queue. When the logic of application requires to change the order of objects in view, then the order of objects in the mover queue is also changed, and the view is refreshed.

As a rule, there are no collisions of the screen objects throughout their movements, so you may look at the whole situation as if each object resides on its own level and can be moved only along its own plane. Occasionally there are tasks in which the movement of an object is restricted by the presence of other objects; several examples of such type, for example, moving through labyrinth, are demonstrated in my book [2].

All movements are done by the mouse, and only three mouse events—MouseDown, MouseMove, and MouseUp—are used for the whole process. For each event, its own method is written, and these are the methods in which `Mover` works and must be mentioned. To organize the moving of objects in the form, several steps must be taken.

1. Declare and initialize a Mover object.

    ```
    Mover mover;
    mover = new Mover (...);
    ```

2. Register with the mover all the screen objects; several methods
    allow you to set the initially needed order of objects in the mover
    queue.

    ```
    mover .Add (...);
    mover .Insert (...);
    ```

3. Write the code for three mouse events.

    ```
    private void OnMouseDown (object sender, MouseEventArgs e)
    {
        if (mover .Catch (...))
        {
            ... ...
        }
    }
    private void OnMouseMove (object sender, MouseEventArgs e)
    {
        if (mover .Move (e .Location))
        {
            Invalidate ();
        }
    }
    private void OnMouseUp (object sender, MouseEventArgs e)
    {
        if (mover .Release (...)
        {
            ... ...
        }
    }
    ```

The calls to three mover methods (one call per each mouse event) are the only mandatory calls in these methods. Three mouse events—MouseDown, MouseMove, and MouseUp—are the standard and often the only places where a mover is used. There are two other events—MouseDoubleClick and Paint—where a mover can be mentioned and used, but this happens only on special occasions.

A double-click was used more widely in my previous programs, but now its use is minimized. First, not all users are happy when they have to use a double-click to start some actions. Second, the double-click may also happen accidentally, and then an unexpected action is started if single- and double-clicks are used for different actions. Because of these two things, there is a limited use of the MouseDoubleClick event in the accompanying program.

- In the examples with many different colored figures, the left double-click on an element brings it on top of all others.

- While I was developing programs for scientists, they asked to add the left double-click as another way to start the tuning of plots and scales; such use of double-clicking is demonstrated in a couple of examples.

In all mentioned cases, the same actions (change of order; start of the tuning) can be also performed through menu commands, so the use of the double-click is nowhere a mandatory thing.

Without a mover at hand (prior to implementing the movable objects), the decision about the clicked object was always done by comparing the mouse location and the boundaries of objects. The mover can do such object detection much better; the mover informs not only about the occurrence of any catch but also about the class of the caught object, its order in the queue, and other useful things. At the moment of initialization, any movable object gets a unique identification number; this ID helps to identify an object when there are several or many objects of the same class.

I think that this is enough for a brief mover description, and now we can look at the movable objects.

An invisible layer that is added to any screen element and provides its movability is an object of the Cover class, so I often write that an object gets a cover. As a rule, Cover has a shape of an object but is slightly bigger; this tiny enlargement for several pixels is caused by the need of a sensitive area along the border. There are objects of many different shapes, and there are covers for all of them. To provide such unlimited variability, covers are constructed of simple elements that are called *nodes* and belong to the CoverNode class. While in general the cover area is only several pixels wider than the area of the associated object, there are special situations when the cover area can be much bigger than the object area; these special and interesting cases are discussed later.

I often write that the mover catches an object, moves an object, releases an object, and so on. There must be an absolutely clear understanding that the mover deals not with an object, as we see it, but only with its cover. Mover doesn't know anything about an object but everything about its cover. Mover sees only the cover nodes. If there are parts of an object that are not covered by the nodes, then for the mover there is no object at those places; this is one of the reasons why an object must be covered by nodes without any gaps. [1]

Screen objects can be of an arbitrary shape, so the nodes available for design must be able to cover an arbitrary area without problems. Three things make this task fairly easy.

- Any number of nodes can constitute a cover; there is at least one node in each cover, but there is no upper limit on the number of them.

- There are no rules or restrictions for positioning those nodes: they can be placed far away from each other or stay side by side or overlap. The only recommendation is the covering of the whole object area without any gaps as users expect some reaction on the mouse press at any point.

- Nodes of three shapes can be used: circles, convex polygons, and rounded strips.

```
enum NodeShape { Circle, Polygon, Strip };
```

Users know that all the screen objects are now movable and resizable. Users know how it works for any object (resize by border, move by any inner point), and users know that everything is done easily with a mouse in a press-move-release process. Users do not know anything about the invisible nodes and covers, but everything is organized through the contact between the cursor and covers, so cover nodes possess the parameters that determine the process to be started when a particular node is pressed.

---

[1]There is a good analog between mover vision and X-rays. When we look at any object, we see the form and colors, while X-rays detect only the elements of some usually hidden structure. For a special case of an entirely metal thing our eyes and X-rays see the same shape, but in all other cases there is a difference, and X-rays don't give information about color and many other features. The mover detects all cover nodes and their parameters, but the mover doesn't detect anything else.

- Each node has its personal number. If there are N nodes in a cover, then their numbers are from the [0, N-1] range, and each node has its own number. When the mover analyzes the cover of an object for the possibility of movement, then this analysis is done node after node in the order of their numbers.

- Each node has parameters that determine its geometry.

- Each node keeps information about the shape that the mouse cursor must have when it is moved across this node. Nodes may overlap, so at any moment the cursor gets its shape from the upper node.

- Each node has a parameter that determines the reaction on the mouse press. Possible behavior is determined by the values of the Behaviour enumeration.

```
enum Behaviour { Nonmoveable, Moveable, Transparent = 4, Frozen };
```

Screen objects are registered in the mover queue. While making the decision about the possibility of catching any object, the mover checks the covers according to the order of objects in the queue, and each cover is analyzed node after node according to its order in the cover. When the first node containing the mouse point is found, then the reaction depends on the Behaviour parameter of this node, as shown here:

Behaviour. Nonmoveable	The object is unmovable by this point. At the same time, such a node does not allow the mover to look anywhere further; all other nodes and objects at this point are blocked from the mover. The analysis at this point is over; if you want to move anything, try another point.
Behaviour. Frozen	The object under the mouse cannot be moved by this point, but it is recognized by the mover as any other object, so, for example, the context menu can be easily called for it.
Behaviour. Moveable	It is the most often used case, and it is the default behavior of any node. For such nodes, the possibility of movement is described by the MoveNode() method of this object according to the number or shape of the node and the movement restrictions, if there are any.
Behaviour. Transparent	The mover skips this and all the following nodes of the same cover and continues the analysis of the situation from the next object in its queue.

Depending on the needed node shape and properties, different sets of parameters are used for the node construction.

Circular node is defined by its central point and radius. The classical constructor for circular node has five parameters, as shown here:

CoverNode (int iNode,	Order number among the nodes of cover
PointF pt,	Circle center
float radius,	Circle radius
Behaviour behaviour,	Node behavior
Cursor cursor)	Cursor shape over node

Only the first two parameters are mandatory, while others can be used in any combination or omitted. The default values of these parameters are determined by the most common use of circular nodes. In the majority of cases, a small circular node is placed over some special point of an object; moving this point results in the change of configuration. Here are the default values for circular nodes:

```
radius    = 3
behaviour = Behaviour.Moveable
cursor    = Cursors.Hand
```

Covers are invisible, so the user does not know about the existence of covers and nodes, but the user knows that an object configuration can be changed by moving some special points. For example, a rectangle can be reconfigured by moving its corner, while a polygon can be reconfigured by moving its vertex. To move any vertex, the user has to press it with the mouse, but it would be unrealistic to expect that at this moment the mouse cursor is placed exactly on the needed point. The cursor is pressed somewhere in the vertex vicinity, so there is a small sensitive area around the needed point; the circular node is just this sensitive area. My experience shows that a circle with the radius of three pixels provides an easy catch though occasionally I increase this radius to four or five pixels. At the beginning of my book [2], there is a simple example that allows readers to play with the sizes of nodes and to select the optimal values.

Polygonal node is described by an array of points representing its vertices. A polygon must be convex! There is no checking of convexity inside the node constructor, so the checking, if needed, must be done prior to calling the constructor.[2]

```
CoverNode (int iNode,
              PointF [] pts,
              Behaviour behaviour,
              Cursor cursor)
```

Two last parameters can be omitted in any combination or at all. Their default values are as follows:

```
behaviour = Behaviour.Moveable
cursor    = Cursors.SizeAll
```

Polygonal nodes are often used in big sizes with the main purpose to cover the whole area of an object. Nodes of this shape are mostly used for moving an object around the screen, so their default cursor shape signals the possibility of movement in any direction. In many cases, the polygonal nodes cover the body of an object, while circular and strip nodes cover its border. Pressing inside or on a border often starts different movements, so I decided to organize different cursor shapes inside and on borders. After all, the mentioned cursor shape is only the default value that can be changed at the moment of construction; you will see it in some examples.

A *strip node* is defined by two points and radius. A strip with two rounded ends can be also looked at as a rectangle with additional semicircles on two opposite sides. Those two mentioned points are the middle points of two opposite sides and the centers of two semicircles; the diameter of those semicircles is equal to the strip width. The classical CoverNode constructor for strip nodes has six parameters:

```
CoverNode (int iNode,

    PointF pt0,              Central point of one semicircle

    PointF pt1,              Central point of another semicircle

    float radius,            Radius of semicircles

    Behaviour behaviour,

    Cursor cursor)
```

---

[2]Checking of convexity can be done, for example, by the `Auxi_Geometry.PolygonConvexity()` method.

The last three parameters can be omitted in any combination or at all. The default values are the same as for circular nodes.

```
radius    = 3
behaviour = Behaviour.Moveable
cursor    = Cursors.Hand
```

Often enough, a thin strip node is stretched along the border segment of an object and is used for resizing this object.

The number of nodes in the cover and their shapes, sizes, and positions are not regulated in any way but are determined by the developer. Usually the lesser number of nodes in a cover is preferable as it requires less code in the MoveNode() method that describes the moving of each node. However, the cover design for objects with the curved border might require including a lot of small (often circular) nodes into the cover. There can be dozens or even hundreds of nodes in such a cover, but the code is usually simple because the behavior of such nodes is identical. Covers of this special type are called *N-node covers*. Years ago such N-node covers were a perfect solution for the resizing of circles and rings. Later these objects get much simpler covers, so the N-node covers are not discussed in this book, but their good explanation can be found in my book [2].

Three different movements can be started by the left button: forward movement, resizing, and reconfiguring. The movement to be started by pressing each node is determined at the stage of design when the cover is constructed. When there is a single node of some shape in the cover, the decision about the movement can be based on the node shape. When there are several nodes of the same shape, the decision can be based on the node number. In some cases, both parameters are considered.

Each class of movable objects is derived from the abstract class GraphicalObject. This class includes three abstract methods that must be overridden in the derived classes.

```
public abstract class GraphicalObject
{
    public abstract void DefineCover ();
    public abstract void Move (int dx, int dy);
    public abstract bool MoveNode (int iNode, int dx, int dy, Point ptMouse,
                        MouseButtons catcher);
```

The DefineCover () method describes the cover construction. The same movements of an object can be organized with different covers, so the exact number of nodes in a cover, their shapes, and their sizes depend only on the developer's ideas. The best solution is to move an object by any inner point and to resize, if needed, by the border. Thus, the entire object area must be covered by the nodes without any gaps. The overlapping of nodes is not prohibited.

Move (dx, dy) is the method for the *forward moving of the whole object* for a number of pixels passed as the parameters. Positive values mean the movement from left to right and from top to bottom. The drawing of any screen object regardless of its complexity is usually based on one or a few simple elements (Point and Rectangle) and some additional parameters (sizes). While an object is moved, the sizes are not changed, so only the positions of the anchor points have to be changed in this method.

MoveNode (iNode, dx, dy, ptMouse, catcher) is the method for *individually moving the nodes*. Each node is used either for moving an object, resizing, or reconfiguring; this method describes the needed reaction on moving each node.

MoveNode (int iNode,	Node number
int dx,	Horizontal movement (in pixels)
int dy,	Vertical movement (in pixels)
Point ptMouse,	Mouse position
MouseButtons catcher);	Mouse button responsible for movement

The pair of parameters (dx, dy) describes the cursor movement that causes the node movement. This pair of parameters is often used when forward movement is described. Parameter ptMouse informs about the current cursor position; this parameter is always used throughout rotation. With the widespread use of the adhered mouse technique that is characterized by the synchronous movement of the mouse and the caught element, this ptMouse parameter turned out to be useful also for all kinds of resizing and reconfiguring. The parameter catcher informs about the pressed mouse button.

All screen objects are derived from the GraphicalObject class, get their covers, and are provided with the methods that define the forward movement of the whole object and personal movements of each node from its cover. Objects are registered with the mover, and then the mover is responsible for all their movements, so let's turn our attention back to the mover.

In the applications of the standard type, the unmovable objects always stay at the places where designers put them, and it is difficult to imagine a situation when some element disappears from view. When all objects are movable, then the case of an object that is moved across the form border and released there becomes absolutely real. It can happen purposely or accidentally, so there is a problem of allowing or not allowing such a move over the border(s). The consequences of moving an object out of view depend on the form border behind which it is left, so different cases might require different solutions.

Suppose that an object is moved across the right or bottom border. If the form is resizable, then it is not a problem at all as the form can be enlarged, and by this an object is returned into play. If an object is moved across the upper or left border of the form, then there is no way to return it into view by resizing the form. The mover can take care of this situation and prevent such a disappearance of objects, but only if the mover is asked to overlook and control this process. For this purpose, the mover has to be initialized with an additional parameter: the form itself. (If a mover works on a page of TabControl or on a panel, then this page or panel is used as a parameter.)

```
mover = new Mover (this);
```

You can find throughout the code of the accompanying application that such a type of mover initialization is used in the majority of examples. In such a case, when the user grabs any object for moving or resizing, the clipping is organized inside the borders of the client area. If any object is caught and the mouse tries to move this object across the border, then the mouse is stopped several pixels from the border. This is done in order to leave some part of an object in view even in the worst situation. Even if an object is caught by its edge and moved in such a direction that nearly the whole body of this object disappears behind the form border, the cursor is stopped several pixels from the border and the remaining, though small, part of an object is still visible.

When there is a menu in the form, then this menu covers a strip along the upper border, and the use of the mentioned constructor will not prevent the disappearance of the remaining small part of an object under the menu. To avoid such a situation, there is another constructor with an additional parameter, which allows you to specify a bigger restricted zone along the upper border of the form.

```
mover = new Mover (this, SystemInformation .MenuHeight);
```

There are different situations when moving objects across the borders can be allowed or forbidden. The level of clipping can be changed with one property of the Mover class; three different levels of clipping are implemented.

```
public enum Clipping { Visual, Safe, Unsafe };
```

• Visual	Throughout any movement, some part of an object is always visible inside the client area.
• Safe	Objects can be moved from view only across the right and bottom borders of the form.
• Unsafe	Objects can be moved from view across any border.

Different Mover constructors set different levels of restrictions on moving objects. A constructor without any parameters sets the Unsafe level of clipping, but you will not find it anywhere in the accompanying program.[3] All other constructors set the Visual level of clipping. There are no constructors that set the Safe level, but this level is used in many applications; the needed clipping level can be set at any moment by the Mover. Clipping property.

When the Clipping.Visual level is used, it does not mean that any object is always fully in view. The clipping is organized not for objects but for the mouse when it has grabbed an object. Under such clipping, the mouse with an object cannot go outside the visible part of the form, so this guarantees that an object cannot be entirely moved beyond the borders. Any part of the caught object can cross the border; it can be a small part or nearly a whole object that goes out of view, but the mouse that is stuck to some point inside an object cannot cross the border, so regardless of where the movement ends, some part of an object is still left in view. By pressing this part, an object can be returned into full view.

I want to underline once more the difference between the well-known mouse clipping that is used for decades and this Mover.Clipping.

---

[3]The possibility of disaster in case of accidental moving of objects over the upper or left border caused me never to use mover initialization without parameters. Such a case is demonstrated only in one of the examples from my book [2]. That example of Form_ClippingLevels.cs is especially designed to compare all possibilities of mover clipping.

- Standard mouse clipping limits mouse movements even for a free mouse not attached to any object.

- The Mover.Clipping property sets the limits of cursor movements only in a situation when some object is caught and the mouse tries to steal it out from the visible area. When the mouse is released, there is no more clipping of this type, and the mouse can be moved anywhere.

The required mover clipping is set at the moment of mover initialization but can be easily changed later by the Mover.Clipping property. Because the mover clipping works only throughout the time when some object is caught by the mover and the mover always knows the class of the caught object, different levels of clipping can be used with different objects. This rarely used feature can be helpful in some cases and is demonstrated in the Form_FillHoles.cs example.

When the Clipping.Visual level is used, it does not mean that an object cannot find itself behind the right or bottom border. Even if an object cannot be moved across the borders, these borders can be moved across objects! (You may not like the rules on the other side of your country border and you may have no wish to be on the other side, but a neighboring ruler may have different views on your property and different plans about its future. There are some crazy rulers in the world.)

Five pages back I already mentioned important methods of the Mover class that are used throughout the MouseDown, MouseMove, and MouseUp events. Let's look at those methods more closely.

Every move of an object starts when an object is pressed with a mouse. The method associated with it—Mover.Catch()—returns the value that indicates if any object is really caught with this press or not. This method has three variants, which can be used in different scenarios depending on what is needed. All three variants have one mandatory parameter—the point where the mouse was pressed—but differ in using other parameters.

`bool Mover.Catch (Point ptMouse, MouseButtons catcher)`	This is the most frequently used variant of the `Catch()` method. The second parameter specifies the mouse button by which an object was caught. In nearly all the situations it is an important parameter as it allows to distinguish the start of rotation from other movements.
`bool Mover.Catch (Point ptMouse)`	The variant without any additional parameter is used rarely enough; you can use it if you do not care by what button an object is caught. In such a case, the system simply substitutes the left button as the default value and goes on.
`bool Mover.Catch (Point ptMouse, MouseButtons catcher, bool bShowAngle)`	This version of the method is often used for the forms with textual comments. For some basic classes of comments included in the library `MoveGraphlibrary.dll` and for comments derived from these classes, this parameter, if its value is `true`, allows to see the comment angle throughout its rotation. Usually, the value of this parameter is controlled by the user and can be changed at any moment, for example, via some context menu.

The mover is the conductor of the whole moving/resizing process for all objects from its queue. All objects are movable, and usually there is only one mover in the form, so all objects are registered in the same queue, and the mover supervises all objects in the form. To some extent, the mover can be associated with the mouse, as it catches the objects by the mouse, moves them with the mouse, and then releases them at the place to which the mouse was moved. When an object is pressed and caught, then a lot of information can be obtained from the `Mover.Move()` call and several properties of the `Mover` class. The return value of the `Mover.Move()` method tells whether any object is moved at the moment. The link between the mover and the mouse is especially strong during the moving process because the only parameter of the `Mover.Move()` method is the mouse position.

`bool Mover.Move (Point ptMouse)`

The valuable information about the currently moved (caught) object includes the order of this object in the mover queue, the number of the pressed node in the cover of this object, and the shape of this node. This information is obtained from three properties of the `Mover` class.

int iObject	= mover .CaughtObject;	// Gets the index of the caught element
int iNode	= mover .CaughtNode;	// Gets the number of the caught node
NodeShape shape = mover .CaughtNodeShape;		// Gets the shape of the caught node

The caught object itself can be received with one of the following calls:

```
GraphicalObject grobj = mover .CaughtSource;
```

or

```
GraphicalObject grobj = mover [mover .CaughtObject] .Source;
```

There is also a property to inform if any object is caught by the mover at the current moment.

```
bool bCaught = mover .Caught;
```

Even if no object is currently caught for moving, the mover can produce all the needed data about the objects that are under the mouse cursor. The mover "senses" the movable objects under the mouse cursor and gives the standard set of information about them.

bool bSensed = mover .Sensed;	// Gets the indication of any movable object under the cursor
int iObject = mover .SensedObject;	// Gets the index of the element underneath
int iNode = mover .SensedNode;	// Gets the number of the node underneath

The mover is like a shark that is not hungry at the moment and lazy to attack but watches carefully and keeps track of everything that is going on. In this way, the mover can produce information not only about the point under the cursor but about any point of the form; the information is returned in the form of a MoverPointInfo object. In addition to the number of objects in the queue, the number of nodes in the cover, and the shape of node, there are also the behavior of the node (of the Behaviour enumeration) and the shape of cursor above this node. It is possible to get either the information about the upper node at the particular point, as follows:

```
MoverPointInfo PointInfoUpper (Point pt)
```

or the information about all the nodes that overlap at this point, as shown here:

```
List<MoverPointInfo> PointInfoAll (Point pt)
```

When the mouse button is released, it is important to know whether any object is released at this moment. This information is provided as the return value of the Mover. Release() method, but variants of this method can provide other pieces of valuable information. These are the order of released object in the mover queue (iObject), the number of the released node in the cover (iNode), and the shape of this node (shape).

```
bool Mover.Release ()
bool Mover.Release (out int iObject)
bool Mover.Release (out int iObject, out int iNode)
bool Mover.Release (out int iObject, out int iNode, out NodeShape shape)
```

Even if the first of these variants is used, the order of released object in the queue can be obtained with the Mover.ReleasedObject property.

```
int iInMover = mover .ReleasedObject;
```

The released object also can be obtained with one of the following calls:

```
GraphicalObject grobj = mover .ReleasedSource;
```

or

```
GraphicalObject grobj = mover [mover .ReleasedObject] .Source;
```

Nearly always it is important to know the class of the released object; this is done by a standard checking of the released object.

```
private void OnMouseUp (object sender, MouseEventArgs e)
{
    ... ...
    int iObj, iNode;
    if (mover .Release (out iObj, out iNode))
    {
        GraphicalObject grobj = mover .ReleasedSource;
        if (e .Button == MouseButtons .Left)
```

```
{
    if (grobj is Button_GR)
    {
        ... ...
    }
    else if (grobj is CheckBox_GR)
    {
        ... ...
    }
    else if (grobj is Rectangle_Unicolored)
    {
        ... ...
    }
    ... ...
```

When the mouse button is released, the mentioned pieces of information allow a program to make a decision about further actions, but there is one more piece that is needed. For example, the forward movement of objects (plus their resizing and reconfiguring) and a command to put an object on top of others are all started with the left button. The rotation of objects and the calling of context menus are started with the right button, so something else must be considered to distinguish the possibilities that are started by the same button. Further action often depends on the distance between the points of mouse press and release.

In the ideal case, the decision must be based on having zero or non-zero distance between two points, but the request of pressing and releasing mouse at exactly the same point and not moving it even for a single pixel between the MouseDown and MouseUp events can be too strong for the majority of users, so I consider the move for "not more than three pixels" as "not moved." (Three pixels for a "not moved" decision is my own suggestion; this number can be easily changed in either direction.) The implementation of this rule in my programs results in the following system of decisions:

Left button	If the mouse is not moved between two events, then it can be a special command (button click, switch of the check box, selection in the list); otherwise, it is simply a move of an object.
Right button	If the mouse is not moved between two events, then it is a menu call; otherwise, it is an object rotation.

The points of two mouse events are obtained not from the mover but from the `MouseEventArgs` parameter of the `OnMouseDown()` and `OnMouseUp()` methods.

Several pages back I wrote about the possible disappearance of objects across the form borders, but the disappearance can be also caused by an unlimited shrinking of objects. To avoid this, the minimum sizes must be declared for any class of resizable objects; these restrictions are used in the `MoveNode()` method to check for the possibility of the proposed movement. As you will see later, the restriction on a minimum size of objects is used in the majority of classes. However, there are cases when such a restriction is purposely not declared, and thus the shrinking to a tiny size or even to zero is considered as a possible user's action.

The first approach is to consider the shrinking of an object to the size less than the predetermined minimum as the user's command to delete this object from view. It is possible, and it is realized this way from time to time, but I still think that the use of the Delete command in the context menu is much better.

In some rare situations, an object can be squeezed to a tiny size or even disappear from view but continue to exist; there is still a possibility to grab this invisible object and increase it, thus making it visible again. This approach is used only on those rare occasions when there are several objects side by side, and still visible neighbors inform users that the empty space between objects is not absolutely empty, but there exists an invisible object that can be found and caught by the mouse. One such example is the manual change of bars in the bar chart. You can move the side of the bar in such a way that the whole bar will disappear from view, and there will be an empty space, but the existence of other bars reminds you that there is something and gives you a tip that the bar can be restored. (A tip is also given by the change of the mouse cursor over this squeezed bar. Though the bar itself is squeezed to zero size, the node over its movable part still has some size; for example, its width is always six pixels, so the cursor over this node changes its shape.)

Technical note. To avoid the screen flicker throughout the moving/resizing of the screen objects, do not forget to switch on the double-buffering in any form where you use the moving/resizing algorithm. This has nothing to do with the described technique, but it is a nice feature from Visual Studio. Moving and resizing can be applied not only to the objects inside any form but also to those that are placed on panels or tab controls. Unfortunately, Visual Studio does not allow you to avoid flicker on panels and tab controls in the same easy way as in forms. To avoid flicker in those situations, the modified (derived) classes must be used. It is easy to do, but to simplify it even more, I included the classes `TabPageWithoutFlickering` and `PanelWithoutFlickering` in the `MoveGraphLibrary.dll`.

Conclusion

You are now familiar with the Mover class, which supervises the whole process of moving all the screen objects, and with the mandatory methods of this class that are used when the mouse is pressed, moved, and released. You know the types of nodes that allow you to make any object movable. Methods that allow you to get information about currently moved or just released objects were also discussed. Now is the time to apply this knowledge to the moving and resizing of simple objects of the most popular shapes.

CHAPTER 2

Simple Objects

This chapter demonstrates the movability of simple objects of the most often used shapes. It is difficult to see an object of a single point, so it is represented by a small spot. Then come the line, rectangle, polygon, circle, ring, and arc. The cover design for each element is discussed. Going from one shape to another, we see that the same basic ideas are applied in the design of different covers. Some ideas, like transparent nodes, may look a bit strange at first, but they allow you to simplify the design of covers for many objects. Each example is simple, but the basic rules of user-driven applications are used from the beginning. At the end of this chapter we have a simple but interesting example: a game.

It is a standard practice to start any explanation of new things with simple objects and simple examples; later more complicated things can be introduced and explained. The complexity of any movable object can be estimated by two factors: involvement in different types of movement and the complexity of the cover design. To some extent, these two estimations correlate with each other but not absolutely, because from time to time you think of a simple cover that provides the same functionality as the previous version did of a much more sophisticated cover. However, if an object contains parts that are involved in individual movements, then these parts must be covered by separate nodes, so the more such parts an object has, the larger the number of nodes in its cover.

A pixel is the smallest element of the screen with which we can deal, so an element of the size of a single pixel is the smallest element that can be moved around the screen. Such an element is not resizable (it is always a single pixel), and even its movement can be questionable because it is often a problem to see it and to press it with a mouse. Let's make the last task easier by associating a pixel with some colored spot. A spot is small enough, but its size allows you to see and press such object without any problems. When we move a spot, we move the pixel associated with this spot.

S. Andreyev, *User-Driven Applications for Research and Science*, https://doi.org/10.1007/978-1-4842-6488-1_2

Spot

File: Form_Spot.cs

Menu position: Simple objects ➤ Spot

Figure 2-1 shows a typical view of Form_Spot.cs, which uses the simplest objects but demonstrates all the features that are used in much more complicated examples. We'll look through all these features a bit later; now let's start with the colored spots.

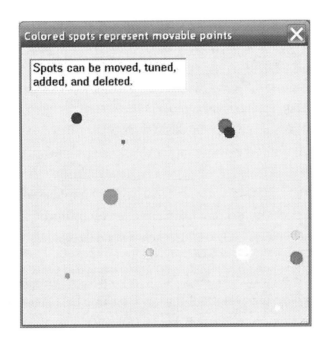

Figure 2-1. *The spot cover consists of a single circular node that is equal to the area of an element*

```
public class Spot : GraphicalObject
{
    Form m_form;
    Mover m_supervisor;
    PointF m_center;
    int m_radius;
    Color m_color;
    static int minRadius = 3;
    static int maxRadius = 12;
```

The spot is a small colored circle with a radius from the [3, 12] range. To initialize such an object, you need to declare the coordinates of its central point, radius, and color.

```
public Spot (Form frm, Mover mvr, PointF ptC, int radius, Color clr)
{
    m_form = frm;
    m_supervisor = mvr;
    m_center = ptC;
    m_radius = Math .Min (Math .Max (minRadius, radius), maxRadius);
    m_color = clr;
}
```

The spot cover is extremely simple and consists of a circular node with the same central point and radius.

```
public override void DefineCover ()
{
    cover = new Cover (new CoverNode (0, m_center, m_radius));
}
```

Forward moving of a spot requires only the change of its central point synchronously with the mouse movement.

```
public override void Move (int dx, int dy)
{
    m_center += new Size (dx, dy);
}
```

Method MoveNode() describes the reaction on movement of any node. The spot can be involved only in forward movement, and there is only one node in the cover, so the MoveNode() method calls the Move() method, and nothing else is needed.

```
public override bool MoveNode (int i, int dx, int dy, Point ptM,
                               MouseButtons catcher)
{
    bool bRet = false;
    if (catcher == MouseButtons .Left)
    {
        Center = ptM;
```

```
        bRet = true;
    }
    return (bRet);
}
```

What happens when an object is pressed with a mouse? More often than not, it is a starting moment of some movement. In general, movement of an object can be restricted by positions of some other screen objects, and the change of sizes is often limited by some ranges. The type of movement nearly always depends on the pressed button, while the limits of further movement depend on the pressed point and the pressed cover node. Thus, at the moment of initial press, a `Press()` method of the particular class (it is a class of the pressed object) is called. Such a method always has the same three parameters.[1]

```
public void Press (Point ptMouse, MouseButtons catcher, int iNode)
```

What the `Spot.Press()` method has to do?

You press a spot in order to move it to another place. Positioning of a spot is done by its central point, but this point is not marked in any way. When the spot is pressed and then the mouse cursor is moved without release, then the spot goes with the mouse. The mouse cursor is perfectly seen, so at any moment you know exactly the position of the arrow point. At the same time, the spot central point is not marked and is always somewhere nearby. The difference between two points never changes throughout movement, but the exact position of the spot central point is not obvious. It would be much better for visual control of spot movement to have the arrow point on the spot central point. It is unrealistic to expect that any user would press a spot exactly at the central point, so it is done by a program. The point of the mouse press is known, and the spot central point is also known, so change the mouse coordinates at this moment, and that is all.

Sounds easy, but there is a catch. At the moment when we need to adjust the cursor position, the spot is already caught by the mover, so any cursor movement is copied by the spot movement with the `Spot.MoveNode()` method, and the spot central point is again at the same initial shift from cursor (something similar to Achilles and tortoise paradox). The only solution is to cut the link between the mover and the caught object,

---

[1] Some older classes from `MoveGraphLibrary.dll` used the `Press()` method with two parameters to start resizing or forward movement and `StartRotation()` method with a single parameter to start rotation. Even for such classes, there is now a `Press()` method with three parameters that can be used instead of older variants.

then to adjust cursor position, and after it to reinstall their link. This is done by the
AdjustCursorPosition() method, which includes two calls of the Mover.MouseTraced
property. (Any object can be used either directly in a form or on a page of TabControl;
this is the reason to have two branches in the code of this method.)

```
private void AdjustCursorPosition (PointF pt)
{
    m_supervisor .MouseTraced = false;
    if (m_tabpage != null)
    {
        Cursor .Position = m_tabpage .PointToScreen (Point .Round (pt));
    }
    else
    {
        Cursor .Position = m_form .PointToScreen (Point .Round (pt));
    }
    m_supervisor .MouseTraced = true;
}
```

Do we need anything else to do at the moment when the spot is pressed? No. Objects
of the Spot class are involved only in forward movement; this movement is done by the
left button. There is a single node in the cover of this class, and regardless of the pressed
point, the cursor is shifted to the central point.

```
public void Press (Point ptMouse, MouseButtons catcher, int iNode)
{
    if (catcher == MouseButtons .Left)
    {
        AdjustCursorPosition (m_center);
    }
}
```

Is there any inconvenience with this initial move of the cursor from one position to
another? The best way to check this situation is to try. The spot radius can be changed
in the [3, 12] range. As you will find further on, the same adjustment is always used in
small circular nodes. The standard radius of such nodes is three pixels; in some cases,
there are circular nodes with a radius of four or five pixels. In all these cases the initial
cursor adjustment at the moment of the mouse press is not even detected by our eyes.
For bigger radius, such movement can be seen, but I never use a bigger radius when a
circular node is positioned over some special point.

Now let's return to our example Form_Spot.cs.

Any movement is started when an object is pressed. In this example, we have objects of only two classes, so in either case the appropriate Press() method is called.

```
private void OnMouseDown (object sender, MouseEventArgs e)
{
    ptMouse_Down = e .Location;
    if (mover .Catch (e .Location, e .Button))
    {
        GraphicalObject grobj = mover .CaughtSource;
        int iNode = mover .CaughtNode;
        if (grobj is Spot)
        {
            spotPressed = grobj as Spot;
            spotPressed .Press (e .Location, e .Button, iNode);
        }
        else if (grobj is Info_Resizable)
        {
            info .Press (e .Location, e .Button, iNode);
        }
    }
    ContextMenuStrip = null;
}
```

The rectangular object with information belongs to the Info_Resizable class, which is included into the MoveGraphLibrary.dll; similar elements are going to appear in many examples of the accompanying application. A rectangle with information can be moved by any inner point and resized by any border point. When the area is decreased, then small circles appear on the right and bottom sides of rectangle; these circles allow you to scroll the information inside the area. Because the information area can be involved in two types of movements, forward movement and resizing, then there must be more than one node in its cover.

When a Spot object is pressed with the left button; the initial adjustment of cursor position happens, and now the spot is pressed at the central point. What happens when the mouse with the pressed button is moved?

The mover knows the class of the caught object and calls the MoveNode() method of this class. Code of the Spot.MoveNode() method was already shown on the previous page; I'll repeat here the needed part.

```
public override bool MoveNode (..., Point ptM, ...)
{
    ... ...
    if (catcher == MouseButtons .Left)
    {
        Center = ptM;
        ... ...
```

The MoveNode() method gets the current cursor position (ptM), and then the Spot. Center property sets the spot central point at the same position.

```
public PointF Center
{
    get { return (m_center); }
    set
    {
        m_center = value;
        DefineCover ();
    }
}
```

Thus, regardless of the mouse movement, the central point of the pressed spot goes with the cursor. This synchronous movement of two different objects is done in two steps.

1. Mouse cursor moves to an arbitrary position.

2. Spot central point moves to the mouse position.

The value returned by the Mover.Move() method signals whether anything is currently caught. If any object is caught, then the returned value is true, and the area must be redrawn.

```
private void OnMouseMove (object sender, MouseEventArgs e)
{
    if (mover .Move (e .Location))
    {
        Invalidate ();
    }
}
```

The third significant event is the release of the mouse button. If any object was caught by the preceding press of mouse button, then this object is released. If an object was pressed with the left button, then it is a rare situation that anything has to be done with the released object. For example, the released push button must be redrawn, but it is an exception from the rule. If an object was previously pressed with the right button and the distance between the points of press and release is negligible (in my programs it happens when the distance does not exceed three pixels), then it is considered as a menu call. Usually each class of elements has its own menu. The same rule of menu call is applied when the press–release pair of events happens at an empty place. Thus, we have three menus in this example (Figure 2-2).

Figure 2-2a. *Menu on spots*

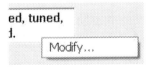

Figure 2-2b. *Menu on information*

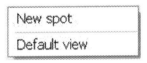

Figure 2-2c. *Menu at empty places*

```
private void OnMouseUp (object sender, MouseEventArgs e)
{
    ptMouse_Up = e .Location;
    double fDist = Auxi_Geometry .Distance (ptMouse_Down, ptMouse_Up);
```

```
    int iObj, iNode;
    if (mover .Release (out iObj, out iNode))
    {
        if (e .Button == MouseButtons .Right && fDist <= 3)
        {
            GraphicalObject grobj = mover .ReleasedSource;
            if (grobj is Spot)
            {
                ContextMenuStrip = menuOnSpot;
            }
            else if (grobj is Info_Resizable)
            {
                ContextMenuStrip = menuOnInfo;
            }
        }
    }
    else if (e .Button == MouseButtons .Right && fDist <= 3)
    {
        ContextMenuStrip = menuOnEmpty;
    }
}
```

The spot is a small and simple object with two parameters that can be changed: color and radius. The change of these parameters is organized via a small tuning form (Figure 2-3).

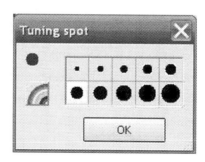

Figure 2-3. *Tuning form for spots*

A small rectangular area with information is an object of the `Info_Resizable` class that is included in `MoveGrapLibrary.dll`. Similar areas with information are used in many examples of the accompanying application, and the work with all these elements is absolutely identical. A small menu that can be called on information (Figure 2-2b) contains a single command that allows you to call a tuning form for information (Figure 2-4). The information area has four parameters that can be changed: the font and color of the text, the background color of the area, and the color of the small circular sliders. Buttons inside the tuning form give access to standard dialogs of the font and color selection; a track bar allows you to change the area transparency. This auxiliary form consists of the elements that are discussed in much more detail in Chapter 5, but I hope that there are not going to be any problems in using all these elements and the form itself prior to their discussion.

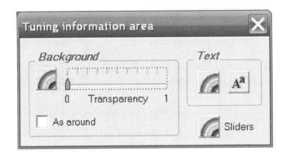

Figure 2-4. *Tuning form for Info_Resizable objects*

File: `Form_Spot_OnLineAndCircle.cs`

Menu position: Simple objects ➤ Spot on line and circle

Let's change our example in such a way that each spot would be allowed to move not freely around the screen but only along some track. Such a track can be either a straight segment or a circle (Figure 2-5). In the current example, the tracks are not movable; such an example will be discussed later. In all my programs, all elements are movable, so the nonmovability of tracks in the current example gives me a feeling of some major fault. I can't move the lines and circles, and I can't resize those circular tracks, so I can't rearrange the general view of this example. Those tracks can be changed through the command of menu for all empty places, but this command sets the new tracks in a random way, so I have no control over this process. This inconvenience can be easily removed, but this will be done a bit later.

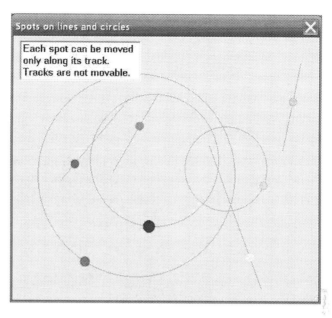

Figure 2-5. *Spots are movable, while tracks in the current example are not movable*

Spots on straight and circular tracks look similar, but they are organized as objects of two different classes. Let's start with the spots on line segments.

```
public class Spot_OnLineSegment : GraphicalObject
{
    PointF ptA, ptB;
    PointF m_center, ptPressed;
    int m_radius;
    Color m_color;
    Pen penLine;
    int minSegmentLength = 30;
    static int minRadius = 3;
    static int maxRadius = 12;
```

To initialize an element of the Spot_OnLineSegment class, you have to declare the segment end points and three parameters for the spot: initial position, radius, and color. If you need the spot to appear exactly at some point on the track, you can calculate this point beforehand and use it as a parameter on initialization. Regardless of the accuracy of your calculations, the spot will appear at such point of segment that is the nearest to the declared initial position.

33

```
public Spot_OnLineSegment (Form frm, Mover mvr, PointF pt0, PointF pt1,
                              PointF ptSpot, int r, Color clrSpot)
{
    ... ...
    m_center = Auxi_Geometry .Segment_NearestPoint (ptSpot, ptA, ptB);
    m_radius = Math .Min (Math .Max (minRadius, r), maxRadius);
```

The DefineCover() and Move() methods for this class are identical to similar
methods of the Spot class. For spots on tracks, I decided to demonstrate the change of
movability, so there is some difference starting with the Press() method. For movable
spot, there is an identical adjustment of cursor position that is moved to the spot central
point. For an unmovable spot, there is no cursor adjustment, but the pressed point is
remembered (ptPressed).

```
public void Press (Point ptMouse, MouseButtons catcher, int iNode)
{
    if (catcher == MouseButtons .Left)
    {
        if (Movable)
        {
            AdjustCursorPosition (m_center);
        }
        else
        {
            ptPressed = ptMouse;
        }
    }
}
```

There are also some changes in the MoveNode() method.

```
public override bool MoveNode (...)
{
    bool bRet = false;
    if (catcher == MouseButtons .Left)
    {
        if (Movable)
```

```
        {
            Center = ptMouse;
            AdjustCursorPosition (m_center);
        }
        else
        {
            AdjustCursorPosition (ptPressed);
        }
        bRet = true;
    }
    return (bRet);
}
```

The Movable spot on the line is nearly identical to the spots from the previous example. How the movement of the new spot is limited only to the straight segment between its end points?

When a spot is pressed with the left button, the same adjustment of the cursor position occurs as was explained for Spot objects several pages back. The cursor is switched to the spot central point. Initially, the spot central point was placed exactly on the line, so now the cursor is also exactly on the line, and the spot is caught.

Then the mouse is moved to some new position (ptMouse). You may try to move the cursor along the line, but with high probability this new point is not exactly on the line but somewhere nearby. The spot must stay strictly on the line, so instead of moving the spot synchronously with cursor, the spot central point (m_center) is moved to such a point of segment that is the closest to the cursor position.

```
public PointF Center
{
    get { return (m_center); }
    set
    {
        m_center = Auxi_Geometry .Segment_NearestPoint (value, ptA, ptB);
        DefineCover ();
    }
}
```

After this, the cursor is moved to the spot central point by the familiar AdjustCursorPosition() method. If you try to move a spot anywhere to the side of the line, it is always returned to the nearest point on the line. If you try to move a spot beyond the end point, it is kept on the end point and not a pixel farther. In the case of restrictions, we have such sequence of movements.

1. The mouse cursor moves to an arbitrary position.

2. The spot central point is moved to the point on line, which is the nearest to mouse position.

3. The cursor is moved to the spot central point.

Compare this sequence of steps with the one from the previous example. There is an obvious and important difference.

For a freely moved object, the cursor goes anywhere, and then the object goes with cursor.

For restricted movement, the cursor goes anywhere, and then object position is determined by cursor and restrictions; after this, the cursor returns to object.

What happens when you press and try to move the *unmovable* spot? The MoveNode() method uses the AdjustCursorPosition() method to keep cursor at initially pressed point. I think that keeping of the pressed mouse at the same position is the best indication of the object immovability.

```
public override bool MoveNode (int iNode, int dx, int dy, Point ptMouse,
                               MouseButtons catcher)
{
    bool bRet = false;
    if (catcher == MouseButtons .Left)
    {
        if (Movable)
        {
            ... ...
        }
        else
        {
            AdjustCursorPosition (ptPressed);
        }
        ... ...
```

What is the difference between keeping a spot on a straight segment and on a circular track? The difference is mostly in the parameters that describe the track.

```
public class Spot_OnCircle : GraphicalObject
{
    PointF centerCircle;
    float radiusCircle;
    PointF m_center, ptPressed;
    int m_radius;
    Color m_color;
    Pen penCircle;
    float minRadius_Circle = 30;
```

The circular track is determined by its central point and radius; other parameters of initialization are identical. First the track is organized. Then the point on the track that is nearest to the one proposed through the parameter is calculated; the spot is positioned at this calculated point.

```
public Spot_OnCircle (Form frm, Mover mvr, PointF ptC_track, float rad_track,
                      PointF ptSpot, int r, Color clrSpot)
{
    ... ...
    centerCircle = ptC_track;
    radiusCircle = Math .Max (rad_track, minRadius_Circle);
    m_center = Auxi_Geometry .PointToPoint (centerCircle,
                 Auxi_Geometry .Angle (centerCircle, ptSpot), radiusCircle);
    ... ...
```

The spot must stay all the time on a track, so the new position is calculated as the nearest to the mouse cursor point on a circle.

```
public PointF Center
{
    get { return (m_center); }
    set
    {
```

```
        m_center = Auxi_Geometry .PointToPoint (centerCircle,
                    Auxi_Geometry .Angle (centerCircle, value),
                    radiusCircle);
        DefineCover ();
    }
}
```

Everything else is absolutely the same as for spots on straight segments.

We discussed the difference in reaction to pressing movable and unmovable spots, but there was no explanation of how the movability of any object is regulated.

Movable and Unmovable Objects

Movability is a feature that is regulated at the level of the base GraphicalObject class. By default, any new object is movable, so when you start the current example with spots on lines and circles, all these spots are movable. To switch the movability of a spot, you call menu on this spot (Figure 2-6) and click the second command; the associated method is executed.

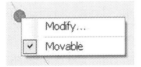

Figure 2-6. *Menu on a spot*

```
private void Click_miMovable_LineSpot (object sender, EventArgs e)
{
    spotPressed_onLine .Movable = !spotPressed_onLine .Movable;
}
```

Classes derived from GraphicalObject do not have a Movable property of their own and use the property of the base class.

```
public bool Movable
{
    get { return (m_movable); }
    set
    {
```

```
            m_movable = value;
            DefineCover ();
        }
    }
}
```

There are two ways to use the movability status of an object. One way is to change the cover according to the needed movability; such a technique is used in some examples from my book [2]. Another way is to use the same cover but to consider the movability value inside the MoveNode() method. Currently I prefer to use this technique, as can be seen in both classes for spots on lines and on circles.

We are only at the beginning of this book, and the demonstrated examples are simple, but it is easy to see how the same technique can be used in much more complex situations. In the Form_SpotOnCommentedWay.cs example from my book [2], the move of similar spot along the system of roads looks like a toy railroad (Figure 2-7). Road parts are either straight segments or arcs; roads can split, merge, and cross. Movement along each road part is organized in the same simple way as along our straight lines and circles. You need only some simple algorithm to decide at any moment (for any spot position) the possibility of further movement from one road segment to another.

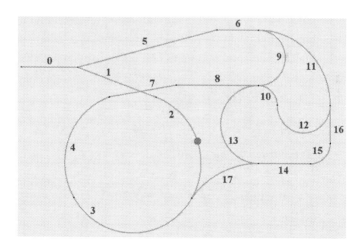

Figure 2-7. *Movement of the spot along these roads is organized in similar way to what is shown with line segments and circles in the current example*

File: Form_ElementOnTrack.cs

Menu position: Simple objects ➤ Element on track

The mouse cursor adjustment to the spot center looks good for small spots and not good at all for bigger circles. The new example demonstrates a different approach to this problem. In the current example, the tracks are not so primitive (Figure 2-8), and two different techniques are used for circles of two different sizes.

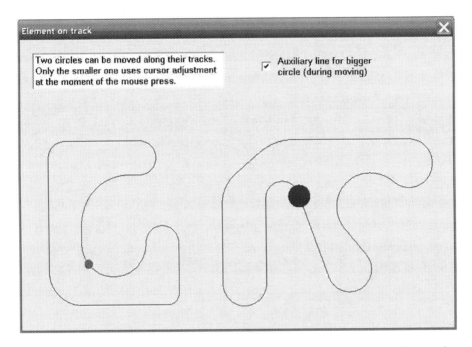

Figure 2-8. *A small circle uses mouse adjustment at the moment of initial mouse press; a bigger circle works without such thing*

Movement of a small red spot is organized in the same way as in the previous example. When an object of the SmallSpotOnTrack class is pressed, the cursor is moved to the spot central point, which is exactly on the track. Until the moment of the mouse release, those two points—the cursor and the spot central point—move synchronously and exactly along the track.

The use of initial cursor adjustment is inaccessible for objects of considerable size, so it is not used for the spot of the BigSpotOnTrack class. At the moment of the initial press, the difference between the cursor position and the spot central point is calculated (m_shift); after that, the copy of the way is constructed, and this copy is shifted from the original way on the same distance.

```
public void Press (Point ptMouse)
{
    m_shift = new SizeF (ptMouse .X - m_center .X, ptMouse .Y - m_center .Y);
    m_wayForMouse = m_way .Copy (m_shift);
}
```

At the moment of the mouse press, as at any other moment, the spot central point is positioned exactly on the original way, while the cursor finds itself on the shifted copy of that way (Figure 2-9). Until the mouse release, there is always the same shift between the mouse cursor and the spot central point. The standard technique of cursor adjustment is used to keep the cursor on its way; the fixed shift between the mouse cursor and spot central point guarantees that the spot central point will be always on its way. In a normal situation, the auxiliary way is not shown. Only the original way is shown, and the spot central point moves along this visible way regardless of the mouse position.

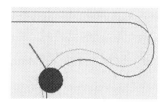

Figure 2-9. *A red line shows the point at which the spot is pressed with a cursor*

In the current example, the quick movement of the mouse cursor will allow you to move the spot from one part of the way to another even across an empty space. There exists an easy-to-use technique that prevents such movements, but it requires bigger code and has nothing to do with the movement explanation. Such code is demonstrated in the examples from my book [2], but it is not used in the current example.

Line

File: Form_Line_Segment.cs

Menu position: Simple objects ➤ Line segment

To move and resize an object, it gets a cover. Each node in a cover is used to start one or another movement. Three different movements are started with the left button press, so each node can start only one of these movements. If an object has a cover consisting of a single node, then such an object can be involved in only one movement, and usually it is a forward move; this was demonstrated in the first example of Form_Spot.cs. The majority of objects are involved both in forward movement and resizing, so there is more than one node in their covers.

Segments of straight lines are the next objects to be explored. In our ordinary life, when we have an elastic string and want to move it, we take it by any place and move the whole string, but if we want to stretch it, we do it by the end point. In the same way, the segments of screen lines can be moved and resized. Pressing of the end points has a different reaction from pressing all other points. In addition, the moving of the caught end can be organized in two different ways.

- It can be moved freely around the screen thus changing simultaneously the segment length and angle.

- The move can be allowed only along the line thus changing the length but not the angle.

Figure 2-10 shows several objects of the Line_Segment class. Auxiliary lines provide information about the currently allowed changes of each segment.If there is a thin line going along the segment beyond its end points, then the ends of this segment can be moved only along this line.

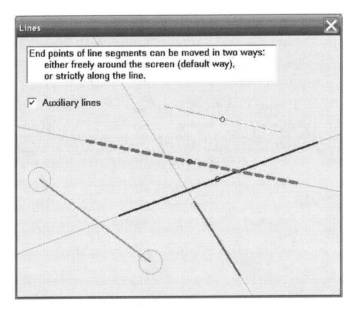

Figure 2-10. *Auxiliary lines can provide some information about the possible change of each segment*

- If there are circles around the end points, then those end points can be moved freely around the screen, but the end point cannot be moved inside the circle around another end point because there is a limit for minimal segment length. This limit works for all segments, but it is not demonstrated for those that can be resized only along the line.

- A small circle in the middle of segment informs that this segment can be rotated and also marks the rotation center.

```
public class Line_Segment : GraphicalObject
{
    EndPointMove m_typeEndMove;
    PointF ptA, ptB;
    Pen m_pen, m_penAuxi;
    bool bResizable, bRotatable, bShowAuxi;
    PointF pt0_limit, pt1_limit, ptPressed;
    float maxWidth = 6;
    float minLen = 20;
```

The cover of such an object consists of three nodes: two circular nodes at the ends and a strip node along the full segment (Figure 2-11). The order of nodes is important. The default diameter of circular nodes is the same as the default width of the strip nodes. The central points of two circular nodes are the same as the central points of semicircles at the ends of the strip node. If you put the strip node at the head, then it will block both circles, and those two nodes will not work. To provide the resizing, both circular nodes have to be placed ahead of the strip node. This is a general rule for the construction of all the covers: if the nodes overlap, then smaller nodes have to be positioned ahead of the bigger nodes.

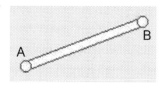

Figure 2-11. *The segment cover consists of one strip and two circular nodes*

```
public override void DefineCover ()
{
    float rad = Resizable ? 4 : 0;
    cover = new Cover (new CoverNode [] {new CoverNode (0, ptA, rad),
                                         new CoverNode (1, ptB, rad),
                                         new CoverNode (2, ptA, ptB)});
    if (TransparentForMover)
    {
        cover .SetBehaviour (Behaviour .Transparent);
    }
}
```

To make the resizing easier, the radius of circular nodes is slightly enlarged from the default value. The radius of circular nodes also depends on the required resizability of a particular segment. The change of segment resizability can be provided in two different ways.

- For a nonresizable segment, two circular nodes can be simply excluded from the cover thus leaving a single node in the cover. In such a case, the number of the strip node for resizable and nonresizable segments will be different, and this will require two different versions of the MoveNode() method.

- Another way is to declare a zero radius for circular nodes of nonresizable segment; then the same MoveNode() method can be used for resizable and nonresizable segments. I prefer to have the same number of nodes in the covers of resizable and nonresizable elements and to squeeze currently unneeded nodes to zero size.

When a line is pressed, then the Line_Segment.Press() method is called. This method includes all the calculations for further movement, which is started by this press.

The *left* button press starts either resizing or forward movement, so calculations depend on the pressed point and the pressed node. If a small circular node is pressed, then the cursor is moved to the line end point, which is covered by this pressed node; in case of a strip node, cursor is moved to the nearest point on the line axis.

```
public void Press (Point ptMouse, MouseButtons catcher, int iNode)
{
    if (catcher == MouseButtons .Left)
    {
        switch (iNode)
        {
            case 0:
                ptPressed = ptA;
                break;
            case 1:
                ptPressed = ptB;
                break;
            case 2:
            default:
                ptPressed =
                        Auxi_Geometry .Segment_NearestPoint (ptMouse,
                        ptA, ptB);
                break;
        }
        AdjustCursorPosition (ptPressed);
        ... ...
```

Additional calculations are needed when the pressed end point can be moved only along the line. There is a limit on minimal segment length (minLen), so the point on the axis nearest to the opposite end and beyond which the pressed end cannot be moved is calculated (pt0_limit). The pressed end would be allowed to move along the line only on one side from this point; to organize such movement, another point (pt1_limit) is calculated as being far away on the same side.

```
        if (Resizable && m_typeEndMove == EndPointMove .Along)
        {
            if (iNode == 0)
            {
                double ang = Angle + Math .PI;
                pt0_limit = Auxi_Geometry .PointToPoint (ptB, ang, minLen);
                pt1_limit = Auxi_Geometry .PointToPoint (ptB, ang, 4000);
```

```
        }
        else if (iNode == 1)
        {
            pt0_limit = Auxi_Geometry .PointToPoint (ptA, Angle,
            minLen);
            pt1_limit = Auxi_Geometry .PointToPoint (ptA, Angle, 4000);
        }
    }
    ... ...
```

Of all possible movements, only rotation is started by the *right* button press. In such a case, the mouse is moved to the nearest point on the line axis; then the angle from the center of rotation to the mouse is calculated (angleMouse) and compensation between this angle and the line angle.

```
public void Press (Point ptMouse, MouseButtons catcher, int iNode)
{
    ... ...
    else if (catcher == MouseButtons .Right)
    {
        ptPressed = Auxi_Geometry .Segment_NearestPoint (ptMouse, ptA, ptB);
        AdjustCursorPosition (ptPressed);
        double angleMouse = Auxi_Geometry .Angle (Center, ptPressed);
        compensation = Auxi_Common .LimitedRadian (angleMouse - Angle);
    }
}
```

Further movement of the pressed line is described by the MoveNode() method. The code depends on the type of movement allowed for end points; let's start with the case of their movement only along the segment line.

The case of the pressed end point allowed *to move only along the line* is similar to the previously discussed case of a small spot on the line segment. The end points of allowed movement—pt0_limit and pt1_limit—were already calculated. The new position of the caught line end can be only on a segment between these points. If a line was pressed somewhere inside, then the entire object (line) is moved.

```
public override bool MoveNode (...)
{
    bool bRet = false;
    if (catcher == MouseButtons .Left)
    {
        if (m_typeEndMove == EndPointMove .Along)
        {
            switch (iNode)
            {
                case 0:
                    Point_A = Auxi_Geometry .Segment_NearestPoint
                    (ptMouse, pt0_limit, pt1_limit);
                    AdjustCursorPosition (Point_A);
                    bRet = true;
                    break;
                case 1:
                    Point_B = Auxi_Geometry .Segment_NearestPoint
                    (ptMouse, pt0_limit, pt1_limit);
                    AdjustCursorPosition (Point_B);
                    bRet = true;
                    break;
                default:
                    if (Movable)
                    {
                        Move (dx, dy);
                        bRet = true;
                    }
                    else
                    {
                        AdjustCursorPosition (ptPressed);
                    }
                    break;
            }
        }
        ... ...
```

For the case of *end points that can move freely* around the screen, the only forbidden area for a pressed end point is a circle around the opposite end; the radius of this forbidden circle is equal to the minimum allowed length of segment.

- If the mouse is placed anywhere outside this circle, then the caught end goes with the mouse.

- If the mouse is moved inside the circle, then the caught end cannot be moved there. Instead, the point on the circle border nearest to the cursor is calculated; the end point is placed there, and the cursor is adjusted to the same position.

When the line is pressed not at the end but anywhere inside, the whole line is moved as in the previous case.

```
... ...
else
{
    double fNewLen;
    switch (iNode)
    {
        case 0:
            fNewLen = Auxi_Geometry .Distance (ptB, ptMouse);
            if (fNewLen >= minLen)
            {
                ptA = ptMouse;
            }
            else
            {
                Point_A = Auxi_Geometry .PointToPoint (ptB,
                        Auxi_Geometry .Angle (ptB, ptMouse),
                        minLen);
                AdjustCursorPosition (ptA);
            }
            bRet = true;
            break;
        case 1:
            fNewLen = Auxi_Geometry .Distance (ptA, ptMouse);
```

```
                    if (fNewLen >= minLen)
                    {
                        ptB = ptMouse;
                    }
                    else
                    {
                        Point_B = Auxi_Geometry .PointToPoint (ptA,
                                    Auxi_Geometry .Angle (ptA, ptMouse),
                                    minLen);
                        AdjustCursorPosition (ptB);
                    }
                    bRet = true;
                    break;
                default:
                    ... ...
```

The *right* button is used for line rotation. The angle between cursor and line never changes throughout the rotation. The compensation angle was calculated at the initial press moment; this compensation is used throughout the rotation to calculate the line angle at any moment. If a line is not rotatable, then the cursor is fixed at the press point in exactly the same way as it is done for an unmovable line.

```
    ... ...
    else if (catcher == MouseButtons .Right)
    {
        if (Rotatable)
        {
            double angleMouse = Auxi_Geometry .Angle (Center, ptMouse);
            Angle = angleMouse - compensation;
            DefineCover ();
            bRet = true;
        }
        else
        {
            AdjustCursorPosition (ptPressed);
        }
    }
    ... ...
```

Regulation of the allowed movements is done through the commands of the menu that is called on the line (Figure 2-12). There is some ambiguity in separate regulation of movability and resizability. Suppose that you used a menu command and declared a segment unmovable. This means you cannot move this segment anywhere by pressing it at any inner point. But does it mean that there is no way to move this segment to another location? In reality you can do it by moving one end of segment and then another. I am not going to block this byroad; it is easy to do, but I am not sure that I have to do it. In the case of complex objects such as plots that are demonstrated closer to the end of this book, I use the fixation of objects; such fixation prevents all possible movements. In the case of simple objects (lines and several others), I prefer to demonstrate all details and different variants.

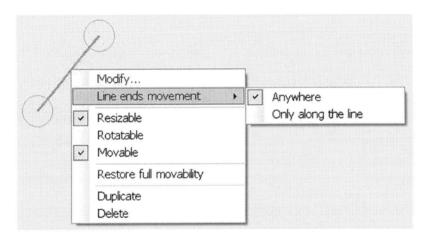

Figure 2-12. *Menu on segment*

I already explained that movability is regulated at the level of the base GraphicalObject class. What about resizability and rotatability? They are needed not for all classes, so they are regulated in each particular class. There are two fields and two properties to change them, but there is a small difference between them. Cover design depends on the current value of resizability, so the change of resizability requires a call of the DefineCover() method. The value of rotatability is simply changed; later it is used by the MoveNode() method.

The same menu (Figure 2-12) includes commands to duplicate the pressed segment, to delete it, or to modify it with the help of a special tuning form Form_Tuning_Line.cs (Figure 2-13).

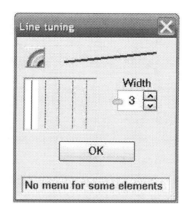

Figure 2-13. *Line tuning*

File: Form_Polyline.cs

Menu position: Simple objects ➤ Polyline

Let's turn to the polyline. Each polyline consists of a sequence of segments. Each segment can be changed in the same way as was just discussed, but there is one additional feature. Polyline configuration can be changed not only by moving the joints and end points, but also by changing the number of segments. See Figure 2-14.

```
public class Polyline : GraphicalObject
{
    List<PointF> m_points = new List<PointF> ();
    Pen m_pen;
    Color clrEnds = Color .DarkGreen;
    Color clrJoints = Color .DarkGray;
    bool bMarkEnds = true;
    bool bMarkJoints = true;
    bool bReconfigurable, bRotatable;
```

Figure 2-14. *Polyline with marked end points and joints*

The cover of such an object is simple: circular nodes are placed at the ends of segments; strip nodes are based on each pair of consecutive points. If there are N points to be connected, then the first N nodes of the cover are circular; after them, there are N-1 strip nodes. If the line is not reconfigurable, then all circular nodes are squeezed to zero size.

```
public override void DefineCover ()
{
    float rad = Reconfigurable ? 4 : 0;
    int nPts = m_points .Count;
    CoverNode [] nodes = new CoverNode [nPts + (nPts - 1)];
    for (int i = 0; i < nPts; i++)
    {
        nodes [i] = new CoverNode (i, m_points [i], rad);
    }
    for (int i = 0; i < nPts - 1; i++)
    {
        nodes [nPts + i] =
                    new CoverNode (nPts + i, m_points [i], m_points
                    [i + 1]);
    }
    cover = new Cover (nodes);
    if (!Movable && Reconfigurable)
    {
        cover .SetCursor (NodeShape .Strip, Cursors .Hand);
    }
    else
    {
        cover .SetCursor (NodeShape .Strip, Cursors .SizeAll);
    }
    ... ...
```

The ends of all segments are used to change the configuration, so we'll deal with circular nodes in the same way as it was done in the Line_Segment class. Strip nodes can be used to move the whole polyline, but a special set of parameters allows you to press the line at the needed point, to add a new joint at this point and, without mouse release, to move this new joint to some needed location. The difference in reaction is signaled by using different cursors.

- When a polyline is movable, then the cursor over its segments takes the standard shape for movable objects: Cursors.SizeAll.

- Adding new joints by pressing segments with the mouse is allowed only for unmovable and reconfigurable polylines; for such combinations, the cursor is changed to Cursors.Hand.

Let's check how this adding of new joints is organized. Everything happens at the moment of mouse press, so we look into the OnMouseDown() method.

```
private void OnMouseDown (object sender, MouseEventArgs e)
{
    ptMouse_Down = e .Location;
    if (mover .Catch (e .Location, e .Button))
    {
        GraphicalObject grobj = mover .CaughtSource;
        int iNode = mover .CaughtNode;
        if (grobj is Polyline)
        {
            linePressed = grobj as Polyline;
            linePressed .Press (e .Location, e .Button, iNode);
            if (mover .CaughtNodeShape == NodeShape .Strip)
            {
                iSegment = iNode - linePressed .PointsNumber;
            }
            else
            {
                iSegment = -1;
            }
            if (!linePressed .Movable && linePressed .Reconfigurable &&
                e .Button == MouseButtons .Left  &&
                mover .CaughtNodeShape == NodeShape .Strip)
            {
                mover .Release ();
                linePressed .InsertPoint (iSegment + 1, e .Location);
                mover .Catch (e .Location, e .Button);
                Invalidate ();
            }
            ... ...
```

53

- The number of the pressed node is provided by the mover (iNode). The order of nodes in the cover is known: first circles, then strips. Circular nodes are numbered from one end of line to another; the numbering of circles and strips start from the same end, so the number of the pressed segment (iSegment) is easily calculated.

```
iSegment = iNode - linePressed .PointsNumber;
```

- The line was pressed on a segment but has to be caught by the new joint, so the mover releases the caught object.

```
mover .Release ();
```

- A new joint is added to the line by the Polyline.InsertPoint() method. Because the numbering of nodes and segments starts from the same end, the segment k is a segment between points k and k+1. Thus, the number of the new point is going to be iSegment+1. Adding a joint causes cover renewal because the number of nodes changes. The DefineCover() method is called from inside the InsertPoint() method.

```
linePressed .InsertPoint (iSegment + 1, e .Location);
```

- The mover gets an order to catch an object under the cursor.

```
mover .Catch (e .Location, e .Button);
```

The cursor did not move anywhere since the moment of the press, and the central point of the new circular node is just under the cursor, so the mover can catch nothing else but the new node and thus the same line. In such way, when you decide to change the line configuration, you declare the line unmovable, then press the segment, and finally you continue to move the mouse with already caught circular node.

Joints are not affected by line movability, so joints can be removed through their menu regardless of the current line movability. If so, then the addition of joints must be also independent of line movability. While the described press-and-move process of adding joints can be used only with unmovable lines, joints can be added also through the menu on segments, and this works regardless of the line movability.

Rectangle

File: `Form_Rectangle.cs`

Menu position: Simple objects ➤ Rectangle

Objects of rectangular shape are the most often used screen elements. A rectangle looks like a simple object, but its transformation can be organized in many different ways; in my book [2], there is a whole chapter dedicated to different types of rectangles. The most general type of resizing allows you to do it by moving any side or corner, but different types of limitations can be imposed. There are rectangles with one fixed side while the moving of the opposite side allows you to change the size of element or even to turn it out. In some cases, the symmetrical move of the opposite side is needed. There is also a case of rectangle with a constant width/height ratio. Different types of resizing require the use of different covers, so for those special cases you better look into my book [2]. In the current example, a classic case of a rectangle with the resizing by all sides and corners is used. Elements of the `Rectangle_Unicolored` class can be freely moved, resized, and rotated. There is only a limit on the minimal size to prevent the accidental disappearance of an object. See Figure 2-15.

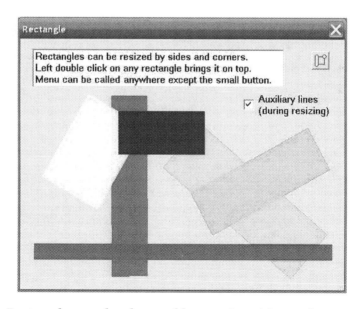

Figure 2-15. *Rectangles can be changed by moving sides and corners*

```
public class Rectangle_Unicolored : GraphicalObject
{
    PointF [] m_points;
    SolidBrush m_brush;
    bool bResizable, bRotatable;
    PointF m_center, ptPressed;
    double m_angle, compensation;
    static int minSide = 20;
```

It is not a rare situation when an object of rectangular shape always has horizontal and vertical sides and is never rotated; an area with information represents such a case. The easiest way to describe such an object is to set the coordinates of its top-left corner and two sizes of the area. An object of the Rectangle_Unicolored class is rotated around its central point, so the easiest way to describe the geometry of such a rectangle is to declare its central point, two sizes, and angle.

```
public Rectangle_Unicolored (Form frm, Mover mvr, PointF ptC,
                             double w, double h, double angleDegree,
                             Color clr)
```

Objects of the Rectangle_Unicolored class have a classical cover design: four circular nodes on the corners, four strip nodes along the sides, and a big rectangular node for the whole area of an object. To catch the corners easier, the radius of circular nodes is slightly enlarged from the default value. For nonresizable rectangles, all eight nodes on the border are squeezed to zero size, and only the big node is unchanged (Figure 2-16).

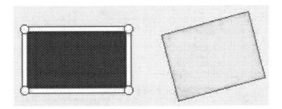

Figure 2-16. *Covers for resizable and nonresizable rectangles*

```
public override void DefineCover ()
{
    float wHalf, rad;
```

```
    if (Resizable)
    {
        wHalf = 3;
        rad = 5;
    }
    else
    {
        wHalf = rad = 0;
    }
    CoverNode [] nodes = new CoverNode [9];
    for (int i = 0; i < 4; i++)
    {
        nodes [i] = new CoverNode (i, m_points [i], rad);
    }
    for (int i = 0; i < 4; i++)
    {
        nodes [i + 4] = new CoverNode (i + 4, m_points [i],
                                       m_points [(i + 1) % 4],
                                       wHalf);
    }
    nodes [8] = new CoverNode (8, m_points);
    cover = new Cover (nodes);
    if (!Movable)
    {
        cover .SetCursor (NodeShape .Polygon, Cursors .NoMove2D);
    }
    ... ...
```

A picture of rectangle with its cover and node numbers (Figure 2-17) can be helpful for further discussion. When a rectangle is pressed, the Rectangle_Unicolored.Press() method is called. Further movements depend on the pressed node, so initial calculations at the press moment also depend on the node number.

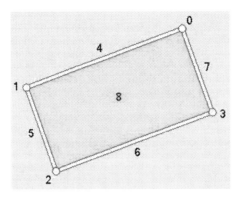

Figure 2-17. *Numbering of the nodes*

- Strip nodes are used to change one size of rectangle, so when a strip node is pressed, the cursor is allowed to move only along the straight line orthogonal to the pressed side. Throughout such cursor movement, this caught side goes with the cursor thus changing only one size of rectangle.

- Circular nodes are used to change both sizes of rectangle, so when a corner is pressed, then it can be moved inside some area, and both sizes can be changed simultaneously.

Because of this difference in reaction on pressing circular and strip nodes, the code in each of the involved methods usually has two branches. Let's start with the case of the pressed corner.

Suppose that the upper corner of the rectangle in Figure 2-17 is pressed (iNode = 0). There exists a minimal allowed size for any side of rectangle (minSide), so the pressed corner cannot be moved closer to two sides than this value. If there is a check mark inside the check box of the form (Figure 2-15), then two thin lines show the sides of the area inside which the pressed corner can be moved (Figure 2-18). (For the purpose of calculations, this area of allowed corner movement is determined as a rectangle. Two sides of this rectangle are shown by these thin lines, while two other sides are out of view because a rectangle is declared as really big.) While the pressed corner is moved around, the corner opposite to the pressed one does not change its position (ptBase). The rectangular area inside which the pressed corner is allowed to move is determined by four corners (ptsAllowed[]). For further use in some methods, I need the border of this area to be represented as a closed polygon, so the same four points are turned into an array of five points (ptsBorderAllowed[]) in which the last value is the same as the first one.

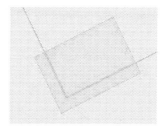

Figure 2-18. *The upper corner of rectangle is pressed; the area allowed for its movement is limited by two gray lines*

When the circular node is pressed, the cursor is switched exactly to the covered corner point by the AdjustCursorPosition() method.

```
public void Press (Point ptMouse, MouseButtons catcher, int iNode)
{
    if (catcher == MouseButtons .Left)
    {
        if (iNode == 8)
        {
            ptPressed = ptMouse;
            return;
        }
        PointF ptNearest;
        if (iNode < 4)        // corners
        {
            ptNearest = m_points [iNode];
            int iBase = (iNode + 2) % 4;
            PointF ptBase = m_points [iBase];
            double angleToNext = Auxi_Geometry .Angle (m_points
            [iBase], m_points [(iBase + 1) % 4]);
            ptsAllowed [0] = Auxi_Geometry .PointToPoint (ptBase,
                        angleToNext + Math .PI / 4, minSide * Math
                        .Sqrt (2));
            ptsAllowed [1] = Auxi_Geometry .PointToPoint (ptsAllowed [0],
                                                angleToNext,
                                                5000);
```

```
            ptsAllowed [2] = Auxi_Geometry .PointToPoint (ptsAllowed [0],
                                        angleToNext + Math .PI / 4,
                                        7000);
            ptsAllowed [3] = Auxi_Geometry .PointToPoint (ptsAllowed [0],
                                        angleToNext + Math .PI / 2,
                                        5000);
            ptsBorderAllowed = Auxi_Geometry .ClosedPolyline
            (ptsAllowed);
        }
        ... ...
        AdjustCursorPosition (ptNearest);
    }
    ... ...
```

From the moment when a corner is pressed and throughout further movement of the pressed mouse, the cursor and the corner point must move together. The opposite corner (in the shown case it is iNode = 2) never changes its position; two other corners must change positions in order to retain the rectangle.

While the cursor moves inside the allowed area, the grabbed corner goes with the cursor without problems.

```
public override bool MoveNode (...)
{
    bool bRet = false;
    if (catcher == MouseButtons .Left)
    {
        if (iNode < 4)        // corners
        {
            PointF ptNext, ptPrev;
            if (Auxi_Geometry .PointInsideConvexPolygon (ptMouse,
            ptsAllowed))
            {
                m_points [iNode] = ptMouse;
                Auxi_Geometry .Distance_PointLine (ptMouse, m_points
                                        [(iNode + 1) % 4],
```

```
                                m_points [(iNode + 2) % 4],
                                            out ptNext);
            Auxi_Geometry .Distance_PointLine (ptMouse,
                                        m_points [(iNode + 2) % 4],
                                        m_points [(iNode + 3) % 4],
                                            out ptPrev);
        m_points [(iNode + 1) % 4] = ptNext;
        m_points [(iNode + 3) % 4] = ptPrev;
        DefineCover ();
        bRet = true;
    }
```

If cursor is moved outside the allowed area, then cursor is returned to the nearest point on the border of this area, and the caught corner goes with the cursor.

```
        else
        {
            m_points [iNode] = Auxi_Geometry .Polyline_NearestPoint (
                                    ptMouse, ptsBorderAllowed);
            Auxi_Geometry .Distance_PointLine (ptMouse,
                                        m_points [(iNode + 1) % 4],
                                        m_points [(iNode + 2) % 4],
                                            out ptNext);
            Auxi_Geometry .Distance_PointLine (ptMouse,
                                        m_points [(iNode + 2) % 4],
                                        m_points [(iNode + 3) % 4],
                                            out ptPrev);
            m_points [(iNode + 1) % 4] = ptNext;
            m_points [(iNode + 3) % 4] = ptPrev;
            DefineCover ();
            AdjustCursorPosition (m_points [iNode]);
            bRet = false;
        }
        ... ...
```

Moving of the side is slightly easier. First, the nearest point on the caught side (ptNearest) and the nearest point on the opposite side (ptOnOppositeSide) are calculated. The line through these points (its angle is angleBeam) is orthogonal to the pressed side (Figure 2-19). The cursor of the pressed mouse is allowed to move only along this line. One end of the cursor way (ptEndIn) is determined by the minimum allowed size of rectangle (minSide), while another end is far away (ptEndOut). Each border of rectangle is covered by a strip node, so when such node is pressed, the cursor is switched to the nearest point of the border under this node (ptNearest). As usual, the adjustment of cursor position is done with the AdjustCursorPosition() method.

Figure 2-19. *The cursor is pressed at the point where the line crosses the side; this line is orthogonal to the pressed side; cursor moves only along this line*

```
public void Press (...)
{
    ... ...
    else                 // sides
    {
        ptNearest = Auxi_Geometry .Segment_NearestPoint (ptMouse,
                        m_points [iNode - 4], m_points [(iNode -
                        3) % 4]);
        ptOnOppositeSide = Auxi_Geometry .Segment_NearestPoint (ptMouse,
        m_points [(iNode + 2) % 4], m_points [(iNode + 3) % 4]);
        double angleBeam = Auxi_Geometry.Angle (ptOnOppositeSide,
                                            ptMouse);
```

```
        ptEndIn = Auxi_Geometry .PointToPoint (ptOnOppositeSide,
                                            angleBeam, minSide);
        ptEndOut = Auxi_Geometry .PointToPoint (ptOnOppositeSide,
                                            angleBeam, 5000);
    }
    ... ...
    AdjustCursorPosition (ptNearest);
}
... ...
```

When any side is moved, only the end points of this side are changed, while two other corners of rectangle stay at their current position. Figure 2-19 shows the case when the mouse is pressed on the right border at the point where this side is crossed with an auxiliary line. Figure 2-17 shows the cover with node numbers and makes it obvious that this is the situation when node 7 was pressed, so only the points 0 and 3 are changed when this side is moved.

```
public override bool MoveNode (...)
{
    bool bRet = false;
    if (catcher == MouseButtons .Left)
    {
        ... ...
        else if (iNode < 8)   // sides
        {
            double newW, newH;
            PointF ptNearest = Auxi_Geometry .Segment_NearestPoint
            (ptMouse, ptEndIn, ptEndOut);
            ... ...
            else    // iNode == 7
            {
```

```
                newW = Auxi_Geometry .Distance (ptNearest,
                                         ptOnOppositeSide);
            m_points [0] = Auxi_Geometry .PointToPoint (m_points [1],
                                              m_angle, newW);
            m_points [3] = Auxi_Geometry .PointToPoint (m_points [2],
                                              m_angle, newW);
        }
        DefineCover ();
        AdjustCursorPosition (ptNearest);
        bRet = true;
    ... ...
```

The case of rectangle perfectly demonstrates the main rules of using the adhered mouse during resizing.

- The border is covered by combination of small circular nodes and thin strips. At the moment of the border press, some adjustment of cursor position might be done. When a circular node is pressed, the cursor is moved to its central point; when a strip node is pressed, the cursor is moved to the nearest point on the strip axis. In any case, the cursor is placed exactly on the border.

- At the same moment, the limits for further cursor movement are calculated. If the cursor is allowed to move only along a straight segment, then two end points of this segment are calculated. If further movement is allowed inside some area; then the border of this area is calculated.

- If cursor movement is allowed along the straight segment, then for any cursor movement the nearest point on this segment is calculated; the cursor is moved to this point and causes the corresponding change of an object. If some area is allowed for cursor movement and the cursor is found outside this area, then the cursor is returned to the nearest point on the border of this area.

The rotation of the Rectangle_Unicolored elements is organized in a way that is standard for all objects, so let's look at the details of this process.

Rotatable and Nonrotatable Objects

Not all the screen objects need rotation, so this feature is not included into the base class but only into the classes that need it. The regulation of rotatability is also included in these classes. By default, rectangles are rotatable. To change the rotatability of particular rectangle, call the menu on this object and use the appropriate command of this menu. The call of the `Rectangle_Unicolored.Rotatable` property does not change the cover, but the value of the `bRotatable` field is used when you try to rotate an object.

```
public bool Rotatable
{
    get { return (bRotatable); }
    set { bRotatable = value; }
}
```

If an object is rotatable, then it has an angle among its parameters. For the `Rectangle_Unicolored` class, the `m_angle` parameter is calculated as an angle from `m_points[1]` to `m_points[0]`. When the rectangle is pressed with the right button, which usually signals the start of rotation, then an angle from the rotation center to the pressed point is calculated (`angleMouse`) and the compensation between this angle and the object angle. This `compensation` angle will be used throughout the whole process of rotation.

```
public void Press (Point ptMouse, MouseButtons catcher, int iNode)
{
    ... ...
    else if (catcher == MouseButtons .Right)
    {
        if (bRotatable)
        {
            m_center = Center;
            double angleMouse = Auxi_Geometry .Angle (m_center,
            ptMouse);
            compensation = Auxi_Common .LimitedRadian (angleMouse - m_
            angle);
        }
```

65

```
        else
        {
            ptPressed = ptMouse;
        }
    ... ...
```

When a rotatable rectangle is caught by the right button and the mouse is moved, rectangle must be rotated. At any moment the angle from the center of rotation to the mouse cursor is calculated, and then the use of compensation angle guarantees that the rectangle will turn on the same angle as the mouse cursor.

```
public override bool MoveNode (...)
{
    ... ...
    else if (catcher == MouseButtons .Right)
    {
        if (Rotatable)
        {
            double angleMouse = Auxi_Geometry .Angle (m_center, ptMouse);
            Angle = angleMouse - compensation;
            bRet = true;
        }
        else
        {
            AdjustCursorPosition (ptPressed);
            bRet = false;
        }
        ... ...
```

I often use the adhered mouse throughout forward movement and resizing of objects but rarely throughout rotation. This is caused not by any difficulties in programming such a thing. When an object is pressed with the right button and rotation has to start, it is easy to calculate the distance from the mouse cursor to the central point of rotation and then to move the cursor along the circle of this radius. Such movement is demonstrated in several examples later in the chapter, but it is done only to demonstrate such a possibility. Rotation accuracy increases with the growth of the radius of cursor movement, so if bigger accuracy of rotation is needed, then it is better to press an object, then move the pressed mouse farther away from the rotation center, and continue the round movement of cursor there.

The Rectangle_Unicolored class demonstrates a classical rotation technique that will be copied for objects of many other classes. There are some objects in which their different points can be placed independently. In such case, a single angle for an object is not enough. Each independently placed special point has its own angle, so the individual compensation angle is calculated for each point at the press moment, and then these compensation angles are used throughout rotation. This was already used in case of the Polyline class; the same will be used later in the Polygon_Elastic class.

When an object is declared nonrotatable, the point of the initial press with the right button is remembered (ptPressed), and the cursor is kept at this point until the mouse release.

Transparency for Mover

While discussing small spots, we already looked at a simple mechanism to regulate the movability of any object. By default, any new object derived from the base GraphicalObject class is movable. This movability is regulated through the GraphicalObject.Movable property. If you try to move an object, then currently the movable object is moved, while for an unmovable object the cursor is kept at the same point until the mouse release. The following piece of code from the Rectangle_ Unicolored.MoveNode() method can be found in nearly any other class. Regardless of whether the pressed object is movable or unmovable, the mover deals only with this object; the existence of other objects does not matter at all.

```
public override bool MoveNode (...)
{
    bool bRet = false;
    if (catcher == MouseButtons .Left)
    {
        ... ...
        else
        {
            if (Movable)
            {
                Move (dx, dy);
                bRet = true;
            }
        }
```

```
        else
        {
            AdjustCursorPosition (ptPressed);
        }
    }
    ... ...
```

There exists one more way to regulate the movability. By using this different mechanism, an object can be turned into unmovable, but the reaction on the mouse press *of this object* depends on the existence of other objects and their relative positions on the screen.

By default, any object derived from the GraphicalObject class and registered in the mover queue is felt by this mover. It can be movable or unmovable, but in each case there is some reaction on the mouse press of such object. Screen objects can overlap. If several objects overlap, then the general expectation is that an object that is shown atop others must react to the mouse press. Is it possible to organize it in such a way as if the mouse press goes through one or several objects and catches (picks for moving) some object underneath? If it can be organized, then there must be an easy-to-use mechanism by which the user decides which object has to be caught.

Such a mechanism exists, and it is called *transparency for mover*. To be used with any object, this transparency for mover feature is included at the level of the base GraphicalObject class and is regulated at the same level.

Suppose that you call the menu at the point where the blue, yellow, and violet rectangles overlap (Figure 2-20). If basic features of the blue rectangle were not changed since the moment of its initialization, then this menu is called for a blue rectangle. The check marks in the menu inform that this blue rectangle is resizable, rotatable, movable, and *not transparent* for the mover.

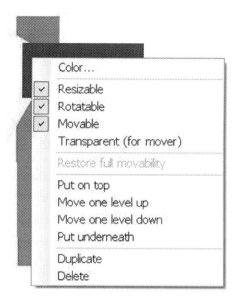

Figure 2-20. *Menu for a rectangle*

Let's turn our blue rectangle into transparent for mover. Click the appropriate command on the menu; this will call the associated method.

```
private void Click_miTransparent (object sender, EventArgs e)
{
    rectPressed .TransparentForMover = true;
}
```

When you use one of three previous commands (Resizable, Rotatable, or Movable), then the corresponding feature simply changes its value to an opposite one, while for transparency the true value is set. Certainly, it is the changing of the transparency value to an opposite one, but I want to underline that this command has different consequences than the use of previous commands.

The Rectangle_Unicolored class has no TransparentForMover property of its own, so the property of the base class GraphicalObject is used.

```
public bool TransparentForMover
{
    get { return (m_transparentForMover); }
    set
```

```
        {
            m_transparentForMover = value;
            DefineCover ();
        }
    }
```

The m_transparentForMover field in the base class gets a true value; then the DefineCover() method is called. At the end of the DefineCover() method *for any class of movable objects* there are absolutely identical lines of code. If an object is declared transparent for mover, then the cover of this object is declared transparent. This means that all nodes of such cover, regardless of their number, types, sizes, and positions, become transparent for mover.

```
    public override void DefineCover ()
    {
        ... ...
        if (TransparentForMover)
        {
            cover .SetBehaviour (Behaviour .Transparent);
        }
    }
```

We declared our blue rectangle transparent for mover; now we need to test the effect of this change. Press the same blue rectangle again at the same point but with the left button. The whole analysis starts at the moment of the mouse press with the Mover. Catch() method.

```
    private void OnMouseDown (object sender, MouseEventArgs e)
    {
        ptMouse_Down = e .Location;
        if (mover .Catch (e .Location, e .Button))
        {
            GraphicalObject grobj = mover .CaughtSource;
            int iNode = mover .CaughtNode;
            ... ...
```

The mover analyzes one object after another according to their order in the mover queue; for each object, the analysis is done node by node according to their order in the cover of an object. When the `Mover.Catch()` method detects a node with the `Behaviour.Transparent` parameter, then not only is this node skipped from the analysis but the whole object to which this node belongs. Don't miss this important thing: not only is the current transparent node ignored, but the whole cover to which this node belongs. The importance of this cannot be demonstrated in the current example because for each rectangle all nodes are either transparent or nontransparent. Later we'll deal with covers that simultaneously contain transparent and nontransparent nodes, and the whole work with such objects depends on the transparency of the first checked node. This will be further on; now let's return to the mouse press on the rectangle that was previously declared transparent for mover.

If there are no more objects underneath the transparent rectangle at the pressed point, then there is no reaction at all. If there are other objects, then the reaction depends on the first nontransparent object found at this point. If the blue rectangle in Figure 2-20 is turned into transparent and then the left button is pressed at the same point, then such a press will catch and move the yellow rectangle. There is no restriction on the number of transparent objects through which the mover can look. If you turn yellow rectangle into transparent for mover and press again at the same point, then a violet rectangle is caught.

There is a catch with turning an object transparent: you can declare an object transparent for mover by using the menu of this object, but you can't declare this transparent object again nontransparent through the same menu. When the `Mover.Catch()` method starts its analysis, it starts with the checking of the `Behaviour` parameter for the node under the cursor. If it is the `Behaviour.Transparent`, then anything else does not matter at all. In such a case, the pressed button is insignificant, this element cannot be moved, and its associated menu cannot be called. The whole object is simply ignored by the mover.

I always underline that both properties (`Movable` and `TransparentForMover`) deal with movability but in different ways. Place two rectangles with initial properties in such a way that they do not overlap. (To reinstall the initial situation, call the menu at any empty place and use the command *Default view*.) Call the menu on one rectangle and make it unmovable; then call the menu on another rectangle and make it transparent for mover. Try to move either of them. Both elements will not move, so from the user's point of view both elements are unmovable because press-and-move doesn't work for either. Call the menu again on the first rectangle (an unmovable one), reinstall its movability, and after this you can move this element around the screen. Try to call the menu on the second rectangle that is transparent, and you will find that it is impossible: instead of a menu for rectangle, you will see a menu for empty places. You cannot call a menu on a transparent for mover object, so it is impossible to turn it back into nontransparent through the command of the same menu.

From time to time I write that the mover does not detect a transparent object. This is correct from the point of reaction (or from the user's point of view) but incorrect from the point of understanding the code and algorithm (from the point of the developer). The mover certainly detects not only a transparent node but the whole cover to which this node belongs; after this, the mover entirely ignores this cover, but for users it looks like the mover doesn't see an object.

Suppose that you declared some object transparent for mover. How do you make this object nontransparent again?

Usually I do it by calling a menu of the upper level. Our objects reside in the form, so for all of them the upper level is the form itself. The menu that can be called at any empty place (Figure 2-21) includes a command to make all elements nontransparent.

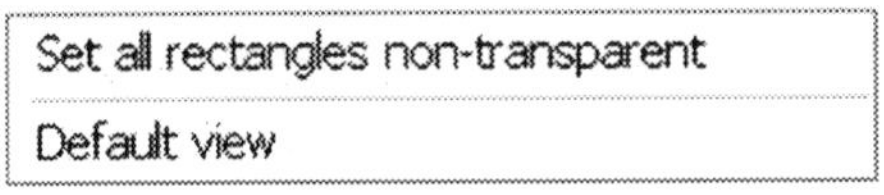

| Set all rectangles non-transparent |
| Default view |

Figure 2-21. *Menu at empty places*

```
private void Click_miAllNontransparent (object sender, EventArgs e)
{
    foreach (Rectangle_Unicolored rect in rects)
    {
        rect .TransparentForMover = false;
    }
}
```

Common Rules of Design

The Form_Rectangle.cs file has all the features that can be found in the majority of further examples; it can be useful to look through these features, their related commands, and implementation.

All objects are movable. To use their movability, a Mover object is initialized, and all objects are registered in its queue. The order of objects in this queue is important because the decision about possible movements is made by analyzing the screen objects one by one strictly according to their order in the queue. The drawing of all objects is done in the opposite order, so it must be considered while the order of objects in the mover queue is decided. To make finding smaller objects easier, they are usually placed ahead of the bigger objects.

If ordinary controls are used in design, they have to precede graphical objects in the mover queue because controls always appear atop all graphical objects. There are no ordinary controls in this example, so the order of elements is decided mostly by the sizes, but not only that way. Information area is comparable in size with rectangles and always exists (only its size can be changed), while the number of rectangles varies because they can be added and deleted. In this and in several examples later in the chapter we have a set of always existing objects and another set of objects the number of which can be changed at any moment. The order of these two sets depends only on developer's preferences. In the current example, such order is organized: button (of the Button_Drawing class), check box (of the CheckBox_GR class), information (of the Info_Resizable class), and a set of rectangles (of the Rectangle_Unicolored class).

```
public void RenewMover ()
{
    mover .Clear ();
    for (int i = 0; i < rects .Count; i++)
    {
        mover .Add (rects [i]);
    }
    info .IntoMover (mover, 0);
    checkAuxi .IntoMover (mover, 0);
    btnCover .IntoMover (mover, 0);
    if (bAfterInit)
    {
        Invalidate ();
    }
}
```

The mover queue is filled by the RenewMover() method. Whenever the number or the order of rectangles is changed, the queue is renewed, and the screen view is refreshed.

This example allows you to visualize the covers of rectangles. It is never done in real applications but can be helpful throughout the discussion of cover design. In my book [2], several variants of cover visualization are discussed; in the current example, only the MovableObject.DrawCover() method is used.

```
private void OnPaint (object sender, PaintEventArgs e)
{
    Graphics grfx = e .Graphics;
    GraphicalObject grobj;
    for (int i = mover .Count - 1; i >= 0; i--)
    {
        grobj = mover [i] .Source;
        if (grobj is Rectangle_Unicolored)
        {
            (grobj as Rectangle_Unicolored) .Draw (grfx);
            if (bShowCovers)
            {
                mover [i] .DrawCover (grfx);
            }
        }
    }
    ... ...
```

Any movement is started when an object is pressed by the mouse. Usually some calculations have to be done at this moment; calculations are done inside the Press() method of the appropriate class. Some of the graphical "controls" can be changed at the press moment, so in such a case the screen view must be refreshed; in the current example, it is required when the button is pressed.

```
private void OnMouseDown (object sender, MouseEventArgs e)
{
    ptMouse_Down = e .Location;
    if (mover .Catch (e .Location, e .Button))
    {
```

```
        GraphicalObject grobj = mover .CaughtSource;
        int iNode = mover .CaughtNode;
        if (grobj is Rectangle_Unicolored)
        {
            rectPressed = grobj as Rectangle_Unicolored;
            rectPressed .Press (e .Location, e .Button, iNode);
            ... ...
        }
        else if (grobj is Button_GR)
        {
            btnCover .Press (e .Location, e .Button, iNode);
            Invalidate ();
        }
        else if (grobj is CheckBox_GR)
        {
            checkAuxi .Press (e .Location, e .Button, iNode);
        }
        else if (grobj is Info_Resizable)
        {
            info .Press (e .Location, e .Button, iNode);
        }
    }
    ContextMenuStrip = null;
}
```

The movement of any object is described with the Move() and MoveNode() methods of its class, so the OnMouseMove() method of the form is usually simple and requires the repainting only if the mover signals that any object is currently caught.

```
private void OnMouseMove (object sender, MouseEventArgs e)
{
    if (mover .Move (e .Location))
    {
        Invalidate ();
    }
}
```

75

When the mouse button is released, some decisions about further actions are made. These decisions depend on the released mouse button, on the released object (if an object is released), and on the released node of the object cover.

When the *left button is released*, then ordinary graphical objects do not require any actions, while the graphical "controls" usually do and always require the screen repainting. (In the current example, there is an unusual repainting after the release of rectangles because the auxiliary lines must be erased.)

```
private void OnMouseUp (object sender, MouseEventArgs e)
{
    ptMouse_Up = e .Location;
    double fDist = Auxi_Geometry .Distance (ptMouse_Down, ptMouse_Up);
    int iObj, iNode;
    if (mover .Release (out iObj, out iNode))
    {
        GraphicalObject grobj = mover .ReleasedSource;
        if (e .Button == MouseButtons .Left)
        {
            if (grobj is Button_GR)
            {
                if (btnCover .Enabled)
                {
                    if (fDist <= 3 && iNode == Button_GR .Node_FullArea)
                    {
                        bShowCovers = !bShowCovers;
                    }
                    btnCover .Pressed = false;
                    Invalidate ();
                }
            }
            else if (grobj is CheckBox_GR)
            {
                if (fDist <= 3)
                {
                    checkAuxi .Checked = !checkAuxi .Checked;
                    Invalidate ();
```

```
            }
        }
        else if (grobj is Rectangle_Unicolored)
        {
            Invalidate ();
        }
    }
```

When the *right button is released* and the distance between the points of mouse press and release is negligible, then some menu must be called because it is a widely used practice to have a context menu for each class of objects and for empty places. In the current example, only the small button has no menu; at any other point some menu can be called.

```
        else if (e .Button == MouseButtons .Right && fDist <= 3)
        {
            if (grobj is Rectangle_Unicolored)
            {
                ContextMenuStrip = menuOnRectangle;
            }
            else if (grobj is CheckBox_GR)
            {
                ContextMenuStrip = menuOnCheckBox;
            }
            else if (grobj is Info_Resizable)
            {
                ContextMenuStrip = menuOnInfo;
            }
        }
    }
    else if (e .Button == MouseButtons .Right && fDist <= 3)
    {
        ContextMenuStrip = menuOnEmpty;
    }
}
```

In the current demo application, whenever there are multiple colored elements in some example, the left double-click can be used to bring the clicked element on top of others.

```
private void OnMouseDoubleClick (object sender, MouseEventArgs e)
{
    if (e .Button == MouseButtons .Left)
    {
        if (mover .Release ())
        {
            GraphicalObject grobj = mover .ReleasedSource;
            if (grobj is Rectangle_Unicolored)
            {
                PopupFigure (grobj .ID);
            }
            ... ...
```

When many objects are used, then several commands to change their order are included into their menu (Figure 2-20). If some objects are involved in different types of movements and those movements must be regulated individually for each object, then the commands of those regulations are included in the same menu. Resizability, rotatability, and ordinary movability of an object can be changed back and forth through these commands at any moment. An object can be set transparent for mover with an analogues command, but no menu can be called with the mover help on a transparent object, so the inverse change of transparency through the same menu is impossible. Something else must be done to turn a transparent for mover object into nontransparent. In this case (and in many others), I use the command of menu for the upper level. Usually it is a menu for a form (Figure 2-21). Commands of menu for a form refer to all objects, so the transparency is reinstalled for all elements.

Movability of elements allows you to change the overall view in any possible way, so there must be a command to reinstall the default view. Such a command is also included into the menu for empty places.

Comment

File: `Form_Comment.cs`

Menu position: Simple objects ➤ Comment

One of the most used elements of the rectangular shape is the comment. Many screen objects speak for themselves; others need some explanation. It can be a short one such as just a word or two, but in many situations, it is impossible to organize a normal interface without them. For example, a tuning form may be used to set several colors. For each color parameter, there is a small button to call a standard dialogue. All buttons to change colors are identical, so they need comments that tell about the parameters associated with these buttons.

A comment can be shown in one or several lines, so one size of the comment area is determined by the font and the number of lines. If there are several lines, then each line has its own length, but to simplify the work with comments, I prefer to determine another size of comment by its longest line. In such a way, any comment has a rectangular area.

Some comments are always horizontal and are not involved in rotation; the position of a horizontal rectangle can be described by its top-left corner. In the `MoveGraphLibrary.dll` file, there is a `Text_Horizontal` class that can be used for such comments.

There are situations when the rotation of comments is needed. Rotation can be organized around any point, but rotation around the comment central point is the most popular variant. Such a rotatable comment can be described by its central point, two sizes, and angle; in such a way, the `Text_Rotatable` class from the `MoveGraphLibrary. dll` file is designed.

Comment is rarely used as a stand-alone object, but you can see such use of comments when you start the accompanying application and look at its main form; the book title is shown as two comments. Usually a comment is associated with another object, and together they form a complex object in which a comment plays a subordinate role. (Complex objects are discussed in the next chapter.) When a comment is associated with some object, then not only the absolute (screen) comment position must be declared but also its relative position to the dominant element. The description of the relative position depends on the shape of dominant element, so there are comments to points (class `CommentToPoint`), to rectangles (class `CommentToRect`), to circles (class `CommentToCircle`), to rings (class `CommentToRing`), and some other. All the mentioned classes are derived from the `Text_Rotatable` class, so all these comments are rotated around their central points.

However, there are many situations when positioning of a comment by its central point is not convenient, and also the rotation around other points can be useful. Objects of the `Comment_Adh` class have nine special points; each of them can be used as an anchor point for positioning and as a central point of rotation.

Let's take a horizontal text, draw its rectangular frame, and mark on the line eight special points according to the cardinal and ordinal directions (Figure 2-22). These points together with the central point of the frame area are described by the `TextBasis` enumeration.

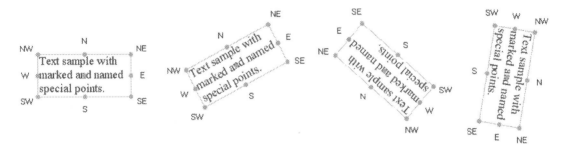

Figure 2-22. *Rectangular area of the text and its special points*

```
public enum TextBasis { NW, N, NE, W, M, E, SW, S, SE };
```

The names of special points stick to their initial marks, and this association does not change throughout the rotation. Figure 2-22 shows the change throughout the rotation around the central point, but rotation can be organized around any of these nine special points.

```
public class Comment_Adh : GraphicalObject
{
    PointF [] m_pts;
    TextBasis m_basis;
    string m_text;
```

```
SizeF m_size;
Font m_font;
double m_angle;        // in radians
Color m_color;
bool m_bRotatable;
```

The design of this class is simple. Among other parameters, any constructor of this class includes the text to be shown (txt) and the font to be used (fnt). These two parameters determine the size of rectangular area. Three other parameters—coordinates of the anchor point (ptAnch), the special point of comment which must be placed at this point (textbasis), and the initial angle (angleDeg)—determine the original comment position. The calculated array m_pts[] contains all the special points according to their order in the TextBasis enumeration.

```
public Comment_Adh (Form frm, Mover mvr, PointF ptAnch, TextBasis
textbasis, string txt, Font fnt, double angleDeg, Color clr)
{
    ... ...
    m_size = Auxi_Geometry .MeasureString (frm, m_text, m_font);
    m_angle = Auxi_Common .LimitedRadian (
                                Auxi_Convert .DegreeToRadian
                                (angleDeg));
    m_basis = textbasis;
    m_pts = Auxi_Geometry .TextGeometry (m_size, m_angle, ptAnch, m_
basis);
    ... ...
```

A comment is not resizable, and its area is always rectangular, so its cover consists of a single rectangular node.

```
public override void DefineCover ()
{
    cover = new Cover (new CoverNode (0, Corners, Cursors .Hand));
    if (!Movable)
    {
        cover .SetCursor (Cursors .NoMove2D);
    }
    ... ...
```

For better demonstration of comments, there is the Form_Comment.cs example (Figure 2-23). This example uses the derived class Comment_withMarks, which allows to show the comment area and all special points with their names.

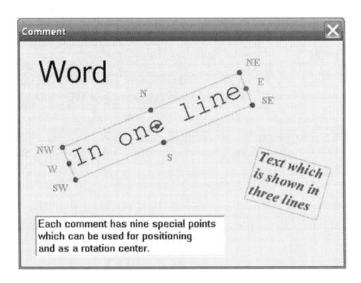

Figure 2-23. *Comment_withMarks objects*

```
public class Comment_withMarks : Comment_Adh
{
    Font m_fntSpotNames;
    Color m_clrSpotNames;
    Color m_clrSpots,
          m_clrAnchorSpot;
    Pen m_penFrame;
    float fSpotRadius = 4;
    float spaceToLetters = 6;
    bool bShowFrame, bShowSpots, bShowSpotNames;
```

The base class Comment_Adh has three parameters that can be changed: font, color, and selected anchor point. The derived class Comment_withMarks has marks on special points and their names; there are also several parameters that regulate the appearance of auxiliary parts. All these parameters are regulated through the menu that can be called on any Comment_withMarks element.

Circle

File: `Form_Circle.cs`

Menu position: Simple objects ➤ Circle

At the beginning of my work on the movability of the screen objects, there were some problems with the resizing of elements with curved borders. Then I thought about the *N-node covers,* and it became a general solution for objects with the curved borders. N-node covers are discussed in my book [2], but they do not appear in the current book for one simple reason. The most popular objects with the curved borders are circles and rings, but for these objects I later invented extremely simple covers that provide all the needed moving and resizing.

Circles of this example are unicolored (Figure 2-24); an auxiliary line is added only for better viewing of rotation.

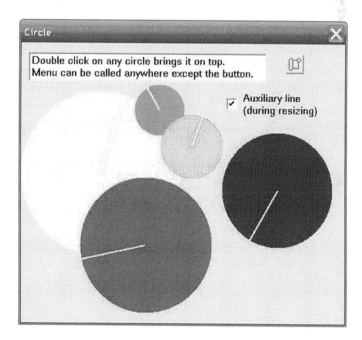

Figure 2-24. *An auxiliary line inside a circle makes the rotation obvious*

```
public class Circle_Unicolored :
                    GraphicalObject
{
    PointF m_center;
    float m_radius;
    double m_angle;
    Color m_color;
    bool bResizable, bRotatable;
    Pen penAuxi;
    static float minRadius = 15;
```

Two different movements must be started by the left button: forward movement of the whole object and resizing. Each node, while pressed by the left button, can start only one movement,[2] so the minimum number of needed nodes is two. The cover of the Circle_Unicolored class has exactly two nodes (Figure 2-25). Both nodes are circular; their sizes slightly depend on the required resizability of an object.

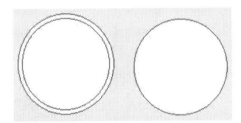

Figure 2-25. *Covers for resizable and nonresizable circles*

- For a nonresizable circle, nodes are identical, so only the first one is seen by the mover; this node is used for the circle movement.

- For a resizable circle, the nodes slightly differ in size. The first node is still used for an object movement. The second node is slightly bigger; its unblocked part forms a narrow ring along the circle border, and this area is used for circle resizing.

---

[2]Throughout all the years of my work with movable objects, I had only one class in which the left press of a node could start two different movements; the decision was based on the point of initial press.

```
public override void DefineCover ()
{
    int delta = Resizable ? 3 : 0;
    cover = new Cover (new CoverNode [] {
                new CoverNode (0, Center, Radius - delta, Cursors
                .SizeAll),
                new CoverNode (1, Center, Radius + delta)});
    if (!Movable)
    {
        cover [0] .Cursor = Cursors .NoMove2D;
    }
    ... ...
```

When the left button is pressed near the border of a resizable circle, the cursor is adjusted to the nearest point on the border (ptPressed). The mouse pressed on the border can be moved only along radius between two points. One end of the segment (ptEndIn) is determined by the minimum allowed radius; another (ptEndOut) is set far away beyond the screen border.

```
public void Press (Point ptMouse, MouseButtons catcher, int iNode)
{
    if (catcher == MouseButtons .Left)
    {
        if (iNode == 0)
        {
            ptPressed = ptMouse;
        }
        else
        {
            double angleBeam = Auxi_Geometry .Angle (Center, ptMouse);
            ptPressed = Auxi_Geometry.PointToPoint (Center, angleBeam,
                                                    Radius);
            AdjustCursorPosition (ptPressed);
            ptEndIn =
                    Auxi_Geometry .PointToPoint (Center, angleBeam,
                                                minRadius);
```

```
            ptEndOut = Auxi_Geometry .PointToPoint (Center, angleBeam,
                                                    4000);

       }
   }
   ... ...
```

At any moment, the cursor of the pressed mouse takes a position on a segment between the two calculated points (ptNearest). Then the circle radius is calculated as the distance between this point and the circle center; in such way, the circle border always follows the cursor.

```
public override bool MoveNode (...)
{
    bool bRet = false;
    if (catcher == MouseButtons .Left)
    {
        if (iNode == 0)
        {
            ... ...
        }
        else
        {
            PointF ptNearest = Auxi_Geometry .Segment_NearestPoint
            (ptMouse, ptEndIn, ptEndOut);
            Radius = Convert .ToSingle (Auxi_Geometry .Distance
                                (Center, ptNearest));
            AdjustCursorPosition (ptNearest);
            bRet = true;
        }
    }
    ... ...
```

At the moment of initialization, the initial angle is declared. For a unicolored circle, rotation cannot be seen, so the radius for the current angle is shown in a special color. In such way, the circle rotation is seen perfectly. The rotation is organized in a standard way as it was explained with rectangles.

Ring

File: `Form_Ring.cs`

Menu position: Simple objects ➤ Ring

The moving and resizing of circles and rings is usually organized in a similar way, so in the case of rings you are going to see familiar things that were discussed with the circles in the previous example. However, there is one new feature in the `Ring_Unicolored` cover because it uses a transparent node. With the use of transparent nodes, the moving/ resizing of some objects becomes easy and elegant, while prior to that, the same cases were the most difficult for development. There are several things about the transparent nodes that you must clearly understand before you start using them.

- The visual transparency of an object and node transparency are different things. They do not correlate, they have nothing in common, and they exist without knowing each other.

- Visual transparency is a smoothly changeable value in the range from, let's say, zero to one. Zero visual transparency means a perfectly seen object through which nothing can be seen. When you smoothly increase the visual transparency of some object, you see better and better the underlying objects but less and less of the object itself. The node transparency is a Boolean value: the node is either detected by the mover or not detected.

- Strictly speaking, the declaration that the *transparent node is not detected by mover* is incorrect. The mover easily detects the transparent node, but this is the only thing that the mover is going to do with such a node. No actions with the transparent node itself are allowed, but there is a bit more. Nodes of the same cover often overlap because this is required by the cover design. The order of nodes in the cover is important as the mover analyzes the cover nodes one by one according to their order. If the mover finds a transparent node at the pressed point, then *the analysis for this object is over*, and the mover starts to analyze the next object at the same point, if there are other objects.

- Transparent nodes of one cover have no effect on the covers of other objects. When the cover consists of nontransparent nodes, then you try to design cover in such a way that nodes cover the object area and maybe several pixels beyond its border (for easier border catch) but do not go farther in order not to block other objects from the mover. When you have transparent nodes in the cover, then their expansion outside the object borders does not matter at all. Transparent nodes of one object can overlap other objects, but they do not block them from the mover. From time to time, big transparent nodes are useful in the design of covers even for small objects; this is perfectly seen in the case of a crescent. In my book [2], there are also interesting examples of circle sectors and arcs; the covers of these objects use big transparent nodes that are much bigger than the elements for which they provide moving and resizing. (Arcs are discussed later in the chapter.)

Figure 2-26 shows several elements of the `Ring_Unicolored` class. You can press a ring that is visible through the hole of another ring or even through the holes of several rings and then move, resize, or rotate such object. Elements of the `Ring_Unicolored` class are resizable by both borders.

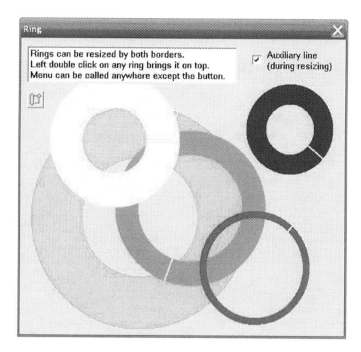

Figure 2-26. *Rings are resizable by both borders*

```
public class Ring_Unicolored : GraphicalObject
{
    PointF m_center;
    float m_radiusInner, m_radiusOuter;
    double m_angle;
    Color m_color;
    bool bResizable, bRotatable;
    Pen penAuxi;
    static float minRadiusInner = 15;
    static float minWidth = 10;
```

The cover of this class consists of four circular nodes; numbering starts from the inner node and goes outside. The smallest node (iNode = 0) is always transparent.

```
public override void DefineCover ()
{
    delta = bResizable ? 3 : 0;
    CoverNode [] nodes = new CoverNode [] {
```

```
                new CoverNode (0, Center, RadiusInner - delta,
                                           Behaviour .Transparent),
                new CoverNode (1, Center, RadiusInner + delta),
                new CoverNode (2, Center, RadiusOuter - delta, Cursors
                .SizeAll),
                new CoverNode (3, Center, RadiusOuter + delta)};
    cover = new Cover (nodes);
    cover .SetClearance (false);
    if (!Movable)
    {
        cover [2] .Cursor = Cursors .NoMove2D;
    }
    ... ...
```

- For a resizable ring, each following node is bigger than the previous
  one, so the working part of each node is only the part that is not
  blocked by the previous node (Figure 2-27). Those four nodes are
  divided into two pairs. The difference in sizes (radii) of the second
  pair makes a narrow strip along the outer border and provides the
  resizing of the ring by the outer border in exactly the same way as was
  explained for circles. The first pair of nodes provides similar resizing
  by the inner border.

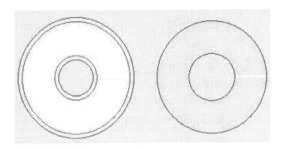

Figure 2-27. *Covers for resizable and nonresizable rings*

- For a nonresizable ring, each node with the odd number is entirely
  blocked by the previous node. As a result, the mover can deal only with the
  node 2, and this node provides forward moving and rotation of a ring.

Each node of the ring cover has its own purpose.

- Node 0 is always transparent and is used to cut out the inner circle.

- Node 1, if accessible, provides the resizing by the inner border. For a nonresizable ring, this node is entirely blocked by the previous one.

- Node 2 provides forward moving and rotation of the whole ring.

- Node 3, if accessible, provides the resizing by the outer border. For a nonresizable ring, this node is entirely blocked by the previous one.

Node 0 is always transparent, so it is mentioned neither in Press() nor in the MoveNode() methods. Resizing starts if node 1 or 3 is pressed. In both cases, the cursor of the pressed mouse is allowed to move only along radius, so the Press() method has to calculate the ends of the allowed cursor movement. In the case of the inner border (node 1), one end point (ptEndIn) is determined by the minimum allowed radius of the hole (MinimumRadiusInner), while another end point (ptEndOut) is determined by the minimum allowed ring width (OuterRadius - MinimumWidth).

```
public void Press (Point ptMouse, MouseButtons catcher, int iNode)
{
    ptPressed = ptMouse;
    if (catcher == MouseButtons .Left)
    {
        angleBeam = Auxi_Geometry .Angle (Center, ptMouse);
        if (iNode == 1)
        {
            ptEndIn = Auxi_Geometry .PointToPoint (Center, angleBeam,
                                                   MinimumRadiusInner);
            ptEndOut = Auxi_Geometry .PointToPoint (Center, angleBeam,
                                                    RadiusOuter -
                                                    MinimumWidth);
            AdjustCursorPosition (Auxi_Geometry .PointToPoint (Center,
                                                   angleBeam,
                                                   m_radiusInner));
        }
        ... ...
```

91

In the case of the outer border (node 3), one end point (ptEndIn) is determined by the minimum allowed ring width (InnerRadius + MinimumWidth), while another end point (ptEndOut) is set beyond the screen border.

```
else if (iNode == 3)
{
    ptEndIn = Auxi_Geometry .PointToPoint (Center, angleBeam,
                              RadiusInner + MinimumWidth);
    ptEndOut = Auxi_Geometry .PointToPoint (Center, angleBeam, 4000);
    AdjustCursorPosition (Auxi_Geometry .PointToPoint (Center,
                              angleBeam, m_radiusOuter));
}
}
```

Ring resizing works in the same way as circle resizing. When a short area near the border is pressed, the cursor is switched to the nearest point on this border, and two end points for the cursor movement are calculated. When the mouse with a pressed left button is moved, the cursor is positioned on the nearest point of the segment between these two points, and the pressed border moves with the cursor.

These are two remarks on the cover design for the Ring_Unicolored class:

- In case of a nonresizable ring, the idea is to make nodes 1 and 3 inaccessible to mover, so these nodes are entirely blocked by their preceding nodes. The same result can be achieved by squeezing these two nodes to a zero size.

- There is a bit of difference between showing covers for circles and rings: while the circles are wiped out and only the node borders can be seen (Figure 2-25), for rings you can see the node borders together with the original ring color (Figure 2-27). This is the result of adding one line into the Ring_Unicolored.DefineCover() method

```
cover .SetClearance (false);
```

This line has no effect on the moving/resizing of objects but helps me in the preparation of pictures for such explanations. In the real applications, covers are never shown, but their views are helpful in the discussion of cover design. In general, circular and strip nodes are used in small sizes, so I decided that wiping out their inner area would increase the visibility of these small nodes. On the contrary, the polygonal nodes often have big sizes, and for them the cleaning of their entire area is not used. Everything can be changed by using different methods of node cleaning. Occasionally you will see the use of such methods for node cleaning, but this is only for the purpose of visibility throughout explanation.

Rounded strip

File: Form_Strip.cs

Menu position: Simple elements ➤ Rounded strip

A rounded strip can be looked at as a rectangle with additional semicircles on two opposite sides (Figure 2-28). A strip can be also looked at as two halves of a circle moved apart with a rectangle filling the gap between them. Such a view on a new figure explains why the strip cover and resizing are similar to those for a circle.

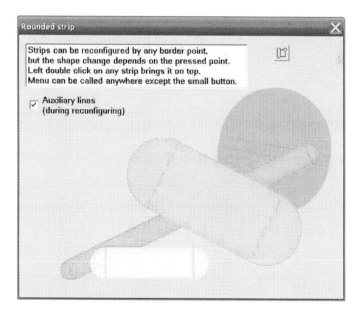

Figure 2-28. *Elements of the Strip_Unicolored class*

```
public class Strip_Unicolored
            : GraphicalObject
{
    PointF ptC0, ptC1;
    double m_angle;
    float m_radius;
    SolidBrush m_brush;
    bool bResizable,
        bRotatable;
    PointF ptEndIn, ptEndOut, ptPressed, m_center;
    CaughtLine caught_line;
    PointF [] m_points;
```

Several points are important for strip resizing. These are the centers of two semicircles and four corners of the rectangular part; all these points are marked in Figure 2-29; numbers correspond to the order of points in the m_points[] array. The strip angle (m_angle) is calculated as an angle from point C0 to point C1.

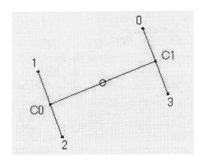

Figure 2-29. *Strip special points*

```
public PointF [] SpecialPoints
{
    get
    {
        return (new PointF [] {
            Auxi_Geometry .PointToPoint (ptC1, m_angle + Math .PI / 2,
                                         m_radius),
            Auxi_Geometry .PointToPoint (ptC0, m_angle + Math .PI / 2,
                                         m_radius),
```

```
        Auxi_Geometry .PointToPoint (ptCO, m_angle - Math .PI / 2,
                                    m_radius),
        Auxi_Geometry .PointToPoint (ptC1, m_angle - Math .PI / 2,
                                    m_radius)
      });
  }
}
```

Whenever I come to something really new in dealing with circle, I try to implement the same new thing for the rounded strip and eventually find the way to do it. Years ago I understood that a cover consisting of two nodes was the best for circles, but some mistake in my thoughts stopped me from propagating the same idea on the rounded strips. As a result, the strips used a cover consisting of five nodes: two thin strip nodes provided the resizing started at the straight border segments, two circular nodes provided the resizing by curves, and a big strip node provided the forward moving. I had no desire to change anything in that cover, but throughout some checking in 2016 I found that for a special combination of sizes there was a tiny area in which resizing worked a bit incorrectly. It was the combination of conditions that made this mistake so difficult to detect: a strip had to be big, its shape had to be close to the circle, the area of wrong resizing was small, and the resizing had to be started in an unusual place. (The variant of cover design with five nodes is still demonstrated with the `Strip_SimpleCoverAdh` class in my book [2], so you can try to find that hiding mistake.) There were several ways to solve the problem, but I found out that the best solution was to switch to the cover consisting of two strip nodes (Figure 2-30).

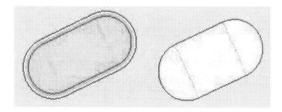

Figure 2-30. *Covers for resizable and nonresizable strips*

```
public override void DefineCover ()
{
    int delta = Resizable ? 3 : 0;
    CoverNode [] nodes = new CoverNode [] {
```

```
                new CoverNode (0, ptC0, ptC1, m_radius - delta, Cursors
                .SizeAll),
                new CoverNode (1, ptC0, ptC1, m_radius + delta)};
        cover = new Cover (nodes);
        cover .SetClearance (false);
        ... ...
```

If not for that evading mistake, I would prefer to use the older cover with five nodes. It looks a bit illogical because if you have two covers that provide all the needed moving and resizing, then the cover with fewer nodes is usually preferable. Why was it better to use the cover with five nodes, and what are the problems with two nodes in the case of a strip? When we deal with a circle, then one node for resizing is perfect and quite enough because the resizing works identically regardless of the pressed border point. In the case of a strip, there are four obviously different parts of the border area, and the reaction on pressing each of these areas is different.

- When a curved part of the border is pressed, then the pressed semicircle can be moved along the strip axis, the opposite semicircle does not move, the radius and width of the strip do not change, and only the length of the straight part changes.

- When the straight part of the border is pressed, then the cursor can only move orthogonally to the strip axis, and the caught side moves with the cursor. The opposite straight part of the border does not move, the length of the straight part does not change, but the width of the strip changes and with it changes the radius of semicircles (and the total strip length).

In each case, the border part opposite to the caught one does not move and can be used as a base for new strip sizes. Because there are four parts of the strip border, I would prefer to use the cover in which each border part is covered by its own node, and the reaction on pressing each node is described by a special piece of code. In the case of a two-node cover, only one node is responsible for all the resizing. In such case, the pressed point determines the part of the border that is pressed, and then one or another variant of resizing is initiated. It is not a problem to determine the pressed part of the border and then continue in the same way as was already done in the old variant, but this is the first example in which I use the parts of the same node for different types of resizing. Maybe it is not bad, maybe I'll find other objects in which such a technique would be useful, but at the moment it is the only example of such type, and for me it is an unusual case.

When the left button is pressed somewhere near the strip border, the first thing to do is to determine the pressed part of the border. Distances to all four parts of the border are calculated (dist[]), and the pressed part (iMinDist) is determined by the minimum value.

```
public void Press (Point ptMouse, MouseButtons catcher, int iNode)
{
    if (catcher == MouseButtons .Left)
    {
        ptPressed = ptMouse;
        if (iNode == 1)
        {
            int iMinDist;
            double angleBeam;
            PointF ptOnCircle, ptCursor, ptBase;
            PointOfSegment typeOfPoint;
            m_points = SpecialPoints;
            PointF [] ptsNearest = new PointF [4];
            double [] dist = new double [] {
                    Auxi_Geometry .Distance_PointSegment (ptMouse,
                    m_points [0], m_points [1], out ptsNearest [0]),
                    Auxi_Geometry .Distance_PointSegment (ptMouse,
                    m_points [2], m_points [3], out ptsNearest [1])
                    Auxi_Geometry .Distance_PointArc (ptMouse, ptC0,
                                            m_points [1], 180, out
                                            ptOnCircle,
                                            out typeOfPoint, out
                                            ptsNearest [2]),
                    Auxi_Geometry .Distance_PointArc (ptMouse, ptC1,
                                            m_points [3], 180, out
                                            ptOnCircle,
                                            out typeOfPoint, out
                                            ptsNearest [3])
                };
```

```
Auxi_Common .MinValue (dist, false, out iMinDist);
ptCursor = ptsNearest [iMinDist];
caught_line = (CaughtLine) iMinDist;
... ...
```

Four parts of the strip border are named in the CaughtLine enumeration.

```
public enum CaughtLine { Straight_01, Straight_23, Curve_C0, Curve_C1 }
```

The first is the straight border between points 0 and 1 (see Figure 2-29), so let's start with this case (Figure 2-31).

Figure 2-31. *The straight segment of the border is pressed at the point where it is crossed by a solid line*

- The cursor is allowed to move only at a right angle to the straight border segments. These segments are parallel to the strip axis, so the line angle (angleBeam) is easily calculated.

- ptBase is the crossing of this line with the opposite side.

- The Strip_Unicolored class has the minimal allowed radius for semicircles (minRadius). The minimum allowed width of the strip is twice as big, and this gives one end point for cursor movement (ptEndIn).

- Another end point (ptEndOut) is calculated as being far away on the same line.

```
caught_line = (CaughtLine) iMinDist;
if (caught_line == CaughtLine .Straight_01)
{
```

```
        angleBeam = m_angle + Math .PI / 2;
        ptBase = Auxi_Geometry .Segment_NearestPoint (ptCursor,
                                        m_points [2],
                                        m_points [3]);
        ptEndIn = Auxi_Geometry .PointToPoint (ptBase,
                                        angleBeam,
                                        2 * minRadius);
        ptEndOut = Auxi_Geometry .PointToPoint (ptBase,
                                        angleBeam,
                                        4000);
    }
    ... ...
```

The movement of the pressed node is described by the Strip_Unicolored.
MoveNode() method. When the straight border segment goes with the cursor, the new
radius is calculated as half of the distance between two straight segments; then the
central points of the two semicircles are calculated. When the new radius is set with the
Strip_Unicolored.Radius property, it also defines the new cover.

```
public override bool MoveNode (...)
{
    bool bRet = false;
    double rNew, dist;
    if (catcher == MouseButtons .Left)
    {
        if (iNode == 0)
        {
            ... ...
        }
        else
        {
            PointF ptNearest = Auxi_Geometry .Segment_NearestPoint
            (ptMouse, ptEndIn, ptEndOut);
            if (caught_line == CaughtLine .Straight_01)
```

```
    {
        rNew = Auxi_Geometry .Distance_PointLine (ptNearest,
                                    m_points [2], m_points
                                    [3]) / 2;
        ptC0 = Auxi_Geometry .PointToPoint (corners [2],
                                    m_angle + Math .PI / 2,
                                    rNew);
        ptC1 = Auxi_Geometry .PointToPoint (corners [3],
                                    m_angle + Math .PI / 2,
                                    rNew);
        Radius = Convert .ToSingle (rNew);
    }
    ... ...
    AdjustCursorPosition (ptNearest);
    bRet = true;
    ... ...
```

Now let's look at the resizing by the curve; let's analyze the situation when the arc around point C0 is pressed (Figure 2-29).

- The cursor is allowed to move only along the line parallel to the strip axis (angleBeam).

- The cursor way is at a right angle to the auxiliary lines shown in Figure 2-32. These two lines mark the sides of rectangular part of the strip; they are also diameters of semicircles. The distance from the pressed point to the nearest of two lines is additionToLength; the imaginary point at which the mouse way crosses another line is ptBase.

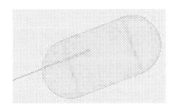

Figure 2-32. *The curved border is pressed at the point where it is crossed by solid line*

- The Strip_Unicolored class has the minimal allowed length of the straight part (minStraight). Throughout the resizing by the curve, the distance between the cursor (which is placed exactly on the curve) and the nearest line shown in the figure never changes (additionToLength), but the distance between the two lines is changed. Thus, the minimal distance between the cursor and remote line is minStraight + additionToLength; this gives one end point for the cursor movement (ptEndIn).

- Another end point (ptEndOut) is calculated as being far away on the same line.

```
public void Press (Point ptMouse, int iNode)
{
    ... ...
    else if (caught_line == CaughtLine.Curve_C0)
    {
        angleBeam = m_angle + Math .PI;
        Auxi_Geometry .Distance_PointLine (ptCursor, m_points [0],
                                        m_points [3], out ptBase);
        additionToLength = Auxi_Geometry .Distance_PointSegment (
                                ptCursor, m_points [1], m_points [2]);
        ptEndIn = Auxi_Geometry .PointToPoint (ptBase, angleBeam,
                                        minStraight +
                                        additionToLength);
        ptEndOut = Auxi_Geometry .PointToPoint (ptBase, angleBeam, 4000);
    }
    ... ...
```

As usual, the results of resizing are determined by the MoveNode() method. The distance to the remote line is calculated (dist); this allows you to calculate the new position for point C0, after which the new cover can be organized.

```
public override bool MoveNode (...)
{
    ... ...
    else if (caught_line == CaughtLine .Curve_CO)
    {
        dist = Auxi_Geometry .Distance_PointLine (ptNearest,
                                    m_points [0], m_points [3]);
        ptCO = Auxi_Geometry .PointToPoint (ptC1, m_angle + Math .PI,
                                    dist - additionToLength);
        DefineCover ();
    }
    ... ...
```

Regular Polygon

File: Form_Polygon_Regular.cs

Menu position: Simple objects ➤ Polygon (regular)

This example deals with elements that belong to the Polygon_Regular class
(Figure 2-33).

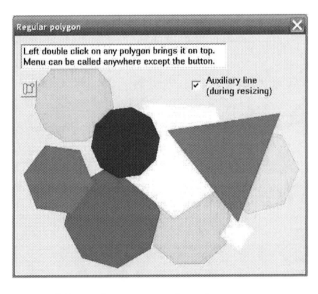

Figure 2-33. *Elements of the Polygon_Regular class*

```
public class Polygon_Regular :
                    GraphicalObject
{
    PointF m_center;
    double m_angle;
    double m_radiusVertices;
    int nVertices;
    SolidBrush m_brush;
    bool bResizable, bRotatable;
    double delta = 3;
    double deltaR;
```

The covers for circles and regular polygons are designed in a similar way. The only difference is in the shape of nodes, and not surprisingly at all, nodes in the cover of the Polygon_Regular class have the shape of regular polygons. Node 0 is used for moving and has the default cursor shape of all polygonal nodes (Cursors.SizeAll); in the case of the unmovable polygon, it is changed to Cursors.NoMove2D. Node 1 is used for resizing. For the resizable polygon, the first node is slightly smaller, and the second node is slightly bigger than the polygon itself. Only a small part of the second node along the object border is not blocked by the previous node and can be used for resizing (Figure 2-34). To signal about the difference in the result of pressing this part, node 1 has another cursor shape (Cursors.Hand). For the nonresizable polygon, the area of the first node is equal to the object itself, while the second node is squeezed to zero size.

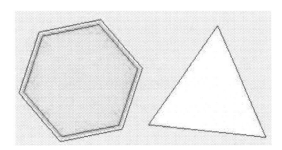

Figure 2-34. *Covers for resizable and nonresizable polygons*

```
public override void DefineCover ()
{
    CoverNode [] nodes = new CoverNode [2];
    if (Resizable)
    {
        nodes [0] = new CoverNode (0, VerticesMinus);
        nodes [1] = new CoverNode (1, VerticesPlus, Cursors .Hand);
    }
    else
    {
        nodes [0] = new CoverNode (0, Vertices);
        nodes [1] = new CoverNode (1, m_center, Of);
    }
    cover = new Cover (nodes);
    ... ...
```

Two polygonal nodes are calculated in such a way that the minimal distance between their borders is six pixels (2 * delta). This is the difference between the straight segments of two borders, while for calculations their vertices are needed. Calculations of two arrays are easy; points for these arrays depend on the number of vertices, on the radius of polygon, and on the required space between two borders. deltaR is the distance between the polygon vertex and the node vertex; both points are on the same radial beam. Vertices for the inner and outer nodes are calculated by the VerticesMinus and VerticesPlus properties.

```
deltaR = delta / Math .Cos (Math .PI / nVertices);
public PointF [] VerticesPlus
{
    get { return (Auxi_Geometry .RegularPolygon (m_center,
                            m_radiusVertices + deltaR, nVertices,
                            m_angle)); }
}
public PointF [] VerticesMinus
{
    get { return (Auxi_Geometry .RegularPolygon (m_center,
                            m_radiusVertices - deltaR, nVertices,
                            m_angle)); }
}
```

When a polygon is resizable and the left button is pressed in the vicinity of the polygon border, the cursor is shifted to the nearest border point (ptNearest). After this, the cursor of the pressed mouse is allowed to move only along the radius. One end point of the way (ptEndIn) is calculated by using the minimum allowed radius for polygon vertices; another end point (ptEndOut) is set beyond the screen border.

```
public void Press (Point ptMouse , MouseButtons catcher, int iNode)
{
    SavePosition ();
    if (catcher == MouseButtons .Left)
    {
        if (iNode == 0)
        {
            ptPressed = ptMouse;
        }
        else
        {
            PointF ptNearest;
            Auxi_Geometry .Distance_PointPolyline (ptMouse, Vertices, true,
                                                out ptNearest);
            AdjustCursorPosition (ptNearest);
            scaling = m_radiusVertices / Auxi_Geometry .Distance
                        (Center, ptNearest);
            angleBeam = Auxi_Geometry .Angle (Center, ptNearest);
            ptEndIn = Auxi_Geometry .PointToPoint (Center, angleBeam,
                                    Polygon_Regular_Adh .MinimumRadius /
                                    scaling);
            ptEndOut = Auxi_Geometry .PointToPoint (Center, angleBeam,
                4000);
        }
    ... ...
```

Throughout the move of the mouse with the pressed button, the border line goes with the cursor. The radius for all vertices is determined by the cursor position with the help of the scaling coefficient, which was calculated in the Press() method.

```
public override bool MoveNode (...)
{
    bool bRet = false;
    if (catcher == MouseButtons .Left)
    {
        if (iNode == 1)
        {
            PointF ptNearest = Auxi_Geometry . Segment_NearestPoint
            (ptMouse, ptEndIn, ptEndOut);
            double dist = Auxi_Geometry .Distance (Center, ptNearest);
            RadiusVertices = dist * scaling;
            AdjustCursorPosition (ptNearest);
            bRet = true;
        }
        ... ...
```

Elastic Polygon

File: Form_Polygon_Elastic.cs

Menu position: Simple objects ➤ Polygon (elastic)

Polygons of the previous example get their shape at the moment of construction. They can be moved and rotated; they can change their size, but not the shape. However, from time to time objects in our programs have to change their shape throughout the work of an application. Let's explore such possibilities by using a different class of polygons.

In my book [2], you can find examples with the convex polygons that can be reconfigured but always stay convex, so their change of shape is limited. Polygons of the current example have no shape limitations. To make the shape transformations more obvious, special points of new polygons are associated with personal colors, and the body of an object is painted by a smooth change of color from point to point. For several years I called such polygons *chatoyant*, so the class name emphasized their painting procedure. From the point of geometry, their main feature is the unrestricted change of shape, so now I prefer to call them *elastic polygons*, though they use the old painting method and continue to be chatoyant.

Figure 2-35 shows an example with several objects of the Polygon_Elastic class.

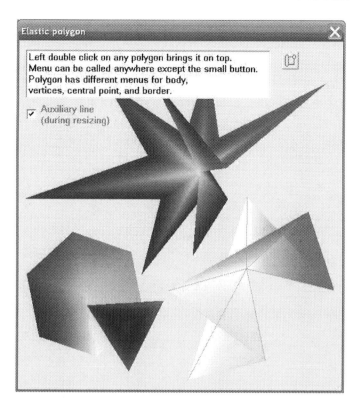

Figure 2-35. *Elastic polygons*

```
public class Polygon_Elastic : GraphicalObject
{
    PointF m_center;
    List<PointF> m_points;
    Color clrCenter;
    List<Color> clrVertices;
    bool bShowRibs, bResizable, bReconfigurable, bRotatable;
```

The flexibility in proposed changes of such polygons determines the set of parameters on initialization.

- There are no restrictions for placing vertices, so an arbitrary array of points can be used for their initialization.

- One more point must be declared on initialization; this point is needed for cover design and for painting. Throughout the later explanation it is called a *central point*, though it can be placed anywhere.

- The central point and each vertex are associated with personal colors, so some colors are initially declared for all these points.

```
public Polygon_Elastic (Form frm, Mover mvr, PointF ptC, PointF [] pts,
                        Color clrC, Color [] clrs)
```

The cover of the elastic polygon contains nodes of all three different shapes (Figures 2-36). As often the case, smaller nodes precede the bigger ones in the cover, so we start with the small circular nodes, next are the strip nodes, while polygonal nodes are the last. For a polygon of N vertices, the cover consists of 3*N + 1 nodes in such an order.

- Each vertex is covered by a small circular node.

- The central point is covered by a small circular node.

- Each pair of consecutive vertices is used to organize a narrow strip node; the last vertex is linked with the first one.

- Each pair of consecutive vertices together with the central point constitutes a polygonal (triangular) node; one more triangular node is constructed by using the last vertex, the first vertex, and the central point.

Throughout further explanation, the set of lines that link consecutive vertices is called a *border*. The easiest way to initialize an elastic polygon is to calculate its points as vertices of a regular polygon, and in such case the lines between consecutive vertices initially constitute a border. Later vertices can be moved in an arbitrary way, vertices can be added and deleted, some vertices can be placed inside the area of the whole polygon, and segments of the original border can cross each other. Regardless of all transformations, the set of lines between consecutive vertices is still called a *border* in this explanation.

If reconfiguring is prohibited, then all circular nodes are squeezed to zero size, but there can be different decisions about the squeezing of the strip nodes.

- In the book *Elements of Total Movability*, I demonstrated similar elastic polygons in which the strip nodes along the border of the nonresizable polygon were squeezed to zero size. It looks absolutely logical from the point of resizing (if a polygon is nonresizable, then it does not need the nodes along its border) but demands an illogical step when you decide to add a vertex to a nonresizable polygon. To add a vertex, you need to mark its place. You cannot simply add it at any screen point, because in such a case it is impossible to decide about the needed object. Even if you press somewhere inside a polygon, it is impossible to set the order of the new vertex among the existing vertices of this polygon. Thus, the obvious way to include a new vertex is to press on the strip node between two vertices, and the new one will be included between them. Vertices are used for reconfiguring; both resizable and nonresizable polygons can be reconfigured. However, if the strip nodes of a nonresizable polygon are squeezed to zero size, then it is impossible to add a new vertex to such a polygon. In such a way, the first step of reconfiguring—adding a new vertex—depends on resizability, and this does not make sense. Resizing and reconfiguring are two different movements, and I don't like the idea of setting some correlation between them.

- In the current version, the size of the strip nodes does not depend on the current resizability, so it is possible to add vertices and reconfigure a polygon regardless of its resizability.

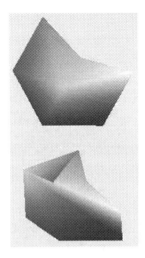

Figure 2-36a. *Two elastic polygons with the central point inside and outside*

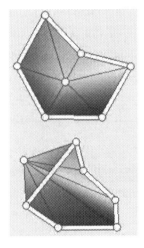

Figure 2-36b. *Visible circular nodes signal about the possibility of reconfiguring*

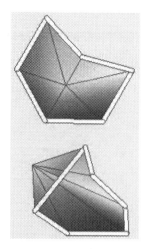

Figure 2-36c. *These are nonreconfigurable polygons, but it is impossible to say whether they are resizable*

All special points can be moved without restrictions, so the central point can also be placed outside. Figure 2-36a shows variants with the central point inside and outside the border line. Without auxiliary lines, it is difficult to detect the central point. When the ribs—the lines between central point and vertices—are visualized, then the central point is obvious.

```
public override void DefineCover ()
{
    CoverNode [] nodes = new CoverNode [3 * VerticesNumber + 1];
    float rad = bReconfigurable ? 5f : 0f;
    for (int i = 0; i < VerticesNumber; i++)
    {
        nodes [i] = new CoverNode (i, m_points [i], rad);
    }
    nodes [VerticesNumber] = new CoverNode (VerticesNumber, m_center,
    rad);
    int k0 = VerticesNumber + 1;
    for (int i = 0; i < VerticesNumber; i++)
    {
        nodes [k0 + i] = new CoverNode (k0 + i, m_points [i],
                                        m_points [(i + 1) %
                                        VerticesNumber]);
```

```
    }
    k0 = 2 * VerticesNumber + 1;
    for (int i = 0; i < VerticesNumber; i++)
    {
        PointF [] pts = new PointF [3] { m_points [i],
                             m_points [(i + 1) % VerticesNumber],
                             m_center };
        nodes [k0 + i] = new CoverNode (k0 + i, pts);
    }
    cover = new Cover (nodes);
    ... ...
```

When the polygon is pressed, different movements can be started. The type of movement depends on the type of node, but in the Press() method the decision is based on the node number.

- If a circular node is pressed, the cursor is switched to the central point of this node by using the standard AdjustCursorPosition() method. Nothing else is needed at this moment because all special points can be freely moved around the screen.

```
public void Press (Point ptMouse , MouseButtons catcher, int iNode)
{
    if (catcher == MouseButtons .Left)
    {
        if (iNode < VerticesNumber)              // vertices
        {
            ptPressed = m_points [iNode];
            AdjustCursorPosition (ptPressed);
        }
        else if (iNode == VerticesNumber)        // center
        {
            ptPressed = m_center;
            AdjustCursorPosition (ptPressed);
        }
        ... ...
```

- If a strip node is pressed, it is the start of resizing. The cursor is moved to the nearest point (ptPressed) on the border segment that is covered by this strip node; then the allowed way for the movement of the pressed mouse is calculated. This way is a straight segment of a line that goes from central point through the border point to which the cursor is moved; angleBeam is the angle of this line. The segment for the allowed cursor movement is described by its two end points ptEndIn and ptEndOut. Scaling coefficients for all vertices are calculated (scaling []); these coefficients will be used throughout resizing.

```
else if (iNode < 2 * VerticesNumber + 1)        // segments
{
    int iSegment = iNode - (VerticesNumber + 1);
    ptPressed = Auxi_Geometry .Segment_NearestPoint (ptMouse,
                                                  m_points
                                                  [iSegment],
                           m_points [(iSegment + 1) %
                           VerticesNumber]);
    if (Resizable)
    {
        distInitial = Auxi_Geometry .Distance (m_center,
                                                  ptPressed);
        double angleBeam = Auxi_Geometry .Angle (m_center,
                                                  ptPressed);
        ptEndIn = Auxi_Geometry.PointToPoint (m_center,
                                                  angleBeam, 20);
        ptEndOut = Auxi_Geometry .PointToPoint (m_center,
                                                  angleBeam,
                                                  4000);
        FillAuxiArrays ();
        for (int i = 0; i < VerticesNumber; i++)
        {
            scaling [i] = radii [i] / distInitial;
        }
    }
    AdjustCursorPosition (ptPressed);
}
```

- If any polygonal node is pressed, only the pressed point is saved.

```
else
{
    ptPressed = ptMouse;
}
```

The reaction on moving any node is described in the MoveNode() method; three types of nodes in this cover are responsible for absolutely different actions, so there are three branches in this method.

- When some circular node is moved, the point associated with this node (it can be a vertex or central point) goes with the cursor.

```
public override bool MoveNode (...)
{
    bool bRet = false;
    if (catcher == MouseButtons .Left)
    {
        if (iNode < VerticesNumber)
        {
            m_points [iNode] = ptMouse;
            bRet = true;
        }
        else if (iNode == VerticesNumber)
        {
            m_center = ptMouse;
            bRet = true;
        }
        ... ...
```

- All polygonal nodes are responsible for moving the whole object, but only if an object is movable.

```
else if (iNode >= 2 * VerticesNumber + 1)
{
    if (Movable)
    {
```

```
            Move (dx, dy);
            bRet = true;
        }
        else
        {
            AdjustCursorPosition (ptPressed);
        }
    }
```

- When some strip node is moved, then the whole object is zoomed.
  The cursor goes along the previously calculated straight segment;
  the border point is moved with the cursor, and the new positions for
  all vertices are determined by the cursor position with the help of
  previously calculated scaling coefficients.

```
    else
    {
        if (Resizable)
        {
            PointF ptNearest = Auxi_Geometry .Segment_NearestPoint (
                                            (ptMouse, ptEndIn,
                                            ptEndOut);
            double distMouse = Auxi_Geometry.Distance (m_
            center,ptNearest);
            List<PointF> ptsNew = new List<PointF> ();
            for (int j = 0; j < m_points .Count; j++)
            {
                ptsNew .Add (Auxi_Geometry .PointToPoint (m_center,
                                    angles [j], distMouse *
                                    scaling [j]));
            }
            m_points = ptsNew;
            DefineCover ();
            AdjustCursorPosition (ptNearest);
            bRet = true;
        }
```

```
            else
            {
                AdjustCursorPosition (ptPressed);
            }
        }
        ... ...
```

Rotation is organized in a standard way around the central point, but the central point is movable, so rotation goes around the current position of the central point. Preliminary calculations are made with the help of the Press() method at the moment when the polygon is pressed by the right button. At this moment two arrays are filled; these arrays contain distances and angles from the central point to all vertices.

```
private void FillAuxiArrays ()
{
    for (int i = 0; i < m_points .Count; i++)
    {
        radii [i] = Auxi_Geometry .Distance (m_center, m_points [i]);
        angles [i] = Auxi_Geometry .Angle (m_center, m_points [i]);
    }
}
```

With those angles already known, the compensation for each vertex is calculated.

```
public void Press (Point ptMouse , MouseButtons catcher, int iNode)
{
    ... ...
    else if (catcher == MouseButtons .Right)
    {
        ptPressed = ptMouse;
        FillAuxiArrays ();
        double angleMouse = Auxi_Geometry .Angle (m_center, ptMouse);
        for (int i = 0; i < VerticesNumber; i++)
        {
            compensation [i] = Auxi_Common .LimitedRadian (angleMouse -
                                angles [i]);
```

```
        }
      }
   }
```

The stored values of radius and compensation for each vertex allow you to calculate the vertex position at any moment of rotation.

```
public override bool MoveNode (...)
{
    ... ...
    else if (catcher == MouseButtons .Right)
    {
        if (Rotatable)
        {
            double angleMouse = -Math .Atan2 (ptMouse .Y - m_center .Y,
                                                ptMouse .X - m_center .X);
            for (int j = 0; j < VerticesNumber; j++)
            {
                m_points [j] = Auxi_Geometry .PointToPoint (m_center,
                    Auxi_Common .LimitedRadian (angleMouse -
                    compensation [j]), radii [j]);
            }
            DefineCover ();
            return (true);
        }
    ... ...
```

A polygon can be reconfigured by moving its vertices and central point, but there is one more option. The number of vertices in elastic polygon can be changed, but several conditions apply to this action. Adding vertices and deleting vertices are organized through the commands of two different menus.

To delete a vertex, use the menu on this vertex; certainly, the command is not available in the case of a triangle. The menu is called on the small circular node that covers this vertex. Such a node has a nonzero size for a reconfigurable polygon only, so this is the only and absolutely reasonable condition: if the polygon is reconfigurable, then there are nonzero circular nodes, and the menu command "Delete vertex" can be used.

To add a vertex, you need to mark its place. You cannot simply add it at any screen point, because in such a case it is impossible to decide about the needed object. Even if you press somewhere inside a polygon, it is impossible to set the order of the new vertex among the existing vertices of this object. Thus, the obvious way to include a new vertex is to press the strip node between two existing vertices. Later the new vertex can be moved to a desired place.

In the case of elastic polygons, the addition of new vertex and its further use are separated. First, you call the menu at the needed point of the polygon border and press the "Add vertex" command. Now you can press this vertex with the left button and move it to any other place thus changing the polygon shape. In the example with polylines, the adding of new joint and its movement are organized in a single press-and-move action. Why is it not done the same way for polygons? An elastic polygon can be resized using any border point, so it would be impossible to predict whether the press of the border with the left button is the start of resizing or a request for a new vertex. (In the case of polylines, an addition of new joints is organized only for unmovable lines, so there is no conflict between two actions.)

The unrestricted change of elastic polygons can produce strange results. I never ran into such situations in real applications throughout all the years of design, and you are not going to see similar strangeness in any of the coming examples, but because these situations are possible, I want to mention them and to explain with the help of Figures 2-37.

Figure 2-37a. *Polygon*

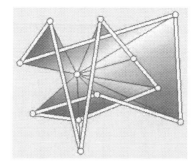

Figure 2-37b. *Full cover*

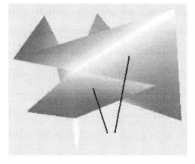

Figure 2-37c. *Cover for nonreconfigurable polygon*

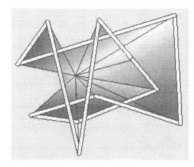

Figure 2-37d. *Places of invisible vertices*

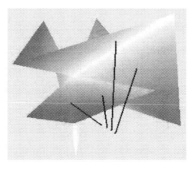

Figure 2-37e. *Places of invisible border*

Figure 2-37a shows a polygon as you see it on the screen. In real applications, the covers are never shown, but their visualization can be helpful for explanation and analysis, so Figure 2-37b shows the cover of the same polygon when all the nodes have real sizes; Figure 2-37c shows the cover for the same polygon when it is declared nonreconfigurable. As you can see, in such a case, all circular nodes are squeezed to zero size. Figures 2-37d and 2-37e mark some interesting places that we need to discuss.

Some strange situations occur because we (users) and the mover have different visions of the same object. We see the same reconfigured polygon in Figure 2-37a regardless of all its parameters. For the mover, there are no colors and no painting, but only the cover, so, depending on the declared Reconfiguration property, the mover sees only nodes in Figure 2-37b or 2-37c. Even this is not all because some further mover actions depend on the currently declared resizability. (I want to remind you that in the `Polygon_Elastic` class the size of the strip nodes does not depend on resizability, so it is impossible to decide by the cover view whether the polygon in Figure 2-37c is resizable or not.)

The polygon is movable by default, and in such case, it is supposed to be movable by any inner point. You move the cursor across this polygon, and nearly everywhere the cursor looks like a cross. But above two small areas marked by the ends of black lines in Figure 2-37d the cross is changed to hand. The mover is constantly looking for the nodes and changes the cursor shape according to the parameter of the first detected node. For our eyes, these are the places of the smooth color change without any special features, but for the mover these are the places of circular nodes, so the cursor shape is changed. You can catch sight of this change if you move the cursor not too fast. If you stop and press the cursor at this moment, then you are going to move not the whole polygon but only the caught vertex. Whether you intend to do it or not is up to you, but you need to know about such a possibility. The vertex can be invisible for the user because it is closed from view by some part of the polygon, but circular nodes of the `Polygon_Elastic` object are the first in its cover and thus the first to be analyzed and grabbed (!) by the mover.

Circular nodes in these polygons are small and the probability of an accidental move of some vertex is negligible. Strip nodes never disappear, and their area is bigger, but the effect of pressing some hidden border part can differ. The cursor shape over the strip nodes is also changed from cross to hand. If you press one of the areas marked by the ends of black lines in Figure 2-37e and the polygon is resizable (it is resizable by default), then you start the resizing. If you do the same for nonresizable polygon, then the cursor is adhered to the pressed point.

There are two ways to add new polygons to the current example. One is to duplicate an existing polygon through the command of its menu. Another is to call a menu at any empty place and to use the "Add polygon" command that calls an auxiliary Form_NewElasticPolygon.cs (Figure 2-38). Elastic polygons from our example Form_Polygon_Elastic.cs can be transformed in an arbitrary way, so I decided that it was not necessary to define the shape of a new polygon in the auxiliary form. The purpose of this auxiliary form is to define a new polygon with the required number of vertices and with the needed colors for all special points. A polygon that is used in this auxiliary form can be resized and rotated, but it is always a regular polygon with additional small circles placed next to its vertices.

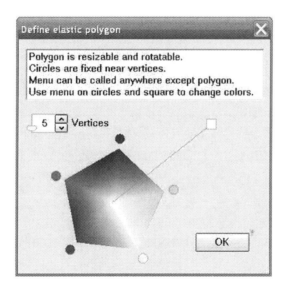

Figure 2-38. *Here the number of vertices and the set of colors for new polygon are defined*

```
public class Polygon_RegChat_withCircles : GraphicalObject
{
    PointF m_center;
    double m_angle;
    double radiusVertices, fRadiusToCenters;
    int nVertices;
    Color clrCenter;
    Color [] clrVertices;
    float fSpaceToCircles, fRadiusSmall;
    bool bResizable, bRotatable;
```

An object of the Polygon_RegChat_withCircles class demonstrates one feature that is rarely seen in the other screen objects. As a rule, a screen object is shown in one piece. An object can be of an arbitrary shape, but it is usually a single piece, so there is usually a cover consisting of overlapping nodes. In the case of this polygon, there are several entirely separated pieces that constitute a single object. For example, you can rotate this polygon by any inner point, and you can do the same by any small circle.

Small circles are placed at a fixed space from vertices (fSpaceToCircles) and at the beams that go from the polygon central point through the vertices, so the polygon geometry together with the known space and radius of these circles (fRadiusSmall) perfectly describes positions of these small parts. Circles cannot be moved individually. The cover for a polygon with N vertices consists of N + 2 nodes. The main part of this object is a regular polygon, so two nodes provide its moving and resizing; N circular nodes cover the small circles.

```
public override void DefineCover ()
{
    CoverNode [] nodes = new CoverNode [VerticesNumber + 2];
    PointF [] ptCircles = Auxi_Geometry .RegularPolygon (Center,
                            fRadiusToCenters, VerticesNumber, Angle);
    for (int i = 0; i < VerticesNumber; i++)
    {
        nodes [i] = new CoverNode (i, ptCircles [i], fRadiusSmall);
    }
    int k0 = VerticesNumber;
    if (Resizable)
    {
        nodes [k0] = new CoverNode (k0, VerticesMinus);
        nodes [k0 + 1] = new CoverNode (k0 + 1, VerticesPlus, Cursors .Hand);
    }
    else
    {
        nodes [k0] = new CoverNode (k0, Vertices);
        nodes [k0 + 1] = new CoverNode (k0 + 1, m_center, 0f);
    }
    cover = new Cover (nodes);
    ... ...
```

What are the reactions on pressing polygon at different places (nodes)?
For the *left button press*:

- If pressed inside the polygon, then the whole object is moved.

- If pressed on the border, then the polygon is resized.

- If pressed on any circle, then the cursor is fixed at the pressed point.

The right button press starts the rotation regardless of the pressed point.

A change of colors is done through menus that can be called on circles and on the small square. A thin line shows that a small square is associated with the central point, so the standard dialog for color selection called through the menu on this square allows you to set the color of the central point.

Arc

File: Form_Arc.cs

Menu position: Simple objects ➤ Arc

Let's turn once more to an object with the curved border. In my book [2], you can find different examples of wide and thin arcs and also several examples with the ring sectors that look exactly like wide arcs. Here I try to unite all those cases into a single class. In addition, the Arc class demonstrates two interesting features.

- Usually the big nodes resemble the shape of an object with which they are used. It is often a case, but it is not a law; there are situations when the shapes of the big nodes have no similarities with the shape of an object itself but such nodes are useful in design of a cover.

- There are cases when the node shape is changed on a fly and depends on some object parameters.

Before going into the details of this Arc class, let's mention some design ideas. Arc, especially a wide arc, looks like part of a ring, so it needs to have some identical parameters, such as the central point, inner radius, and outer radius. In addition, there are two angles that describe the arc ends.

When you look at any arc, you don't see any difference between its two ends. In the same way, we don't see any difference between four corners of rectangle, but when you press any corner, the mover knows exactly which one is pressed because each corner is covered by a node with its personal number. To make two arc ends movable, they are covered by nodes; these nodes have their numbers, so the mover knows which one is pressed. In the code, one end is called the *head*, and the angle from the central point to this end is named angleHead. Another end of arc is called the *tail*; the angle from head to tail is called angleArc. I want to remind you that angles in the counterclockwise direction are positive. The head of an arc can be marked by the letter *H* (Figure 2-39).

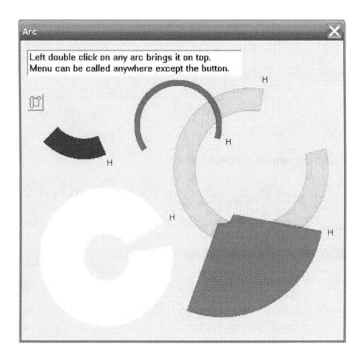

Figure 2-39. *Several objects of the Arc class*

```
public Arc (Form frm, Mover mvr, PointF ptC, float rIn, float rOut,
            double angleHead_Degree, double angleArc_Degree, Color clr)
```

Arcs of this class have movable ends; by moving one or another end, the arc angle is changed. This angle can be changed only inside a range. The limit on the minimum angle (minDegree_Arc = 10) prevents arc disappearance. The limit on the maximum angle (maxDegree_Arc = 350) prevents the arc from turning into a ring; the yellow arc in Figure 2-39 demonstrates the nearly maximum allowed arc angle.

Inner and outer borders of an arc are movable. Theoretically the width of an arc can be decreased to a single pixel thus turning an arc into a curved line, but in doing so the sensitive ring along one border will be blocked by the similar sensitive ring along another. The cover of the `Ring_Adh` class that was discussed 35 pages back includes coaxial circular nodes that go from the smallest one to the biggest. Nodes in the cover of the `Arc` class go in the same order, and this may cause a deadlock in the case of a thin arc.

Suppose that you squeeze the arc inner border to its minimal size and then start to squeeze the outer border. If the width of the arc body is allowed to be squeezed to one pixel and you do it and release the outer border, then there is no way to change or move this arc anymore. The node over inner border blocks the nodes on the body and on the outer border, but the inner border cannot be moved because it already has the minimum allowed radius. To avoid such situation, there is a limit on the minimal allowed width of an arc (`minWidth = 10`). Such a limit guarantees that at any moment there is a possibility to move an arc around the screen and to move its outer border.

```
public class Arc : GraphicalObject
{
    PointF m_center;
    float rInner, rOuter;
    double rCursor;
    double angleHead, angleArc, compensation, angleFixedTail;
    SpecArea curArea;
    SolidBrush m_brush;
    bool bChangeableWidth, bMovableHead, bMovableTail, bRotatable;
    float minRadius_Inner = 20;
    float minWidth = 10;
    double minDegree_Arc = 10;
    double maxDegree_Arc = 350;
```

In general, the arc can be changed by any part of its border, and there are several parameters that regulate the possible movements of border parts. The arc border has four different parts: inner border, outer border, and two end borders. It is not a problem at all to organize the independent regulation of movability for these four parts, but in the current version of the `Arc` class, the resizing by the inner and outer borders is changed synchronously. The arc cover depends on the declared movability of border parts and on the current arc angle (!); variants are shown in Figure 2-40.

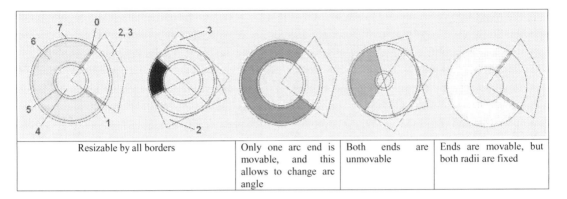

Figure 2-40. *Cover variants for the* Arc *class*

The cover always consists of eight nodes; all of them are marked on the left arc. The first two nodes cover the arc ends; by moving them, the arc angle is changed. There are situations when the arc angle has to be fixed (the cyan arc in Figure 2-40) or only one end is allowed to be moved (the *green* arc in Figure 2-40).

```
public override void DefineCover ()
{
    CoverNode [] nodes = new CoverNode [8];
    double angleTail = angleHead + angleArc;
    float wHalf = bMovableHead ? 3 : 0;
    double rClean;
    nodes [0] = new CoverNode (0,
                Auxi_Geometry .PointToPoint (m_center, angleHead,
                rInner),
                Auxi_Geometry .PointToPoint (m_center, angleHead,
                rOuter), wHalf);
    wHalf = bMovableTail ? 3 : 0;
    nodes [1] = new CoverNode (1,
                Auxi_Geometry .PointToPoint (m_center, angleTail,
                rInner),
                Auxi_Geometry .PointToPoint (m_center, angleTail,
                rOuter), wHalf);
    ... ...
```

The arc gap has to be covered by transparent nodes. Though an arc is part of a ring, those transparent nodes are polygonal, while their geometry depends on the arc angle (or the gap angle).

- When the arc angle does not exceed 180 degrees (the blue arc in Figure 2-40), there are two different rectangular nodes. Each one stands next to the arc end and erases half of the outer circle.

```
if (Math .Abs (angleArc) <= Math .PI)
{
    PointF ptA, ptB;
    double angleA, angleB;
    if (angleArc >= 0)
    {
        angleB = angleHead;
        angleA = angleTail;
    }
    else
    {
        angleA = angleHead;
        angleB = angleTail;
    }
    rClean = rOuter + wHalf;
    ptA = Auxi_Geometry .PointToPoint (m_center, angleA, rClean);
    ptB = Auxi_Geometry .PointToPoint (m_center, angleB, rClean);
    PointF [] ptsA = new PointF [] {ptA,
        Auxi_Geometry .PointToPoint (ptA, angleA + Math .PI / 2, rClean),
        Auxi_Geometry .PointToPoint (m_center, angleA + 3 * Math
        .PI / 4,
                                     rClean * Math .Sqrt (2)),
        Auxi_Geometry .PointToPoint (m_center, angleA - Math.PI,
        rClean) };
    PointF [] ptsB = new PointF [] {ptB,
        Auxi_Geometry .PointToPoint (m_center, angleB - Math .PI,
        rClean),
```

```
            Auxi_Geometry .PointToPoint (m_center, angleB - 3 * Math
            .PI / 4, rClean * Math .Sqrt (2)),
            Auxi_Geometry .PointToPoint (ptB, angleB - Math .PI / 2,
            rClean) };
        nodes [2] = new CoverNode (2, ptsA, Behaviour .Transparent);
        nodes [3] = new CoverNode (3, ptsB, Behaviour .Transparent);
    }
```

- When the arc angle exceeds 180 degrees (the yellow arc in Figure 2-40), the gap can be closed with a single polygonal node, but it is easier to deal with the same number of nodes in all the cases, so the needed polygon is calculated, and then two identical nodes are organized.

```
else
{
    double angleGap;
    if (angleArc > 0)
    {
        angleGap = angleArc - 2 * Math .PI;
    }
    else
    {
        angleGap = angleArc + 2 * Math .PI;
    }
    rClean = (rOuter + wHalf) * Math .Sqrt (2);
    PointF [] pts = new PointF [] { m_center,
            Auxi_Geometry .PointToPoint (m_center, angleHead, rClean),
            Auxi_Geometry .PointToPoint (m_center,
                                        angleHead + angleGap / 2,
                                        rClean),
            Auxi_Geometry .PointToPoint (m_center, angleHead +
            angleGap,
                                        rClean) };
        nodes [2] = new CoverNode (2, pts, Behaviour .Transparent);
        nodes [3] = new CoverNode (3, pts, Behaviour .Transparent);
    }
```

The last four nodes are organized in a way that was already described with the ring cover. These four nodes are circular; the first of them is transparent and erases the hole, two of them provide the resizing by inner and outer border, and the remaining one provides the forward moving of the whole arc. The resizing by inner and outer borders in this version of the Arc class is changed simultaneously, so neither inner nor outer radius of the pale-yellow arc in Figure 2-40 can be changed.

```
int delta = bChangeableWidth ? 3 : 0;
nodes [4] = new CoverNode (4, m_center, rInner - delta,
                                Behaviour .Transparent);
nodes [5] = new CoverNode (5, m_center, rInner + delta);
nodes [6] = new CoverNode (6, m_center, rOuter - delta, Cursors
.SizeAll);
nodes [7] = new CoverNode (7, m_center, rOuter + delta);
if (!Movable)
{
    nodes [6] .Cursor = Cursors .NoMove2D;
}
cover = new Cover (nodes);
... ...
```

The change of arc radii is organized in the same way as in the Ring_Adh class. Two interesting things are demonstrated throughout the change of the arc angle, and both of them are worth mentioning.

The first is the cursor path when the arc end is caught for moving. While writing about the rotation of any object, I always underline that for greater accuracy the cursor must be moved farther away from rotation center, and that is why the radius of the cursor movement is never fixed throughout rotation. However, if from the aesthetic or any other point of view you want to keep the cursor at the same circular path, it is easy to organize; this is demonstrated in the current example. When an arc end is pressed, the distance between the arc center and the pressed point is calculated (rCursor).

```
public void Press (Point ptMouse, MouseButtons catcher, int iNode)
{
    if (catcher == MouseButtons .Left)
    {
        if (iNode < 2)
```

```
        {
            double angle = (iNode == Node_Head) ? angleHead
                                                 : (angleHead + angleArc);
            ptEnd = Auxi_Geometry .Segment_NearestPoint (ptMouse,
                        Auxi_Geometry .PointToPoint (m_center, angle,
                        rInner),
                        Auxi_Geometry .PointToPoint (m_center, angle,
                        rOuter));
            rCursor = Auxi_Geometry .Distance (m_center, ptEnd);
            AdjustCursorPosition (ptEnd);
            ... ...
```

The possible trail for the pressed cursor is then calculated as an arc with such radius (rCursor).

Throughout the movement of the ends, cursor position is calculated as the nearest point on this arc with the help of the NearestPointOnTrail() method.

```
    public override bool MoveNode (...)
    {
        bool bRet = false;
        if (catcher == MouseButtons .Left)
        {
            if (iNode == Node_Head)
            {
                ptNew = NearestPointOnTrail (ptMouse);
                ... ...
            }
            else if (iNode == Node_Tail)
            {
                ptNew = NearestPointOnTrail (ptMouse);
                ... ...
```

The second feature of the end movement is maybe more interesting. There are limits on the minimum and maximum arc angles, so there must be a mechanism to keep the arc angle inside this range. When you need to keep the cursor between the end points of a straight segment, it is easy to organize by calculating the distance to cursor. When you have the circular track, the same task is a bit tricky because the angles do not grow infinitely but always stay inside the same range of [-180, 180] degrees. An additional check must be done. Throughout the years, I used different techniques to keep an arc inside the allowed angles range; I want to demonstrate and explain the currently used technique with the help of another example. Keeping the arc angle inside some range or moving a spot along a nearly circular trail with only a small gap and preventing this spot from jumping over the gap are the equivalent tasks, but the second one is more obvious and easier for understanding.

File: Form_Spot_OnArc.cs

Menu position: Simple objects ➤ Spot on arc

Figure 2-41 shows three elements of the Spot_OnArc class. We already had an example with similar spots on the line segments and circles. In that old example, spots were movable, but their tracks were not. In the new example, a spot can be moved along its track, but a track can be also moved and rotated.

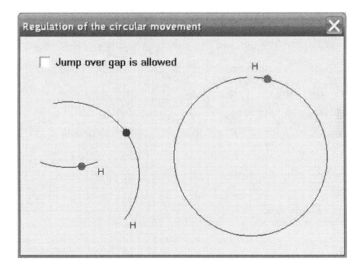

Figure 2-41. *Objects of the Spot_OnArc class*

Three tracks of the current example demonstrate arc tracks with arc angles from a small one to nearly a full circle. In all three cases, the same code is used, but the most interesting one is the track with a small gap. The basic idea of keeping a spot on a track is always the same. You press a spot and then move cursor with the pressed button. For any new position of cursor, the nearest allowed point on a track is calculated; the spot is moved to this point, and the cursor is placed at the spot central point. If this new point is somewhere in the direction of cursor movement, then everything looks like a smooth spot movement. If this nearest allowed point is somewhere in the opposite direction from the cursor movement, then it looks like the spot is frozen at the arc end point; this happens if you try to move blue or green spots over the ends of their tracks. What is the problem of having a small gap on a circular track?

Suppose that in the situation depicted in Figure 2-41 you press the red spot and slowly move it to the left. The spot will move to the line end but will not move across the gap if you try to do it slowly. There is an easy way to calculate the nearest point not only on the full circle, but also on any part of a circle (on arc). If you move the pressed spot slowly, then the cursor can go several pixels beyond the right end point, but the nearest point on the arc will be still to the right of the gap, so the cursor will be always returned there. The whole process will look like a spot frozen on the right side of the gap.

Now press the red spot at the same place (Figure 2-41) and move the cursor to the left quickly. The cursor will easily cross such a small gap, and the nearest point on the arc will be somewhere to the left from the gap. This proposed next point for a spot can be also reached by the long way around the circle, so the point to the left of the gap is an appropriate point for a spot. If the jump over a gap is allowed, then such a small gap is not a hurdle at all for the spot movement. If the jump over a gap is not allowed, then some additional instrument to prevent such a jump must be used.

The spot position is always described by the angle from the arc central point. When a spot is slowly moved along the arc, the angle from the arc center is constantly calculated; if the new angle is inside the arc range, then such a new position is allowed. When the red spot is moved all the way around its track, then at any moment its angle is inside the allowed range, and the spot is moved from one place to another. When the cursor is quickly moved across the gap, then the new position is also inside the allowed range. To avoid such a jump, the whole plane of possible spot movements is divided into three areas: an area to the right of the gap, an area to the left of the gap, and the remaining territory. The direct switch between left and right areas is prohibited, while all other movements are allowed. Those two special areas cover two quarters of a circle with their common border placed in the middle of the gap (Figure 2-42).

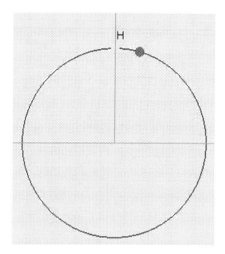

Figure 2-42. *Boundaries of two special areas are shown by thin violet lines*

An arc with a spot on it can be organized as a complex object consisting of two parts; instead, it is organized as a single object with parameters for both parts.

```
public class Spot_OnArc : GraphicalObject
{
    PointF center_Arc;
    float radius_Arc;
    double m_angleHead, m_angleArc;
    bool bJumpOverGapAllowed = false;
    SpecArea curArea;
    Pen m_penArc;
    double compensationForArc, compensationForSpot;
    PointF [] areaPlus = new PointF [3];
    PointF [] areaMinus = new PointF [3];
    PointF m_ptSpot;
    int m_radiusSpot;
    Color m_colorSpot;
```

The constructor gets parameters both for the arc and for the spot.

```
public Spot_OnArc (Form frm, Mover mvr, PointF ptC_track, float rad_track,
                   double angleHead_Degree, double angleArc_Degree,
                   PointF ptSpot, int rSpot, Color clrSpot)
```

The cover for this class is similar to the cover of the Arc class but simpler because the track (the arc) is thin and it is enough to have one pair of circular nodes for it. The gap is always covered by two nodes, but, depending on the gap angle, these nodes are either different or identical; the explanation was given for the Arc class (see Figure 2-40). The spot is covered by a small circular node that must be the first in the cover. Thus, the cover consists of five nodes of which only the first and the last are nontransparent. The first node is responsible for moving the spot along the arc, while the last one provides all movements of the arc. The small spot has the default cursor of all circular nodes: Cursors.Hand. The last node in the cover is also circular. To give a tip about its different movement, and because a track can be moved freely around the screen, the cursor over this circular node is changed to Cursors.SizeAll.

```
public override void DefineCover ()
{
    double angleEnd = Auxi_Common .LimitedRadian (m_angleHead + m_angleArc);
    float wHalf = 3;
    float rOuter = radius_Arc + wHalf;
    CoverNode [] nodes = new CoverNode [5];
    nodes [0] = new CoverNode (0, m_ptSpot, m_radiusSpot);
    if (Math .Abs (m_angleArc) <= Math .PI)
    {
        ... ...
        nodes [1] = new CoverNode (1, ptsA, Behaviour .Transparent);
        nodes [2] = new CoverNode (2, ptsB, Behaviour .Transparent);
    }
    else
    {
        ... ...
        nodes [1] = new CoverNode (1, pts, Behaviour .Transparent);
        nodes [2] = new CoverNode (2, pts, Behaviour .Transparent);
    }
    nodes [3] = new CoverNode (3, center_Arc, radius_Arc - wHalf,
                                Behaviour .Transparent);
    nodes [4] = new CoverNode (4, center_Arc, radius_Arc + wHalf,
                                Cursors .SizeAll);
    cover = new Cover (nodes);
    ... ...
```

There are two nontransparent nodes in the cover, so there are two branches in the Press() method.

```
public void Press (Point ptMouse, MouseButtons catcher, int iNode)
{
    if (catcher == MouseButtons .Left)
    {
        if (iNode == 0)
        {
            AdjustCursorPosition (m_ptSpot);
            SetTriangles ();
            curArea = InsideArea (m_ptSpot);
        }
        else
        {
            PointF pt = NearestPointOnArc (ptMouse);
            AdjustCursorPosition (pt);
        }
        ... ...
```

The interesting one is the case of the pressed spot (iNode == 0). At this moment, two areas shown in Figure 2-42 are calculated.

```
private void SetTriangles ()
{
    double angleGapMiddle = Auxi_Common .LimitedRadian (
                                        m_angleHead + m_angleArc / 2 +
                                        Math .PI);
    areaPlus [0] = center_Arc;
    areaPlus [1] = Auxi_Geometry .PointToPoint (center_Arc,
                    angleGapMiddle, 4000);
    areaPlus [2] = Auxi_Geometry .PointToPoint (center_Arc,
                                        angleGapMiddle + Math .PI /
                                        2, 4000);
    areaMinus [0] = center_Arc;
    areaMinus [1] = Auxi_Geometry .PointToPoint (center_Arc,
                    angleGapMiddle, 4000);
```

```
    areaMinus [2] = Auxi_Geometry .PointToPoint (center_Arc,
                                        angleGapMiddle - Math .PI /
                                        2, 4000);
}
```

Then the area in which the pressed spot resides at this moment is determined.

```
private SpecArea InsideArea (PointF pt)
{
    if (Auxi_Geometry .Point_InsideConvexPolygon (pt, areaPlus))
    {
        return (SpecArea .Plus);
    }
    else if (Auxi_Geometry .Point_InsideConvexPolygon (pt, areaMinus))
    {
        return (SpecArea .Minus);
    }
    else
    {
        return (SpecArea .Outside);
    }
}
```

The returned value is remembered.

```
        curArea = InsideArea (m_ptSpot);
```

As usual, all movement of all the caught nodes is described in the MoveNode()
method. The cursor can be moved anywhere from the caught spot; for any new cursor
position (ptMouse), the nearest point on the track is calculated (ptNew). Further actions
depend on whether a jump over the gap is allowed.

- If such a jump is allowed, then the spot is moved to the new
  calculated point.

- If a jump across the gap is not allowed, then there is additional
  checking. The area for the new proposed position is determined
  (newArea). If the comparison of two values signals the proposed

switch from one side of the gap to another, then the cursor is returned
to the current spot position; otherwise, the spot is moved to the
proposed position, and the area for this position is remembered.

```
public override bool MoveNode (...)
{
    bool bRet = false;
    if (catcher == MouseButtons .Left)
    {
        if (iNode == 0)
        {
            PointF ptNew = NearestPointOnArc (ptMouse);
            if (m_bJumpOverGapAllowed)
            {
                m_ptSpot = ptNew;
            }
            else
            {
                SpecArea newArea = InsideArea (ptNew);
                if ((curArea == SpecArea.Plus && newArea == SpecArea.
                Minus) ||
                    (curArea == SpecArea.Minus && newArea == SpecArea.
                    Plus))
                {
                }
                else
                {
                    m_ptSpot = ptNew;
                    curArea = newArea;
                }
            }
            AdjustCursorPosition (m_ptSpot);
        }
        ... ...
```

Like Swiss Cheese

File: Form_FillHoles.cs

Menu position: Applications ➤ Fill the holes

At the end of this chapter, we'll have a funny example for diversion. Small kids learn to distinguish objects of different shapes by filling the holes in the plastic forms with the appropriate plugs. We'll have similar task.

Figure 2-43 demonstrates all elements that are used in this example. There is a board with holes; there is a group of buttons to initialize the needed plug, and there is also a plug. When a plug is alive (as shown in Figure 2-43), then all buttons are disabled, so not more than one plug can be used at any moment. To close some hole with a plug, the plug can be moved, resized, and rotated. When a plug matches with some hole, then both the plug and the hole disappear, and buttons inside the group become enabled. (My book [2] includes a similar example that allows you to have simultaneously several boards and any number of plugs. For the current book, I decided to simplify this example.)

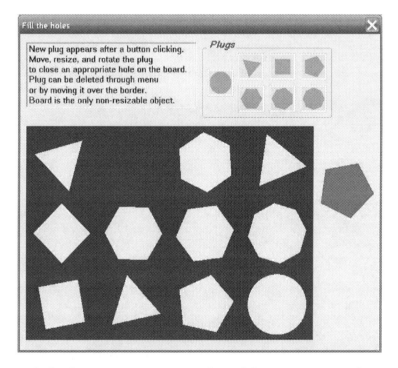

Figure 2-43. *Click a button to activate a plug of the appropriate shape. To match the plug with some hole, the plug can be moved, rotated, and resized*

The rectangular board with the holes belongs to the AreaWithHoles class.

```
public class AreaWithHoles : GraphicalObject
{
    RectangleF m_rc;
    int nRow, nCol;
    List<Hole> holes = new List<Hole> ();
    SolidBrush m_brush;
    float spaceAroundHole = 10;
```

The board is a nonresizable rectangle with the holes positioned by rows and columns. This object has a simple but interesting cover in which all but the last node are transparent. These transparent nodes are used one per each hole.

```
public override void DefineCover ()
{
    int nHoles = holes .Count;
    CoverNode [] nodes = new CoverNode [nHoles + 1];
    for (int i = 0; i < nHoles; i++)
    {
        if (holes [i] .VerticesNumber == 0)
        {
            nodes [i] = new CoverNode (i, holes [i] .Center, holes [i]
            .Radius, Behaviour .Transparent);
        }
        else
        {
            nodes [i] = new CoverNode (i, holes [i] .Vertices,
                                        Behaviour .Transparent);
        }
    }
    nodes [nHoles] = new CoverNode (nHoles, m_rc);
    cover = new Cover (nodes);
}
```

The board has a single nontransparent node, so this node is used for moving the whole board.

```
public override bool MoveNode (...)
{
    bool bRet = false;
    if (catcher == MouseButtons .Left)
    {
        Move (dx, dy);
        bRet = true;
    }
    return (bRet);
}
```

Throughout such board movement, the positions of all the holes are changed synchronously.

```
public override void Move (int dx, int dy)
{
    m_rc .X += dx;
    m_rc .Y += dy;
    SizeF size = new SizeF (dx, dy);
    for (int i = 0; i < holes .Count; i++)
    {
        holes [i] .Center += size;
    }
}
```

Each hole is either a circle or a regular polygon. Variants are the same as for plugs and are listed in the Plug_Shape enumeration.

```
public enum Plug_Shape { Circle, RegPoly };
```

Parameters of a hole describe its geometry, but hole is not a movable object, so it is not derived from the GraphicalObject class.

```
public class Hole
```

```
{
    Plug_Shape shape;
    PointF m_center;
    float m_radius;
    int nVertices;
    double m_angle;
```

The plug object has the same set of parameters to describe its geometry, but a plug is movable, resizable, and rotatable.

```
public class Plug : GraphicalObject
{
    Plug_Shape m_shape;
    PointF m_center;
    float m_radius;
    double m_angle;
    SolidBrush m_brush;
    int nVertices;
```

We already discussed covers for circles and regular polygons. In both cases, two nodes provide all the needed movements, and in both cases these nodes copy the shape of an object with the first node being slightly smaller and the second node slightly bigger than an object itself.

```
public override void DefineCover ()
{
    CoverNode [] nodes = new CoverNode [2];
    if (m_shape == Plug_Shape .Circle)
    {
        nodes [0] = new CoverNode (0, m_center, m_radius - delta,
                                    Cursors .SizeAll);
        nodes [1] = new CoverNode (1, m_center, m_radius + delta);
    }
    else
    {
        nodes [0] = new CoverNode (0, VerticesMinus);
        nodes [1] = new CoverNode (1, VerticesPlus, Cursors .Hand);
```

```
        }
        cover = new Cover (nodes);
    }
```

A plug is moved, resized, and rotated in the same way as circles and regular polygons, but there is one interesting thing related to a plug movement. Suppose that you clicked the wrong button, and a plug of the unneeded shape appeared on the screen. You can delete it through the command of its menu, but there is also another and more interesting way to do the same: the unneeded plug can be moved over the border and released there. The program does not allow you to move any other object but plug across the border. How is it organized?

The mover is initialized in a standard way with the form itself as a parameter.

```
public Form_FillHoles ()
{
    InitializeComponent ();
    mover = new Mover (this);
    ... ...
```

This means that the mover clipping is set at the Clipping.Visual level, and no object can be moved across the borders. Only when a plug is pressed for moving (and not for resizing!) is this clipping level changed to Clipping.Unsafe. Of the two nodes in the plug cover, the first one is used for moving and the second one for resizing, so there is an additional check by the number of the pressed node.

```
private void OnMouseDown (object sender, MouseEventArgs e)
{
    ptMouse_Down = e .Location;
    if (mover .Catch (e .Location, e .Button))
    {
        GraphicalObject grobj = mover .CaughtSource;
        int iNode = mover .CaughtNode;
        if (grobj is Plug)
        {
            m_plug .Press (e .Location, e .Button, iNode);
            if (e .Button == MouseButtons .Left && iNode == 0)
            {
```

```
        mover .Clipping = Clipping .Unsafe;
    }
... ...
```

With such a level of mover clipping, the caught plug can be moved across any border. The reset of the Clipping.Visual level is done when the mouse button is released.

```
private void OnMouseUp (object sender, MouseEventArgs e)
{
    ... ...
    mover .Clipping = Clipping .Visual;
}
```

The main purpose of this example is not the plug relocation across the border, so let's check what happens when a plug is released. First, there is a checking of whether it was released inside or outside the form. If the plug is released out of sight, then its life is over, and all buttons in the group become enabled, so another plug can be initialized.

```
private void OnMouseUp (object sender, MouseEventArgs e)
{
    ptMouse_Up = e .Location;
    double fDist = Auxi_Geometry .Distance (ptMouse_Down, ptMouse_Up);
    int iObj, iNode;
    if (mover .Release (out iObj, out iNode))
    {
        GraphicalObject grobj = mover .ReleasedSource;
        if (e .Button == MouseButtons .Left)
        {
            ... ...
            else if (grobj is Plug)
            {
                Rectangle rcClient = ClientRectangle;
                Rectangle rcPlug = Rectangle .Round (plug .RectAround);
                if (Rectangle.Empty == Rectangle .Intersect (rcPlug,
                rcClient))
                {
```

```
                    plug = null;
                    BtnsStatus ();
                    RenewMover ();
            }
```

If the plug is released anywhere in view, then it is still alive and must be compared with all the board holes; such comparison is done by the CheckMatch() method.

```
            if (plug != null)
            {
                    CheckMatch ();
            }
```

If there is a good match between the plug and some hole, then the plug disappears, the hole also disappears, and buttons inside the group become enabled. If the last hole on the board was closed, then the new set of holes is organized, and the same process can be started again.

```
private bool CheckMatch ()
{
        ... ...
        if (bHoleClosed)
        {
            plug = null;
            BtnsStatus ();
            board .Holes .RemoveAt (iHole);
            if (board .Holes .Count == 0)
            {
                board .RenewHoles ();
            }
            board .DefineCover ();
            RenewMover ();
        }
        ... ...
```

Conclusion

In this chapter, we found out how to make movable the objects of the most popular shapes. These objects can be moved, resized, and rotated. The discussed objects are called simple because each one has its own cover and can be involved in all the needed movements without paying attention to all the other screen objects. However, it is a common situation when, in addition to individual movements, elements can be involved in synchronous or related movements with other elements. The design of such complex objects is discussed in the next chapter.

CHAPTER 3

Complex Objects

While discussing the movability of objects in the previous chapter, we made an assumption that their movements could be discussed without paying attention to anything else. However, often, in addition to individual movements, objects are involved in related and/or synchronous movements. How does this affect the algorithm of movability, and how does this affect the design of user-driven applications? These questions are discussed in this chapter. Throughout this discussion we make a big step in the design of complex plotting areas, which often consist of the plots associated with unlimited number of scales and comments. It is an important step because the majority of scientific and engineering applications work with such plotting areas.

The objects discussed in the previous chapter were involved in different movements. All movements are organized on the basis of covers, which may include a different number of nodes. There is some correlation between the number of not transparent nodes in a cover and the number of different movements in which these objects are involved because the left button press on any node can start only one movement.

- A small square (class `Square_Sample`) and a board with holes (class `AreaWithHoles`) have a single nontransparent node in a cover, so such elements can be involved only in forward movement.

- A regular polygon (class `Polygon_Regular`) and circle (class `Circle_Unicolored`) have two nodes in their covers, so they can be moved and resized.

- Elastic polygons (class `Polygon_Elastic`) have nodes of all three types in their covers, so they can be moved, resized, and reconfigured.

With the increase of nodes in a cover, objects look more and more complex. Yet, all these objects were discussed in Chapter 2 because I distinguish simple and complex objects not by the number and variety of nodes but by the way of cover design.

© Sergey Andreyev 2020
S. Andreyev, *User-Driven Applications for Research and Science*, https://doi.org/10.1007/978-1-4842-6488-1_3

- If an object has a single cover that provides all the required movements of all its parts, then it is a simple object.

- If parts of an object have individual covers that are registered in the mover queue by separate commands, then it is a complex object.

There are objects that can be designed in both ways, and both variants would provide the same movability. By playing with such an object, it would be impossible to say whether it is designed as a simple or a complex one. Thus, it's only for the developer to decide about the design of a particular class. Spot_OnArc is an excellent example of objects that can be easily designed as complex.

There are objects that tell from the beginning that they must be designed as complex. The most common case of a complex object is some simple element united with a comment, and the most often case of such a union is a nonrotatable rectangle with one or several comments.

Rectangle with Comments

File: Form_Rectangle_withComments.cs

Menu position: Complex objects ➤ Rectangle with comments

In Figure 3-1, there are several objects of the Rectangle_withComments class. Each rectangle of this class can be associated with an unlimited number of comments. Whenever a rectangle or comment is pressed, their parameters are shown in two lists inside the group. A small colored rectangle inside the group is used as a reminder about the rectangle which parameters are shown. Let's begin with this small rectangle because from the point of cover design and all possible movements, it is designed in an identical way.

```
public class Rectangle_SizeRange : GraphicalObject
{
    PointF [] ptsCorner;
    Resizing m_resize;
    RectRange m_range;
    bool bShowFrame;
    RectFrameType typeFrame;
    Pen penLine = new Pen (Color .DarkGray);
    Delegate_Draw m_draw = null;
    static int minSide = 20;
```

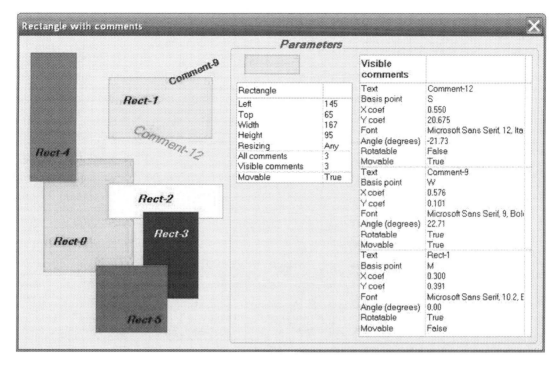

Figure 3-1. *Parameters are shown when some object is pressed*

The sides of such rectangle are always horizontal and vertical. It cannot be rotated but allows you to set different types of resizing, which are described by the `Resizing` enumeration.

```
public enum Resizing { None, NS, WE, Any };
```

Parameters of initialization include the original size and two ranges for changing width and height; by comparison of these parameters, the current type of resizing (`m_resize`) is set. The numbering of points in the `ptsCorner` array starts from the top-left corner and goes clockwise.

```
public Rectangle_SizeRange (Form frm, Mover mvr, RectangleF rc,
                            RectRange range, Delegate_Draw drawmethod)
{
    ... ...
    ptsCorner = new PointF [4] { new PointF (rc .X, rc .Y),
                       new PointF (rc .X + w, rc .Y),
                       new PointF (rc .X + w, rc .Y + h),
                       new PointF (rc .X, rc .Y + h) };
    ... ...
```

The cover consists of nine nodes (Figure 3-2). The positions and numbering of the first four nodes coincide with the points of the ptsCorner[] array.

```
public override void DefineCover ()
{
    float rad = (m_resize == Resizing .Any) ? 5 : 0;
    float wHalf_WE =
                (m_resize == Resizing .Any || m_resize == Resizing .WE)
                ? 3 : 0;
    float wHalf_NS =
                (m_resize == Resizing .Any || m_resize == Resizing .NS)
                ? 3 : 0;
    CoverNode [] nodes = new CoverNode [9] {
                new CoverNode (0, ptsCorner [0], rad, Cursors
                .SizeNWSE),
                new CoverNode (1, ptsCorner [1], rad, Cursors
                .SizeNESW),
                new CoverNode (2, ptsCorner [2], rad, Cursors
                .SizeNWSE),
                new CoverNode (3, ptsCorner [3], rad, Cursors
                .SizeNESW),
                new CoverNode (4, ptsCorner [0], ptsCorner [3],
                wHalf_WE, Cursors .SizeWE),
                new CoverNode (5, ptsCorner [1], ptsCorner [2],
                wHalf_WE, Cursors .SizeWE),
                new CoverNode (6, ptsCorner [0], ptsCorner [1],
                wHalf_NS, Cursors .SizeNS),

                new CoverNode (7, ptsCorner [3], ptsCorner [2],
                wHalf_NS, Cursors .SizeNS),
                new CoverNode (8, ptsCorner) };
    cover = new Cover (nodes);
    ... ...
```

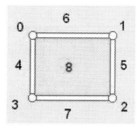

Figure 3-2. *The cover and the numbering of nodes*

There are always nine nodes, but depending on the needed type of resizing, the number of sizable (nonzero) nodes can be one, three, or nine. All possible variants are shown in Figure 3-3 in the same order as in the Resizing enumeration.

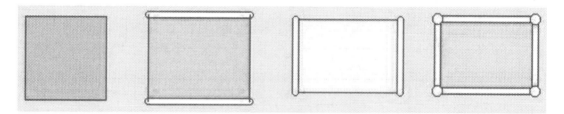

Figure 3-3. *Covers for all variants of resizing*

The resizing of rectangles is organized in the same way as explained in the previous chapter. If a circular node is pressed, then the cursor is adjusted to the corner position and is allowed to move only inside some rectangular area that is determined by minimum and maximum allowed sizes for the pressed rectangle. If a strip node is pressed, then the cursor is adjusted to the covered border and is allowed to move only orthogonally to the pressed side; the limits of cursor movement are determined by the same minimum and maximum allowed sizes of the pressed rectangle.

From the solitary rectangle, we can move to the Rectangle_withComments class. The rectangle has the same cover, so it is moved and resized in identical way. The most interesting thing is the teamwork of rectangle and comments.

When two elements—in our case they are rectangle and comment—are united for coordinated work, then one of them must be declared a dominant element while another is a subordinate element. Usually a rectangle is bigger than its comment and contains more important information, so the obvious choice is to make rectangle a dominant element in such a pair. In the case of the Rectangle_withComments class, there can be not one but several subordinates.

```
public class Rectangle_withComments : GraphicalObject
{
    PointF [] ptsCorner;
    Resizing m_resize;
    SolidBrush m_brush;
    List<Comment_ToRectangle> m_comments = new List<Comment_
    ToRectangle> ();
    static int minSide = 20;
```

Individual and related movements of rectangle and its associated comments are organized according to such rules.

- When a rectangle is moved, all its comments move synchronously.

- When a rectangle is resized, all its comments move in order to keep their relative positions to the rectangle.

- Any comment can be moved and rotated individually; such movements have no effect on anyone else.

Comments to a rectangle are derived from the Comment_Adh class, which was discussed in the previous chapter (see Figure 2-22). The Comment_ToRectangle class has a few fields of its own; these fields are used to organize the teamwork of rectangle and comments.

```
public class Comment_ToRectangle : Comment_Adh
{
    RectangleF m_rcParent;
    double m_xCoef;
    double m_yCoef;
```

The Comment_Adh object has nine special points (Figure 2-22). When the Comment_ToRectangle object is initialized, one of these points is declared as an anchor point, and two positioning coefficients for this point are calculated.

```
public Comment_ToRectangle (Form frm, Mover mvr, RectangleF rc,
                            PointF ptAnch, TextBasis textbasis, string txt,
                                Font fnt, double ang_Deg, Color clr)
    : base (frm, mvr, ptAnch, textbasis, txt, fnt, ang_Deg, clr)
```

```
    {
        m_rcParent = rc;
        Auxi_Geometry .CoefficientsByLocation (m_rcParent, ptAnch,
                                            out m_xCoef, out m_yCoef);
    }
```
Comments can be associated with rectangle by the AddComment() method.
```
    public void AddComment (Comment_ToRectangle cmnt)
    {
        cmnt .ParentRect = MainElementArea;
        cmnt .ParentID = ID;
        m_comments .Add (cmnt);
    }
```

Two lines of this simple method are important for further united work of elements. First, the comment stores the ID of rectangle with which it is associated. Later this will provide an easy identification of the related rectangle when any comment is pressed with a mouse.

```
        cmnt .ParentID = ID;
```

Second, the comment is informed about the area of the dominant element.

```
        cmnt .ParentRect = MainElementArea;
```

To participate in synchronous and related movements with a rectangle, any comment needs two things: the area of rectangle and a pair of coefficients that describe the position of comment anchor point in relation to this rectangle. Coefficients along both scales are calculated in a similar way, so it is enough to look at the rules for calculating the horizontal coefficient.

- If the comment anchor point is anywhere to the left of the rectangle, then the coefficient is equal to the distance from the point to the left border of the rectangle and has a negative sign.

- If the anchor point is to the right of rectangle, then the coefficient is equal to the distance from the point to the right border of the rectangle and has a positive sign. To be exact, in this case, `coefficient = distance + 1`.

- If the point is between the left and right borders of rectangle, then the coefficient belongs to the [0, 1] range with 0 on the left border and 1 on the right. (For the vertical coefficient, the upper border of the rectangle is associated with 0 and the lower border with 1.)

At any moment, the comment position is determined in two different ways: there is a PointF value of its anchor point and another definition through the rectangle and a pair of positional coefficients. On any movement of the rectangle or comment, only one of parameters is changed directly and causes the recalculation of another parameter.

- When the rectangle is moved or resized, all its associated comments are informed about the change by the InformRelatedElements() method.

```
private void InformRelatedElements ()
{
    RectangleF rc = MainArea;
    foreach (Comment_ToRectangle cmnt in m_comments)
    {
        cmnt .ParentRect = rc;
    }
}
```

Each comment gets the new value of rectangle area through its ParentRect property; the unchanged coefficients {m_xCoef, m_yCoef} are used to calculate the new comment position.

```
public RectangleF ParentRect
{
    get { return (m_rcParent); }
    set
    {
        m_rcParent= value;
        AnchorPoint = Auxi_Geometry .LocationByCoefficients (m_rcParent,
                                               m_xCoef, m_yCoef);
    }
}
```

- When the comment is moved, its new location is determined by the Move() method of the base class, which changes the coordinates of the comment anchor point. Then the new coefficients are calculated.

```
public override void Move (int dx, int dy)
{
    base .Move (dx, dy);
    CoefficientsByLocation ();
}
private void CoefficientsByLocation ()
{
    m_xCoef = Auxi_Geometry .CoefficientByCoor (m_rcParent .Left,
                         m_rcParent .Right, AnchorPoint .X);
    m_yCoef = Auxi_Geometry .CoefficientByCoor (m_rcParent .Top,
                         m_rcParent .Bottom, AnchorPoint .Y);
}
```

I already mentioned that visually there is no strict division between simple and complex objects. The track bar is just the case of an object that can be designed in both ways, and there would be no difference in using a "simple" track bar or a "complex" track bar. Yet, there is one way simple and complex objects are absolutely different: the way they are registered with the mover.

A simple object can be extremely simple and may be involved in one movement only (like a nonresizable rectangle or circle) or can consist of different parts involved in different movements (elastic polygon or arc), but in all these cases an object has a single cover that provides all these movements. Such an object is registered in the mover queue by one of two methods:

```
Mover .Add (GraphicalObject grobj)
```

or

```
Mover .Insert (int iPos, GraphicalObject grobj)
```

You can find in the previous examples that simple objects can be also registered by the GraphicalObject.IntoMover() method. This is possible because all movable objects are derived from the GraphicalObject class, and the GraphicalObject.IntoMover() method simply calls the Mover.Insert() method.

```
public void IntoMover (Mover mover, int iPos)
{
    mover .Insert (iPos, this);
}
```

You can use this method to register any simple graphical object, and it will work correctly.

A complex object consists of several parts (at least two) that have individual covers. In the current case of rectangle with comments, the rectangle has its cover, and each comment has its own cover. If you try to use the GraphicalObject.IntoMover() method with a complex object, it will register the main part but not the associated components because the mover has no information about the possible existence and the number of components. To organize the correct registering of any complex object, you need to write such a method for your particular class and always use only this method for registering.

Here is the code of the Rectangle_withComments.IntoMover() method:

```
public void IntoMover (Mover mvr, int iPos)
{
    mvr .Insert (iPos, this);
    for (int i = m_comments .Count - 1; i >= 0; i--)
    {
        if (m_comments [i] .Visible)
        {
            mvr .Insert (iPos, m_comments [i]);
        }
    }
}
```

First the cover of rectangle is inserted into the mover queue at the required position iPos; then all the associated comments are inserted ahead of their "parent" rectangle. Thus, a rectangle will be correctly registered together with all its comments regardless of their number.

It is a standard practice that subordinate parts of any complex object are registered ahead of their dominant element. Screen objects are drawn in the opposite order to their registering in the mover queue. The same rule is applied to the parts of a complex object, so first the rectangle is drawn, and then all its comments in the order opposite to their registering.

```
public void Draw (Graphics grfx)
{
    grfx .FillPolygon (m_brushBack, ptsCorner);
    ... ...
    for (int i = m_comments .Count - 1; i >= 0; i--)
    {
        m_comments [i] .Draw (grfx);
    }
}
```

There are many different things that can be done with rectangles in this example; many different actions are started via the commands of menu that can be called on a rectangle (Figure 3-4a).

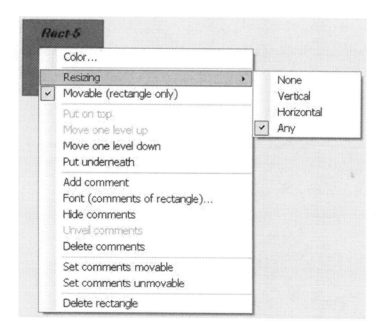

Figure 3-4a. *Context menu for rectangles*

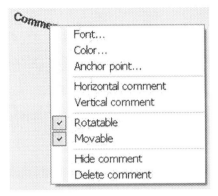

Figure 3-4b. *Menu on rectangle comments*

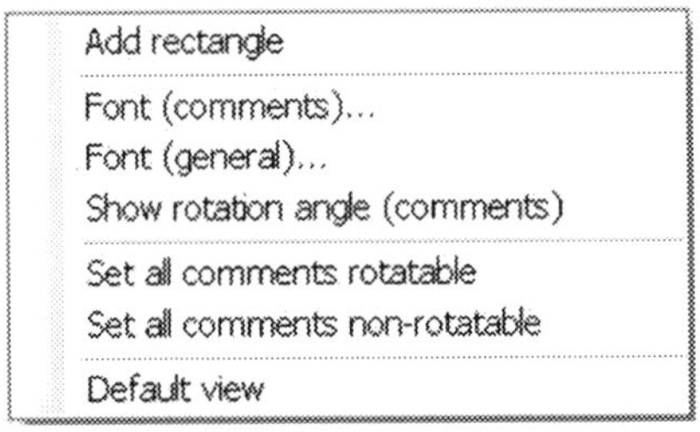

Figure 3-4c. *Menu at empty place*

Comments can be temporarily hidden, and this can be done individually through their menu (Figure 3-4b) or synchronously for all comments of the rectangle through the menu for the dominant element (Figure 3-4a). Hidden comments are not registered in the mover queue (see the code of the `IntoMover()` method), so the menu cannot be called on the hidden comment; such comments can be returned into view only via the menu on the dominant element (Figure 3-4a).

One more thing is demonstrated in this example, though it can be useful in much more complicated applications.

Later I'll write about the engineering and scientific applications that often use a lot of plotting. When you have a plotting area with different graphs, then in the case of a classical design with unmovable elements, there is always a problem of positioning some comments that must obviously correspond to the lines and at the same time not block them from view. The movability and rotatability of comments are useful in organizing the view that the user needs, but there can be a small inconvenience. The comment rotation and the call of the comment menu are both started with a right-click, and while calling a menu, the user can slightly rotate this comment. Two things help to deal with this problem.

First, there is an indicator (its appearance is regulated by the user) that allows you to set (or restore) the needed angle of the comment. To make easier the positioning of comments along the sides of the rectangles, two commands from the menu on the comment allow you to make it strictly horizontal or vertical (Figure 3-4b). Second, the rotatability of comments can be regulated either individually (Figure 3-4b) or synchronously for all (Figure 3-4c).

To demonstrate all the features of comments and a lot of possibilities in dealing with them, I included a significant number of commands in their menu (Figure 3-4b). The `Comment_ToRectangle` objects are used in many different classes; for example, they are used with nearly all classes of graphical controls that substitute ordinary controls. (Graphical analogues of ordinary controls appear in nearly every example starting from the beginning of this book, but they will be discussed later in Chapter 5.) Whenever such a comment is used, there is always some menu that can be called on a comment, but usually the menu on the comment has fewer commands than in the current example. The font and color are always changeable, but with all other commands there can be variants. In nearly half of all cases, the anchor point selection is not used. If I don't see any need in the comment rotation, then such a comment can be initialized as nonrotatable. From time to time a comment is declared rotatable, but only a command to set it strictly horizontal is left in the menu. When you see some small menus on comments, keep in mind that all missing commands from the big menu (Figure 3-4b) can be easily added.

To demonstrate the design of complex objects and interaction of its parts, abstract rectangles were used. A similar interaction between the parts of real object is demonstrated in the next example.

> File: `Form_Scrolling.cs`

> Menu position: Complex objects ➤ Scrolling

Programs often have to show the names of some files. Usually a filename with the whole path is so long that scrolling is used for the area in which a filename is shown. Engineering and scientific programs often use several input files for data of different types; to distinguish these files, each area needs a comment. Figure 3-5 demonstrates one object of the `FilenameViewer_withSlider` class.

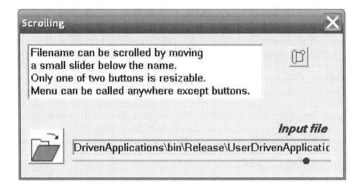

Figure 3-5. *Rectangular area to show the filename is accompanied by comment*

The main area of this object includes a rectangle to show the filename and a thin rail along which the small slider is moved.

The cover for this class consists of only four nodes. First is a small circular node on a spot that is moved along the rail at the bottom of this element (Figure 3-6). Next are two strip nodes on the sides of rectangular area; these nodes are used to change the size of an element. The rectangle, which covers the filename area and the rail below it, is used as an area of the dominant part. The last node covers this rectangle and is used for moving the whole object. The comment of the Comment_ToRectangle class is associated with this area.

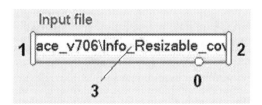

Figure 3-6. *Cover for the filename viewer*

There is nothing new in the work of this filename viewer; all the details were already discussed in the previous examples. When the left or right border is pressed, the cursor is adjusted exactly to the pressed border, the end points for horizontal mouse move are calculated, and the pressed mouse is allowed to move only between these points. When the circle is pressed, the cursor is adjusted to its central point, the end points for cursor movement along the rail are calculated, and the circle with the cursor can be moved only between these points.

The only thing that is worth mentioning is the font change. Call the menu anywhere inside the filename area and select the needed font with the help of a standard dialog. When the font is selected, the NameFont property of the class gets the new value. This NameFont property adjusts the height of the filename rectangle (hFrame) to the height of the new font and makes the needed adjustments in positions of other parts (rail, ball, comment).

```
public Font NameFont
{
    get { return (m_font); }
    set
    {
        if (value != null)
        {
            m_font = value;
            sizeFilename = Auxi_Geometry .MeasureString (m_form, filename,
                                        m_font);
            float hFrame = 2 * fShift_side + Auxi_Geometry .MeasureString (
                                        m_form, "File name", m_font)
                                        .Height;
            rcTextFrame .Height = hFrame;
            rcRail .Y = rcTextFrame .Bottom + fRadius;
            ... ...
```

Simple? Yes. Expected? Yes. Correct? No!

Each time I reread the previous page and see the words about the adjustment of rectangle height to the font size, I immediately see the wrong action, rush to correct the code, and only then remember that it was done this way and left here on purpose.

At the beginning of the book I formulated the rules of user-driven application. Rule 3 declares that "...no additions or expanded interpretation [of the commands] by developers are allowed." Through the menu command you ordered to change the font, but there was no demand for anything else. The automatic adjustment of the area height after the font change is definitely wrong in user-driven applications. I assume that the majority of users would expect such an adjustment, but it is still incorrect. The best solution would be to add one more parameter and let users decide whether they agree with such automatic adjustment. If the user disagrees, then there must be an easy way to change also the vertical size of the filename area. I hope to demonstrate such a solution in another example later, but for now simply remember this case and do not forget that even the solutions that looked correct without any doubts for many years may be not so correct in applications of the new type.[1]

I am not going to change this example, but the correct version of the filename viewer would need a different cover, which would allow users to change the height of the area. The standard cover with circular nodes on the corners and strip nodes along the sides would work perfectly.

Circle with Comments

File: Form_Circle_withComments.cs

Menu position: Complex objects ➤ Circle with comments

Forward movement and resizing of circles was demonstrated in the previous chapter with the help of simple unicolored elements. Circular diagrams, which are used in many areas, have the same shape, but to demonstrate the needed data, those diagrams are shown as circles divided into sectors. If a user needs to change the ratio between sectors, then sector partitions must be movable.

Circles consisting of sectors need two types of comments (Figure 3-7). Comments of both types react identically to circle movement and resizing, but usually they have different reactions to circle rotation. Individual movements of comments of two types are absolutely different.

---

[1]Users can decide about possible adjustment of the height to the selected font in the case of Label_GR objects, which are discussed in Chapter 5.

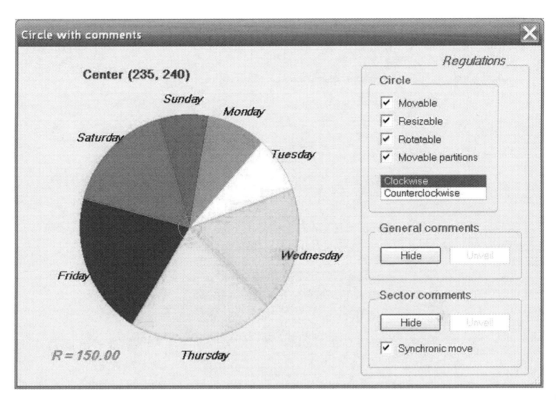

Figure 3-7. *Circle with general and sector comments*

- First, there are comments that apply to the whole circle; these comments are called *general*; in the current example, these comments belong to the `Comment_ToCircle` class. The user decides whether each of these comments reacts or does not react to the circle rotation. These comments can be moved freely around the screen. The number of general comments is unlimited. A change of comment parameters is more obvious when you can visually compare comments with different settings, so in this example there are two comments of such a type.

- There are other comments that are associated with sectors; they are called *sector* comments. Each sector has a single comment of such type, so the number of comments is equal to the number of sectors. To demonstrate the association between comment and sector, such a comment cannot be moved freely around the screen. In the current example, I use the `Comment_OnCircleRadius` class; each object of this class is positioned on the bisector of the associated sector. Individually comment can be moved only along this bisector line.

163

Each comment has its own cover. The circle is a dominant element, while all comments are its subordinates.

```
public class Circle_withComments : GraphicalObject
{
    CircleData m_data;
    bool bResizable, bRotatable, bMovablePartitions;
    Comment_OnCircleRadius [] cmntSector;
    List<Comment_ToCircle> cmntsGeneral = new List<Comment_ToCircle>
();
```

Before showing the code of the cover design for this class, I want to mention the implemented ideas.

- This circle is resized by any border point in the same way as was explained for the `Circle_Unicolored` class, so the cover includes the same pair of big circular nodes with a small difference in their radii. These two nodes will be the last in the cover of the new class.

- To make all the partitions movable, each one is covered by a strip node from the central point to the circle border. When such a node is caught by the left button, the mouse cursor is allowed to move only along the circular trail, so pressing closer to the circle border provides higher accuracy in sector changes.

- Near the central point, those strip nodes overlap, and the user can't estimate beforehand which partition is caught at one or another point. Even if the needed partition is caught very close to the central point, the movement of the caught partition at such a small radius is limited, and the change of sectors is inaccurate. To avoid all these problems, I put a small circular node around the central point. It is the first node in the cover, and its area is shown by a thin line. This node is used to move the whole object.

```
public override void DefineCover ()
{
    float wHalf = MovablePartitions ? 3 : 0;
    int delta = Resizable ? 3 : 0;
    double [] partition_angle = PartitionAngles;
    int nSectors = m_data .SectorsNumber;
    CoverNode [] nodes = new CoverNode [1 + nSectors + 2];
```

```
nodes [0] = new CoverNode (0, Center, radInner, Cursors .SizeAll);
for (int i = 0; i < nSectors; i++)          // nodes on borders
                                                between sectors
{
    nodes [i + 1] = new CoverNode (i + 1, Center,
        Auxi_Geometry .PointToPoint (Center, partition_angle [i],
        Radius), wHalf);
}
nodes [nSectors + 1] = new CoverNode (nSectors + 1, Center,
Radius - delta, Cursors .SizeAll);
if (!Movable)
{
    nodes [0] .Cursor = Cursors .NoMove2D;
    nodes [nSectors + 1] .Cursor = Cursors .NoMove2D;
}
nodes [nSectors + 2] = new CoverNode (nSectors + 2, Center,
                                    Radius + delta);
cover = new Cover (nodes);
... ....
```

As usual, all preliminary calculations for further movement are done at the moment when an object is pressed.

- The minimum number of sectors in such a circle is two. When any partition is pressed with the left button, then there is some neighboring partition in the clockwise direction and another in the opposite direction. (In the case of two sectors, it is the same neighboring partition in both directions, but usually they are different.) The direction of the drawing can be changed; in the current example, it is done through the list box. To avoid the disappearance of sectors, there is a minimum allowed angle for any sector (0.05 radian). Thus, the movement of the caught partition is limited by its neighbors. The numbering of partitions is done in the direction of a drawing, so in the code, the neighboring partitions are named as previous and next.

```
public void Press (Point ptMouse, MouseButtons catcher, int iNode)
{
    if (catcher == MouseButtons .Left)
    {
        ... ...
        else        // partitions
        {
            int iPartition = iNode - 1;
            double [] sector_angle = SectorAngles;
            double [] partition_angle = PartitionAngles;
            iPartition_Prev = (iPartition == 0) ? (nSectors - 1)
                                                 : (iPartition - 1);
            int iPartition_Next = (iPartition + 1) % nSectors;
```

- Throughout the movement of partition, the ratio between the angles of sectors on two sides can be changed, but their sum (angleArc_TwoSectors) does not.

```
            anglePartition_Prev = partition_angle [iPartition_Prev];
            anglePartition_Next = partition_angle [iPartition_Next];
            angleArc_TwoSectors = sector_angle [iPartition_Prev] +
                                  sector_angle [iPartition];
```

- The radius of further cursor movement (rCursor) is determined by the point of the initial press.

```
            double anglePartition = partition_angle [iPartition];
            ptPressed = Auxi_Geometry .Segment_NearestPoint
            (ptMouse, Center, Auxi_Geometry .PointToPoint (Center,
            anglePartition, Radius));
            rCursor = Auxi_Geometry .Distance (Center, ptPressed);
```

- Further cursor movement is organized along the arc trail, which is determined by the angle of one end (angleWay_Head) and the arc angle (angleWay_Arc).

```
        if (DrawingDirection == DrawingDirection .Clockwise)
        {
            angleWay_Head =
                        partition_angle [iPartition_Prev] -
                        minSectorAngle;
            angleWay_Arc = sector_angle [iPartition_Prev] +
                sector_angle [iPartition] + 2 * minSectorAngle;   //
                negative
        }
        else
        {
            angleWay_Head = partition_angle [iPartition_Prev] +
                            minSectorAngle;
            angleWay_Arc = sector_angle [iPartition_Prev] +
                sector_angle [iPartition] - 2 * minSectorAngle;   //
                positive
        }
        SetTriangles ();
        curArea = InsideArea (ptPressed);
        ... ...
```

The movement of the cursor along the arc and not beyond its ends is organized in the same way as was explained with the Spot_OnArc and Arc classes. While the cursor of the pressed mouse moves along this arc, the pressed partition goes with the cursor, and angles of two sectors on its sides change.

The main purpose of this chapter is to investigate the teamwork of different elements that are united into some complex object. The circle can be moved, resized, and rotated.

- When the circle is moved, its central point is changed through the Center property.

- When the circle is resized, its radius is changed through the Radius property.

- When the circle is rotated, its angle is changed through the Angle property.

When the circle is moved or resized, the change of positions for both types of comments is done in an identical way. The position of any comment (position of its anchor point) is determined by an angle from the circle center and special coefficient. For points inside the circle, this coefficient changes from zero (at the circle center) to one (at the circle border). For points outside the circle, this coefficient is equal to the distance from the circle. (To be exact, `coef = dist + 1`.)

When the circle is rotated, all the sector comments rotate synchronously because they are kept on the associated bisector lines. By default, general comments ignore circle rotation. The user can change such behavior via the menu command.

Movement of a sector comment along the bisector line is similar to a spot movement along the line segment, which was demonstrated at the beginning of this book. Only in case of the `Comment_OnCircleRadius` class, there is no mouse adjustment at the press moment. When a sector comment is pressed with the left button, the shift between the comment anchor (central) point and the pressed point is calculated. After that, the cursor is moved along the line that is parallel to the bisector line, and this causes the anchor point of the comment to move exactly along the bisector.

Plot Analogue

It was the immovability of plots in scientific applications that years ago triggered my work on the movability of the screen objects, so plots were the first objects on which the algorithm of movability was tested. Maybe it was not the best choice because plots are complex objects with lots of parameters, but just this complexity demanded such clarity and generality from the developed algorithm that later it could be applied without problems to many different objects in other areas. Later in this book we'll come to real plots that are used in scientific and engineering applications; just now I want to discuss some simplified analogs of such plots.

> File: `Form_PlotAnalogue.cs`

> Menu position: Complex objects ➤ Plot analogue

The main part of each plot is a rectangular area in which the plotting is done. This area may have an arbitrary number of horizontal and vertical scales; each scale is associated with some range of values. The end values are usually shown next to the scale, but for easier evaluation of the intermediate values, the scale often has a number of ticks. For bigger accuracy in the estimation of the graphs, shorter subticks can appear between the ticks. Not only the scale end values but also the tick values can be shown. In addition, there can be comments associated with the plotting area and each scale. This is a general view of the plotting area with all its associated elements, while in the current example we use its simplified version.

In the current example, a plotting area is represented by a colored rectangle, while the scale is shown as a main line with a fixed number of ticks that divide scale into five intervals. Subticks and associated numbers are not used; all ticks have the same length. Comments can be associated with the plotting area and any scale. Figure 3-8 shows several objects of the `Plot_analogue` class. These are classical complex objects.

We already discussed an example of rectangle with comments; the main plotting area with its comments is another object of such a type. Here we have even more complicated case because scales are subordinate elements of the main area, so it is another complex object. Scale might have its own subordinates of comments, so we have a chain of three associated elements. Let's start with the main elements: the plotting areas.

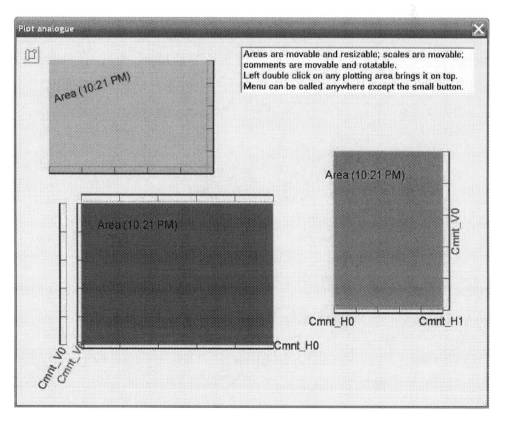

Figure 3-8. *A plot analog consists of the main rectangular area and an arbitrary number of scales. The main area and any scale can be associated with an arbitrary number of comments*

```
public class Plot_analogue : GraphicalObject
{
    PointF [] ptsCorner;
    SolidBrush m_brush;
    bool bResizable;
    List<HorScale_analogue> m_horScales = new List<HorScale_analogue> ();
    List<VerScale_analogue> m_verScales = new List<VerScale_analogue> ();
    List<Comment_ToRectangle> m_comments = new List<Comment_ToRectangle> ();
```

The cover for the Plot_analogue class (Figure 3-9) is absolutely the same as shown for the Rectangle_SizeRange class on page 82: four circular nodes on the corners, four strip nodes along the sides, and a rectangular node for the whole element. Instead of four types of resizing that were used in the older class, the new class has only two variants, so each area is either resizable or not. If the plotting area is not resizable, then all eight nodes on the border are squeezed to zero size. Moving and resizing of the plotting area are done in a standard way. The difference with the previously discussed Rectangle_withComments class is in the type of the associated elements. In the case of a plot analogue, subordinates belong to different classes, but each one has a property to get the new value of the dominant rectangle.

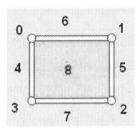

Figure 3-9. *Plot_analogue cover*

```
private void InformRelatedElements ()
{
    RectangleF rc = PlottingArea;
    foreach (Comment_ToRectangle cmnt in m_comments)
    {
        cmnt .ParentRect = rc;
    }
```

```
        foreach (HorScale_analogue scale in m_horScales)
        {
            scale .ParentRect = rc;
        }
        foreach (VerScale_analogue scale in m_verScales)
        {
            scale .ParentRect = rc;
        }
    }
```

The scales of the Plot_analogue class can be placed outside the main area, or partly overlap with this area, or be entirely inside this area; Figure 3-8 shows all these variants. To have access to the scales regardless of their positions, all scales are registered ahead of their dominant element.

```
    new public void IntoMover (Mover mvr, int iPos)
    {
        mvr .Insert (iPos, this);
        for (int i = m_comments .Count - 1; i >= 0; i--)
        {
            if (m_comments [i] .Visible)
            {
                mvr .Insert (iPos, m_comments [i]);
            }
        }
        for (int i = m_horScales .Count - 1; i >= 0; i--)
        {
            m_horScales [i] .IntoMover (mvr, iPos);
        }
        for (int i = m_verScales .Count - 1; i >= 0; i--)
        {
            m_verScales [i] .IntoMover (mvr, iPos);
        }
    }
```

Horizontal and vertical scales are very much alike. It is possible to use a single class for both types of scales, to have an additional field that will determine the direction of a particular scale, and to have two variants inside nearly every method of such a class. Instead, I decided to have two similar but different classes. Because they are very much alike, it is enough to look at the code and work of one of them. Let's look at horizontal scales.

```
public class HorScale_analogue : GraphicalObject
{
    RectangleF rcParent;            // main plotting area
    PointF pt_LT, pt_RB;            // end points of the main line
    double posCoef;                 // positioning coefficient of the main
                                    //    line in relation to rcParent
    List<Comment_ToRectangle> m_comments = new List<Comment_ToRectangle> ();
    Side sideTicks = Side .N;        // N or S
    float lenTicks = 12;
    Pen penLine, penTicks, penDots;
```

A scale analogue is a classical complex object that consists of a dominant element associated with an arbitrary number of subordinates: comments. At the same time, it is nearly a unique complex object because the dominant element is simple. It is a primitive nonresizable (directly) element that can be moved only orthogonally to its main line. The length of this main line is equal to one size of the plotting area. Another size of the scale is equal to the fixed length of the ticks, so scale has a rectangular area, and its cover consists of a single rectangular node. The cursor over this node gives a tip about the possible direction of the scale movement. The horizontal scale can be moved only up and down, so its cursor shape is Cursors.SizeNS.

```
public override void DefineCover ()
{
    cover = new Cover (new CoverNode (0, MainArea, Cursors .SizeNS));
    if (!Movable)
    {
        cover .SetCursor (Cursors .NoMove2D);
    }
    ... ...
```

While looking into the case of a comment associated with a rectangle, we already discussed the positioning coefficients used in the Comment_ToRectangle class. The same coefficient is used to determine the scale position, but because each scale can be moved along only one axis, then it is enough to have a single coefficient. This coefficient determines the position of the scale main line in relation to the plot rectangle.

```
public HorScale_analogue (Form frm, Mover mvr, RectangleF rcRel, double coef,
                          Side sideOfTicks, Color clr)
{
    ... ...
    rcParent = rcRel;
    posCoef = coef;
    MainLineByCoefficient ();
    ... ...
```

The coefficient (posCoef) allows you to calculate the coordinate of the scale main line.

```
public void MainLineByCoefficient ()
{
    float cy = Auxi_Geometry .CoorByCoefficient (rcParent .Top,
                                                 rcParent .Bottom,
                                                 posCoef);
    pt_LT = new PointF (rcParent .Left, cy);
    pt_RB = new PointF (rcParent .Right, cy);
}
```

Ticks are orthogonal to the main line, but they can be placed on one or another side. The scale area depends on the side of the scale ticks.

```
public RectangleF MainArea
{
    get {
        float cyTop = (sideTicks == Side.N) ? (pt_LT.Y - lenTicks) :
        pt_LT.Y;
        return (new RectangleF (pt_LT.X, cyTop, pt_RB.X - pt_LT.X,
        lenTicks));
    }
}
```

User-driven applications are based on the movability of absolutely all elements, and the first thing to do with each new class is to organize its cover in such a way that it provides all the needed movements. At the same time, the full control over new applications is given to users, and, among other things, users control the movability of all the screen elements. When you have an application with only a few screen objects and a lot of extra space, then the regulation of movability looks not so important, and all elements can be used as fully movable all the time. In an application with lots of movable elements, the working space becomes overcrowded, so the regulation of movability (and resizability) of each and all turns into an important thing. As a rule, scientific and engineering programs have a lot of elements on the screen. It is often a case that the user tries to organize the view in the best possible way by moving and resizing the involved objects. Moving is done easily at any moment, but if the user organizes some view and after that wants to avoid the unneeded (often accidental) movements, then the commands to fix elements are needed. If there are commands to fix anything, then there must be commands to unfix.

The movability of each element can be regulated through the commands of its menu, but the cases of complex objects have a lot of variants because, if needed, the movability of each part of a complex object can be regulated individually. The current example is a simple case of a scientific application. Users of real scientific applications always told me that they did not need too many variants of regulated movability. They definitely needed the movability for each and all, but when scientists organized the view they preferred, they would like to have a single command to fix everything to avoid accidental changes.

In the current example, the movability regulation is organized through the commands of several context menus.

- The menu for empty places (Figure 3-10a) includes commands that are applied to all objects of the form.

- The menu for plotting areas (Figure 3-10b) allows you to set the same movability for the pressed area, its scales, and all their comments.

- The menu for scales (Figure 3-10c) allows you to declare the same movability for the pressed scale and its comments.

- Only the menu on comments (Figure 3-10d) does not have a command to regulate the movability of the pressed comment. I simply do not see any sense in the individual regulation of movability for the pressed comment, but if you think that it can be useful, such a command can be easily added.

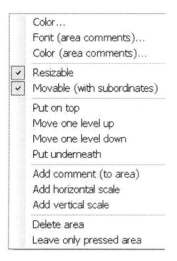

Figure 3-10a. *Menu for empty places*

Add area
Font (all comments)...
Fix everything
Unfix everything
Default view

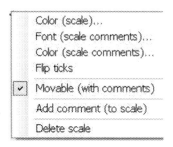

Figure 3-10b. *Menu for plotting areas*

Color...
Font (area comments)...
Color (area comments)...
✓ Resizable
✓ Movable (with subordinates)
Put on top
Move one level up
Move one level down
Put underneath
Add comment (to area)
Add horizontal scale
Add vertical scale
Delete area
Leave only pressed area

Figure 3-10c. *Menu for scales*

Color (scale)...
Font (scale comments)...
Color (scale comments)...
Flip ticks
✓ Movable (with comments)
Add comment (to scale)
Delete scale

Figure 3-10d. *Menu for comments*

Font...
Color (comment)...
Anchor point...
✓ Horizontal comment
Vertical comment
Delete comment

Here are some remarks about total movability and immovability.

In general, the screen objects can be moved around, resized, and rotated. I consider these three types of changes as three different movements; they are regulated by three different fields (these fields also belong to different classes) through different methods and properties. If a plotting area is declared unmovable but still resizable, then by moving one border after another, you can still produce the same result as if an area is movable. It takes more time and looks a bit awkward, but the resizable and unmovable area can be relocated from one place to another, which is strange for an object that is declared unmovable. I think that when a user wants to fix everything, then the user wants to avoid any kind of changes, so the "Fix everything" and "Unfix everything" commands in the menu at empty places (Figure 3-10a) deal simultaneously with movability, resizability, and rotatability of all the elements.

```
private void Click_miFix_All (object sender, EventArgs e)
{
    foreach (Plot_analogue area in areas)
    {
        area .TotalMovability = false;
        area .Resizable = false;
    }
    AllCommentsRotatability = false;
    info .Movable = false;
    info .Resizing = Resizing .None;
    btnCover .Movable = false;
    Invalidate ();
}
```

While looking at the code of the Click_miFix_All() method earlier and at the code of the twin Click_miUnfix_All() method, do not forget about the initial design of all the involved objects.

- The information area and plotting areas are movable and resizable.

- The button and all the scales are movable and nonresizable.

- The comments are movable and nonresizable; they are also the only rotatable elements in this example.

Call the menu at any empty place and click the command "Fix everything." The plotting areas, scales, and comments are then fixed, and when the mouse is moved over these elements, the cursor shape (`Cursors.NoMove2D`) informs about the immovability of underlying element. If in such a situation the mouse is pressed on any object, then the cursor is adhered to the pressed point until the mouse release.

Let's turn to one tiny problem that I'm sure you haven't run in to yet. This problem can be called a tiny one by the size of an area where it happens, but years ago when I ran into it while designing sophisticated scientific applications, this problem was a big one for me until I found an interesting and unusual solution. See Figure 3-11.

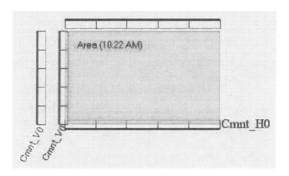

Figure 3-11a. *A Plot_analogue object with the standard positioning of scales along the sides of the plotting area*

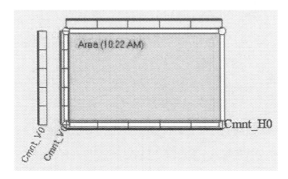

Figure 3-11b. *The cover visualization helps to understand the problem with the resizing by the corners of the plotting area*

Try to resize the green plotting area of our example (Figure 3-11a). The best way to do this is to move its corner, but depending on the direction of the needed change, you might find the task either easy or impossible to do. As a user of a scientific application, I would not expect any problems with all the corners, but in the current case there are no problems with the top-right corner, little problems with the top-left corner, and an inability to move both corners on the lower side.

You might immediately think that the problems occur at the sides over which the scales are positioned. You are absolutely right about the cause of the problem, but it does not eliminate the problem itself. Figure 3-11b shows the covers for the involved elements (at least, for the majority of them), but the problem is not only in the sizes of those nodes but also in the order of covers. The code of the `Plot_analogue.IntoMover()` method can be seen several pages back, and it makes it obvious that covers of all scales and comments appear in the mover queue ahead of the cover of their dominant element.

The positioning of the scales along the plotting area sides is the most common situation, so the view in Figure 3-11a is not rare. Let's see what happens with the small circular nodes in the corners of the plotting area.

- The node in the top-right corner is not blocked by anything, so there are no problems with moving this corner.

- Half of the node in the top-left corner is blocked by the cover of the vertical scale. When the cursor is moved into the vicinity of this corner, it will show different shapes for points near the corner. With a tiny cursor move of one or two pixels, you can catch the moment when the cursor takes a shape of the arrow inclined for 45 degrees. If the mouse button is pressed at such moment, then the plotting area can be resized by its top-left corner.

- Three-quarters of the circular node in the bottom-left corner of the green rectangle are blocked by two scales. Now take into consideration that the comment cover is not shown, but it has a rectangular area around the text of comment, so the remaining quarter of the same circular node is blocked by a comment.

- In the bottom-right corner, one-half of the circle is blocked by the scale, while the another half is blocked by the comment.

Thus, on two corners at the bottom, the inclined cursor will not appear at all, so the area cannot be resized by those corners. There is an obvious solution to this problem: move the neighboring scales and comments slightly aside, resize the plotting area, and return scales and comments back to their positions next to the plot. This solution is obvious but inconvenient. It looks at least strange if, to change some object, you need to move back and force several other objects.

Scales and comments must be shown atop their associated plotting area, so they must stay ahead of this area in the mover queue, and this order of elements cannot be changed. To have an easy resizing by the corners regardless of the scales and comments positions, I only need the appearance of circular nodes ahead of all scales and comments, but with the used cover design, this is impossible because the nodes of one cover must stay one after another and cannot be interrupted by another cover. It is impossible to place in the mover queue several nodes of the plotting area, then put ahead of them the covers for scales and comments, and then put ahead of them the remaining nodes (circles) from the cover of the main area.

For some time, I couldn't find a solution. When I finally found one, it turned out to be simple. This is often the case: when such a solution is found, it is difficult to understand why it took so long to organize because the solution is obvious.

- The best solution would be to split the cover of the main area into two parts and to register them separately with the covers of all other parts registered between them. This is impossible, so why not add one more element with the cover consisting of only four circular nodes? If this element is registered ahead of all other parts, then its four circular nodes would be never blocked.

- Let's say that we have this additional element with the cover consisting of four circular nodes. This new element is registered ahead of other parts, so this element must be painted after all other parts and must appear on top of them. But we already have the needed view of the plotting area with all the needed parts. What kind of object can be painted on top of everything in such a way as not to mar the existing view? This must be an invisible element or better to say an element that doesn't need any painting.

- Thus, we have a new element that is always invisible. This element has a bit strange geometry as it consists of four points that stay far apart. Up till now we had the elements in which the cover nodes were positioned side by side and often overlapped; in the new element, the nodes never move close to one another. This new element must work as another subordinate element for the dominant plotting area.

Regardless of its unusual geometry (four points and nothing else), its strange feature (always invisible), and its strange positioning of cover nodes (they never move close to each other), such an element perfectly solves the problem. To not to make the code too complicated, I decided to demonstrate the solution in a separate but absolutely similar in view example that uses plotting areas of the Plot_analogue_advanced class.

File: Form_PlotAnalogue_Advanced.cs

Menu position: Complex objects ➤ Plot analogue (advanced)

```
public class Plot_analogue_advanced : GraphicalObject
{
    PointF [] ptsCorner;
    SolidBrush m_brush;
    bool bResizable;
    RectCornerPoints m_rectcorners;
    List<HorScale_analogue> m_horScales = new List<HorScale_analogue> ();
    List<VerScale_analogue> m_verScales = new List<VerScale_analogue> ();
    List<CommentToRect> m_comments = new List<CommentToRect> ();
```

The plotting areas of the new class use the same scales and comments, but there is a new RectCornerPoints field.

The cover of the Plot_analogue_advanced class (Figure 3-12a) is simpler than in the Plot_analogue class (Figure 3-9). The circular nodes in the corners will be always blocked by the circular nodes of the new element, so the circular nodes in the cover of rectangle itself are not needed. The cover of the new main element consists of only five nodes: four strip nodes along the sides and one rectangular node for the whole area (Figure 3-12a).

```
public override void DefineCover ()
{
    float wHalf = bResizable ? 3 : 0;
    CoverNode [] nodes = new CoverNode [] {
        new CoverNode (0, ptsCorner [0], ptsCorner [3], wHalf, Cursors
        .SizeWE),
        new CoverNode (1, ptsCorner [1], ptsCorner [2], wHalf, Cursors
        .SizeWE),
        new CoverNode (2, ptsCorner [0], ptsCorner [1], wHalf, Cursors
        .SizeNS),
        new CoverNode (3, ptsCorner [2], ptsCorner [3], wHalf, Cursors
        .SizeNS), new CoverNode (4, ptsCorner) };
    cover = new Cover (nodes);
    ... ...
```

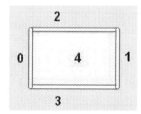

Figure 3-12a. *Cover of the Plot_analogue_advanced class*

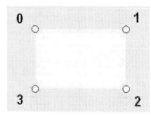

Figure 3-12b. *Cover of the RectCornerPoints class*

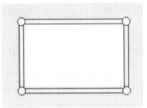

Figure 3-12c. _Combined view of two covers_

The MoveNode() method of the new rectangle is also a simplified version of a similar method from the Plot_analogue class; just remove the part that is initiated by the corner nodes, and everything else is absolutely the same. When a rectangle is moved or resized, all the subordinates must be informed about the change. The only difference with the previous example is an addition of one more subordinate element, called m_rectcorners.

```
private void InformRelatedElements ()
{
    RectangleF rc = PlottingArea;
    m_rectcorners .ParentRect = rc;
    foreach (Comment_ToRectangle cmnt in m_comments)
    {
        cmnt .ParentRect = rc;
    }
    ... ...
```

There is one new thing at the moment when a new rectangle is initialized; the RectCornerPoints element is also initialized.

```
public Plot_analogue_advanced (Form frm, Mover mvr, RectangleF rc,
Color clr)
{
    ... ...
    float w = Math .Max (minSide, rc .Width);
    float h = Math .Max (minSide, rc .Height);
    ptsCorner = new PointF [4] { new PointF (rc .X, rc .Y),
                                 new PointF (rc .X + w, rc .Y),
                                 new PointF (rc .X + w, rc .Y + h),
                                 new PointF (rc .X, rc .Y + h) };
```

```
        m_brush = new SolidBrush (clr);
        bResizable = true;
        m_rectcorners = new RectCornerPoints (frm, mvr, PlottingArea,
        bResizable,
                                            CornersRelocated);
        m_rectcorners .ParentID = ID;
    }
```
The RectCornerPoints element consists of only four points.
```
    public class RectCornerPoints : GraphicalObject
    {
        PointF [] ptsCorner;
        bool bResizable;
        Delegate_Rect InformParent = null;
```

The cover of such an element consists of circular nodes centered on those four points (Figure 3-12b). Four circular nodes have the same radius, which depends on resizability.

```
    public override void DefineCover ()
    {
        float rad = bResizable ? 5 : 0;
        CoverNode [] nodes = new CoverNode [] {
                        new CoverNode (0, ptsCorner [0], rad, Cursors
                        .SizeNWSE),
                        new CoverNode (1, ptsCorner [1], rad, Cursors
                        .SizeNESW),
                        new CoverNode (2, ptsCorner [2], rad, Cursors
                        .SizeNWSE),
                        new CoverNode (3, ptsCorner [3], rad, Cursors
                        .SizeNESW) };
        cover = new Cover (nodes);
    }
```

When the RectCornerPoints element is initialized, it gets the area of the dominant rectangle, positions its own four points in the corners of this rectangle, and synchronizes its own resizability with the resizability of the dominant element. The new element also gets a method (inform), which provides the feedback from this subordinate to the dominant element.

```
public RectCornerPoints (Form frm, Mover mvr, RectangleF rc, bool
resizable, Delegate_Rect inform)
{
    ... ...
    float w = Math .Max (minSide, rc .Width);
    float h = Math .Max (minSide, rc .Height);
    ptsCorner = new PointF [4] { new PointF (rc .X, rc .Y),
                                 new PointF (rc .X + w, rc .Y),
                                 new PointF (rc .X + w, rc .Y + h),
                                 new PointF (rc .X, rc .Y + h) };
    bResizable = resizable;
    InformParent = inform;
}
```

From the point of relations between the parts of the complex rectangle, this special element is subordinate to the main plotting area and is informed about any change of the parent area in line with all other subordinates (see the Plot_analogue_advanced. InformRelatedElements() method two pages back). But the RectCornerPoints class has a unique feature: whenever it changes the position of its points, it has to inform about this change the dominant element, and then the dominant element will change its own size and inform all the subordinates about such a change. The Plot_analogue_ advanced.CornersRelocated() method provides this feedback from four corner points.

```
private void CornersRelocated (RectangleF rc)
{
    ptsCorner [0] .X = ptsCorner [3] .X = rc .Left;
    ptsCorner [1] .X = ptsCorner [2] .X = rc .Right;
    ptsCorner [0] .Y = ptsCorner [1] .Y = rc .Top;
    ptsCorner [2] .Y = ptsCorner [3] .Y = rc .Bottom;
    DefineCover ();
    InformRelatedElements ();
}
```

The two-way communication provides the synchronous movements, though movable sides belong to one element and movable corners to another. Figure 3-12c shows the combined view of two covers when the scales are moved aside and do not overlap with these two elements. More often the scales overlap with them, and the difference in two variants become much more obvious when all parts stay nearby.

Figure 3-13a shows an object of the `Plot_analogue_advanced` class. The new class uses the same scales and comments as the `Plot_analogue` class, so visually the objects of two classes are indistinguishable from each other. With such positions of scales and comments, as shown in Figure 3-13a, two lower corners of the main area would be inaccessible in the case of a `Plot_analogue` object. Figure 3-13b makes it obvious why the `Plot_analogue_advanced` class has no such problems: all four circular nodes on the corners are never blocked regardless of the scales and comments positions.

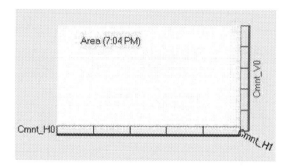

Figure 3-13a. *The object of the Plot_analogue_advanced class uses the same scales and comments as the Plot_analogue class*

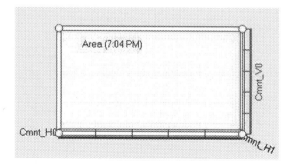

Figure 3-13b. *The cover of the RectCornerPoints element is placed ahead of all other subordinates, so the four circular nodes are never blocked regardless of the positions of all scales and comments*

185

Conclusion

In this chapter, we discussed the design of complex objects. Each part of such an object has its own cover, so each part can be involved in an individual movement, but parts are also involved in related movements, so there are some aspects of their overall design. Not rare is the situation when several objects are united to deal with some subtask, so such a set of objects must move and work as a group. This is discussed in the next chapter.

CHAPTER 4

Groups

A set of objects can be involved in dealing with some subtask; the union of these objects must be visually obvious. There must be an easy way to move the whole group of objects around the screen and an easy way to change their relative positions without losing a view of their union.

> File: `Form_Group_ArbitraryElements.cs`
>
> Menu position: Groups ➤ With arbitrary elements

A group of screen objects is an abstract concept that is easy to demonstrate but difficult to define. In general, it is a set of elements that are united for some task or subtask. This whole book is about the movability of screen objects and about the design of new programs on the basis of total movability, so three chapters about simple objects, complex objects, and groups must introduce objects that differ in the way their movability is organized and supervised.

- A *simple object* has a single cover for all its parts. Usually, but it is not a mandatory feature, parts of simple object stay together. A simple object has no subordinate elements that have their separate covers.

- A *complex object* consists of several elements with a personal cover for each part. These covers are individually registered in the mover queue; as a rule, the order of these parts in the mover queue is important. One part of complex object plays the dominant role, while other parts are its subordinates. Parts of complex object can be involved in synchronous, related, and individual movements. As a rule, forward movement of the dominant part causes the synchronous movement of all subordinates, resizing of the dominant part causes the related movement of subordinates, and movement of any subordinate has no effect on all other parts.

© Sergey Andreyev 2020
S. Andreyev, *User-Driven Applications for Research and Science*, https://doi.org/10.1007/978-1-4842-6488-1_4

- A *group* contains a set of objects with an individual cover for each one; the group itself has its own cover. Some groups allow only specific inner elements; other groups can work with arbitrary elements. Usually, there is no dominant element in a group, so each one moves individually and has no effect on others. The group itself is used to visualize the union of those inner elements and provides an easy way of moving all of them synchronously. Correlation between the movement of inner elements and the movement of the group can be organized in different ways.

As you see, these definitions often use words *as a rule* or *usually*. This is because there are classes that perfectly and without any doubts can fit into one or another category, but there are also boundary cases that fit for two of them. There are also objects that change their behavior depending on the user's commands. In my book [2], I demonstrate an interesting example with several nearly identical objects that differ only by color (for better explanation). Each element can be moved and resized individually without affecting others, so it is just a bunch of simple objects. But at any moment the user can declare any one of them as dominant, and then all others automatically turn into subordinates, so from this moment it is a classical complex object.

The union of elements into a group can be organized in many different ways, so the chapter "Groups" is one of the biggest in my other book [2]. It demonstrates different types of groups that I designed and used throughout the years of my work on movable objects.

When a set of objects is united into a group, it is helpful to have some visual element that informs about this union. More often than not, a set of inner objects is rounded with a frame; such a frame can also include a title that informs about the purpose of the group. In accordance with the main design ideas, a group can be moved by any inner point, but there is one interesting aspect of interaction between the frame and inner elements. There can be two absolutely different views on organizing such interaction.

Frame can be considered as the restriction for moving and changing inner objects. If you decide to organize such a ruling, you have to decide on the results of frame resizing and its effect on inner elements. The frame resizing can affect inner elements in three ways.

- Sizes of inner elements are changed *without changing their relative positions.*

- Sizes of inner elements are not changed, but their *relative positions are changed.*

- Sizes and relative positions of inner elements *are changed simultaneously.*

You can compare and discuss the advantages and disadvantages of these variants, but from my point of view, they are all wrong. All of them break one of the main rules of user-driven applications that "users' commands on moving/resizing of objects... must be implemented exactly as they are; no additions or expanded interpretation by developer are allowed." Regardless of the variant that you prefer and implement in your application, this is exactly the expanded interpretation against which I write. One solution is to implement all three variants and let users choose the needed one; such an example is demonstrated in my other book [2]. But I think that the only correct decision is to change the overall view on the role of the group frame.

Ruling of the group frame over inner elements immediately causes the break of one of the main rules of user-driven applications. From the beginning, this signaled to me that the mentioned ruling is inadmissible in new applications. Understanding this basic flaw triggered the design of different groups. In a group of new type, the frame has no ruling over inner elements, so none of three mentioned variants is used. The frame is not considered as independently resizable element but only as an element of decoration and information. Regardless of the new frame role, it still has to inform about the union of inner elements, so the frame has to adjust its size and position to any change inside. In addition, and only for easiness of moving the whole set of elements, a group can be moved by any point inside the frame. Thus, the idea of new group was born. See Figure 4-1.

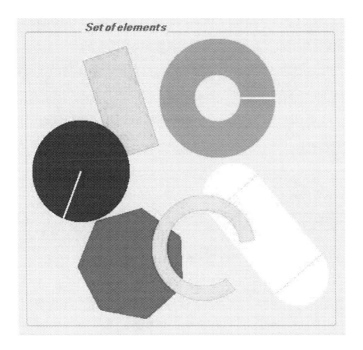

Figure 4-1. *The object of the Group_ArbitraryElements class can contain any elements*

The objects of the Group_ArbitraryElements class already appeared in the previous examples (see Figures 3-1 and 3-7) but without any discussion; now is the time to look into the details. Such a group can be moved by any point, but there is no direct resizing. The group area has a rectangular shape (m_rcBigNode), which is determined by the combined area of inner elements with some extra space around.

```
public class Group_ArbitraryElements : GraphicalObject
{
    RectangleF rcFrame, rcBigNode, rcTitle;
    GroupParameters paramsSet;
    string title;
    bool bTitleMovable = true;
```

For a movable and nonresizable rectangle, it is enough to have a single node cover, but there is a small addition. The group title can be used to inform about the group purpose. The title is a short text (often a single word) that is placed at the top of the group area. As any text, it has a rectangular area (rcTitle). I decided to make the title movable between the left and right borders. Thus, the group cover consists of two rectangular nodes. If there is no title, then one node is squeezed to zero size.

```
public override void DefineCover ()
{
    rcBigNode = RectangleF .FromLTRB (rcFrame .Left, rcFrame .Top,
                                      rcFrame .Right + 1, rcFrame.
                                      Bottom);
    CoverNode [] nodes = new CoverNode [2];
    if (TitleExist)
    {
        nodes [0] = new CoverNode (0, rcTitle);
        if (bTitleMovable)
        {
            nodes [0] .SetBehaviourCursor (Behaviour.Moveable, Cursors.
            SizeWE);
        }
    }
    else
    {
        nodes [0] = new CoverNode (0, rcFrame .Location, Of);
    }
    nodes [1] = new CoverNode (1, rcBigNode);
    cover = new Cover (nodes);
    ... ...
```

There are several main actions that a group must provide.

- Drawing

- Synchronous movement of inner elements

- Registering in the mover queue

When the allowed classes of inner elements are known beforehand, it is possible to design a group with the predefined methods for all these actions; such groups of the ElasticGroup class are demonstrated in a couple of examples in Appendix A. When inner elements can belong to arbitrary classes, the only way is to provide the needed methods at the moment of the group initialization. Here is the most general case of constructor:

```
public Group_ArbitraryElements (Form frm,      // form in which the group is used

    Mover mvr,                                 // mover

    PointF ptFrame,                            // top-left frame corner

    GroupParameters viewparams,                // visibility parameters

    string strTitle,                           // title

    Delegate_Bounds onCalcBoundsElems,         // method to calculate the area of inner
                                               // elements

    Delegate_Draw onDrawElems,                 // method to draw inner elements

    Delegate_Move onSynchroMoveElems,          // method for synchronous movement of
                                               // the elements

    Delegate_IntoMover onIntoMoverGroup)       // method to register the group with the
                                               // mover
```

Figure 4-1 shows a group from the `Form_Group_ArbitraryElements.cs` example. All the inner elements of this group were already discussed. In the current example, they are all movable and resizable. Only the color can be changed for inner elements, so this example is focused only on the group behavior. Inner elements are initialized, and then the group is organized around them.

```
void DefaultView ()
{
    rectangle = new Rectangle_Unicolored (...);
    ring = new Ring_Unicolored (...);
    strip = new Strip_Unicolored (...);
    circle = new Circle_Unicolored (...);
    polygon = new Polygon_Regular (...);
    arc = new Arc (...);
    arc .MarkHead = false;
    group = new Group_ArbitraryElements (this, mover, new PointF (30, 30),
                                         "Set of elements",
                                         ElemsArea_group, DrawElems_
                                         group,
```

```
                                    SynchroMove_group, IntoMover_
                                    group);
    group .Update ();
}
```

Four methods that are used on the group initialization are simple.
The first method returns the combined area of all inner elements.

```
private RectangleF ElemsArea_group ()
{
    return (RectangleF .Union (RectangleF .Union (RectangleF .Union (
                            RectangleF .Union (RectangleF .Union (
            rectangle .RectAround, ring .RectAround), strip
            .RectAround),
            circle .RectAround), polygon .RectAround), arc
            .RectAround));
}
```

The second method provides the drawing of inner elements. The drawing of
elements must be organized in the opposite order to their inclusion into the mover
queue.

```
private void DrawElems_group (Graphics grfx)
{
    rectangle .Draw (grfx);
    ring .Draw (grfx);
    strip .Draw (grfx);
    circle .Draw (grfx);
    polygon .Draw (grfx);
    arc .Draw (grfx);
}
```

The third method provides the synchronous move of inner elements.

```
void SynchroMove_group (int dx, int dy)
{
    rectangle .Move (dx, dy);
    ring .Move (dx, dy);
```

```
        strip .Move (dx, dy);
        circle .Move (dx, dy);
        polygon .Move (dx, dy);
        arc .Move (dx, dy);
    }
```

The fourth method provides the registering in the mover queue. This is the only method that mentions the group itself.

```
    void IntoMover_group (Mover mv, int iPos)
    {
        mv .Insert (iPos, group);
        rectangle .IntoMover (mv, iPos);
        ring .IntoMover (mv, iPos);
        strip .IntoMover (mv, iPos);
        circle .IntoMover (mv, iPos);
        polygon .IntoMover (mv, iPos);
        arc .IntoMover (mv, iPos);
    }
```

Any group has a set of general parameters that are used for some auxiliary calculations and for drawing. These parameters are kept as a GroupParameters object.

There is one thing to be remembered while using the Group_ArbitraryElements class. The group does not contain the list of its inner elements, so the group cannot adjust itself to any change of inner elements. Such adjustment is done by using the Group_ArbitraryElements.Update() method, so there are several obvious situations when this method must be called.

- Whenever anything is moved or resized

```
    private void OnMouseMove (object sender, MouseEventArgs e)
    {
        if (mover .Move (e .Location))
        {
            group .Update ();
            Invalidate ();
        }
    }
```

- On adding elements into a group or deleting inner elements

- When a group is modified

  A special tuning form (Figure 4-2) can be used to modify any
  Group_ArbitraryElements object. A tuning form is called by the
  Group_ArbitraryElements.ParametersDialog() method; one
  of the parameters is the method to be executed on any group
  change.

```
private void Click_miModify_Group (object sender, EventArgs e)
{
    group .ParametersDialog (this, ParamsChanged_group,
                            PointToScreen (ptMouse_Up));
}
private void ParamsChanged_group (object sender, EventArgs ea)
{
    group .Update ();
    Invalidate ();
}
```

I have two remarks about this chapter.

- In my other book [2], the chapter called "Groups" is one of the
  biggest, while here it is the smallest one. The explanation is simple:
  in my other book [2], I try to demonstrate many different variants,
  while in the current book only the final product in group design is
  demonstrated.

- You are going to see other classes of groups with similar behavior.
  Because all those groups use inner elements of predetermined
  types, then on some of the mentioned occasions they are updated
  automatically, while on other occasions their Update() methods
  must be called.

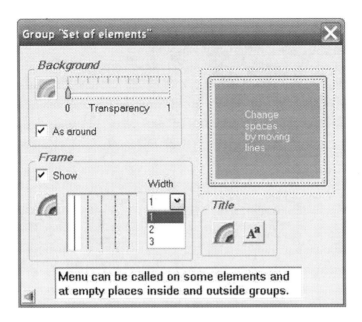

Figure 4-2. *Tuning form for Group_ArbitraryElements objects*

Conclusion

Screen elements can be simple or complex; such individual elements can be also united into groups. These three cases were discussed in the previous chapters. All the demonstrated objects are graphical, and all of them perfectly fit into the algorithm of movability. However, from the beginning of the PC era, the majority of serious programs were developed on the basis of controls, and many programmers cannot imagine the design of programs without controls. The same algorithm of movability allows you to use standard controls; this is discussed in Appendix A. For user-driven applications, it would be much better to have not standard controls but their graphical analogs. They are discussed in the next chapter.

CHAPTER 5

Graphical Analogs of Ordinary Controls

It would be a huge boost for user-driven applications if standard controls could be substituted with graphical objects with analog features. Such graphical analogs for the most popular controls are discussed in this chapter.

For many years, standard controls were the cornerstones of program design, so the majority of developers cannot imagine program design without such elements. Controls are very well designed, but… their treatment by the operating system as high-level elements causes such problems in user-driven applications that prevail over their declared advantages.

I advocate for programs that are fully controlled by users, so I do not like the idea of having a special type of objects that is mostly controlled by the operating system. Controls always appear on top of all graphical objects, so the user cannot even change the order of elements on the screen if controls are among them. Controls have useful functionality, so I like to use them in my programs if they behave like all other elements and are controlled by users in exactly the same way as graphical objects. "If the mountain won't come to Muhammad, then Muhammad must go to the mountain." There are some doubts that ordinary controls are going to change according to my view, so the only way is to design graphical elements that behave like the needed controls. Table 5-1 lists the most popular ordinary controls and their graphical analogs that are discussed in this chapter.

© Sergey Andreyev 2020
S. Andreyev, *User-Driven Applications for Research and Science*, https://doi.org/10.1007/978-1-4842-6488-1_5

Table 5-1. *Popular Ordinary Controls and Their Graphical Analogs*

Control from Visual Studio	Analog from MoveGraphLibrary.dll	Comments
Button	Button_GR, Button_Text Button_Drawing, Button_Image	Button_GR is an abstract class; three derived classes represent variants with different types of information on button top.
Label	Label_GR	
NumericUpDown	NumericUpDown_GR	
TrackBar	Trackbar_GR	
ListBox	ListBox_GR	Not more than one element can be selected.
ComboBox	ComboBox_DDList	Classical combo box has three variants; graphical analog demonstrates only the one with the DropDownList style.
CheckBox	CheckBox_GR	
ListView	ListView_GR	Not more than one element can be selected.
RadioButton GroupBox	RadioButton_GR Group_RadioButtons	Radio buttons are used only in groups, so there is a class of buttons and a class for their groups.

Figure 5-1 shows the view of these ordinary controls. Of all the standard controls that I have used for years, only the TextBox has no graphical analog.

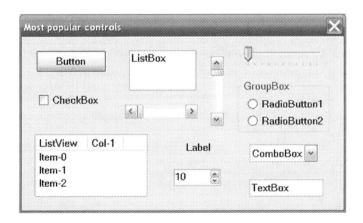

Figure 5-1. *View of ordinary controls*

Graphical controls have several general features that I want to mention before starting the discussion of their analogs. Later I am going to write only about graphical controls, so I can skip the word *graphical* and discuss all new elements simply as controls. If I have to mention the classical controls, I call them *ordinary controls*.

Controls can be simple or complex; controls require the regulation of movability and resizability like any other graphical object, so all these things will be discussed with the new classes. But controls have one feature by which they differ from all previously discussed graphical objects. Many controls have some status (for example, a control can be checked or unchecked), and depending on the parameters of the working application, the change of this status is either allowed or blocked. Thus, a control can be declared enabled or disabled. The difference between enabled and disabled controls must be visible.

Here are several rules that are implemented for all controls:

- Controls can be used with or without additional comment; as all controls are rectangular, then all of them use comments of the `Comment_ToRectangle` class. There are controls that include text as an important part, and this text conveys enough information about the purpose of an element. These are check boxes and radio buttons, so objects of the `CheckBox_GR` and `RadioButton_GR` classes do not have comments. Buttons of the `Button_Text` class have text on top, and usually it gives sufficient information about such a button. If additional information is needed, such a button can be used with a comment. Each control has no more than one comment; the only exception is the `Trackbar_GR` class with an unlimited number of comments.

- Any control can be either enabled or disabled; the only exception is the `Label_GR` class. Disabled means that some status or value associated with an object cannot be changed; label has no such value, so the `Label_GR` class has no `Enabled` property. Disability does not affect the movability of an object, so enabled and disabled objects are moved and resized in the same way. The basic `GraphicalObject` class does not include the field and property to regulate the enabled/disabled status, so this is implemented in each class of controls.

- The Enabled property of the class is used in three different places.

  - In the Draw() method of the class, because enabled and disabled objects must look differently.

  - In the OnMouseDown() method to block those clicks of a disabled object that starts with a change of its status (value). Be careful not to block the start of resizing or moving as both actions are allowed for disabled objects.

  - In the OnMouseUp() method to block the change of status (value) of the disabled object.

Push Button

File: Form_Button.cs

Menu position: *Graphical controls* ➤ *Push button*

The majority of elements in this example are buttons (Figure 5-2), but they belong to three different classes.

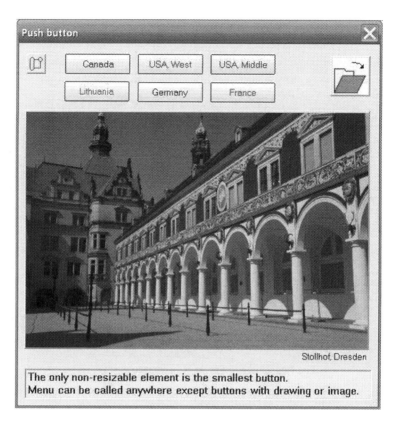

Figure 5-2. *All three types of buttons—with text, drawing, or image—are used in this example*

```
Button_Drawing btnCover;
Button_Image btnOpen, btnImage;
Button_Text btnCanada,
            btnUSA1, btnUSA2,
            btnLithuania,
         btnGermany, btnFrance;
```

As shown in Figure 5-2, push buttons are used with text, a drawing, or an image on top. This is the only way in which buttons differ from each other, so they are all derived from the abstract Button_GR class, which contains their main features such as cover design, moving, and type of allowed resizing.

201

```
public abstract class Button_GR
                : GraphicalObject
{
    PointF [] ptsCorner;
    Resizing resize;
    bool bEnabled;
    bool bPressed;
    Comment_ToRectangle m_cmnt = null;
```

Buttons have a standard cover for rectangular objects: four circular nodes on the corners, four strip nodes along the sides, and a rectangular node for the whole area (Figure 5-3). Strip nodes along the sides have a default width (six pixels), while circular nodes on the corners are slightly enlarged. When a button is declared unmovable, the cursor shape over its big node is changed from the standard Cursors.SizeAll to Cursors.NoMove2D.

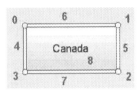

Figure 5-3. *Nodes in the cover of the Button_GR class*

```
public override void DefineCover ()
{
    float rad = (resize == Resizing .Any) ? 5 : 0;
    float wHalf_WE = (resize == Resizing.Any || resize == Resizing.WE)
    ? 3 : 0;
    float wHalf_NS = (resize == Resizing.Any || resize == Resizing.NS)
    ? 3 : 0;
    CoverNode [] nodes = new CoverNode [9] {
                new CoverNode (0, ptsCorner [0], rad, Cursors .SizeNWSE),
                new CoverNode (1, ptsCorner [1], rad, Cursors .SizeNESW),
                new CoverNode (2, ptsCorner [2], rad, Cursors .SizeNWSE),
                new CoverNode (3, ptsCorner [3], rad, Cursors .SizeNESW),
                new CoverNode (4, ptsCorner [0], ptsCorner [3], wHalf_WE,
```

```
                                                   Cursors
                                                    .SizeWE),
           new CoverNode (5, ptsCorner [1], ptsCorner [2], wHalf_WE,
                                                   Cursors
                                                    .SizeWE),
           new CoverNode (6, ptsCorner [0], ptsCorner [1], wHalf_NS,
                                                   Cursors
                                                    .SizeNS),
           new CoverNode (7, ptsCorner [3], ptsCorner [2], wHalf_NS,
                                                   Cursors
                                                    .SizeNS),
           new CoverNode (8, ptsCorner) };
    cover = new Cover (nodes);
    ... ...
```

Buttons use four standard variants of resizing. Depending on the particular type of resizing, some of the nodes can be squeezed to a size of zero; Figure 3-3 shows all four variants. Button moving and button resizing are organized in the same way as explained for the Rectangle_Unicolored class; however, buttons are not rotatable.

The constructor of the Button_GR class uses a rectangle to set the initial area of an object but does not describe the range of possible size changes. By default, any button is fully resizable without upper limits, but there is a limit on the minimum allowed size (minSide = 10) to avoid the accidental disappearance through resizing.

```
public Button_GR (Form frm, Mover mvr, RectangleF rc)
{
    ... ...
    float w = Math .Max (minSide, rc .Width);
    float h = Math .Max (minSide, rc .Height);
    ptsCorner = new PointF [4] {rc .Location, new PointF (rc .X + w,
    rc .Y),
                               new PointF (rc .X + w, rc .Y + h),
                               new PointF (rc .X, rc .Y + h) };
    bEnabled = true;
    bPressed = false;
    resize = Resizing .Any;
}
```

Any button can be associated with a comment. Buttons are rectangular, so the easiest way is to use the comments of the Comment_ToRectangle class. As a rule, buttons with the text on top do not need any additional comment because the text itself clearly informs about the purpose of an object. Buttons with the image or drawing on top often need some comment. For example, a tuning form may include identical buttons to change different color parameters, and it would be impossible to select the needed button without some comments. In the current example, only the button on which pictures appear is used with comments. The button with comments behaves in the same way as was explained for the Rectangle_withComments class.

The main difference between the three types of buttons is in their drawing, but before going into their details, I want to remind you about some features of the programs based on ordinary controls and about some details of drawing the ordinary Button controls because graphical buttons have to copy their behavior and view as much as it is needed.

Controls were introduced more than 30 years ago. Prior to the introduction of the mouse, the keyboard was the users' main instrument. Years ago, even with the mouse at hand, a lot of users preferred to use the keyboard to control applications, so when screen controls were designed, they were supposed to provide (through visualization) the needed information for keyboard control of a program. For this purpose, the idea of focus is used. Regardless of the number of controls in any form (long ago the word *form* was not even used but only *window* or *dialog*), at any particular moment only one screen control has the focus, and this is the control that obtains commands from the keyboard. The focus can be moved from one control to another by pressing the Tab key. All controls of the dialog are set in order, and the focus is moved from control to control according to this order. The focus is also moved to the control when it is clicked by a mouse, but if somebody prefers to use the keyboard, then passing the focus from one element to another in a dialog with a significant number of controls can require a number of the Tab key clicks. The focus is passed only between controls, while graphical objects, which are considered by the system as elements of lesser importance, are not included in this game. There are different ways to highlight focus; it can differ by the control class and the system version, but usually there is an additional dotted frame inside the control or wider (or of different color) frame around the element.

From my point of view, ordinary controls are superfluous and whenever possible must be substituted with graphical analogs. Also, it is enough to have a mouse as the only instrument of control in applications, so focus is not used. At any moment, a button is either enabled or disabled. The enabled button is either idle (not pressed) or pressed. These three situations—disabled button, pressed, or idle—must be visually distinguishable.

A button drawing consists of two parts: the border drawing and the drawing of the inner area. If I am not mistaken, buttons in the earlier versions of Windows had frames that imitated the third dimension, but the background of those buttons was unicolored. Later the frame was simplified to an ordinary line, while the background got the color gradient from pale gray at the top to pale blue at the bottom. In such a way, the normal (idle) buttons are shown, while for the pressed button the same color gradient is used in the opposite direction, and such a switch of colors perfectly signals the moment of button press or release.

Now we are ready to move from abstract buttons to real. The mentioned color gradient from pale gray to pale blue is used for Button controls with text on the top, so let's start with the Button_Text class. In the current example (Figure 5-2), there are six objects of the Button_Text class.

```
public class Button_Text : Button_GR
{
    string m_text;
    Font m_font;
    Color m_color;
    ButtonBackType typeBack = ButtonBackType .Gradient;
    SolidBrush brushBack;
```

The constructor of the Button_Text class has six parameters; three of them are for the base class constructor; three others are for the text on the top.

```
public Button_Text (Form frm, Mover mvr, RectangleF rc,
                    string txt, Font fnt, Color clr)
    : base (frm, mvr, rc)
{
    m_text = CheckedText (txt);
    m_font = fnt;
    m_color = clr;
    brushBack = new SolidBrush (Background);
    ... ...
```

Two background types were used in the past in Button controls: unicolored background and color gradient. By default, Button_Text objects are organized with the color gradient, but this class provides both views and lets users decide on the particular view of any button at any moment. The difference in views exists only for enabled buttons.

```
public override void Draw (Graphics grfx)
{
    ... ...
    Rectangle rc = Rectangle .Round (MainElementArea);
    RectangleF rcClip = new RectangleF (rc .Left + 2, rc .Top + 2,
                                        rc .Width - 4, rc .Height - 4);
    Color clrText;
    if (Enabled)
    {
        ButtonState btn_state = Pressed ? ButtonState .Pushed
                                        : ButtonState .Normal;
        if (typeBack == ButtonBackType .Unicolor)
        {
            ControlPaint .DrawButton (grfx, rc, btn_state);
            grfx .FillRectangle (brushBack, rcClip);
        }
        else
        {
            Auxi_Drawing .Button (grfx, rc, btn_state, Background);
        }
        clrText = m_color;
    }
    else
    {
        grfx .FillRectangle (Brushes .White, rc);
        grfx .DrawRectangle (Pens .LightGray, rc);
        clrText = Color .LightGray;
    }
    ... ...
```

The text on the top is shown exactly as it is prepared; if the text includes special symbols of the line change, then such text is shown in several lines. Usually the text does not have such symbols, and then it is shown in one line. In any case, the text is centered to the middle point of the button. If the text is longer than the button width and there are spaces inside the text, then such text can be divided into parts at those places and can be shown in several lines, but only if the combined height of all those text lines is less than the button height. Maybe it is easier to understand this explanation by looking at Figure 5-4.

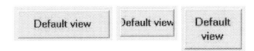

Figure 5-4. *The text is changed to several lines if there are spaces inside the text and the combined height of several lines is less than the button height*

At first the button width was enough to show the text in one line. Then I started to squeeze the button by the side; the text was still shown in one line, though its length was bigger than the button width. In this situation, the text is not shown in two lines, because the button height is not enough for the two text lines. I stopped changing the width and started to increase the button height. The text consists of two words separated by a space; when the button height reached the height of two lines, only at that moment did the text appear in two lines.

Ordinary controls are designed with a large number of associated events. To organize the needed reaction on the click of a standard button, you write the method and then associate this method with the Click event of the button.

Graphical buttons have no events of their own; as with all other graphical objects, everything is organized through the MouseDown and MouseUp events of the form. When a graphical button is pressed by the mouse, the Button_GR.Press() method is called.

```
private void OnMouseDown (object sender, MouseEventArgs e)
{
    ptMouse_Down = e .Location;
    if (mover .Catch (e .Location, e .Button))
    {
        if (e .Button == MouseButtons .Left)
        {
            GraphicalObject grobj = mover .CaughtSource;
```

```
            int iNode = mover .CaughtNode;
            if (grobj is Button_GR)
            {
                btnPressed = grobj as Button_GR;
                btnPressed .Press (e .Location, e .Button, iNode);
                Invalidate ();
            }
            ... ...
```

The reaction to the button press is provided at the moment of the mouse release, but the need of any reaction depends on the released node and the distance between the points of mouse press and release.

- If one of the border nodes is released (regardless of whether it is a corner or a side), then it is resizing, which is done by the Button_GR.MoveNode() method. When the resizing is over, no further action is needed.

- If the big node is released (iNode == Button_GR.Node_FullArea), then the reaction depends on the distance between the points of the mouse press and release. The case of an ordinary movement (fDist > 3) is under the jurisdiction of the Button_GR.MoveNode() method, which, in this particular situation, calls for help to the Button_GR.Move() method.

The OnMouseUp() method of the form has to deal with the remaining situation of the button click on the big node, when the distance between the two mentioned points is negligible (fDist <= 3). The reaction depends on the clicked button, which is easily identified by its unique ID.

```
private void OnMouseUp (object sender, MouseEventArgs e)
{
    ptMouse_Up = e .Location;
    double fDist = Auxi_Geometry .Distance (ptMouse_Down, ptMouse_Up);
    int iObj, iNode;
    if (mover .Release (out iObj, out iNode))
    {
        GraphicalObject grobj = mover .ReleasedSource;
```

```
long id = grobj .ID;
if (e .Button == MouseButtons .Left)
{
    if (grobj is Button_GR && btnPressed .Enabled)
    {
        if (iNode == Button_GR .Node_FullArea && fDist <= 3)
        {
            ... ...
```

- When the button ![icon] is clicked, then the standard form for file selection is opened, and any image file can be selected for viewing. (This button is of the Button_Image class, so I am slightly jumping ahead, but, as you can see from the code, the analysis inside the OnMouseUp() method uses the base class Button_GR.)

```
if (id == btnOpen .ID)
{
    SelectFileName ();
}
```

- Clicking the button ![icon] switches on/off the visualization of covers. (This button is of the Button_Drawing class.)

```
else if (id == btnCover .ID)
{
    bShowCovers = !bShowCovers;
}
```

- Clicking any Button_Text element of this example results in the appearance of an image associated with the pressed button.

```
else
{
    ShowPredefinedImage (id);
}
}
```

When any button is released, its status is set by the `Pressed` property, and the view is refreshed.

```
btn .Pressed = false;
Invalidate ();
... ...
```

`Button_Text` elements have a few changeable parameters that can be changed in a special tuning form (Figure 5-5).

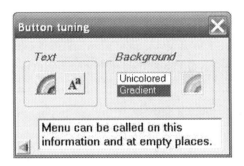

Figure 5-5. *Tuning of the Button_Text elements*

A small menu for the `Button_Text` elements of this example includes a command to switch the pressed button between the enabled/disabled modes. In any real application, this is regulated only by the logic of a program, but I purposely added this command to demonstrate all the possibilities of the `Button_Text.Draw()` method.

The small button 🔳 belongs to the `Button_Drawing` class. This class has a single field of its own; this field represents a method that is used to draw on the button area.

```
public class Button_Drawing : Button_GR
{
    Delegate_DrawInRect m_draw = null;
```

The simplest `Button_Drawing` constructor has three parameters for the base class plus the needed drawing method.

```
public Button_Drawing (Form frm, Mover mvr, RectangleF rc,
                    Delegate_DrawInRect drawmethod)
    : base (frm, mvr, rc)
{
    m_draw = drawmethod;
}
```

The drawing method that is passed on initialization has two parameters. The second one is the button area without frame. The result of drawing is shown in this area, but it does not mean at all that the whole drawing by your method must be done strictly inside this rectangle. Usually, this is the case, and for simple cases like drawing an arrow on top of a button, it is done inside the provided rectangle, and everything looks fine. But there are situations when the drawing on the button has to be some part of much bigger picture. In such a case, you calculate the area of the big picture in relation to the passed rectangle and draw the full picture without thinking of any limitations; the clipping is done automatically, so only that part of the drawing that fits into the declared rectangle will appear on the screen. In such way not only is the drawing easier, but the drawing can depend on the button position, on relative position of the button and other screen elements, and on many other things. The size of the button can also depend on its position (for example, an unneeded button can be moved to the side of the form and shrink), and the drawing can depend on the button size with more details appearing in bigger area. A lot of interesting things can be done with the Button_Drawing objects.

Small buttons that are used to call standard dialogs for font and color selection are usually declared as nonresizable, but this is done only to avoid them becoming too small. By default, all Button_Drawing elements are resizable. In Form_FillHoles.cs (Figure 2-43), a group of several buttons is used to select the needed plug. When that example was discussed at the end of Chapter 2, it was too early to attract attention to some features of the group or the buttons that were used inside. Now it is easy to understand that the moving/resizing of the inner Button_Drawing elements automatically changes the group of the Group_ArbitraryElements class, so the original view of the group can be changed in seconds. If some user has a problem with ordering a plug with seven or eight vertices in the original group, there must be no such problems with a slightly changed group (Figure 5-6). It is for the user to decide about the size and position of each button, so there can be innumerable variants.

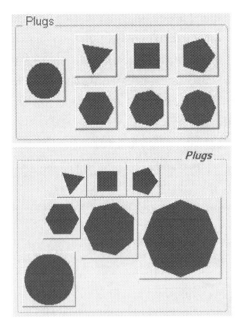

Figure 5-6. *All elements inside this group are the buttons of the Button_Drawing class.. The initial view of the group is shown at the top*

Two elements of the Button_Image class are used in the current example. One field of the Button_Image class contains the path to the image; another field is for the image itself.

```
public class Button_Image : Button_GR
{
    string strImage = "";
    Image m_image = null;
```

Four parameters are used on initialization. Three of them are standard parameters for the base class, while the last one is the path to the file with an image. This parameter can include either the full name or the relative path to the file; in any case, the full path is stored in the designed button.

```
public Button_Image (Form frm, Mover mvr, RectangleF rc, string image_name)
```

The image on top of any Button_Image object is centered both horizontally and vertically. For the drawing, the Auxi_Drawing.ShowImage() method is used, which analyzes the image proportions and fits this image into the proposed rectangle. There is no image cropping; if the button and the image have different proportions, then you see empty strips on two opposite sides. Buttons are usually resizable, so you can change them to the needed size and then change them a bit more according to the image proportions. Figure 5-7 demonstrates four views of the btnOpen element: a small one, two variants of enlarging button in one direction only, and the bigger version in which I tried to keep the original proportions.

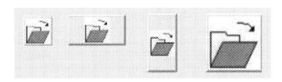

Figure 5-7. *The results of resizing the same Button_Image object*

This example uses six photos representing picturesque places on Earth. I purposely selected some pictures with different proportions, so you can play with the sizes of the Button_Image object on which the images appear.

Rectangles can be resized in different ways. In my other book [2], there is a demonstration of a rectangle that is resized with the fixed width/height ratio. It is easy to organize a class derived from the Button_Image class that will resize the button according to the proportions of the currently shown picture. I decided not to do it here, but it can be a good exercise.

Label

File: Form_Label.cs

Menu position: Graphical controls ➤ Label

A label is a simple control that was designed to display a text. If the text is too long to be shown in one line, then in the ordinary Label control it is wrapped and shown on several lines. The logic of showing text inside the Label_GR objects is different: there is no text wrapping.

Four objects of the Label_GR class are shown in the Form_Label.cs example (Figure 5-8). Text inside two labels represents different views of the same time period. These two labels together with their comments are united into a group.

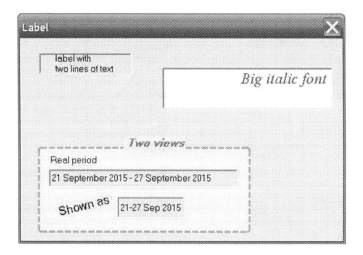

Figure 5-8. *Several Label_GR objects*

The Label_GR class has the same cover as was demonstrated for buttons 12 pages back.

```
public class Label_GR : GraphicalObject
{
    PointF [] ptsCorner;
    Resizing resize;
    string m_text;
    Font fntText;
    Color clrText;
    bool bHeightAdjustmentToFont = false;
```

Any constructor of the Label_GR class specifies the label area and text; other parameters can be declared or set by default.

```
public Label_GR (Form frm, Mover mvr, RectangleF rc, string txt,
            Font fnt_txt, Color clr_txt, RectFrameType frtype, Color
            clrBack)
```

Label_GR objects have a special tuning form (Figure 5-9). Some parts of this form, for example, the whole Background group, will be repeated again and again in the tuning forms of other elements.

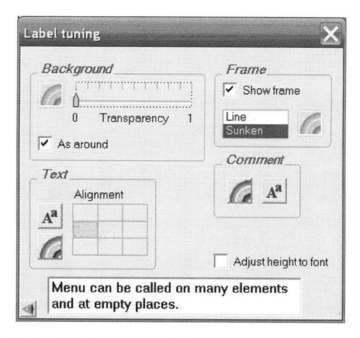

Figure 5-9. *Tuning form for Label_GR objects*

Any Label_GR object is used to show some text inside the rectangular area; the sizes of this area can be changed by direct resizing. The text also has a rectangular shape with the sizes determined by the used font. I always write that the font change, while causing the change of the text area, must not affect the label area. By default, these sizes are independent, and there is an easy way to change the text positioning inside the label area through the tuning form.

Though I prefer the independence of the font size and label height, some users might prefer to see their correlation, so there is a possibility to organize such a thing. If you put the mark inside the check box "Adjust height to font," then the height of the label area will be changed with any font change, but not more. This mark does not change the width of the label area, and this mark does not block the direct label resizing.

NumericUpDown

File: Form_NumericUpDown.cs

Menu position: Graphical controls ➤ NumericUpDown

An ordinary NumericUpDown control has two instruments to change the value: there are two small buttons to increase and decrease the current value by a predetermined step, and there is a direct editing of the value. The NumericUpDown_GR class has no editing, but there is a small slider that allows you to go quickly through the whole range of values. My experience with NumericUpDown controls is too small to insist that such addition suits very well for any required range, but in all the situations where I needed to use NumericUpDown_GR elements, they worked perfectly.

Nearly all the NumericUpDown_GR objects in Figure 5-10 have sliders on the left side. There is also one object with the slider at the bottom, one with the slider at the top, and one object without slider at all. These objects demonstrate that sliders can be positioned in different ways and that a new element without a slider looks exactly like an ordinary control.

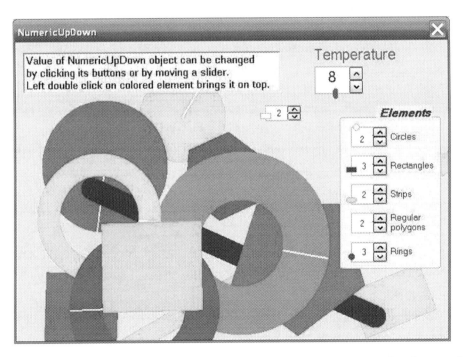

Figure 5-10. *The value of the NumericUpDown_GR element can be changed either by clicking the two buttons or by moving the slider*

```
public class NumericUpDown_GR : GraphicalObject
{
    PointF [] ptsCorner;
    Resizing resize;
    int minVal, maxVal, curVal, stepVal;
```

```
Font m_font;
SideAlignment alignValue;
Side sideSlider;
bool bSliderShow = true;
NumericSliderShape shapeSlider = NumericSliderShape .Rectangle;
```

The possible slider shapes are determined by the NumericSliderShape enumeration; Figure 5-10 shows all the variants.

```
public enum NumericSliderShape { Circle, Rectangle, Strip };
```

The cover for the NumericUpDown_GR object consists of 12 nodes (Figure 5-11).

- For the enabled element with the shown slider, node 0 covers the slider; the shape of this node is determined by the slider shape. For the disabled object, this node is squeezed to a size of zero.

- Four small circular nodes on the corners (1–4) and four strip nodes along the sides (5–8) cover the whole border and are used for resizing. There are four standard variants of resizing (the same that were discussed with buttons), so depending on the selected type, some or all of these eight nodes can be squeezed to a size of zero.

- Rectangular nodes 9 and 10 cover two buttons with arrows.

- Rectangular node 11 covers the whole area and is used for moving an object.

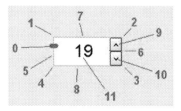

Figure 5-11. *Numbering of nodes*

Occasionally the numbering of nodes can be changed, so while writing programs, it is better to rely on the names of the crucial nodes: Node_Slider, Node_ArrowUp, and Node_ArrowDown.

The slider shape defines the shape of the first node; the mouse cursor for this node depends on the side where the slider is positioned. Only the right side is forbidden for the slider because the two buttons with arrows are placed next to this side.

The slider can be moved only along the border on which it resides. If the border is movable, then it can be moved only orthogonally to its own line. Both nodes have a cursor in a shape of an arrow with two heads, but these arrows point in orthogonal directions because the movements of the two nodes are orthogonal.

At the beginning of this chapter, I mentioned three places where the enabled/disabled status of an element must be checked. For objects of the NumericUpDown_GR class, this status also affects the cover design: the first node of the disabled elements is squeezed to a size of zero. For the enabled object and with the slider in view, the calculation of the first node is easy but depends on the slider side and shape, so it is a bit lengthy to be shown here. The remaining part of the DefineCover() method is simple. To make the resizing by corners easier, the radius of circular nodes is slightly increased from the default value.

```
public override void DefineCover ()
{
    CoverNode [] nodes = new CoverNode [12];
    if (bSliderShow && bEnabled)
    {
        ... ...
    }
    else
    {
        nodes [0] = new CoverNode (0, ptsCorner [3], 0f, Cursors .Hand);
    }
    float rCorner = (m_resize == Resizing .Any) ? 5 : 0;
    float wHalf_WE =
            (m_resize == Resizing .Any || m_resize == Resizing .WE) ?
            3 : 0;
    float wHalf_NS =
            (m_resize == Resizing .Any || m_resize == Resizing .NS) ?
            3 : 0;
    nodes [1] = new CoverNode (1, ptsCorner [0], rCorner, Cursors
    .SizeNWSE);
```

```
nodes [2] = new CoverNode (2, ptsCorner [1], rCorner, Cursors
.SizeNESW);
nodes [3] = new CoverNode (3, ptsCorner [2], rCorner, Cursors
.SizeNWSE);
nodes [4] = new CoverNode (4, ptsCorner [3], rCorner, Cursors
.SizeNESW);
nodes [5] = new CoverNode (5, ptsCorner [0], ptsCorner [3], wHalf_WE,
                                              Cursors
                                              .SizeWE);
nodes [6] = new CoverNode (6, ptsCorner [1], ptsCorner [2], wHalf_WE,
                                              Cursors
                                              .SizeWE);
nodes [7] = new CoverNode (7, ptsCorner [0], ptsCorner [1], wHalf_NS,
                                              Cursors
                                              .SizeNS);
nodes [8] = new CoverNode (8, ptsCorner [3], ptsCorner [2], wHalf_NS,
                                              Cursors
                                              .SizeNS);
nodes [9] = new CoverNode (9, rcBtnUp, Cursors .Hand);
nodes [10] = new CoverNode (10, rcBtnDown, Cursors .Hand);
nodes [11] = new CoverNode (11, ptsCorner);
if (!Movable)
{
    nodes [11] .Cursor = Cursors .NoMove2D;
}
cover = new Cover (nodes);
... ...
```

The idea of fixing the cursor at the pressed point of an unmovable object is implemented with elements of many classes. For NumericUpDown_GR objects, the same cursor fixing happens whenever those two small buttons are pressed, regardless of whether the object is movable or not.

```
public override bool MoveNode (...)
{
    bool bRet = false;
```

```
        if (catcher == MouseButtons .Left)
        {
            ... ...
            else if (iNode == Node_ArrowUp || iNode == Node_
            ArrowDown)    // buttons
            {
                AdjustCursorPosition (ptFixed);
                bRet = false;
            }
            ... ...
```

For any movable element, its Press() method is called at the moment of the mouse press. The NumericUpDown_GR class is among those few that require you to use their Release() method at the moment when an object is released by the left mouse button. To be absolutely correct, the use of this method is needed only if one of the two buttons with the arrow is released, but because the same actions are needed in cases of released buttons and slider, then it was easier to unite these three cases.

```
    private void OnMouseUp (object sender, MouseEventArgs e)
    {
        ptMouse_Up = e .Location;
        double fDist = Auxi_Geometry .Distance (ptMouse_Down, ptMouse_Up);
        int iObj, iNode;
        if (mover .Release (out iObj, out iNode))
        {
            GraphicalObject grobj = mover .ReleasedSource;
            long id = grobj .ID;
            if (e .Button == MouseButtons .Left)
            {
                if (grobj is NumericUpDown_GR && numericPressed .Enabled)
                {
                    if (iNode == NumericUpDown_GR .Node_Slider ||
                        iNode == NumericUpDown_GR .Node_ArrowUp ||
                        iNode == NumericUpDown_GR .Node_ArrowDown)
                    {
                        ... ...
```

```
            numericPressed .Release ();
        }
        Invalidate ();
    }
    ... ...
```

The parameters of any NumericUpDown_GR object can be changed in the special tuning form (Figure 5-12).

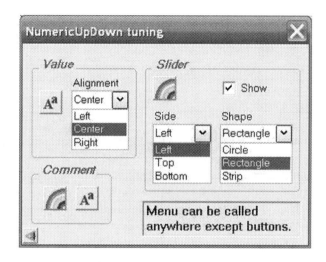

Figure 5-12. *Tuning form for NumericUpDown_GR objects*

Track Bar

File: Form_Trackbar.cs

Menu position: Graphical controls ➤ Track bar

Track bars are well-known elements of the interface design. The idea of an object in which a small slider moves along a thin bar and allows you to select any value from some range can be useful in many situations. Unfortunately, the implementation of this control in Visual Studio is so clumsy that after each attempt to use an ordinary TrackBar control, I had to reject it. But the main idea of the track bar is perfect, and a good element of such a type is so desirable from time to time that it has to be used. I designed several classes of track bars; here I want to demonstrate the Trackbar_GR class. You are already familiar with the use of such an object because it is used in all tuning forms with the change of the background color (Figures 2-4, 4-2, and 5-9).

```
public class Trackbar_GR : GraphicalObject
{
    RectangleF rcTicks;
    PointF ptLT_rail_axis, ptRB_rail_axis, ptSliderAnchor;
    RectangleF rcRail;          // narrow rectangle
    RectangleF rcFrame;         // includes rcTicks and the area which is
                                   covered by movable slider

    bool bEnabled = true;
    bool bResizable = true;
```

The track bars in Figure 5-13 are shown in their classical view with all their parts visible. However, the only mandatory parts to be shown are the thin rail and a slider, which can be moved along this rail.

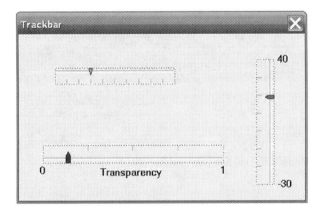

Figure 5-13. *Elements of the Trackbar_GR class*

A track bar can be vertical or horizontal; the direction is determined by the rail. In each case, there are two possible directions in which the slider can look. There are two variants of slider shape (triangle or pentagon), and there are variations in sizes.

The Trackbar_GR class has two constructors. One of them requires a number of parameters to define the appearance of slider and ticks, while in the second case many of these parameters get the default values. In the current example, both horizontal track bars use constructors with a full list of parameters, while the vertical track bar is constructed with a minimum of parameters. This minimal set of parameters includes the side in which the slider is looking, the top-left coordinate of the rail, the rail length, and the slider coefficient. All other parameters get default values, but the slider color and the number of ticks are changed with the help of some properties.

```
void DefaultView ()
{
    ... ...
    trackbars .Add (new Trackbar_GR (this, mover, Side .S, new PointF
    (60, 60),
                                200, 0.3, SharpSlider .Triangle,
                                12, 4,
                                true, 6, 8, 11));
    Trackbar_GR elem = new Trackbar_GR (this, mover, Side .N,
                                new PointF (40, 200), 300, 0.14,
                            SharpSlider .Pentagon, 12, 8, true,
                                2, 8, 5);
    elem .SliderColor = Color .Blue;
    ... ...
    elem = new Trackbar_GR (this, mover, Side .W,
                            new PointF (440, 50), 200, 0.3);
    elem .SliderColor = Color .Red;
    elem .TicksNumber = 8;
    ... ...
```

The track bar cover consists of four nodes.

- One node covers the slider; if the track bar is disabled, then this node is squeezed to a size of zero.

- Two nodes cover the opposite sides of the track bar area and allow you to change the track bar length. The track bar can be resized only along the rail. For the nonresizable track bar, both nodes on the sides are squeezed to a size of zero.

- The last node covers the whole area of an element.

```
public override void DefineCover ()
{
    CoverNode [] nodes = new CoverNode [4];
    float wHalf = bResizable ? 3 : 0;
    if (sideHead == Side .N || sideHead == Side .S)      // horizontal
                                                            rail
    {
```

223

```
            nodes [0] = new CoverNode (0, ptsSlider, Cursors .SizeWE);
            nodes [1] = new CoverNode (1, rcFrame .Location,
                                    new PointF (rcFrame .Left, rcFrame
                                    .Bottom),
                                    wHalf, Cursors .SizeWE);
            nodes [2] = new CoverNode (2, new PointF (rcFrame.Right,
            rcFrame .Top),
                                    new PointF (rcFrame.Right, rcFrame
                                    .Bottom),
                                    wHalf, Cursors .SizeWE);
        }
        else
        {
            nodes [0] = new CoverNode (0, ptsSlider, Cursors .SizeNS);
            nodes [1] = new CoverNode (1, rcFrame .Location,
                                    new PointF (rcFrame .Right, rcFrame
                                    .Top),
                                    wHalf, Cursors .SizeNS);
            nodes [2] = new CoverNode (2,
                                    new PointF (rcFrame .Left, rcFrame
                                    .Bottom),
                                    new PointF (rcFrame.Right, rcFrame
                                    .Bottom),
                                    wHalf, Cursors .SizeNS);
        }
        nodes [3] = new CoverNode (3, m_rcFrame, Cursors .SizeAll);
        if (!Enabled)
        {
            nodes [0] = new CoverNode (0, ptSliderAnchor, 0f);
        }
        if (!Movable)
        {
            nodes [3] .Cursor = Cursors .NoMove2D;
        }
        cover = new Cover (nodes);
        ... ...
```

Surprisingly for such a simple object, there are enough parameters that can be tuned; all tuning is done in a special form (Figure 5-14). I already mentioned that a thin rail and a slider that can be moved along this rail are always shown. The appearance of ticks and the frame are regulated from this tuning form.

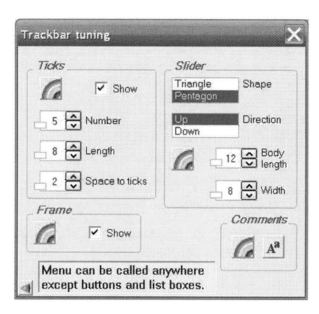

Figure 5-14. *Tuning form for track bars*

List Box

File: Form_ListBox.cs

Menu position: Graphical controls ➤ List box

The list box contains a set of strings. The ordinary ListBox control can be used with single or multiple selections; the proposed ListBox_GR class allows only a single selection (or no selection at all).

In general, the height of the ListBox_GR element does not correlate with the combined height of the included strings. If the area height is not enough to show all the strings, then a scroll bar appears next to the right border. If the area height exceeds the combined height of all the strings, then an empty space appears at the bottom. Figure 5-15 shows all the variants.

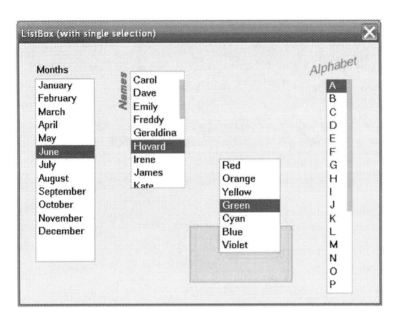

Figure 5-15. *ListBox_GR objects*

```
public class ListBox_GR :
            GraphicalObject
{
    PointF [] ptsCorner;
    Resizing resize;
    int m_iSel;
    List<string> m_strs = new List<string> ();
    Font m_font;
    bool bEnabled = true;
    float minWidth = SystemInformation .VerticalScrollBarWidth * 2;
    float minHeight = 22;
```

The minimum allowed width of the list (minWidth) and the minimum allowed height (minHeight) prevent an accidental disappearance through the resizing. In general, there is no upper size limit, though it can be set if needed. The cover is nearly standard for all rectangular objects (four circular nodes on the corners, four strip nodes along the sides, and a big node for the whole area), but an extra node for a scroll bar is included at the head. When the scroll bar is not needed, this node is squeezed to a size of zero.

```
public override void DefineCover ()
{
    float rCorner = (resize == Resizing .Any) ? 5 : 0;
    float wHalf_WE = (resize == Resizing.Any || resize == Resizing.WE)
    ? 3 : 0;
    float wHalf_NS = (resize == Resizing.Any || resize == Resizing.NS)
    ? 3 : 0;
    CoverNode [] nodes = new CoverNode [] {
            new CoverNode (0, ptsCorner [1], 0f, Cursors .SizeNS),
            new CoverNode (1, ptsCorner [0], rCorner, Cursors .SizeNWSE),
            new CoverNode (2, ptsCorner [1], rCorner, Cursors .SizeNESW),
            new CoverNode (3, ptsCorner [2], rCorner, Cursors .SizeNWSE),
            new CoverNode (4, ptsCorner [3], rCorner, Cursors .SizeNESW),
            new CoverNode (5, ptsCorner [0], ptsCorner [3], wHalf_WE,
                                                        Cursors
                                                        .SizeWE),
            new CoverNode (6, ptsCorner [1], ptsCorner [2], wHalf_WE,
                                                        Cursors
                                                        .SizeWE),
            new CoverNode (7, ptsCorner [0], ptsCorner [1], wHalf_NS,
                                                        Cursors
                                                        .SizeNS),
            new CoverNode (8, ptsCorner [3], ptsCorner [2], wHalf_NS,
                                                        Cursors
                                                        .SizeNS),
            new CoverNode (9, ptsCorner, Cursors .Hand) };
    if (m_hStrings > Height)
    {
        nodes [0] = new CoverNode (0, rcSlider, Cursors .SizeNS);
    }
    if (!Movable)
    {
        nodes [9] .Cursor = Cursors .NoMove2D;
    }
    cover = new Cover (nodes);
    ... ...
```

Parameters for the list box initialization include an initial rectangular area, a set of strings, the font, and the selected line.

```
public ListBox_GR (Form frm, Mover mvr, RectangleF rc, string [] txts,
                   Font fnt, int iSel)
```

The font size determines the combined height of all the strings (m_hStrings). If the combined height is less than the declared height of rectangle, then you see an empty space below the whole list. In the current example, this happens with the listboxMonths, which is shown on the left in Figure 5-15.

```
private void DefaultView ()
{
    ... ...
    listboxMonths = new ListBox_GR (this, mover,
                                    new RectangleF (20, 50, 100, 280),
                                    Auxi_Common .strMonths,
                                    fntSelected, 5);
    ... ...
```

The last parameter in the constructor is the number of the selected line. When the selection is not needed, the selected line is declared as -1; this is the case of the list with color names.

```
    listboxColors = new ListBox_GR (this, mover, new RectangleF (...),
                                    Auxi_Colours .strRainbowColorNames,
                                    fntSelected, -1);
```

A forward move of a ListBox_GR object is started with the left button press at any inner point. A list box is used not only to demonstrate a set of strings but also for selection among them. Selection is done by the left button click of the needed string, so two different actions are started in an identical way at the same point. The decision about one or another action is based on the estimation of distance between the mouse points of press and release. If this distance is negligible (fDist <= 3), then it is a command to select the pressed line; selection is done by the ListBox_GR.SelectByPoint() method.

```
private void OnMouseUp (object sender, MouseEventArgs e)
{
    ptMouse_Up = e .Location;
    double fDist = Auxi_Geometry .Distance (ptMouse_Down, ptMouse_Up);
    int iObj, iNode;
    if (mover .Release (out iObj, out iNode))
    {
        GraphicalObject grobj = mover .ReleasedSource;
        if (e .Button == MouseButtons .Left)
        {
            if (grobj is ListBox_GR)
            {
                if (fDist <= 3 && listPressed .Enabled &&
                                iNode == ListBox_GR .Node_FullArea)
                {
                    listPressed .SelectByPoint (e .Location);
                    ... ...
```

If some string in the list box is pressed, then the number of this string is calculated. There is no selection if an empty space beyond the last string is pressed, but there are situations when this cannot be allowed, and the perfect solution would be a list box without empty space. This is easily achieved by setting the maximum allowed height of the rectangle equal to the combined height of all strings.

By default, any ListBox_GR object has an unlimited height, but this can be changed by the ListBox_GR.MaxHeightLimit property. An optimal list height means a size in which all the strings are simultaneously in view; such a height can be set with the OptimalHeight() method. Both things are demonstrated with the list box that contains the names of colors.

```
private void DefaultView ()
{
    ... ...
    listboxColors = new ListBox_GR (...);
    listboxColors .MaxHeightLimit = ListBoxMaxHeight .Optimal;
    listboxColors .OptimalHeight ();
    ... ...
```

A list box with the color names is resizable. It can be squeezed, and then the scroll bar will appear next to the right border, but empty space would never appear beyond its last string, so any click inside the `listboxColors` selects a color.

One of the rules of user-driven applications declares that the change of visibility parameters must not affect the element sizes. However, here we purposely link the maximum allowed size of the list box with the combined height of the strings. Because this combined height depends on the font size, we organized the condition for breaking the mentioned rule.

Call the menu on the `listboxColors` as shown in Figure 5-15 and increase the font. The size of the list box will not change, but each string will grow in size, part of the strings will be out of rectangle, and the scroll bar on the right side of the rectangle will appear. Try to increase the list box height. At first it grows, but when you reach the new maximum allowed size, it will stop, and the scroll bar will disappear. You will have a similar figure with all the strings in view but shown in a bigger font. Now call the menu again and decrease the font. The new maximum allowed height also decreases, and to avoid empty space at the bottom, the real height of the list box is decreased. As you see, the change of visibility parameter (font) affects the object sizes only when it is absolutely needed and when the list box is ordered to limit its height by "no empty space" rule. For all other list boxes, there is no such order, and there is no correlation between the font size and maximum list box height.

The `ListBox_GR` class uses standard colors from the `SystemColors` class. The font is the only changeable parameter, so this is the only class of graphical controls without its tuning form. Selection of the needed font is organized through the menu command.

Combo Box

File: `Form_ComboBox.cs`

Menu position: Graphical controls ➤ Combo box

The combo box unites a text box with a list box. The text box can be editable or noneditable; the list can be always in view or can be dropped down and then hidden again after the selection of some string. In the ordinary `ComboBox` control, three of these four variants are represented; the needed variant is determined by the value from the `ComboBoxStyle` enumeration. My graphical combo box uses a noneditable text box, so this is the case with the `DropDownList` style; this is even mentioned in the name of the new class. Because there is no text box in the new object, then it is better to call two parts the *head* and the *list*.

When the list is hidden, the remaining visible part can be resized only horizontally. When the list is dropped down, the rectangular area of the `ComboBox_DDList` object can be resized in a standard way by its corners and sides. If the height of the list box is not enough to show all the strings, then a scroll bar appears next to the right side. The maximum height of a new element is limited by the combined height of all the strings, so a space at the bottom is never shown.

In the `Form_ComboBox.cs` example, elements of the `ComboBox_DDList` class are used with and without comments; there are also stand-alone objects and a whole set of combo boxes united into a group (Figure 5-16).

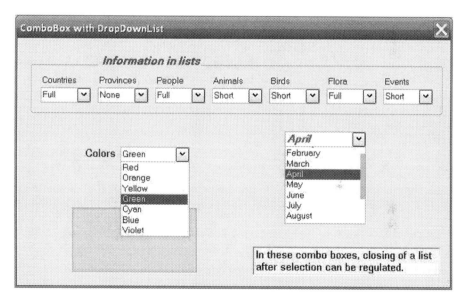

Figure 5-16. *Objects of the ComboBox_DDList class*

```
public class ComboBox_DDList : GraphicalObject
{
    PointF [] ptsCorner;
    Resizing resize;
    bool bDroppedDown, bArrowPressed, bAutoHideOnClickSelect;
    int m_iSel;
    string [] m_strs;
```

```
Font fntHead, fntList;
bool bEnabled = true;
float wBtn = SystemInformation .VerticalScrollBarWidth;
float minWidth = SystemInformation .VerticalScrollBarWidth * 5 / 2;
float minListHeight = 30;
```

Colors for the list part are taken from the standard `SystemColors` class. The new class of combo boxes allows you to use two different fonts for the head and the list; from my point of view, the increased head font can be useful. It is also possible to use a different color for the head string.

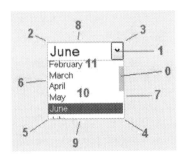

Figure 5-17. *Numbering of nodes for the ComboBox_DDList cover*

The geometry of the combo box is described by its four corners (`PointF []` `ptsCorner`); the numbering of points starts from the top-left corner and goes clockwise. The head has a special arrow square on the right. The width of this area (`wBtn`) is determined by one value from the `SystemInformation` class. The height of this area cannot be less than the width, but the height is increased if the big font is used for the head.

The cover for a `ComboBox_DDList` object consists of 12 nodes.

- If the scroll bar is in view, it is covered by rectangular node 0; otherwise, this node is squeezed to a size of zero.

- Rectangular node 1 covers the arrow square.

- Four circular nodes on the corners (2–5) and four strip nodes along the sides (6–9) cover the whole border and are used for resizing. There are four standard variants of resizing, so depending on the selected type, some or all of these eight nodes can be squeezed to a size of zero.

- With the list in view, node 10 covers the list area.

- The last node (node 11) covers the whole area of an object. Certainly, when the list is in view, the bigger part of this node is blocked by the previous one.

```
public override void DefineCover ()
{
    float wHalf_WE = (resize == Resizing.Any || resize == Resizing.WE)
    ? 3 : 0;
    CoverNode [] nodes;
    if (bDroppedDown)
    {
        float rCorner = (resize == Resizing .Any) ? 5 : 0;
        float wHalf_NS =
                    (resize == Resizing .Any || resize == Resizing .NS)
                    ? 3 : 0;
        nodes = new CoverNode [] {
                new CoverNode (0, ptsCorner [1], 0f, Cursors .SizeNS),
                new CoverNode (1, ArrowSquare, Cursors .Hand),
                new CoverNode (2, ptsCorner [0], rCorner, Cursors .SizeNWSE),
                new CoverNode (3, ptsCorner [1], rCorner, Cursors .SizeNESW),
                new CoverNode (4, ptsCorner [2], rCorner, Cursors .SizeNWSE),
                new CoverNode (5, ptsCorner [3], rCorner, Cursors .SizeNESW),
                new CoverNode (6, ptsCorner [0], ptsCorner [3], wHalf_WE,
                                                            Cursors
                                                            .SizeWE),
                new CoverNode (7, ptsCorner [1], ptsCorner [2], wHalf_WE,
                                                            Cursors
                                                            .SizeWE),
                new CoverNode (8, ptsCorner [0], ptsCorner [1], wHalf_NS,
                                                            Cursors
                                                            .SizeNS),
                new CoverNode (9, ptsCorner [3], ptsCorner [2], wHalf_NS,
                                                            Cursors
                                                            .SizeNS),
```

```
                new CoverNode (10, new PointF [] {
                        new PointF (ptsCorner [0] .X, ptsCorner [0] .Y +
                        hHead),
                        new PointF (ptsCorner [1] .X, ptsCorner [0] .Y +
                        hHead),
                        new PointF (ptsCorner [2] .X, ptsCorner [2] .Y),
                        new PointF (ptsCorner [3] .X, ptsCorner [3] .Y)},
                                Cursors .Hand),
                new CoverNode (11, ptsCorner, Cursors .SizeAll) };
        if (hStrings > Height_listpart - 2)
        {
            nodes [0] = new CoverNode (0, rcSlider, Cursors .SizeNS);
        }
    }
}
... ...
```

That was the code for the cover design in case of the drop-down list (Figure 5-17). When the list is hidden, the number of nodes does not change, but two-thirds of them are squeezed to a size of zero. Of the four remaining nodes, two more nodes are squeezed to a size of zero if horizontal resizing is prohibited.

```
    else
    {
        // only four nodes are used (1, 6, 7, 11)
        nodes = new CoverNode [] {
                new CoverNode (0, ptsCorner [0], 0f, Cursors .Hand),
                new CoverNode (1, ArrowSquare, Cursors .Hand),
                new CoverNode (2, ptsCorner [0], 0f, Cursors .Hand),
                new CoverNode (3, ptsCorner [1], 0f, Cursors .Hand),
                new CoverNode (4, ptsCorner [2], 0f, Cursors .Hand),
                new CoverNode (5, ptsCorner [3], 0f, Cursors .Hand),
                new CoverNode (6, ptsCorner [0], ptsCorner [3], wHalf_WE,
                                                             Cursors
                                                             .SizeWE),
                new CoverNode (7, ptsCorner [1], ptsCorner [2], wHalf_WE,
```

```
                                                        Cursors
                                                          .SizeWE),
                new CoverNode (8, ptsCorner [0], Of, Cursors .Hand),
                new CoverNode (9, ptsCorner [0], Of, Cursors .Hand),
                new CoverNode (10, ptsCorner [0], Of, Cursors .Hand),
                new CoverNode (11, ptsCorner, Cursors .SizeAll) };
    }
    if (!Movable)
    {
        nodes [10] .Cursor = Cursors .NoMove2D;
        nodes [11] .Cursor = Cursors .NoMove2D;
    }
    cover = new Cover (nodes);
    ... ...
```

Occasionally the numbering of nodes can be changed, so it is better to rely on the names of the crucial nodes: Node_Slider, Node_Arrow, and Node_List.

There are two main changes in the drawing of the ComboBox_DDList objects in comparison to an ordinary ComboBox control; both changes are caused by the lack of focus.

- When the list of the ComboBox control is hidden and this combo box has focus, then the text in the text box is highlighted. In the ComboBox_DDList objects, the head is always shown in standard colors.

- When the mouse moves across the list of the ComboBox control, then the current line under cursor is highlighted; this is not duplicated in the ComboBox_DDList objects because I prefer the currently selected line to be highlighted all the time.

When an object is pressed, the ComboBox_DDList.Press() method is called. Resizing by corners and sides works in the same way as in other rectangular objects. A combo box can be moved by any inner point except the area of the small button with the arrow. This small area is used only to change the list view (shown or hidden), so when this button is pressed, the cursor is fixed at the pressed point. Two interesting things happen when the button is pressed.

```
public void Press (Point ptMouse , MouseButtons catcher, int iNode)
{
    ... ...
    if (Enabled)
    {
        if (iNode == ComboBox_DDList .Node_Arrow)
        {
            ArrowPressed = !ArrowPressed;
            DroppedDown = !DroppedDown;
        }
    }
    ... ...
```

- The ArrowPressed property gets the opposite value, and the background of the arrow square gets a different view. (This area looks like a button with the gradient of colors. When the square is pressed, the same colors are used in reverse order.)

- The DroppedDown property gets the opposite value, and the list either appears or disappears.

The reaction when pressing a combo box depends on the node of release.

- If the arrow square is released, then the ComboBox_DDList. ArrowPressed property gets the false value, and the background of the arrow square gets normal view.

```
private void OnMouseUp (object sender, MouseEventArgs e)
{
    ... ...
    int iObj, iNode;
    if (mover .Release (out iObj, out iNode))
    {
        GraphicalObject grobj = mover .ReleasedSource;
        if (e .Button == MouseButtons .Left)
        {
            if (grobj is ComboBox_DDList && comboPressed.Enabled &&
            fDist <= 3)
```

```
{
    if (iNode == ComboBox_DDList .Node_Arrow)
    {
        comboPressed .ArrowPressed = false;
        Invalidate ();
    }
```

- If the list area is released and this is not the end of movement, but a selection (fDist <= 3), then the selected line is determined by the ComboBox_DDList.SelectByPoint() method. In an ordinary ComboBox control, the list is automatically hidden after line selection. In the new class, the list hiding is regulated through the ComboBox_DDList.AutoHideOnClickSelect property; its value can be changed inside the tuning form. There can be some "outer" reaction to the change of the selected line; in the current example, it happens only with the comboColors object—the auxiliary rectangle is painted with the selected color.

```
    else if (iNode == ComboBox_DDList .Node_List)
    {
        comboPressed .SelectByPoint (e .Location);
        if (comboPressed .AutoHideOnClickSelect)
        {
            comboPressed .DroppedDown = false;
        }
        if (comboPressed .ID == comboColors .ID)
        {
            SetSampleColor ();
        }
        Invalidate ();
    }
}
... ...
```

Preventing the automatic list hiding may look like a small feature, but in some cases it can be very helpful. It is not a rare situation when each selection changes something on the screen, and before making the final decision, you would like to see and visually compare (or estimate) all the possibilities. This process becomes really tiresome if each time you have to start with an arrow and click in order to see the list. The usefulness of the new feature is demonstrated with the group of combo boxes.

In the current example, we have a set of combo boxes united into a group (Figure 5-16). A similar-looking group was demonstrated in one of the examples in my other book [2], and that old example used ordinary ComboBox controls. My main complaint against that variant was about the inability to see simultaneously all possible variants from all those combo boxes. An ordinary ComboBox with the DropDownList style hides its list after selection, so at any moment only a list of one ComboBox can be seen. For the ComboBox_DDList objects, the closing of the list at the moment of selection is not mandatory. Through menu commands, you can open simultaneously the lists for all combo boxes or only for those that are needed, make all the selections, and then close all the lists with a single command of menu.

Now let's pay attention to one unusual aspect of using comments in the ComboBox_DDList class. All controls have a rectangular shape, so all graphical analogs of ordinary controls use comments of the Comment_ToRectangle class. I didn't expect any problems while adding a comment to this class because it was already done in an absolutely identical way to other classes of rectangular elements, but then I understood that there was a problem.

Up until that moment, any comment was used with *manually resizable rectangles*. The relative position of a comment is determined by two coefficients, and while the size of rectangle is changed by moving its borders, the comment position is recalculated by using those two coefficients. The manual resizing means a smooth change of rectangle sizes, so the anchor point of the comment also moves smoothly. In previous years, there was not a single case of abrupt change of the parent rectangle, so there was not a single case of comments jumping from one position to another. The combo box area can change abruptly, so something different must be thought out for comments of the combo boxes. The difference is not in using another class of comments; the difference is in calculating the comment position in the reaction to cause of an abrupt change of the dominant rectangle.

When a ComboBox_DDList object is moved or resized, then its area is changed smoothly. In these cases, the associated comment can be informed about the change through its ParentRect property, and everything works fine.

```
public override void Move (int dx, int dy)
{
    for (int i = 0; i < 4; i++)
    {
        ptsCorner [i] .X += dx;
        ptsCorner [i] .Y += dy;
    }
    ... ...
    InformComment ();
}
public void InformComment ()
{
    if (CommentExist)
    {
        m_cmnt .ParentRect = MainElementArea;
    }
}
```

But the combo box has one more possibility of changing its geometry by showing or hiding the list of strings. Depending on the number of strings in the list, such a change can be abrupt. If there are N strings in the list, then the height change can be described by the ratio $1 : (N + 1)$, and the use of the same ParentRect property throughout such change can cause problems.

The combo box view is regulated by the ComboBox_DDList.DroppedDown property; the associated comment is informed by this property about the rectangular area of the main part. There are two ways to associate positions of the main rectangle and its comment; in each case, the comment gets the new rectangle, but there is a difference in reaction.

- When the CommentToRect.ParentRect property is used, then two existing coefficients are used to change the comment position.

- When the CommentToRect.SetParentRect() method is used, the comment position is not changed, but the new coefficients are calculated.

At first I used InformComment() on any change of the combo box area, so the ParentRect property was called in all the cases; there were situations when I liked the result, and there were others that I did not. At last I understood that in some cases the SetParentRect() method gave better results, and the selection between two cases had to be based on the initial comment position (on the position of its anchor point). Figure 5-18 shows two areas (they are bordered by the red lines) for which the SetParentRect() method is called; in all other cases, the InformComment() method is called, and this method uses the ParentRect property.

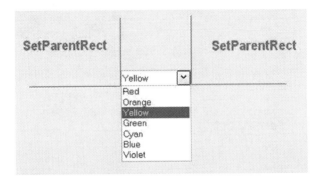

Figure 5-18. *The SetParentRect() method is used when a comment is initially inside one of two marked areas; in all other cases, the ParentRect property is used*

```
public bool DroppedDown
{
    get { return (bDroppedDown); }
    set
    {
        ... ...
        PointF ptA = m_cmnt .AnchorPoint;
        if ((ptA.X < MainElementArea.Left || MainElementArea.Right <
        ptA.X) &&
            ptA .Y <= MainElementArea .Top + hHead)
        {
            m_cmnt .SetParentRect (MainElementArea);
        }
```

```
else
{
    InformComment ();
}
... ...
```

The `ComboBox_DDList` object can be tuned together with its comment with the help of a special tuning form (Figure 5-19). At the same time, users are not aware of the system of classes, and if they want to change a comment, they call the menu on this comment and can do the same changes through the commands of this menu.

Figure 5-19. *Tuning form for ComboBox_DDList objects*

Check Box

File: `Form_CheckBox.cs`

Menu position: Graphical controls ➤ Check box

For starters, an ordinary `CheckBox` control is mostly used in a two-state variant (checked or unchecked) but also has a three-state alternative. Though it is not a problem to design a three-state graphical replica, the currently demonstrated `CheckBox_GR` class has only a two-state version.

```
public class CheckBox_GR : GraphicalObject
{
    RectangleF rcCheck, rcText;
    float m_space;
    Side sideText;
    SideAlignment alignParts;
    string m_text;
    Font m_font;
    Color m_color;
    bool bChecked = true;
    bool bEnabled = true;
    bool bFixMouseOnUnmovable = true;
```

Each check box consists of two absolutely different parts: a small square and text. An ordinary CheckBox control allows you to change the relative position of these parts, but I have never seen any other variants except the text positioned to the right of the square. The CheckBox_GR class allows 12 variants of relative position; this and several other parameters are regulated through the tuning form.

One important remark about the meaning of the sideText field that determines the relative position of square and text is that the square is small while the text is either bigger or significantly bigger (see Figure 5-20). Regardless of this discrepancy in sizes, the square is the anchor part of any check box, so the sideText field defines *the side of the square at which the text is positioned.* All check boxes except one in Figure 5-20 demonstrate the most often used case of the text positioned to the right of the square; in such a case, sideText = Side.E. This is also the default value for the sideText field when the appropriate parameter is skipped in the CheckBox_GR constructor.

Figure 5-20. *A check box consists of a small square and text*

A check box consists of two obvious parts. Each part is a nonresizable rectangle, so it looks like it would be enough to have two nodes in the cover, but there are three. For a better view of an object, there is a small space between two parts, and I do not like the idea of catching another object through this gap, so the gap is covered by an additional polygonal node. The size of a square is fixed (nSquare = 18), while the size of the text varies. Depending on the ratio of these two sizes, the extra node is either a rectangle or a trapezium. Calculating the corner points (PointF [] pts) for this node is simple but too lengthy to be shown here.

```
public override void DefineCover ()
{
    PointF [] pts = new PointF [4];
    ... ...
```

243

```
CoverNode [] nodes = new CoverNode [] {
                                    new CoverNode (0, rcCheck, Cursors
                                    .Hand),
                                    new CoverNode (1, rcText),
                                    new CoverNode (2, pts) };
if (!Movable)
{
    nodes [1] .Cursor = Cursors .NoMove2D;
    nodes [2] .Cursor = Cursors .NoMove2D;
}
cover = new Cover (nodes);
... ...
```

Selecting or unselecting a check box is done by clicking any point of an object, so for the purpose of changing the check status, both parts—the square and the text—work identically. Moving an object is allowed only by the text, while the mouse cursor pressed inside the square is fixed until the mouse release. The check box cover and the logic of check box work are so simple that the only reaction on the check box press is the storing of the pressed point.

```
public void Press (...)
{
    ptPressed = ptMouse;
}
```

The reaction on the element press is determined at the moment of the mouse release and depends on the distance between the points of mouse press and release. If the distance is negligible (fDist <= 3), then it is considered as the change of the check status, which is done by the Checked property. This is the only possible reaction on a click inside the square as the cursor position is fixed and the mouse can be released only at the same point.

```
private void OnMouseUp (object sender, MouseEventArgs e)
{
    ptMouse_Up = e .Location;
    double fDist = Auxi_Geometry .Distance (ptMouse_Down, ptMouse_Up);
    int iObj, iNode;
```

```
if (mover .Release (out iObj, out iNode))
{
    GraphicalObject grobj = mover .ReleasedSource;
    if (e .Button == MouseButtons .Left)
    {
        if (grobj is CheckBox_GR && checkPressed .Enabled &&
        fDist <= 3)
        {
            checkPressed .Checked = !checkPressed .Checked;
            ButtonsVisibililty ();
            RenewMover ();
        }
    ... ...
```

The movement of an object is described by the MoveNode() method of its class. If the pressed node is used to move the whole object, then there is a standard for all objects and simple code.

- For a movable object, its Move() method is called.

- For an unmovable object, the cursor is fixed at the pressed point.

For the CheckBox_GR class, the cursor is always fixed if the press happens inside the small square, but the following code is nearly standard:

```
public override bool MoveNode (...)
{
    bool bRet = false;
    if (catcher == MouseButtons .Left)
    {
        if (Movable)
        {
            if (iNode == 0)
            {
                AdjustCursorPosition (ptPressed);
            }
            else
```

```
        {
            Move (dx, dy);
            bRet = true;
        }
    }
    ... ...
```

As shown in the previous code, the standard reaction is implemented for movable check boxes, while there is something different for unmovable elements. Before looking at the case of pressing an unmovable check box, let's ask a more general question: what do you expect as a reaction on pressing an *unmovable element*?

Movable and unmovable elements do not differ visually, so the current movability status of any element can be revealed only as a reaction on mouse press-and-move attempt. The movable element simply moves with the mouse, but there can be two absolutely different reactions when an unmovable object is pressed.

- The cursor can be fixed at the pressed point, and no mouse move would be allowed until the mouse release.

- The cursor can be freely moved around without any element movement.

I prefer the first variant, so in the majority of the demonstrated classes, the idea of a mouse fixing on an unmovable element is implemented. However, the best way to form your personal opinion is to compare both variants. To make such a comparison easier, in the CheckBox_GR class both reactions are possible.

Several extra lines in the CheckBox_GR.MoveNode() method allow you to have two variants.

```
public override bool MoveNode (...)
{
    bool bRet = false;
    if (catcher == MouseButtons .Left)
    {
        if (Movable)
        {
            ... ...
        }
```

```
        else
        {
            if (bFixMouseOnUnmovable)
            {
                AdjustCursorPosition (ptPressed);
            }
        }
    }
    return (bRet);
}
```

In the current example, the check boxes inside the group are used in their standard way, so if all the images that can be shown here are available, then all these check boxes are enabled. To demonstrate some special situations, the check box outside the group has a different menu. The commands of this menu allow you to compare the cases of fixed and free cursors for unmovable check boxes and to see the change of the view when a check box becomes disabled.

The tuning of the CheckBox_GR objects is organized via the special form Form_ Tuning_CheckBox.cs (Figure 5-21). The check box is simple in view, so its tuning form is also simple. The relative position of the square and the text is set by moving a small square around a rectangle with the word *Text*.

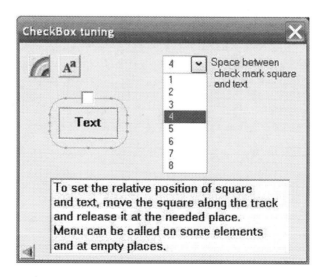

Figure 5-21. *Tuning form for CheckBox_GR objects*

Pay attention to one thing. In the tuning form, it is more convenient to move a small square around a bigger rectangle, but in the original check box that is currently under tuning, the square plays the role of an anchor element, so the square will be unmoved, but its text will take the new position.

The first example in this chapter used several pictures to demonstrate the `Button_Image` class. Buttons use the nearly standard covers for all rectangles with nodes on the sides and on the corners. Such a system of nodes along the border allows you to resize a rectangle in an arbitrary way. This is the best type of resizing for many rectangles, but such arbitrary resizing is redundant for pictures. Photos have different width/height ratios, but for each particular picture this ratio is fixed and does not need any change throughout the resizing. In the current example, objects of the `Rectangle_Image` class are used for a picture demonstration. These rectangles are resized only by the corners, and throughout such a process their width/height ratio never changes, so the rectangle always has optimal sizes for demonstration of a particular picture. The menu on rectangles allows you to change the order of their appearance on the screen.

List View

File: `Form_ListView.cs`

Menu position: Graphical controls ➤ List view

Earlier we discussed the list box and combo box; these objects use a single column of strings from which any item can be selected. The list view allows you to show more complex data consisting of multiple parts. To do this, the list view presents this data in rows and columns with each cell showing some piece of data as a string. The list view is a compact way to show a big chunk of data. See Figure 5-22.

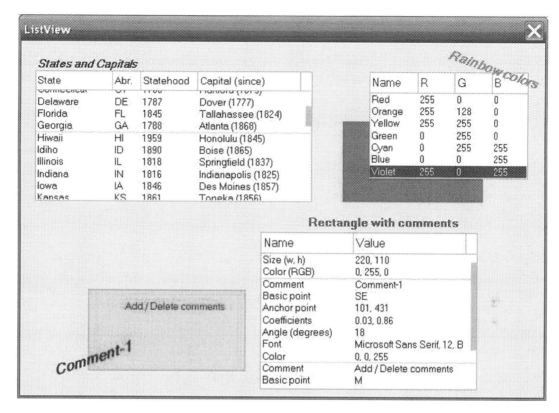

Figure 5-22. *ListView_GR objects*

A `ListView_GR` object looks similar to a `ComboBox_DDList` object with the list in view, and there are many similarities between their covers; compare Figure 5-23a with Figure 5-17. There is one feature in which the cover of the `ListView_GR` class differs from the covers for other graphical controls: the number of nodes in the new cover is not constant. The number of nodes depends on the number of columns; for a list of N columns, the number of nodes is 9 + N.

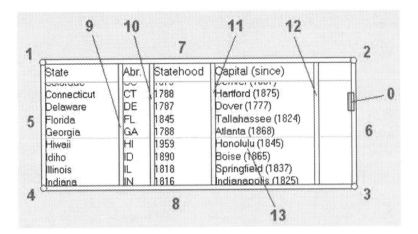

Figure 5-23a. *The cover view when the vertical grid inside the list is shown*

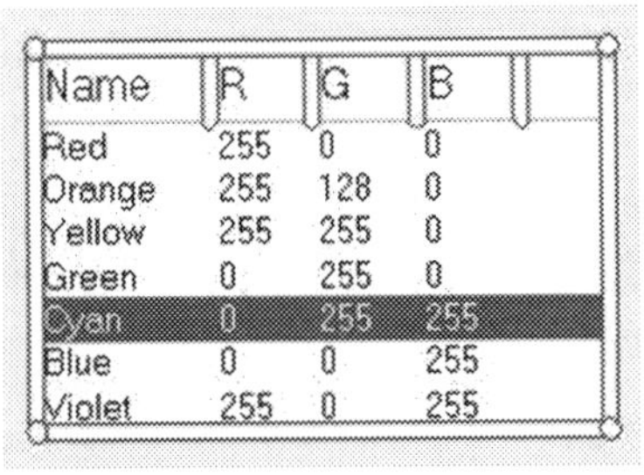

Figure 5-23b. *The cover view when the vertical grid is not shown*

- The scroll bar is covered by rectangular node 0; if the scroll bar is not needed, then this node is squeezed to a size of zero.

- Four circular nodes on the corners (1–4) and four strip nodes along the sides (5–8) cover the whole border and are used for resizing. There are four standard variants of resizing, so depending on the selected type, some or all of these eight nodes can be squeezed to a size of zero.

- Data is shown in columns. The headers of these columns are always separated by the thin lines, while the appearance of the vertical grid in the main area of the list is determined by the user. These vertical lines are covered by nodes, but the length of these nodes depends on the grid appearance; Figure 5-23 demonstrates both variants. The number of these nodes depends on the number of columns; in Figure 5-23a, these are nodes 9–12.

- The last node covers the whole area of the list view. In our list of five columns, it has the number 13

A similarity in the view of the `ListView_GR` and `ComboBox_DDList` objects means the use of the same parameters, and this means the similarity in tuning forms. The tuning form for the `ListView_GR` objects (Figure 5-24) is nearly identical to the tuning form for combo boxes (Figure 5-19).

From my point of view, different fonts for headers and the main part of the list make the view of an object much better, so it can be organized from the moment of construction. Strings for all the cells are provided in a single array; the order of strings is from top to bottom and for each row from left to right.

```
public ListView_GR (Form frm, Mover mvr, RectangleF rc,
                    string [] strHeads, Font fntHead,
                    string [] strInner, Font fntList, int iSel)
```

There can be different types of interaction between a `ListView_GR` object and other elements of the surrounding form.

- No interaction at all.

- A change of selection in the list may cause some changes of other elements.

- A change of elements may cause the change of the `ListView_GR` object.

Three `ListView_GR` objects of the current example illustrate these three different cases.

Figure 5-24. *Tuning form for ListView_GR objects*

The list with the information on states and their capitals–listStates–illustrates the simplest case without any interaction. This list gets the data at the moment of construction, and the data is never changed after this moment. The headers of this list use the same type of font as the main part but are slightly enlarged.

```
private void DefaultView_listStates (PointF ptLT)
{
    listStates = new ListView_GR (this, mover,
                                new RectangleF (ptLT .X, ptLT .Y,
                                200, 210),
                new string [] { "State", "Abr.", "Statehood", "Capital
                (since)" },
                                Auxi_Common .FontZoomed (fntSelected,
                                1.1),
                            Auxi_Common .strStatesCapitals,
                            fntSelected, -1);
    listStates .MaxHeightLimit = ListMaxHeight .Optimal;
    listStates .OptimalWidth ();
    listStates .UnderlinedItems = new int [] { 9, 19, 29, 39 };
    ... ...
```

Several important features of the ListView_GR class are mentioned in this code.

- By default, the height of an object can be changed regardless of the number of rows and their combined height, so an empty space can appear beyond the last row. However, if the selection (by a mouse click) of any particular row causes some further action, then the click at an empty space is meaningless. To avoid the appearance of empty space, the list height can be limited by the last row with the help of the MaxHeightLimit property.

```
listStates .MaxHeightLimit = ListMaxHeight .Optimal;
```

- The user can change the width of any column at any moment, while the ListView_GR.OptimalWidth() method determines the width of each column by its longest string with an additional space of several pixels for better view.

```
listStates .OptimalWidth ();
```

- With the large number of rows in a list, the underlining of some rows makes reading easier. There is an instrument to organize the arbitrary underlining of rows in a list. In this list, every 10th row is underlined.

```
listStates .UnderlinedItems = new int [] { 9, 19, 29, 39 };
```

listStates shows only the previously prepared data, while listColors represents the case when changing the selection in the list causes some changes in other elements of the form. Changing the selection is done by the ListView_GR.SelectByPoint() method. The change of selection in the current list causes the change of color in the associated rectangle.

```
private void OnMouseUp (object sender, MouseEventArgs e)
{
    ptMouse_Up = e .Location;
    double fDist = Auxi_Geometry .Distance (ptMouse_Down, ptMouse_Up);
    int iObj, iNode;
    if (mover .Release (out iObj, out iNode))
    {
        GraphicalObject grobj = mover .ReleasedSource;
```

```
            if (e .Button == MouseButtons .Left)
            {
                if (grobj is ListView_GR && listPressed .Enabled)
                {
                    if (iNode == listPressed .NodesCount - 1 && fDist <= 3)
                    {
                        listPressed .SelectByPoint (e .Location);
                        if (listPressed .ID == listColors .ID)
                        {
                            SetSampleColor ();
                        }
                        ... ...
// ----------------------------
private void SetSampleColor ()
{
    if (listColors .SelectedIndex >= 0)
    {
        brushSample .Color =
                        Auxi_Colours .RainbowColors [listColors
                        .SelectedIndex];
    }
    else
    {
        brushSample .Color = Color .White;
    }
}
```

The third list—listRect—is also associated with a rectangle, but this one is an element of the Rectangle_withComments class, and the change of this rectangle or its associated comments causes the change of data in the list. Not only the strings inside the cells of the list are changed, but even the number of rows in the list depends on the parameters of the associated rectangle.

```
private void DefaultView_listRect (PointF ptLT)
{
    Font fntHead = Auxi_Common .FontZoomed (fntSelected, 1.2);
    string [] strs = PrepareListStrings_listRect ();
```

```
listRect = new ListView_GR (this, mover,
                              new RectangleF (ptLT .X, ptLT .Y,
                              210, 160),
                              new string [] { "Name", "Value" },
                              fntHead,
                              strs, fntSelected, -1);
    ... ...
```

The first three rows of this list show the parameters of rectangle itself, so these three rows always exist.

```
string [] PrepareListStrings_listRect ()
{
    Comment_ToRectangle cmnt;
    List<string> strs = new List<string> ();
    strs .Add (listRect_rectNames [0]);
    strs .Add (Auxi_Convert .PointToStr (rectWithComments .Location));
    strs .Add (listRect_rectNames [1]);
    strs .Add (rectWithComments .Width .ToString ("F0") + ", " +
               rectWithComments .Height .ToString ("F0"));
    strs .Add (listRect_rectNames [2]);
    strs .Add (Auxi_Convert .ClrToStr (rectWithComments .Color,
                                       ColorStr .NUMBER_COMA_SPACE));
    ... ...
```

For each comment on a rectangle, there are seven rows of data in the list, so the total number of rows is determined by the number of associated comments.

```
for (int i = 0; i < rectWithComments .Comments .Count; i++)
{
    cmnt = rectWithComments .Comments [i];
    strs .Add (listRect_cmntNames [0]);
    strs .Add (cmnt .Text);
    strs .Add (listRect_cmntNames [1]);
    strs .Add (namesTextBasis [(int) cmnt .TextBasis]);
    strs .Add (listRect_cmntNames [2]);
    strs .Add (Auxi_Convert .PointToStr (cmnt .AnchorPoint));
```

```
            strs .Add (listRect_cmntNames [3]);
            strs .Add (cmnt .XCoefficient .ToString ("F2") + ", " +
                        cmnt .YCoefficient .ToString ("F2"));
            strs .Add (listRect_cmntNames [4]);
            strs .Add (cmnt .Angle_Degree .ToString ("F2"));
            strs .Add (listRect_cmntNames [5]);
            strs .Add (Auxi_Convert .FontInDetails (cmnt .Font));
            strs .Add (listRect_cmntNames [6]);
            strs .Add (Auxi_Convert .ClrToStr (cmnt .Color,
                                        ColorStr .NUMBER_COMA_SPACE));
        }
        ... ...
```

It is not a problem to renew the whole list by calling the same PrepareListString_ listRect() method on any change of rectangle or its comment, but I prefer to demonstrate several other possibilities. We have only one rectangle with comments in this example; so, for the rectangle itself, no additional identification is needed. The number of comments associated with this rectangle can vary, so the press of any comment requires comment identification.

```
    private void OnMouseDown (object sender, MouseEventArgs e)
    {
        ptMouse_Down = e .Location;
        if (mover .Catch (e .Location, e .Button, bShowAngle))
        {
            GraphicalObject grobj = mover .CaughtSource;
            ... ...
            else if (grobj is Comment_ToRectangle)
            {
                cmntPressed = grobj as Comment_ToRectangle;
                CommentIdentification ();
                cmntPressed .Press (e .Location, e .Button, iNode);
            }
            ... ...
```

This simple identification gives the order number of the pressed comment (jCmntRWC) among all the comments of the rectangle; this also determines the rows of the listRect in which the data of the pressed comment is shown.

```
private void CommentIdentification ()
{
    jCmntRWC = -1;
    if (cmntPressed .ParentID == rectWithComments .ID)
    {
        for (int j = 0; j < rectWithComments .Comments .Count; j++)
        {
            if (cmntPressed .ID == rectWithComments .Comments [j] .ID)
            {
                jCmntRWC = j;
                break;
            }
        }
    }
}
```

The majority of changes for rectangle or its pressed comment require you to change the data in some particular cell, which is done with the ListView_GR.Subitem() method. For example, here is the change of font for the pressed comment.

```
private void Click_miFont_Cmnt (object sender, EventArgs e)
{
    ... ...
    if (jCmntRWC >= 0)
    {
        listRect .Subitem (3 + 5 + jCmntRWC * 7, 1,
                           Auxi_Convert .FontInDetails (cmntPressed
                           .Font));
    ... ...
```

New comments can be added through the menu command. The new comment is included at the head of associated comments; a number of rows must be included in the list, so it is easier to renew the whole list. For easier reading of data, the rows associated with each comment are separated by the line, so on each change of the number of comments (addition or erasing), the array of underlined items is calculated by the ListRect_HorLines() method.

```
private void Click_miAddComment (object sender, EventArgs e)
{
    double xCoef, yCoef;
    Auxi_Geometry .CoefficientsByLocation (rectWithComments
    .MainElementArea,
                                          ptMouse_Up, out xCoef, out
                                          yCoef);
    rectWithComments .InsertComment (0, xCoef, yCoef,
                             "Comment-" + rectWithComments .Comments
                             .Count);
    string [] strs = PrepareListStrings_listRect ();
    listRect .RenewTexts (strs);
    ListRect_HorLines ();
    RenewMover ();
}
```

Radio Buttons

Three types of buttons are widely used in interface design: push buttons, check boxes, and radio buttons. We already have the graphical analogs for the first two; now it is the time for radio buttons. One thing makes them different not only from other buttons but also from all other controls: radio buttons are never used individually but only in groups. Having an individual radio button makes no sense because the only purpose of these controls is to organize a single selection among N possibilities. Ordinary RadioButton controls are usually united into a group by a GroupBox, though this can be also done with a Panel. The graphical analog of a radio button is also used only in a group, but certainly no controls are used for this purpose. Before going into the details of graphical radio buttons, let's talk a bit about some features of the ordinary RadioButton and GroupBox controls.

- The `RadioButton` object consists of a small circle and associated text. It is possible to organize different types of their relative positions, but I had never seen anything else except both of them placed on the same horizontal line with the text to the right of the circle. I assume that positioning of the circle to the right of the text would be more appropriate for countries with the rule of writing from right to left, but I have never worked with such applications.

- `RadioButton` objects are used only in groups. Inside the group, there can be an arbitrary positioning of those buttons, but the standard practice is to position their circles strictly on a single vertical line. In one program, I have seen a group in which radio buttons were placed in several columns, but I remember it as a single case throughout the decades. In my other book [2], there is an example in which ordinary radio buttons are positioned along the inclined line, but this shows only that strict vertical placement is not mandatory.

- `RadioButton` objects are usually positioned at the equal distances from each other. In the same example from my other book [2], there is one more group of radio buttons with uneven distances between neighbors. These radio buttons are associated with other elements of the form, which are positioned outside the group. Those "outer" objects are of different types and sizes, so I used the uneven distribution of radio buttons inside the group in such a way as to place each button opposite its associated elements outside. Such positioning of buttons makes this association much more obvious. There is nothing wrong in having different distances between buttons, but I never saw it in other programs.

File: `Form_RadioBtnsLight.cs`

Menu position: Graphical controls ➤ Radio buttons (light version)

Let's start our work on the graphical radio buttons with a light version that provides exactly the type of buttons that we usually see in programs. In this light version, the circle and the text are always positioned on the same horizontal line with the text to the right of the circle. Such radio buttons can be organized into a light version of a group—the `Group_RadioBtnsLight` class—in which all circles are positioned along the same vertical line and the buttons can be moved only up or down.

```
public class RadioButton_Light : GraphicalObject
{
    PointF ptCenter;
    string m_text;
    Font m_font;
    Color m_color;
    bool bSwitched;
    bool bEnabled = true;
    static float rBig = 8;
    RectangleF rcText;
```

The button text is placed not next to the circle but is moved aside for half a circle radius (rBig). The cover of the RadioButton_Light object consists of three nodes. The first node covers the circle, the second node covers the text, and the third node covers the gap between the circle and the text.

```
public override void DefineCover()
{
    PointF [] pts = new PointF [] {
                    new PointF (ptCenter .X, ptCenter .Y - rBig),
                    new PointF (rcText .Left,
                             Math .Max (ptCenter .Y - rBig, rcText
                             .Top)),
                    new PointF (rcText .Left,
                             Math .Min (ptCenter .Y + rBig, rcText
                             .Bottom)),
                    new PointF (ptCenter .X, ptCenter .Y + rBig) };
    CoverNode [] nodes = new CoverNode [] {
                             new CoverNode (0, ptCenter, rBig),
                             new CoverNode (1, rcText, Cursors
                             .SizeNS),
                             new CoverNode (2, pts, Cursors
                             .SizeNS) };
```

```
if (!Movable)
{
    nodes [1] .Cursor = Cursors .NoMove2D;
    nodes [2] .Cursor = Cursors .NoMove2D;
}
cover = new Cover (nodes);
... ...
```

Button selection is done by clicking at any point; the last two nodes can also be used to move the button up or down. Regardless of the point at which the button is pressed, this point is remembered (ptPressed). Nothing else is done at the moment of the mouse press.

```
public void Press (...)
{
    ptPressed = ptMouse;
}
```

Possible movements are described by the MoveNode() method.

- The radio button is not moved by its circle; when the circle is pressed (iNode == 0), no movement is allowed, and the cursor is kept at the same point until the mouse release.

- When a movable button is pressed outside the circle, the cursor is allowed to move only vertically, and throughout such movement the button moves with the cursor.

- When an unmovable button is pressed outside the circle, the cursor is kept at the same point until the mouse release.

The cursor is kept at the pressed point or on a straight line by the familiar AdjustCursorPosition() method.

```
public override bool MoveNode (...)
{
    bool bRet = false;
    if (catcher == MouseButtons .Left)
    {
```

```
        if (iNode == 0)
        {
            AdjustCursorPosition (ptPressed);
        }
        else
        {
            if (Movable)
            {
                Move (0, dy);
                bRet = true;
                AdjustCursorPosition (new Point (ptPressed .X, ptMouse .Y));
            }
            else
            {
                AdjustCursorPosition (ptPressed);
            }
        }
    }
    return (bRet);
}
```

Radio buttons are used only inside groups. This example (Figure 5-25) demonstrates three groups of the Group_RadioBtnsLight class. The design ideas of these groups are the same as were used for the Group_ArbitraryElements class.

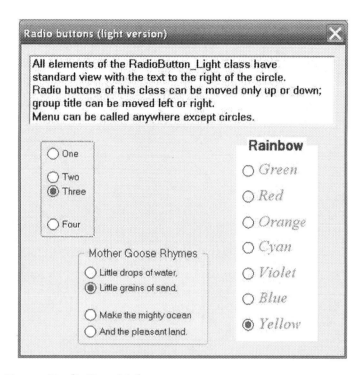

Figure 5-25. *Form_RadioBtnsLight.cs*

- There is a set of inner elements; in the current case, all elements belong to the `RadioButton_Light` class.

- Inner elements are movable. It is possible to declare these elements unmovable to prevent accidental movement, but this must be the user's decision. All inner elements can be moved up or down without any restrictions, so the user is free to change the distances between elements, to position them in visually obvious subgroups, and to change their order.

- The group area can be marked by the frame, by different a background color, or by both. The group area is automatically adjusted to any change of inner elements.

- The group can be used with or without a title. The group width is determined by the larger of two elements: the title, if it exists, and the longest button. If the group width allows, the title can be moved left and right; the adhered mouse technique is used for such movement. The user can regulate the title movability.

```
public class Group_RadioBtnsLight : GraphicalObject
{
    RectangleF m_rcFrame, m_rcBigNode, m_rcTitle;
    List<RadioButton_Light> m_elements = new List<RadioButton_Light> ();
    string m_title;
    bool bTitleMovable = true;
    Font fntTitle;
    Color clrTitle;
    Pen penFrame;
```

The cover for such a group consists of two nodes. The first one covers the title rectangular area (m_rcTitle); for a group without a title, this node is squeezed to a size of zero. The second node is also rectangular and covers the frame area (m_rcBigNode).

```
public override void DefineCover ()
{
    m_rcBigNode = RectangleF.FromLTRB (m_rcFrame .Left, m_rcFrame .Top,
                                        m_rcFrame .Right + 1, m_rcFrame.
                                        Bottom);
    CoverNode [] nodes = new CoverNode [2];
    if (TitleExist)
    {
        nodes [0] = new CoverNode (0, m_rcTitle);
        if (bTitleMovable)
        {
            nodes [0] .SetBehaviourCursor (Behaviour.Moveable, Cursors.
            SizeWE);
        }
    }
    else
    {
        nodes [0] = new CoverNode (0, m_rcFrame .Location, 0f);
    }
    nodes [1] = new CoverNode (1, m_rcBigNode);
    cover = new Cover (nodes);
    ... ...
```

The visibility parameters of groups and their buttons must be under the users' control. For the light version of radio buttons, the light version of tuning is used, so some less important parameters in this example are not tunable. All tuning is organized via the menu commands (Figure 5-26). To change the parameters of a particular button or to spread its parameters on all the siblings, you call the menu on the button (Figure 5-26a).

Figure 5-26a. *Menu on radio buttons*

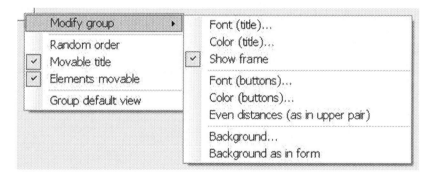

Figure 5-26b. *Menu on groups*

The group menu (Figure 5-26b) can be called at any empty place inside a group. This menu allows you to define the title view, to regulate the frame drawing, to set parameters for all buttons, to use the distance of the upper pair as a sample for all pairs of neighboring buttons, and to set the group background. There are also commands to restore the group default view and to regulate the movability of the title and buttons.

The "Modify group" line has a submenu with a good number of commands (Figure 5-26b). In such a case, a tuning form with all these possibilities is more convenient. I decided to organize the tuning in different ways for light and normal versions of the group, so the normal variant of a group has an expected tuning form covered a bit later in the chapter.

The user can easily change the order of radio buttons inside the group, so the selection is based only on the ID of the pressed button. The button ID is set once and for all at the moment of the button construction. This ID does not depend on all further movements or a change of parameters.

```
private void OnMouseUp (object sender, MouseEventArgs e)
{
    ptMouse_Up = e .Location;
    double fDist = Auxi_Geometry .Distance (ptMouse_Down, ptMouse_Up);
    int iObj, iNode;
    if (mover .Release (out iObj, out iNode))
    {
        GraphicalObject grobj = mover .ReleasedSource;
        if (e .Button == MouseButtons .Left)
        {
            if (grobj is RadioButton_Light && radiobtnPressed .Enabled)
            {
                if (fDist <= 3)
                {
                    groupAround .SelectButton (
                            groupAround .ButtonSearch
                            (radiobtnPressed .ID));
                }
                ... ...
```

The group menu (Figure 5-26b) includes a command to regulate the movability for all buttons. Selection and tuning work regardless of this movability.

The "Random order" command of the group menu is enabled only for the Rainbow group. This command uses the current button's coordinates but changes their order. This Rainbow group has one more interesting feature; you can find it out if the buttons are placed in the correct rainbow order.

File: Form_RadioButtons.cs

Menu position: Graphical controls ➤ Radio buttons

Light versions of radio buttons and their groups are designed with these three restrictions:

- Button view   Text is placed to the right of circle, and the central points are on the same horizontal line.
- Group view   Circles of all buttons in a group are placed along the same vertical line.
- Movement   Buttons can be moved only up or down.

Almost all radio buttons in all applications that you have seen throughout the years had such a view, so you would consider it the expected one and would not think about these three rules as being any kind of limitation. However, the ordinary RadioButton class allows you, for example, to position a circle above its associated text and to position radio buttons inside the GroupBox in an arbitrary way. There are some interesting things that developers can do with the ordinary RadioButton controls, but regardless of designers' ideas, the users have to deal with whatever they are given and cannot change anything themselves. In user-driven applications, the full control is passed to the users, so the new version of radio buttons has to work without any mentioned restrictions, and the new classes must implement easy ways of changing relative positions inside the pair circle—the text and button position inside group. Because in the majority of applications the mentioned restrictions do not look like any limitations at all, I decided to include in the new classes an easy way of switching between the variants of limited and unlimited movements. The variants of the new radio buttons are described by the RadioButtonType enumeration; from the names of these variants you can see that the free unlimited movements and the arbitrary positioning of new radio buttons are considered as normal.

```
public enum RadioButtonType { Normal, Light };
```

Radio buttons are never used as stand-alone objects but only in groups. The buttons of the RadioButton_GR class are organized into the groups of the Group_RadioButtons class; two such groups are demonstrated in the current example (Figure 5-27). It is impossible to use inside the same group the buttons with limited and unlimited movement as this will produce the same mess as a simultaneous use of movable and unmovable objects. Thus, if the user decides to change the button behavior inside any group, then this change is implemented simultaneously for all buttons of this group.

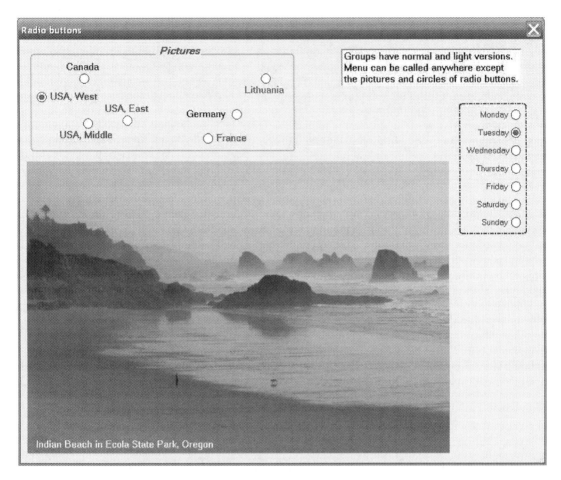

Figure 5-27. *Objects of the Group_RadioButtons class*

For any radio button, the position of the text in relation to the circle is described in the same way as in the check boxes, so the text can be placed at any side of the circle, and for each side there are three variants of the circle-text alignment.

```
public class RadioButton_GR : GraphicalObject
{
    RadioButtonType typeBtn = RadioButtonType .Normal;
    PointF ptCenter;
    Side sideText;
    SideAlignment alignParts;
    string m_text;
    Font m_font;
```

```
Color m_color;
bool bSwitched;
bool bEnabled = true;
```

The cover of the RadioButton_GR class is designed in the same way as in the light variant: one node over the circle, another node over the text, and an additional node over the space between them. This third node is always polygonal, but its exact shape depends on the sizes and relative positions of the circle and text. The calculation of this node is easy, but this part of code is too lengthy to be shown here.

```
public override void DefineCover ()
{
    CoverNode [] nodes = new CoverNode [3];
    nodes [0] = new CoverNode (0, ptCenter, rBig);
    PointF [] pts = new PointF [4];
    if (typeBtn == RadioButtonType .Normal)
    {
        nodes [1] = new CoverNode (1, rcText, Cursors .Hand);
        ... ...
        nodes [2] = new CoverNode (2, pts, Cursors .Hand);
    }
    else
    {
        nodes [1] = new CoverNode (1, rcText, Cursors .SizeNS);
        ... ...
        nodes [2] = new CoverNode (2, pts, Cursors .SizeNS);
    }
    if (!Movable)
    {
        nodes [1] .Cursor = Cursors .NoMove2D;
        nodes [2] .Cursor = Cursors .NoMove2D;
    }
    cover = new Cover (nodes);
    ... ...
```

There is nothing new in the cover design of the group (class `Group_RadioButtons`) and inner radio buttons (class `RadioButton_GR`); only the cursor shape over radio buttons is changed from the default. When the mouse cursor is moved across the group area, it passes over the inner elements and over unoccupied places of the group. In both cases, there is some polygonal node under the mouse, so without any additional changes, the cursor would have the same default shape and would not give a tip about the possible movement. To distinguish visually the possibility of moving the group or inner element, the cursor for one of them must be changed. I tried both variants and decided to keep the standard cursor (`Cursors.SizeAll`) for the group itself while the cursor for buttons is changed to `Cursors.Hand`.

A simple group with the names of the weekdays can demonstrate a lot of things that can be done with such groups. For a lot of readers (I think, for majority) the shown order of days in Figure 5-27 looks strange, but depending on traditions, there are countries in which the first weekday is either Sunday or Monday; there are (or at least there were not long ago) some countries in which the week starts on Saturday, so the upper line in the list of days might be different. This application does not need to check the traditions of the country from which it is started; if you need to change the starting day, you simply move the upper line to the bottom of the list or vice versa.

Suppose that you want to distinguish visually (with font and color) the working days and the weekend. In many countries, there are five working days, while in other countries, people work six days. These are all general cases, but there can be also personal requirements. You might work on a special schedule with only two, three, or four working days; you may have classes in the morning on some days and in the evening on others. For all such cases you can organize a special view of this group. Figure 5-28 shows several variants, but there can be many others. All changes are done in seconds and at any moment whenever it is needed. Even if you decide to place Friday between Tuesday and Wednesday, it is not prohibited.

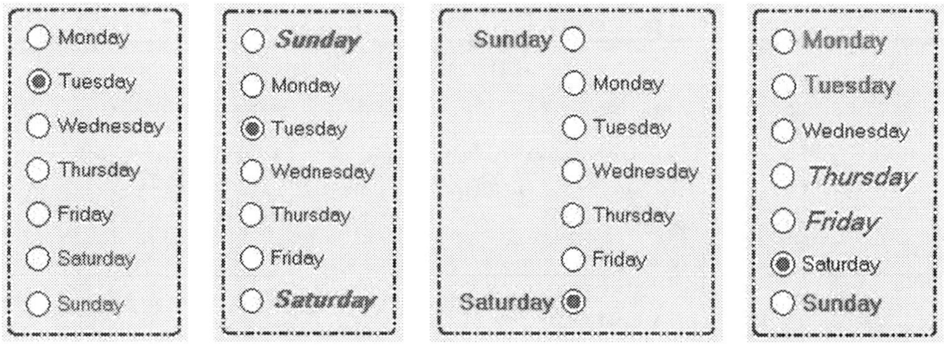

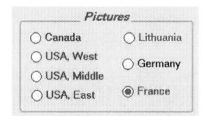

Figure 5-28. *Several views of the same group are organized by changing the parameters of radio buttons, by changing the relative position of the circle and text in some of them, and by changing the order of buttons*

It so happened that in all four variants of this group the buttons are positioned in one column. Certainly, there are no restrictions on the positions of buttons inside a group, and there are variants of relative positions inside each circle-text pair. Figure 5-29 shows this in another group of this example.

Figure 5-29a. *Buttons of two columns represent North America and Europe*

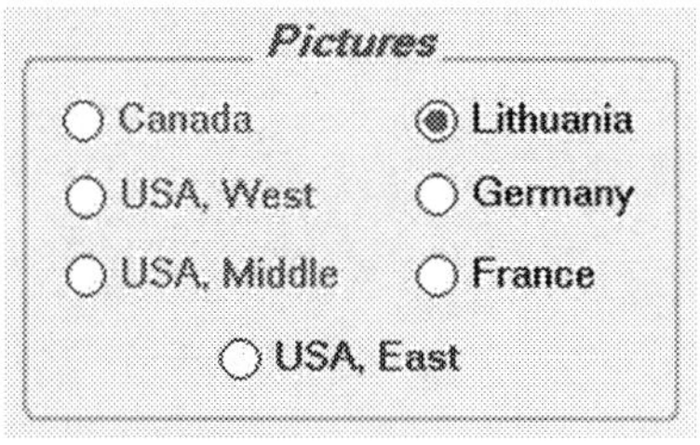

Figure 5-29b. *Buttons of the left column are associated with Nature pictures, while buttons on the right - with buildings*

There are seven buttons in this group. Selecting a button shows the associated picture; this is the thing that I, as a developer, have to provide. This selection must work regardless of any changes that the user would like to do with this group and its buttons. The default positioning of buttons in this group (Figure 5-27) resembles the location of the associated places at the world map. The user can reorganize the group under absolutely different ideas. For example, two columns of buttons from Figure 5-29a are associated with pictures from North America and Europe. In the variant in Figure 5-29b, the left buttons open pictures with nature, while the right buttons show pictures with buildings. One button is placed in the middle, because there are no buildings, but the main element is road.

Even with such simple examples I try to underline one main idea of user-driven applications. The programmer is responsible only for the correct working of an application, so each radio button, when selected, must show the associated photo regardless of any changes of a program view. How a program must look is decided by the user.

Group parameters are regulated in two different ways. Movability and some other general things are regulated via the commands of the context menu, while all visibility parameters can be changed in a special tuning form (Figure 5-29). The Group_RadioButtons class is designed similarly to the Group_ArbitraryElements class, so it is not surprising at all that their tuning forms are designed in a similar way.

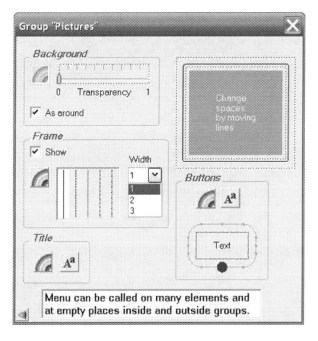

Figure 5-30. *Tuning of Group_RadioButtons*

Conclusion

This chapter discussed the graphical analogs of the most popular controls. Before switching the focus of discussion from elements to the overall design of user-driven applications, let's look at the design of some really complex and often used elements.

CHAPTER 6

Elements of Data Visualization

It is useful to analyze the design of complex objects that have parts involved in different movements and a lot of features that require tuning. Some objects that are used in financial applications can be the best for such discussions.

The movability of the screen objects can be used in programs from many different areas, but there is one general rule: the less the developer can predetermine the future needed view of an application, the bigger the advantages of a switch to a user-driven application. In the next chapter, I'll illustrate this rule by moving from a simple program with only a few possibilities to applications in which the scenario of users' work cannot be predicted at all.

Suppose that an application gets some data that has to be shown in different ways. Data visualization is only a preliminary step for analysis, but depending on the used visualization, it can either hide or perfectly demonstrate some features hidden in the data, so the outcome of this analysis greatly depends on the data view. It depends not only on the view itself but on the coincidence of the data view with the expectations and preferences of a particular user. Because popular applications have a significant number of users, developers cannot provide the best view for each particular user. The main goal of user-driven applications is not to prepare the best view for everyone (this is impossible), but to provide an easy-to-use instrument that allows each user to see the data in the most preferable and advantageous way.

How did scientists analyze data throughout past centuries and up to modern times? Researchers draw graphs on the sheets of paper and then look at these sheets and try to understand the processes behind those graphs. There can be one graph per sheet, or there can be sets of graphs on some sheets. Graphs can vary in sizes; lines may differ in style, color, and type. There can be a lot of data, and the results of analysis often depend on such placement of the sheets that the view of the neighboring graphs can give a

© Sergey Andreyev 2020
S. Andreyev, *User-Driven Applications for Research and Science*, https://doi.org/10.1007/978-1-4842-6488-1_6

hint for further analysis. Nothing new is done when you substitute the sheets of paper with the computer screen. You have the graph areas and the lines, but instead of the simplicity of drawing lines and placing the sheets in an arbitrary but preferable way on your desk, you get a system of commands that you have to learn and a lot of restrictions when you try to see graphs on the screen. Often (nearly always) you are limited in the number of plotting areas that can be seen simultaneously, and you are limited in the positioning of the graphs and in their views. Scientists always have to work inside the bounds that developers of applications decided are ample for researchers' work.

Data visualization is used in many different areas. My work on the movability of the screen objects was ignited by the requirements in the area of scientific and engineering applications. In this wide area, the most popular is a rectangular graphical area with the scales along the sides; the discussion of such graphs is included in the next chapter. Research and analysis in financial and economic areas deal not only with the same standard type of graphs but also with special data views. It was interesting for me to apply movability to some screen objects with which otherwise I would never work. I have no desire to design the movable versions of all different types of plots that are used in the financial area, so I am going to discuss here only two popular elements: bar charts and pie charts. Both of them are discussed in detail in my other book [2], so I want to stress that regardless of all the similarities in the examples from the older and current books, the classes that are used in these examples are different.

Bar Chart

File: Form_BarChart.cs

Menu position: Complex objects ➤ Bar chart

Usually, a bar chart has a rectangular area for plotting and a pair of scales (Figure 6-1).

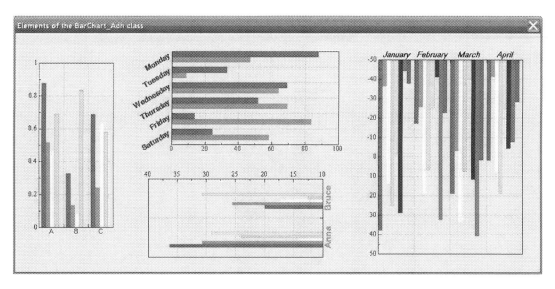

Figure 6-1. *Objects of the BarChart_Adh class with different bar orientations*

The data can be shown in different ways, but the most common is the case with the colored bars. The length of bars can be determined by the data and thus fixed, or the bars can be changeable. In some versions, the bars can be changed by two opposite ends, but the most popular is the case of bars based on one border of the plotting area, while the opposite end of the bars can be moved. The bars are stretched along the scale with numbers; this makes the estimation easier. The orthogonal scale contains a textual explanation for different parts (segments) of the main area. The main plotting area and scales can be associated with comments. Figure 6-2 gives better view of a single BarChart_Adh object. More often than not, the main lines of each scale are placed exactly on the border of the plotting area (Figure 6-1), but for a better view of some details, one scale in Figure 6-2 is moved slightly aside.

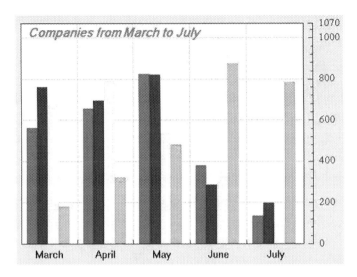

Figure 6-2. *Bar chart with its scales*

In Chapter 3, we discussed an object consisting of a rectangular plotting area with scales. We also discussed the problem of resizing when scales are placed along the borders and they block the corner nodes of the main area; that problem was solved by using an additional invisible element with four circular nodes placed on the corners of the plotting area. The BarChart_Adh class has the same problem, which is solved in the same way by using an additional element of the RectCorners_Adh class.

A bar chart is a complex object that consists of different parts and has a lot of changeable parameters. The scales themselves are also complex objects with a significant number of regulated parameters. The scales with numbers belong to the Scale_Numbers class; scales with text belong to the Scale_Texts class; and comments, regardless of whether they are used with the main plotting area or with one of the scales, belong to the CommentToRect class.

```
public class BarChart_Adh : GraphicalObject
{
    PointF [] ptsCorner;
    RectCorners_Adh rectCorners;
    bool bResizable = true;
    Scale_Texts scaleTexts;
    Scale_Numbers scaleNumbers;
    TextsDrawingDirection dirDrawing;
```

```
Side sideBase;           // side of rectangle at which the unmovable
                         sides of all bars are placed
List<CommentToRect> m_comments = new List<CommentToRect> ();
```

All the parameters of visibility for comments, scales, and main areas are modified with the help of auxiliary tuning forms. As a rule, a more complex object has more regulated parameters, so it needs to have a more complex tuning form with more elements. All those tuning forms are constructed from the graphical analogs of ordinary controls, so you are going to see again and again the same elements that were discussed in the previous chapter. The rules of user-driven applications must be applied at all levels, so all elements inside the tuning forms are also tunable; their tuning forms were also discussed in the previous chapter.

This system of elements that has tuning forms consisting of elements with their own tuning forms sounds like a complicated system that is impossible to understand and remember. In reality, it is simple because everything is based on several simple rules of design.

- Any element is tunable.

- Tuning is never mandatory and always starts only on a user's request.

- All the results of tuning are saved and restored when you start an application the next time or call the tuning form again.

The examples in this chapter are not the real applications (this will be the case for the examples in the next chapter), but these examples are developed like real applications. This means that any parameter of each screen element is under the user's control. The user doesn't need to read and learn the instructions for each new example because they are the same for all of them.

A bar chart is a complex object with a lot of tunable parameters, but moving/resizing bar charts is really simple. The main area is a rectangle that can be moved by any inner point and resized by its borders; its cover is simple and is the same as was discussed with the plot analogs in Chapter 3. Any scale is a nonresizable rectangle, because its size can be changed only indirectly when the main plotting area is resized. A nonresizable rectangular object has the simplest cover consisting of a single rectangular node. In addition, a scale can be moved only orthogonally to its main line. All movements are the same as were discussed with the example of a plot analog. The interesting thing in the current example of bar charts is not the cover design or movement, but the overall design of this example with all the tuning forms and menus.

A menu can be called at any place of this example regardless of whether it is an element or an empty place. If a menu is called on an element, then the first command allows you to call a tuning form for the pressed element. (Menus are shown and discussed later in this section.) Scales with text are simpler in design than scales with numbers, so let's start with the simpler objects.

Figure 6-3 shows a `Scale_Texts` object and its tuning form; such positioning makes the explanation and understanding much easier.

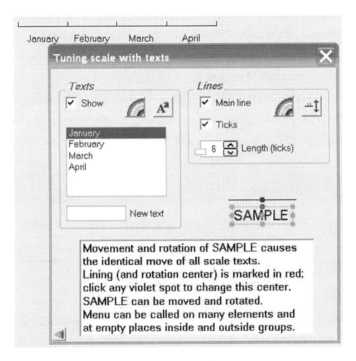

Figure 6-3. *Scale_Texts object with its tuning form*

The scale consists of three parts: main line, ticks on the side of the main line that show the borders of segments, and text associated with segments. The drawing of lines and text is based on absolutely different and unrelated parameters, so their tuning is organized inside two different groups.

The main line, ticks, and text can appear in any combination, and only the disappearance of all of them is prohibited; therefore, the program would not allow you to switch OFF all three check boxes simultaneously. If a scale must be hidden, it is done through the command of its menu.

Tuning in the group Lines. The main line and ticks always have the width of one pixel and are shown in the same color. Ticks can appear on either side of the main line; all ticks have an equal length from the [3, 20] range.

Tuning in the group Texts. Text is shown in the same font and color.

"Sample for texts" is a special element that allows you to line and rotate all text. This object consists of a short line and a SAMPLE word. (Figure 6-3 demonstrates a tuning form for horizontal scale; for vertical scale, you'll see a nearly identical form but with a vertical line for a sample.) Each text of the scale is positioned to the central point of the corresponding segment; in the tuning form, this central point is marked by a blue spot in the middle of a short line. The SAMPLE word represents text. In Chapter 2, in the example about comments, nine special points of any text were explained. The same nine points are marked on the SAMPLE. The point that is currently used for lining and as a center of rotation is shown in red; the other eight points are violet. This pair of elements—line + SAMPLE—can be moved synchronously by moving the short line. While the SAMPLE is moved or rotated, all text along the scale move and rotate in the same way. By clicking one of the special marks on the SAMPLE, you change the lining and rotation center for all the scale texts.

Text along the scale has different lengths, and their lengths differ from the SAMPLE length. While you select another basic point on the SAMPLE, this word doesn't move, and only two small spots exchange colors. At the same moment, the same change of basic points occurs for all text along the scale, but because the text lengths are different and they copy the shift between the basic and anchor points from SAMPLE, then all text along the scale would be moved. The best way to position text along a scale is to move and rotate the SAMPLE word but at the same time watch the position of the text.

Later in the section I'll demonstrate an auxiliary form to prepare a new bar chart. That form provides several variants for the scale text, but real bar charts would probably need other text. In the scale tuning form, you see the list of currently used text and a text box to type the needed text. Select the text you want to change, type the new text, and press Enter.

Figure 6-4 shows a `Scale_Numbers` object with its tuning form, which is significantly more complex than the tuning form for scales with text.

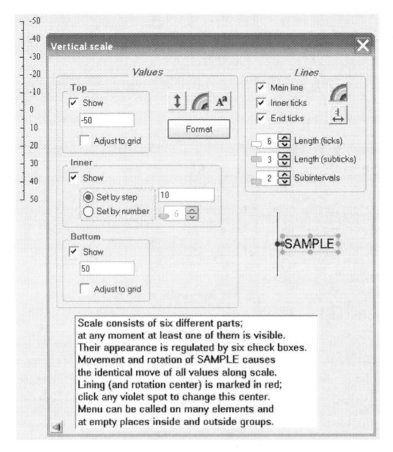

Figure 6-4. *Tuning form for vertical Scale_Numbers object*

The group Lines is more complex here. In addition to the main line, there are ticks and subticks that are shown at one side of the main line. Three different parts—main line, ticks, and subticks—are shown independently, so there are three check boxes to regulate their appearance. The number of subintervals between the neighboring ticks can be changed; the number of subticks is less by one than the number of subintervals. The lengths of ticks and subticks are regulated individually, but of these two, the ticks are always bigger. The main line, ticks, and subticks are always shown in one color, and the width of all lines is always one pixel.

The group Values is mostly responsible for the complexity of this tuning form. For the purpose of drawing (and tuning), all numbers are divided into three groups with two of them representing the border values and the third group for all inner values. The numbers of these three groups are tuned independently; they can appear in any combination or not appear at all; this is regulated by three check boxes.

The number of inner values is determined either by the step between neighboring values or by the required number of inner lines that correspond with the values. In the last case, the program either uses the declared number or slightly increases it to provide a rounder step, which is better for visual estimation. (If you do not like the proposed change of the tick number, you can set the value of the needed step.)

If the value on the border slightly differs from the nearest inner value, then two numbers on the screen can overlap and make their reading difficult. One solution is to switch OFF the showing of the border value. Another solution is to adjust the border value to the grid step; this can be done independently for both end values.

Several buttons inside the Values group allow you to change the font and color of the shown numbers, to swap the end values, and to change the format in which all the numbers are shown.

The menu on bar chart allows you to rotate the pressed object by 90 degrees in one or another direction. Each turn transforms vertical scale into horizontal, and vice versa. Such transformation of the scale with text requires a minimal change of its tuning form in which only the direction of the auxiliary line in the Lines group (see Figure 6-3) has to be changed. The tuning form for the scale with numbers requires more changes because instead of the top and bottom values, now the left and right values must be tuned. Also, it is better to have the default view of the tuning form, which does not confuse users and clearly informs about the direction of the tuned scale. Thus, the tuning form for horizontal scale with numbers has the same set of elements but a different default view (Figure 6-5).

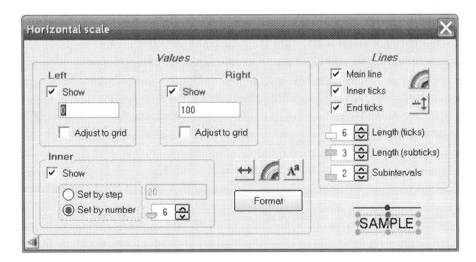

Figure 6-5. *Tuning form for horizontal Scale_Numbers object*

Three check boxes inside the Lines group regulate the appearance of lines; three Show check boxes inside the Values group regulate the appearance of numbers along the scale. Switching of these six check boxes ON/OFF allows you to select exactly those parts that you want to see. The only prohibited combination is all six check boxes in the OFF mode, so the form would not allow you to do it; all other combinations are possible.

Default views of the tuning forms (Figures 6-4 and 6-5) look a bit complicated and occupy a significant part of the valuable screen space, but users are not forced to deal only with the default views of these forms. Suppose that you set the preferable length of ticks and subticks, the preferable number of subintervals, and the needed appearance of numbers along the scale. If you do not need the tuning of these parameters in the nearest future, you can hide a lot of elements of the tuning form and leave in view only the elements you really need. Red ellipses in Figure 6-6 mark the elements that can be hidden through their menus. I want to stress that you are not forced to hide all of them or none; you can hide any combination of the 13 marked elements, but if you hide all of them, then the original tuning form (Figure 6-5) can be reduced to something much smaller (Figure 6-7). This tuning form is designed under the standard rules of user-driven applications. If anything is hidden, it can be unveiled through the menu of the upper level, so elements of the Lines group can be unveiled through the menu of this group. Elements of the Left, Inner, and Right groups can be unveiled through the menu of the appropriate group, while all elements of the Values group can be unveiled through its menu.

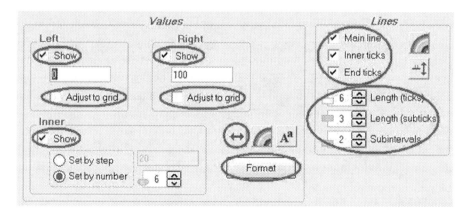

Figure 6-6. *Marked elements can be hidden through their menu commands.*

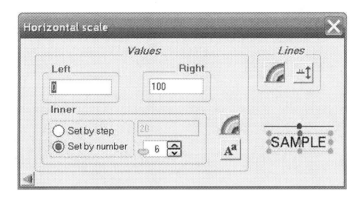

Figure 6-7. *Different view of the same tuning form*

We are done with the tuning of both types of scales, and now we can look at the tuning of the bar chart main area (Figure 6-8). Surprisingly, it might look simpler than the tuning of some scales.

- The frame of the plotting area and grids from both scales are tuned independently but in a similar way. Each of them can be shown or not; if shown, then the line color and style can be selected. Positions of the grid lines are determined by the positions of the ticks on the scales, but the appearance of ticks and grids are independent, and they are regulated in different tuning forms.

- The background is tuned in a standard way as was shown for different groups and controls (Figures 4-2, 5-9, and 5-30).

- The group "Colors and filling" allows you to regulate the filling of the main area with the bars and to select the bar colors. The left and right ends of the horizontal bar inside the group can be moved, and this changes the filling of each segment of the bar chart. As a researcher, I prefer bar charts with some space between segments, so I always move the ends of this horizontal bar from their extreme positions to the center. Whether to move one or both ends, and how much to move, usually depends on the filling of the particular bar chart.

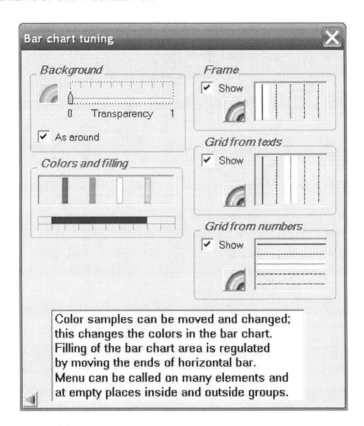

Figure 6-8. *Tuning of the bar chart main area*

Another area inside the group contains the samples of the bar colors. The number of samples cannot be less than the number of sets but can be bigger; colors are used starting from the left end. It is possible to change the order simply by moving the samples inside the area and dropping the caught sample at another location. It is also possible to change the color of any sample (and thus to change the color of the associated bars). For this you call the menu on the sample. The same menu allows you to delete the pressed sample, but only if the number of samples exceeds the number of sets in the bar chart. To add more colors, call the menu at an empty place inside the area of samples. If you want to add more colors without changing the existing order, add new colors by calling the menu to the right of the last sample.

Tuning forms deal with the visibility parameters and thus change an object appearance on the screen; other parameters are changed through the commands of menus. There are menus for each class of the used elements, and there is a menu for empty places (Figure 6-9d). The menu for a plotting area has the most commands

(Figure 6-9a). Scales belong to different classes, but their menus are identical (Figure 6-9b). The simplest element—the comment—has the simplest menu (Figure 6-9c). The menu that can be called on the information area consists of a single command to start the tuning of this area, so I decided not even to show this tiny menu.

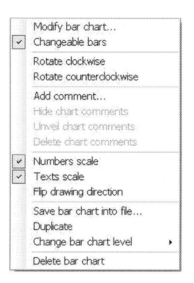

Figure 6-9a. *Menu on plotting area*

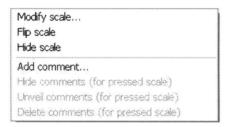

Figure 6-9b. *Menu on scale*

Figure 6-9c. *Menu on comment*

Figure 6-9d. *Menu at empty place*

Some of menu commands that are used in this example might look a bit strange for specialists on economic and financial programs, so there are two reasons for the appearance of these commands. First, I am more familiar with the requirements of scientific applications, and many commands were simply copied from that area. I spent a lot of time while developing the system of classes for scientific/engineering applications. Those classes will be demonstrated in the next chapter, but there are a lot of similarities between the drawing of Y(x) functions and bar charts, so some parameters and related commands were copied from one area to another. Second, I used the current example to check the involved classes and their features.

The menu on comments calls a standard tuning form to modify the pressed comment. The menu also allows you to fix/unfix the pressed comment, to hide it, and to delete it. Each comment can be fixed or unfixed through the command of the same menu, but for fixed comments, the text of the second command will be different. It is impossible to call the menu on a hidden element, so the hidden comment can be unveiled through the menu of its parent, which can be either the scale or the bar chart main area.

The menu on a scale allows you to hide, unveil, and delete comments; all three commands are applied simultaneously to all comments associated with the scale. For a scale with numbers, there is an obvious difference between the numbers and comments; for a scale with text, the difference is not so clear because all of them are shown as text, and the same font and color can be used. The difference is in tuning and moving. Texts are tuned and moved synchronously in the scale tuning form, while comments are modified individually through another tuning form. The same form is used when the command "Add comment" is clicked.

There is an interesting situation with the "Flip scale" command. Imagine a line that is parallel to the main line of the scale and that goes through the central point of the plotting area. The "Flip scale" command has to mirror the scale to the opposite side of this line. It is easily done for the scale line and ticks, but there is a problem with text (and numbers). Remember how you tried to understand some text mirrored in the show window? We are not taught to read such text, and we expect to see normal text when the scale is mirrored, but then some of the parameters must be changed. When the scale is flipped, the original rectangular area of the text is mirrored, and the text is drawn inside the new rectangle in such a way that makes this text readable. For any scale flip, the angle and the basis point of all texts are changed (Figures 6-10 and 6-11). For strictly horizontal text, its angle is not changed, but in any other case, reading from top to bottom (or from bottom to top) is changed on the opposite one.

Figure 6-10. *Flip of vertical scale*

Figure 6-11. *Flip of horizontal scale*

Let's look into the biggest menu of this example—the menu on a bar chart (Figure 6-9a).

Changeable bars	The check mark indicates whether bars can be changed directly or not. A bit later I'll demonstrate an auxiliary form in which new bar charts are organized. In that form, any bar can be changed, and throughout this process the value of the bar is shown, so the setting of the values can be done precisely. In the main form of the current example, the indication of the bar value is not included, though it is easy to add. A bar chart is moved around the screen by any point of the plotting area. There is a possibility that, while pressing inside the main rectangular area, the user would press on the movable end of some bar and would start the unneeded change. To avoid this, the user can switch the bars into the unchangeable mode. This command is applied only to the pressed bar chart. If there is a need to set the same mode for all bar charts, then a similar command must be added to the menu that is called at empty places.
Rotate counterclockwise *Rotate clockwise*	Two commands are used to rotate a bar chart. Figure 6-12 demonstrates the clockwise rotation, though the same figures can be reordered, and then they will illustrate the counterclockwise rotation. The text of the original bar chart (left figure) can be horizontal, vertical, or inclined. Throughout the further steps of rotation, some of the text appears not in the best view for reading, and it is obvious how they have to be changed for a much better view at each step of rotation. Is it possible to include such improvements into the `BarChart_Adh.Rotate()` method? Yes, it is easy to do, but it would be a huge mistake, and I am not going to do it. Rule 3 of user-driven applications states that "Users' commands on moving and resizing … must be implemented exactly as they are; no additions or expanded interpretation by developer are allowed." If you want to demonstrate your skills in improving the bar chart after rotation, you can do so by adding another command like "Rotation with adjustment." Then the user can try both variants, compare the results, and select the one the user prefers. The selection will be only the user's decision, and the control over the application will still be in the user's hands. Don't try to force users into something they didn't request.

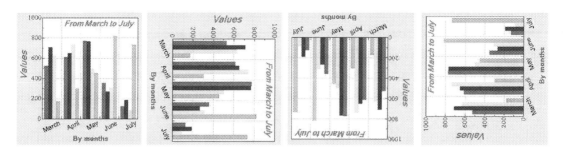

Figure 6-12. *The original bar chart is rotated clockwise step-by-step. The same views, though in a different order, can be obtained with a counterclockwise rotation*

Numbers scale
Texts scale

Two commands regulate the visibility of scales.

Flip drawing direction

Figure 6-13 demonstrates the result of this command, which affects only the main plotting area and the scale with text but in different ways. The bars are mirrored over the central line of the plotting area. Text has to be associated with the same segments, so the positions of the text are mirrored over the same line, but the angle of this text is not changed.

Preparation of this figure gave me a chance to illustrate the use of the previous command by which the scale can be hidden and unveiled. The change of drawing direction does not affect the scale with numbers, so I simply turned OFF its visualization after the flip of drawing direction.

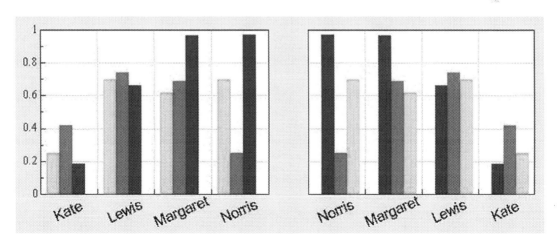

Figure 6-13. *A change of drawing direction affects the scale with text and the appearance of the bars*

Save bar chart into file	This command is used with another one, which can be seen in the menu for empty places. When you deal with lots of plots, there is always a chance that you have more plots than you want to see at any particular moment. You don't want to lose the charts that you'll need at another moment, so there must be some way to delete the charts by saving them in some storage from which they can be returned at any moment. There exist different solutions for this problem of extra storage and temporary eviction from the screen; one of the solutions is demonstrated in the Function Viewer program, which is discussed in the next chapter. In the current example, a simple solution is demonstrated. By using this command, the pressed bar chart can be saved in a binary file. The unneeded bar chart can be deleted with another command of the same menu (Figure 6-9a). Later another menu can be called at any empty place, and the bar chart can be restored from the file with a command of this menu (Figure 6-9d).

The remaining commands of the menu on a bar charts speak for themselves and do not require any explanation. Let's look at some commands from the menu at empty places (Figure 6-9d).

Show moving area dimensions	The user can move and resize the bar charts; throughout such changes, the exact size and location of any area are not important. But as I already mentioned, some commands for this example were simply copied from the scientific applications, so the request for these commands was born there. Scientists often include screen images as illustrations into their articles. To prepare the best view of the needed figures, they would like to have some specified size or proportion of the plotting area or to place several plots of identical size next to each other without any unneeded shift. Some people do not see a tiny shift, while others easily catch even a single pixel shift and are annoyed by it. To make the preparation of figures easier, I added the temporary demonstration of the sizes for a plotting area, which is currently moved or resized (Figure 6-14). This information is not needed throughout the normal use of application, so its appearance is regulated through the menu command.

(continued)

Font for temporary information

This command is an addition to the previous one. Whenever the user wants to change the font for some object, the menu is called on this object, and an appropriate command of the menu allows you to use the standard dialog for font selection. A small area with information about the size and location appears at the moment of the mouse press on a bar chart and disappears when the mouse is released. Thus, it is impossible to press this temporary information to change its font. The command in the menu at empty places allows you to select the font for this temporary information, but the results of the selection can be seen only the next time a bar chart is pressed.

Add bar chart

This command allows you to organize a new bar chart, which is done in an auxiliary Form_NewBarChart.cs (Figure 6-15). This form allows you to set the main valuable parameters: number of sets, number of segments, and values for all bars. The value of any bar can be changed by moving its top; throughout such movement, the current value from the [0, 1] range is shown in a small area next to the moving line. There is a limited selection of text for the scale. Only the standard colors are used with the possibility to select the first one.

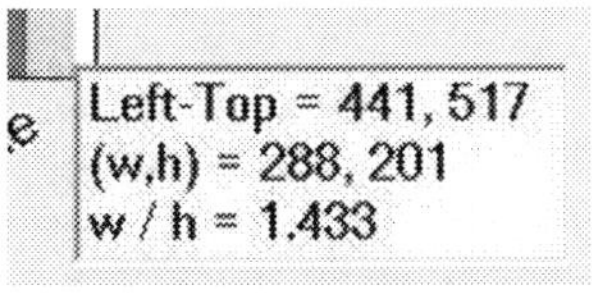

Left-Top = 441, 517
(w,h) = 288, 201
w / h = 1.433

Figure 6-14. *Temporary information about current size and position of the bar chart area*

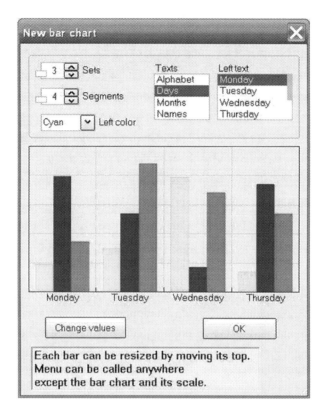

Figure 6-15. *Preparation of the new bar chart*

Is it enough to have not full tuning of a new bar chart? Yes, because it is an auxiliary form in which a sketch of the needed bar chart is prepared. When you click the OK button, a new bar chart appears in the main form, where the new bar chart can be tuned like any other.

For the same reason, the bar chart area and the only visible scale in this auxiliary form are not tunable, while all other elements of this form can be modified.

Pie Chart

File: `Form_PieChart.cs`

Menu position: Complex objects ➤ Pie chart

In Chapter 3, we already discussed circles with two types of comments. One type of comments was associated with a circle as a whole; such comments reacted only to circle resizing and ignored the circle rotation, while the moving of those comments around the screen was not limited in any way. Circles were divided into sectors, and other comments were associated with those sectors. Each comment of that type was placed and could be moved only along the bisector of the associated circle sector. Elements of the PieChart_Adh class that are discussed in the current section have similar design. This limitation on the movement of the sector comment is not mandatory; in my other book [2] I demonstrated the PieChart class in which sector comments could be freely moved around. Pie charts of the current example (Figure 6-16) are similar to the circles with comments that were discussed in Chapter 3, but they have a slightly different behavior for sector comments.

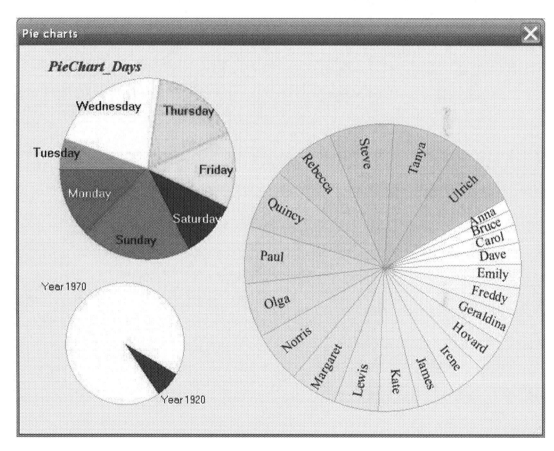

Figure 6-16. *Objects of the PieChart_Adh class*

```
public class PieChart_Adh : GraphicalObject
{
    PointF m_center;
    float m_radius;
    DrawingDirection dirDrawing;
```

```
bool bResizable, bRotatable, bMovablePartitions;
List<Color> m_clrs = new List<Color> ();        // one color per each
                                                            sector
CommentToPieChartSector [] commentsForSectors;
List<CommentToCircle> commentsForCircle = new List<CommentToCircle> ();
```

A pie chart is a complex object that consists of the dominant circular part and subordinate comments of two different types. By default, the main part is resizable, rotatable, and with movable partitions, but all three things are easily regulated through menu commands. Regardless of the type of comment, each one can be rotated around its central point.

- Comments associated with the whole circle are called *general*. These are elements of the `CommentToCircle` class. Any pie chart can be associated with an arbitrary number of general comments. Such a comment moves synchronously when a circle is moved, retains its relative position when a circle is resized, and ignores the circle rotation.

- Comments of the `CommentToPieChartSector` class are associated with sectors; there is one comment of such type for each sector. The central point of such a comment is placed on the bisector of the associated sector, and a comment can be moved only along this line. There is no synchronous move of all sector comments, but they can be placed at the same distance by using a menu command.

Comments of both types are pure strings, so for them only the font, color, and text can be changed. This is done in a tiny auxiliary form that is the same for both types of comments. Visually, comments of the two types are undistinguishable, but they have different sets of commands in their menus.

A general comment can be modified, hidden, or deleted.

A sector comment can be hidden but not deleted, because the number of these comments is always equal to the number of sectors. This type of comment can be shown in many different ways.

A pie chart is associated with some value that is distributed via the sectors, so each sector is associated with some smaller value and with the percent of the sum. A comment on the sector can include a combination of pure text, value, and percent; there are variants to show them in one or two lines. All variants are shown in Figure 6-17 starting at the yellow sector with comment January and going counterclockwise.

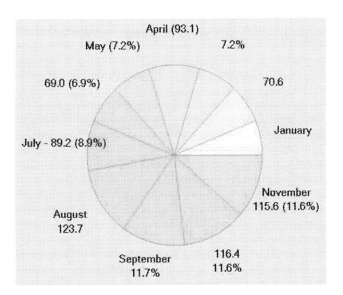

Figure 6-17. *Different views of sector comments*

Though the number of general comments is not limited, I doubt that there would be more than one comment of this type. On the other hand, the number of sector comments is at least two (minimum number of sectors) but can be big enough. Each comment can be modified individually, but there is a possibility that the user would like to spread some parameters of some sector comment to all its siblings; this is done through the menu.

General comments and sector comments look similar; all of them can be moved and rotated, but to organize all these movements correctly, only one of their classes has to be mentioned in the OnMouseDown() method. Why? General comments belong to the CommentToCircle class, which is derived from the TextRotatable class. The mover knows how to move and rotate elements of this class without any instruction. On the other hand, sector comments belong to the CommentToPieChartSector class, which is not derived from the TextRotatable class, so the CommentToPieChartSector.Press() method must be called.

```
private void OnMouseDown (object sender, MouseEventArgs e)
{
    ptMouse_Down = e .Location;
    if (mover .Catch (e .Location, e .Button))
    {
```

```
GraphicalObject grobj = mover .CaughtSource;
... ...
else if (grobj is CommentToPieChartSector)
{
    sectorcmntPressed = grobj as CommentToPieChartSector;
    sectorcmntPressed .Press (e .Location, e .Button, iNode);
}
... ...
```

Figure 6-18 shows a tuning form for the PieChart_Adh objects. The colors can be changed individually or all together. For individual changes, you have to call the menu on a particular color sample and then use the standard dialog. You can also change the order of colors by moving any sample to another location. Samples can be moved only inside the framed rectangular area, but the area itself is resizable, so it can be easily enlarged if you have to deal with a lot of colors like in the case of the biggest pie chart in Figure 6-16. The number of samples can be bigger than the number of sectors, but the colors to be used are always taken starting from the left side.

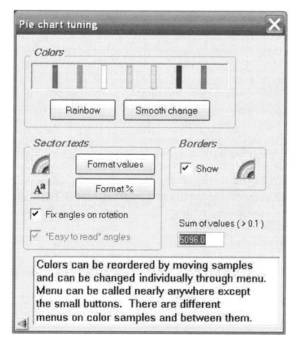

Figure 6-18. *Tuning form for pie charts*

Two buttons inside the group Colors allow you to change all colors simultaneously. One button sets the rainbow order of colors; if more than seven colors are needed, then they are repeated. Another button sets the smooth change of colors from the left sample to the right one.

The "Sector texts" group deals simultaneously with all sector comments. Different formats can be selected for values and percentages, which are shown in comments. Two check boxes allow you to play with the angles of sector comments.

When a new pie chart is organized, all its sector comments are horizontal (Figure 6-19a) and are positioned at the same distance from the circle center. Each comment can be moved and rotated individually (Figure 6-19b). By default, the angles of sector comments are fixed throughout the circle rotation; the "Fix angles on rotation" check box in Figure 6-18 demonstrates a check mark, and this automatically disables another check box. With the angles of comments fixed throughout the rotation, each comment retains its angle regardless of the sector position (Figure 6-19c). Thus, the change in Figures 6-19b–6-19c is the result of rotation when the angles of the sector comments are fixed.

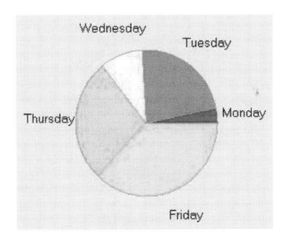

Figure 6-19a. *By default a new pie chart has all horizontal sector comments*

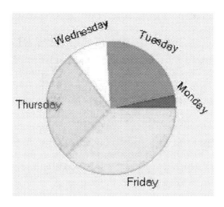

Figure 6-19b. *Comments are moved and rotated*

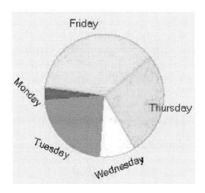

Figure 6-19c. *The pie chart is rotated*

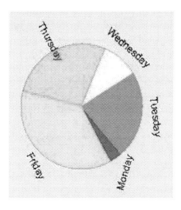

Figure 6-19d. *The angle of each comment changes synchronously with the pie chart angle*

Now rotate the pie chart back to the situation in Figure 6-19b, open the tuning form, and switch OFF the fixing of angles on rotation. The second check box becomes enabled, but it is still checked. Now rotate the pie chart to the view shown in Figure 6-19d. When the comment angle is not fixed on rotation, it is changed in the same way as the pie chart angle, so *Thursday* is shown along the bisector and *Wednesday* is orthogonal to the bisector line. An interesting thing happened to *Monday*. In Figure 6-19b, the angles for *Tuesday* and *Monday* are nearly the same, and in Figure 6-19d these two comments look like they are in nearly opposite directions. This happens because the second check box in the tuning form has a mark, and this does not allow any comment to appear upside down. Take this mark out, and comments will appear upside down whenever the circle rotation will turn them this way. The change in Figures 6-19b–6-19d is the result of rotation when the angles of sector comments are not fixed.

The biggest pie chart in Figure 6-16 shows one more way in which the angles of sector comments can be changed. Such a view can be obtained by using the command "Sector comments looking to center" from the menu on a pie chart.

Some commands to regulate the comment angle can be used together, while others cannot. For example, the "Sector comments looking to center" command allows you to use any mode of the "Easy to read" angles check box, but the same command automatically switches OFF the fixing of angles on rotation.

New pie charts are organized through an auxiliary form (Figure 6-20). This form allows you to set some parameters, but the main tuning is done in the main form when the new pie chart appears there.

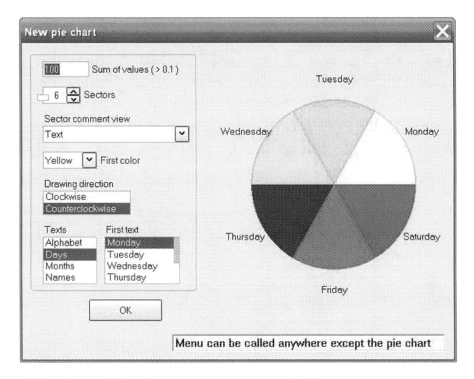

Figure 6-20. *An auxiliary form to prepare new pie charts*

Conclusion

This chapter deals with only two well known complex objects but demonstrates with them the standard way to deal with complex objects in all the user-driven applications.

All parameters require tuning, so there must be a system of menus associated with different parts of the complex object. Each class of complex objects needs a special form in which user can organize new elements. Some limited level of tuning can be used for this preparation because when a new object is organized, the full tuning can be applied to it at any place where it is used.

CHAPTER 7

Examples

User-driven applications can be constructed only on the basis of total movability, so the previous chapters were mostly about the design of absolutely different movable objects. Step-by-step we moved from simple objects of the most often used shapes (rectangle, circle, polygon, ring, and so on) to complex objects and groups that can include any type of objects. I think that examples from the previous chapters demonstrated well enough how absolutely different objects can be turned into movable ones and how they can be used in applications of the new type. Nearly all of the previous examples were developed in such a way as to demonstrate the most important features of the proposed algorithm and their implementation.

This chapter is not about some aspects of movability that were not discussed yet. This chapter is about the overall design of real user-driven applications with well-known purposes. The following examples were developed as stand-alone applications, and only later I included them as parts of the program accompanying this book.

Calculator

I use the standard Windows Calculator only on those rare occasions when I need to divide two big numbers and I'm too lazy to do it with a pen on a sheet of paper. Maybe it is a result of my rare use of this program, but each time when I have to use it, I have a problem finding the needed buttons with the correct numbers because they are definitely not where I would put them as a designer. I was taught years ago (and still continue) to read and write from left to right and from top to bottom, so considering the fact that the order of digits from zero to nine didn't change throughout the centuries and the Calculator designers were taught by the same rules, it is just a puzzle to me why the same digits in the Windows Calculator start at the bottom and go up the screen (Figure 7-1a). There had to be some great idea behind such placement, but I cannot

© Sergey Andreyev 2020
S. Andreyev, *User-Driven Applications for Research and Science*, https://doi.org/10.1007/978-1-4842-6488-1_7

understand it. On each occasion when I use this program, I spend some extra time searching for the needed keys. Eventually I find them, get the needed result, and forget about this search until the next time.

Years ago, after I included ordinary controls into my algorithm of movability, I was thinking about some good example to demonstrate this part of an algorithm. Then I thought about the Calculator program that was a perfect candidate for demonstration because it was entirely designed with controls, and everyone was familiar with this program. My first version of Calculator had limited functionality but re-created the view of the original program and perfectly demonstrated the movability of all elements (Figure 7-1).

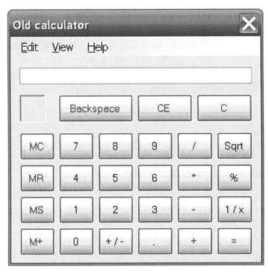

Figure 7-1a. *Default view of the original Calculator program*

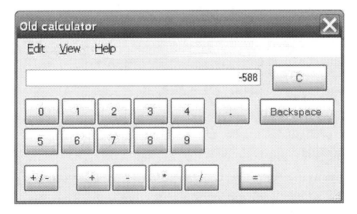

Figure 7-1b. *Movability allows each user to organize the preferable view*

I had no intention of doing anything else with the Calculator, but several years later during a conversation with one of my colleagues I heard a complaint: having poor vision, this colleague had big trouble with the standard Calculator program because even the combined efforts of several specialists did not reveal any way to increase the font used by this application. So, I sat down and developed another Calculator that the colleague could use. As it was not for me, the program had to work as a normal Calculator with operations and functions. Certainly, changing the font was not the only thing that I allowed users to do in this program; it was designed according to all the rules of user-driven applications.

The second version of my Calculator had the same view as shown in Figure 7-2; only the text of the short information was slightly different because the second version of my Calculator was still designed with ordinary controls. Several more years have passed, and in the next version of Calculator, no ordinary controls were left. This program is shown in Figure 7-2, and this is the program that I want to discuss now.

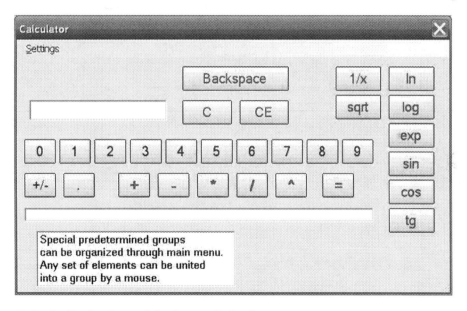

Figure 7-2. *Default view of the latest Calculator*

File: Form_Calculator.cs

Menu position: Applications ➤ Calculator

I had no intention of designing a program that could compete with the Windows analog. The new Calculator had to be used by a particular person; this person never used the memory operations of the original program, so there are no buttons for memory operations in my program.

One remark before further explanation: in the following text, the expression *all elements* means all elements except the one with information.

All but two elements of the new application are buttons of the Button_Text class. These buttons are divided into four groups; in Figure 7-2 they are easily distinguished by different text colors.

- Buttons with digits have their texts shown in blue. From the point of view of mathematics, the dot and sign are definitely not numbers, but they are used as parts of notation while writing numbers, so in this program these two buttons are included in the group of *numbers*.

```
Button_Text btn_0, btn_1, btn_2, btn_3, btn_4, btn_5, btn_6, btn_7,
btn_8, btn_9, btnSign, btnDot;                        // Numbers
```

- Buttons with operations are shown in red.

```
Button_Text btnPlus, btnMinus, btnMultiply, btnDivide, btnDegree,
btnEqual;
```

- Buttons for *functions* have their text shown in violet. I could easily add more functions, but the person for whom I designed this program said that this set of functions would be enough. You can add more functions into this program, but carefully check the code and make changes in all the places where this group is used.

```
Button_Text btnLn, btnLog, btnExp, btnSin, btnCos,
            btnTg, btnInverse, btnSqrt;
```

- Three buttons with the green text are united into a group of *cleaners* because they are used to delete some or all of the prepared data.

```
Button_Text btnBackspace, btnClearAll, btnClearEdit;
```

For the purpose of better showing the results, there are two auxiliary areas; one of them is used to show the current number, and the other shows the whole expression.

```
Label_GR labelValue, labelExpression;
```

Calculator is designed to fulfill its main purpose, but this is a user-driven application with all the possibilities of moving, resizing, tuning, saving, and restoring. Let's start with moving.

Moving can be applied to individual objects, to elements of three predetermined groups (numbers, operations, and functions), and to the temporary group of elements. An individual move of an element is organized in a standard way: press it with the left button and move it to another location.

Groups of numbers, operations, or functions (Figure 7-3) can be organized via the menu commands; I will write about menus a bit later. Thus, the organized "standard" group includes only the elements of that predefined set and nothing else, even if some other objects happen to be inside the frame when the group is called. Thus, the Functions group always includes exactly eight buttons with the names of the functions; the two other elements inside the frame in Figure 7-3 (one with the digit and another with the equal sign) do not belong to this group.

Figure 7-3. *Functions group includes eight buttons*

A temporary group can include an arbitrary set of elements. Press the left button at any empty place and move the mouse cursor without releasing the button. Throughout such movement, you will see the rectangular frame; two opposite corners of this rectangle are the initial press point and the current mouse position. If at the moment of the mouse release there is more than one object inside this rectangle, then a temporary group of these rounded objects is organized. For example, the temporary group in Figure 7-4 includes eight buttons from the Numbers group, three buttons from the Operations group, one button from the Cleaners group, and one label.

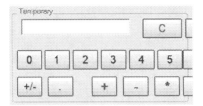

Figure 7-4. *Temporary group*

Any group, regardless of whether it is a predefined one or a temporary one, belongs to the Group_ArbitraryElements class, so it can be moved by any inner point. The frame adjusts its size and position to any changes of inner elements. I would say that any group organized in Calculator serves like a temporary one and is used only for the purpose of moving some set of elements; that is why there is no command to modify a group.

Without an information area, there are 31 elements in the Form_Calculator.cs file (Figure 7-2). These 31 objects are divided between two Lists. The names of these Lists make it obvious that one of them includes all elements of the currently existing group; the remaining elements go into another List.

```
List<CalcElem> elemsInGroup = new List<CalcElem> ();
List<CalcElem> elemsSingle = new List<CalcElem> ();
```

The distribution of elements between two Lists is done either at the moment of calling an appropriate command from the Settings menu (Figure 7-5) or when a mouse is released with a drawn rectangle in the view. In both cases, the SetGroup() method is called but with different parameters.

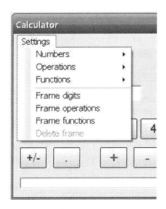

Figure 7-5. *The Settings menu*

When a menu command is called and one of the predefined groups is ordered to be marked, then the SetGroup() method gets as a parameter the particular type of elements to be framed. As a preliminary step, all elements are included into the elemsSingle in a predetermined order while the elemsInGroup is cleared.

```
private void ElemsDefaultOrder ()
{
    elemsSingle .Clear ();
    elemsSingle .Add (new CalcElem (labelValue));
    elemsSingle .Add (
                new CalcElem (labelExpression));
    ... ...
    elemsInGroup .Clear ();
}
```

Now all elements of the specified type are moved from the elemsSingle into the elemsInGroup.

```
private void SetGroup (CalcElemType elem_type)
{
    ElemsDefaultOrder ();
    for (int i = elemsSingle .Count - 1; i >= 0; i--)
    {
        if (elemsSingle [i] .ElemType == elem_type)
        {
            elemsInGroup .Insert (0, elemsSingle [i]);
            elemsSingle .RemoveAt (i);
        }
    }
    ... ...
```

When a rectangle is painted by a mouse and then the mouse is released, another version of the SetGroup() method is called. In this case, the rectangle is used as a parameter.

```
private void OnMouseUp (object sender, MouseEventArgs e)
{
    ptMouse_Up = e .Location;
    double fDist = Auxi_Geometry .Distance (ptMouse_Down, ptMouse_Up);
    int iObj, iNode;
    if (mover .Release (out iObj, out iNode))
    {
        ... ...
    }
    else
    {
        if (e .Button == MouseButtons .Left)
        {
            if (bRectInView)
            {
                SetGroup (new Rectangle (Math .Min (ptMouse_Down .X, e .X),
                                         Math .Min (ptMouse_Down .Y, e .Y),
                                         Math .Abs (e .X - ptMouse_Down .X),
                                         Math .Abs (e .Y - ptMouse_Down .Y)));
                bRectInView = false;
            }
        }
        ... ...
```

All elements are checked for being inside this rectangle; everyone found inside is included into the elemsInGroup.

```
private void SetGroup (RectangleF rc)
{
    elemsInGroup .Clear ();
    group = null;
    ElemsDefaultOrder ();
```

```
    if (MoreThanOneInside (rc))
    {
        for (int i = elemsSingle .Count - 1; i >= 0; i--)
        {
            if (rc .Contains (elemsSingle [i] .RectAround))
            {
                elemsInGroup .Insert (0, elemsSingle [i]);
                elemsSingle .RemoveAt (i);
            }
        }
        ... ...
```

If at the end there is more than one element in the elemsInGroup, those elements constitute a group.

```
    private void SetGroup (CalcElemType elem_type)
    {
        ... ...
        RectangleF rcElems = ElemsArea_group ();
        PointF ptLT =
                new PointF (rcElems .Left - GroupParameters
                                .DefaultFrameSpaces [0],
                            rcElems .Top - GroupParameters
                                .DefaultFrameSpaces [1]);
        group = new Group_ArbitraryElements (this, mover, ptLT, grparams,
                                                strTitle,
                                                ElemsArea_group, DrawElems_
                                                group,
                                                SynchroMove_group, IntoMover_
                                                group);
        GroupMovability ();
    }
```

A group can be eliminated by using the "Delete frame" command (Figure 7-5), but the condition of having more than one element in a group shows one more way to do it. Simply draw a new rectangle that contains no elements or a single element. In each of these situations, no group will be organized, but if some group is shown at this moment, then it will disappear. Even the drawing of a rectangle is not needed; it is enough to click with the left button at any empty spot.

There is one more way to rearrange the positions of elements, but this method works only with the three predefined groups. The submenu in Figure 7-6 shows three commands that can be applied to the Numbers group; identical submenus are opened when the menu Operations or Functions is selected.

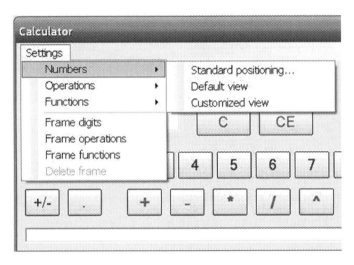

Figure 7-6.   *The Standard positioning menu command opens an auxiliary form that allows you to select some standard positioning of elements for the predefined group*

The Settings ➤ Numbers ➤ Standard positioning command opens the Form_ BtnPlaces_Numbers.cs file (Figure 7-7a); this form allows you to select among the standard positioning of elements for the Numbers group. The groups Functions and Operations have similar forms to select among their standard views, but these groups have fewer elements and fewer combinations to select from (Figures 7-7b and 7-7c).

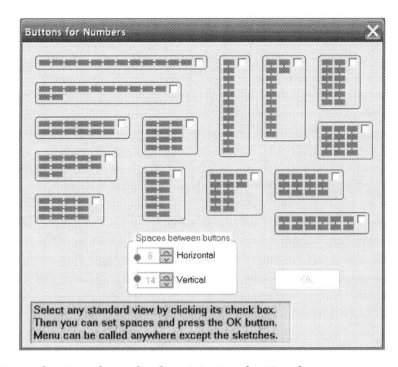

Figure 7-7a. *Selection of standard positioning for Numbers group*

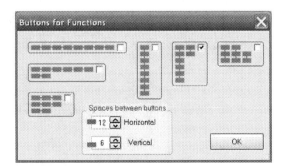

Figure 7-7b. *Selection of standard positioning for Functions group*

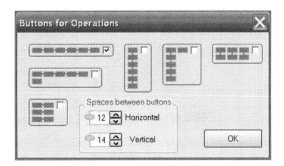

Figure 7-7c. *Selection of standard positioning for Operations group*

Each variant of the standard positioning is shown as a sketch with an additional check box to select this variant. Each sketch consists of a set of rectangles representing the real controls. These tiny rectangles are linked by the lines that show the order of elements in the group. Otherwise, it would be impossible to distinguish similar variants in which elements can be positioned either by rows or by columns. When the `Form_BtnPlaces_Numbers.cs` file is closed by clicking the OK button, the buttons of the Numbers group in Calculator are lined according to the selected variant. It does not matter whether the Numbers group has or does not have the frame at this moment; the standard positioning works regardless.

Each auxiliary form for selecting the standard positioning has a small group containing two `NumericUpDown_GR` elements; in Figure 7-7 these groups are shown in different colors. A change of values inside these elements has no effect on the sketches view, so when these values are changed, then there is no reaction inside the auxiliary form. But if any standard positioning is selected and the OK button is pressed, then elements of the group in Calculator are placed according to the selected case, and the distances between elements are determined by those two values. Let's continue with the Calculator, but after that, I will return to the discussion of sketches in Figure 7-7.

Any element in Calculator can be resized individually. Now suppose that you want to change the size of buttons in the Numbers group; you experiment with one button and set the right size. What are you going to do next? Do you want to keep the button different from other buttons of the group or to change the size of the other 11 buttons in the Numbers group in the same way? Are you going to do it manually one by one? Some people may like to organize the steadily growing size of the buttons according to the increase of the numbers on them or organize other extraordinary views (nothing is prohibited in user-driven applications!), but I have a feeling that the majority of users would prefer to set the same size for all buttons of a group. I also think that the manual standardizing of buttons in a big group one after another is not going to be a popular operation.

Certainly, there is a better way: an element can be used as a sample for all its siblings. The variations are only in choosing the parameters for spreading and also in deciding on which group of buttons to spread the selected parameter.

Figure 7-8 shows the menu that can be called on any button of the Numbers group. The first command calls an auxiliary form for tuning such buttons (see Figure 5-5); the submenu of the second command allows you to spread parameters on the other buttons of the group; the last command allows you to set the same size for the buttons of the two groups. The buttons of the Numbers and Operations groups initially have the same size; the last command allows you to keep this equality in sizes.

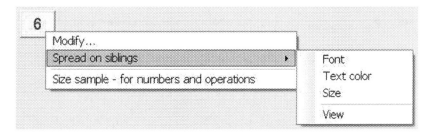

***Figure 7-8.** Menu on buttons of the Numbers group*

Nearly identical menus can be called for the buttons of the Operations and Functions groups. A similar but smaller menu can be called on buttons of the Cleaners group.

Usually applications are built on elements of different classes, and the selection of the appropriate menu is done by analyzing the class of the clicked element. In this Calculator, selecting an element by the class is not enough as the majority of elements belong to the same Button_Text class, so an additional ID checking is used.

```
private void OnMouseUp (object sender, MouseEventArgs e)
{
    ptMouse_Up = e .Location;
    double fDist = Auxi_Geometry .Distance (ptMouse_Down, ptMouse_Up);
    int iObj, iNode;
    if (mover .Release (out iObj, out iNode))
    {
        GraphicalObject grobj = mover .ReleasedSource;
        long id = grobj .ID;
        if (e .Button == MouseButtons .Left)
        {
            ... ...
        }
        else if (e .Button == MouseButtons .Right && fDist <= 3)
        {
            if (grobj is Button_Text)
            {
                if (id == btn_0 .ID || id == btn_1 .ID || id == btn_2 .ID ||
                    id == btn_3 .ID || id == btn_4 .ID || id == btn_5 .ID ||
                    id == btn_6 .ID || id == btn_7 .ID || id == btn_8 .ID ||
```

```
                    id == btn_9 .ID || id == btnSign .ID || id ==
                    btnDot .ID)
                {
                    ContextMenuStrip = menuOnNumbers;
                }
                else if (id == btnPlus .ID || id == btnMinus .ID ||
                        id == btnMultiply .ID || id == btnDivide .ID ||
                        id == btnDegree .ID || id == btnEqual .ID)
                {
                    ContextMenuStrip = menuOnOperations;
                }
                else if (id == btnLn .ID || id == btnLog .ID ||
                        id == btnExp .ID || id == btnSin .ID ||
                        id == btnCos .ID || id == btnTg .ID ||
                        id == btnInverse .ID || id == btnSqrt .ID)
                {
                    ContextMenuStrip = menuOnFunctions;
                }
                else
                {
                    ContextMenuStrip = menuOnCleaners;
                }
            }
        ... ...
```

Total movability is the feature that changes our work with applications, but this movability, as any other feature, is also under users' control. Suppose that after moving and resizing of objects you have organized a view of the Calculator that you like and you do not want to damage this view by an accidental move of any element. You can preserve the view by setting the elements to be unmovable. In Calculator, the movability is changed synchronously for all the elements via the menu at empty places.

```
private void Click_miFixUnfixAll (object sender, EventArgs e)
{
    bMovable = !bMovable;
    Resizing resize = bMovable ? Resizing .Any : Resizing .None;
```

```
    for (int i = 0; i < elemsSingle .Count; i++)
    {
        elemsSingle [i] .Movable = bMovable;
        elemsSingle [i] .Resizing = resize;
    }
    if (group != null)
    {
        GroupMovability ();
    }
    info .Movable = bMovable;
    info .Resizing = resize;
    RenewMover ();
}
```

The same movability is declared for inner elements of the group, for the group itself, and for the group title.

```
private void GroupMovability ()
{
    Resizing resize = bMovable ? Resizing .Any : Resizing .None;
    for (int i = 0; i < elemsInGroup .Count; i++)
    {
        elemsInGroup [i] .Movable = bMovable;
        elemsInGroup [i] .Resizing = resize;
    }
    group .Movable = bMovable;
    group .TitleMovable = bMovable;
}
```

Now let's return to the discussion of sketches, which are used in three auxiliary forms (Figure 7-7). All elements inside these forms are movable, so you can rearrange their views by positioning those sketches in any way you want. Don't be afraid to do anything: the default view of the form can be reinstalled at any moment through the menu at empty places.

Whenever you develop user-driven applications, you have to design from time to time movable objects with some interesting and nonstandard features because the requirements are nonstandard. I think it is the most interesting in programming when you have to think about something nontrivial.

Sketches in those three forms belong to the `ButtonsSketch` class. A sketch is a graphical object with the majority of its fields representing its geometry.

```
public class ButtonsSketch :
GraphicalObject
  {
    bool bSelected;                    // indicator of the sketch selection
    Rectangle m_rc;                    // the whole area of an object
    Rectangle rcSelect;                // the rectangle of a fictional check box
    Point [] ptBtn;                    // positions of all the "buttons" on the sketch
    int w = 16;                        // sizes for the "buttons"
    int h = 8;
    int spaceInside = 4;               // spaces between "buttons"
    int spaceOnBorders = 6;            // spaces on the sides
    int sideSelectSquare = 14;
```

Sketches in each auxiliary form demonstrate variants of positioning buttons for a particular group. Each standard group has its fixed number of buttons, so all the sketches in one auxiliary form demonstrate variants of positioning for the same number of buttons; let's call this number N. Figure 7-9 shows some variants for N = 12.

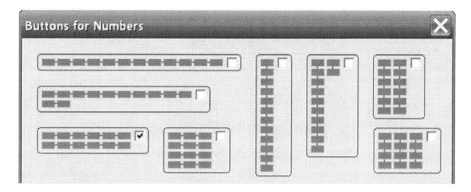

Figure 7-9. *Several sketches for the case of N = 12*

- Each button is represented by a small dark rectangle; its size is 16*8 pixels (w*h).

- The distances between the neighboring small rectangles of the sketch are always the same and equal to 4 pixels (spaceInside).

- A sketch has a rounded frame; the distance between this frame and the inner elements is 6 pixels (spaceOnBorders).

- To select the needed positioning of the group buttons, the needed sketch must be marked; this is done with the help of a small check box inside the frame. This special check box occupies a rectangle with a side of 14 pixels (sideSelectSquare).

- The positioning of N buttons by rows and columns can be done in many different ways, but there are two boundary variants: all buttons in one row and all buttons in one column. To describe the position of the "buttons" on a sketch, I use a matrix of N*N size. The numbering of positions starts with 0 in the top-left corner and goes to the right along the upper row; then it goes down row by row; in each row the numbering starts on the left position and increases to the right. Thus, the left position in the second row has the number N; the position in the bottom-right corner of the matrix has the biggest possible number of N*N-1. All sketches in Figure 7-9 are designed for the case of N = 12. An array of positions is one of the parameters for the initialization of a sketch. Next you can see the code for initializing the checked sketch in the bottom-left corner of Figure 7-9.

```
ButtonsSketch sketch_2rows = new ButtonsSketch (nCode, false,
                    new Point (rect .Left, rect .Bottom + 20),
                    new int [] { 0, 1, 2, 3, 4, 5, 12, 13, 14, 15, 16, 17 },
                    brushBtns);
```

- Sketches may have the same number of rows and columns but differ by the order of elements. For example, two sketches in Figure 7-9 have four rows and three columns each; however, in the left sample the elements have to be positioned along the rows, while in another one they have to be positioned along the columns. To distinguish between such cases visually, the consecutive elements of the sketch inside the row or column are connected by the lines.

```
public void Draw (Graphics grfx)
{
    Pen penConnect = new Pen (brushBtns .Color, 2);
    Auxi_Drawing .CurvedFrame (grfx, m_rc, penFrame);
    for (int i = 0; i < ptBtn .Length; i++)
    {
        grfx .FillRectangle (brushBtns, ptBtn [i] .X, ptBtn [i] .Y, w, h);
        grfx .DrawRectangle (Pens .DarkGray, ptBtn [i] .X, ptBtn [i]
        .Y, w, h);
        if (i > 0)
        {
            if (ptBtn[i].X == ptBtn [i - 1].X || ptBtn[i].Y == ptBtn
            [i - 1].Y)
            {
                grfx .DrawLine (penConnect,
                        ptBtn [i] .X + w / 2, ptBtn [i] .Y + h / 2,
                        ptBtn [i - 1] .X + w / 2, ptBtn [i - 1] .
                        Y + h / 2);
            }
        }
    }
    ControlPaint .DrawCheckBox (grfx, rcSelect,
                    bSelected ? ButtonState .Checked : ButtonState
                    .Normal);
}
```

A sketch is movable by any inner point with the exception of the check box area, so the ButtonsSketch cover consists of two rectangular nodes. As usual, the smaller node that covers the rectangle for the check mark (rcSelect) must precede the bigger one that is responsible for moving the whole object.

```
public override void DefineCover ()
{
    CoverNode [] nodes = new CoverNode [] {
                            new CoverNode (0, rcSelect, Cursors .Hand),
                            new CoverNode (1, m_rc, Cursors .SizeAll) };
    cover = new Cover (nodes);
}
```

The sketch moving is done only if the bigger node (with number 1) is pressed.

```
public override bool MoveNode (...)
{
    bool bRet = false;
    if (catcher == MouseButtons .Left)
    {
        if (i == 1)
        {
            Move (dx, dy);
            bRet = true;
        }
    }
    return (bRet);
}
```

Sketches are movable but nonresizable. When a sketch is moved, the values of all the basic points are changed synchronously.

```
public override void Move (int dx, int dy)
{
    m_rc .X += dx;
    m_rc .Y += dy;
    for (int i = 0; i < ptBtn .Length; i++)
    {
```

321

```
            ptBtn [i] .X += dx;
            ptBtn [i] .Y += dy;
        }
        rcSelect .X += dx;
        rcSelect .Y += dy;
    }
```

These are all interesting things that can be found inside the ButtonsSketch class.
One more important thing related to the class is mentioned in the form where sketches
are used, for example, in Form_BtnPlaces_Numbers.cs. The selection of the needed
sketch is done by clicking inside the special area that is shown as a check box; this small
square is covered by node zero of the ButtonsSketch class. Only one sketch in a form
can be marked at any time, so the selection through the set of radio buttons would be
more correct, but because the same selection with small squares is used in the older
example, I decided not to change the view.

```
private void OnMouseUp (object sender, MouseEventArgs e)
{
    ptMouse_Up = e .Location;
    double fDist = Auxi_Geometry .Distance (ptMouse_Down, ptMouse_Up);
    int iObject, iNode;
    if (mover .Release (out iObject, out iNode))
    {
        GraphicalObject grobj = mover .ReleasedSource;
        if (e .Button == MouseButtons .Left)
        {
            if (grobj is ButtonsSketch && iNode == 0)
            {
                ButtonsSketch sketch = grobj as ButtonsSketch;
                for (int i = 0; i < sketches .Count; i++)
                {
                    sketches [i] .Selected = false;
                }
                sketch .Selected = true;
```

```
        viewSelected = (Calculator_FunctionsGroupView) (sketch
        .Code);
        places = sketch .Places;
        numericHor .Enabled = true;
        numericVer .Enabled = true;
        btnOK .Enabled = true;
        Invalidate ();
    }
... ...
```

Years ago, I designed the first version of Calculator to demonstrate how a program based entirely on ordinary controls could be transformed into a user-driven application. Now we have a similar-looking application with the same functionality but designed only with graphical elements. Certainly, as a user-driven application this variant is much better, but...do I have to find another demonstration program with ordinary controls?

Family Tree

The main example in this section is a real application that I use myself. Since the moment when I first wrote about this example in an article at the beginning of 2013, it attracted the attention of programmers all around the world. There are several other areas (electric circuits is one of them) in which the design is similar to the design of family trees, so specialists from those areas were also interested in the current example.

Before we come to the final program in this section—the real Family Tree application—there is a whole set of simple examples that demonstrate the development step-by-step. While writing code for this application, I thought again about the members of the Hogben family who could construct some extremely sophisticated devices from primitive elements.[1] In this Family Tree application, I use only straight lines, rectangles, and the simplest comments. At the end of this section, you will see what can be developed on such a primitive basis.

---

[1]Members of the Hogben family could, among other things, construct an ultrasonic device on the basis of an old battery and several wires. See *Exit the Professor* by Henry Kuttner and C.L. Moore.

The Family Tree program is a standard user-driven application in which everything can be modified by users, and all these changes are saved and restored. There is the possibility that some elements of the preliminary examples are not saved and restored, but this is done only because I want the auxiliary examples always to have the best view for my explanations.

It is easy to take a sheet of paper and start drawing your own family tree. Years ago, I did it under the supervision of my grandmother, and I still keep those old sheets of paper. A lot of people in many families are doing the same thing at one moment or another, and nearly everyone has an idea of how such a family tree must look. Family trees can be found in many books on history, and those professionally prepared trees differ from the simple drawings in pen or pencil only by some tiny details. Any sketch of a family tree looks like Figure 7-10. However, this particular sketch shows a small and simple family tree representing three generations. To simplify the sketch and discussion, I took out the information about the birth and death of each person though it is usually shown; you will see this in later examples.

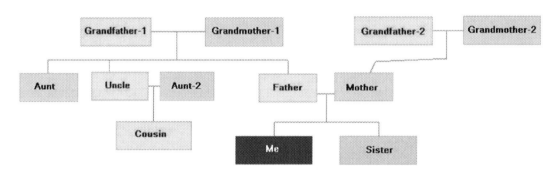

Figure 7-10. *An example of a family tree for three generations*

Even a simple sketch (Figure 7-10) can say a lot about the rules to be implemented in the Family Tree application. Each person is represented by a small rectangle, and a lot of information is shown by the set of connections between the rectangles. Usually, a couple is shown as a pair of rectangles placed close to each other with a short straight line (*bus*) between them. If a couple has children, then there is another bus going down from that intermediate line (Figure 7-11), but the view of the next generation depends on the number of children. If there is only one child, then this line goes down straight to the rectangle representing this person (Figure 7-12). In the case of several children, there is an intermediate bus between two generations; this bus has connections down to each child and up to the line between their parents. For example, the couple that is shown at the top of Figure 7-13 has three children.

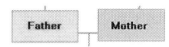

Figure 7-11. *Couple with children*

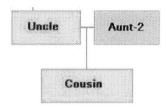

Figure 7-12. *Couple with one child*

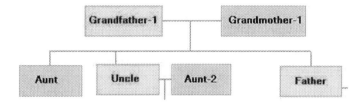

Figure 7-13. *Couple with three children*

When you draw the part containing only the immediate family, you usually know all the needed information, and there are no problems at all. When you try to draw some peripheral parts of the family tree, there can be a lack of information, and you either have to draw some empty rectangles without any information or go with what you know even if it is against the simple rules of biology (Figure 7-14).

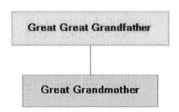

Figure 7-14. *The case is not correct from the point of biology, but there is no more information*

The Family Tree program has to include commands that simplify the process of adding some standard parts (spouse, parents, one child, several children). As a developer, you have to think about the most often needed variants and provide a system

325

of commands to answer such requests, but no system of commands can cover all the possible variants of relations. This is a classical situation where a user-driven application is much better than any program with a fixed system of variants, and this is one of the examples where a user-driven application can be the only really good solution.

Let's look at the Figure 7-10 once more. As mentioned, there are rectangles and lines that in the current program are called *buses*. Some buses connect the rectangles, some buses connect other buses, and there are buses between buses and rectangles. The flexible system of buses allows you to draw whatever you need, so let's start our work on the Family Tree application by developing some flexible buses.

```
public class Bus : GraphicalObject
{
    Pen m_pen;
    bool bMarkJoints = true;
    bool bMarkEnds = true;
    Color clrEnds = Color .Red;
    Color clrJoints = Color .White;
    bool bRegisteredWithMover = true;
    bool bUseWarningColor = true;
    Pen penWarn = new Pen (Color .Magenta, 2);
    List<PointF> m_pts = new List<PointF> ();
    List<BusConnection> headsConnected = new List<BusConnection> ();
    List<BusConnection> tailsConnected = new List<BusConnection> ();
```

Any bus consists of a set of straight segments connected into a chain one after another; there is at least one segment in each bus, but there is no upper limit on the number of segments. Each segment is described by two points, and the end point of the previous segment is the starting point of the next one. Thus, the minimal number of points for a bus is two, and the number of segments is always one less than the number of points. A bus can be initialized either by a List of points or only by two points; in the last case, the bus consists of a single segment.

```
public Bus (Form frm, Mover mvr, List<PointF> points, Pen pen)
{
    ... ...
    m_pen = new Pen (pen .Color, pen .Width);
    m_pen .DashStyle = pen .DashStyle;
```

```
        m_pts = points;
        Movable = false;
    }
```

The bus cover consists of small circular nodes on all the points from the List and of another set of strip nodes covering the segments.

```
    public override void DefineCover ()
    {
        int rad = Math .Max (4, Convert .ToInt32 (Width / 2));
        int nCircles = pts .Count;
        int nStrips = pts .Count - 1;
        CoverNode [] nodes = new CoverNode [nCircles + nStrips];
        for (int i = 0; i < nCircles; i++)
        {
            nodes [i] = new CoverNode (i, m_pts [i], rad);
        }
        for (int i = 0; i < nStrips; i++)
        {
            nodes [nCircles + i] = new CoverNode (nCircles + i, m_pts [i],
                                        m_pts [i + 1], rad, Behaviour
                                        .Frozen);
        }
        cover = new Cover (nodes);
        if (Movable)
        {
            cover .SetBehaviour (NodeShape .Strip, Behaviour .Moveable);
            cover .SetCursor (Cursors .SizeAll);
        }
    }
```

By moving the circular nodes, the length and angle of segments can be changed; in this way, the bus configuration is changed.

Now is the time to start our design step-by-step and to go from one preliminary example to another. All these auxiliary examples are divided into three groups. In the first group of examples only free buses are used. The examples in the second group demonstrate connected buses. In the third group, the Person objects are used.

Free Buses

File: Form_FreeBuses.cs

Menu position: Applications ➤ FamilyTree design step by step ➤ Free buses

The first preliminary example demonstrates two buses; one of them consists of a single segment, while another has four segments (Figure 7-15). A bus can be initialized by a pair of points or by a List of points; both cases are demonstrated in the current example. The points for the second bus are provided by the PointsForLine() method; these are random points from the form area but with one restriction. Buses are constructed after the information area, so the PointsForLine() method guarantees that at the moment of initialization no bus special point is hidden behind the information area.

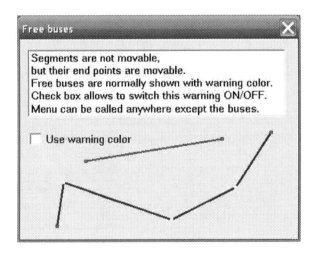

Figure 7-15a. *To see the colors of free buses, the warning is switched OFF*

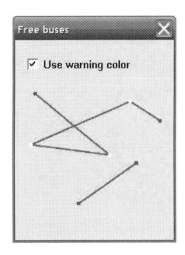

Figure 7-15b. *The warning is switched ON*

```
private void DefaultBuses ()
{
    bus_2 = new Bus (this, mover, new PointF (100, 220), new PointF
                     (300, 400), new Pen (Color .Green, 3));
    bus_5 = new Bus (this, mover, PointsForLine (5), new Pen (Color
    .Blue, 3));
    bus_2 .UseWarningColor =
    bus_5 .UseWarningColor = checkboxWarning .Checked;
}
```

These two buses are initialized with two different pens, but to see the colors of free buses, a special warning has to be switched OFF (Figure 7-15a). A bus that is not connected to anything and even a bus with one free end are abnormal situations for buses in a family tree, and such buses are shown with a special warning color. Several preliminary examples include a check box that allows you to switch this warning ON/OFF and to see even free buses in those colors that were declared on their initialization. The use of warning color for each bus is regulated via the Bus.UseWarningColor property. Later in this section, the tuning form for buses is demonstrated; this form contains a check box to regulate the use of the warning color. In a preliminary example such as this one, the mandatory switch to normal colors can be useful, and the view of buses in Figure 7-15a is better than in Figure 7-15b, but in a real application such a warning is helpful, and I would recommend not switching it OFF.

A bus is a relatively simple object. Its main part is a line with all three parameters of visualization—color, width, and line style—packed into a single field (m_pen). Two additional colors are used to mark the bus end points (clrEnds) and the joints between segments (clrJoints), but there are some conditions for the appearance of these special marks. Marks at all special points (ends and joints) are shown only for unmovable buses, and even then there are two Boolean parameters—bMarkEnds and bMarkJoints—that regulate the appearance of these marks. The Bus.Draw() method starts by checking a full list of conditions under which the line has to be shown with a warning color. We'll explore all these conditions in later examples.

```
public void Draw (Graphics grfx)
{
    if (((bHeadConnected != bTailConnected) ||
        (bHeadConnected == false && bTailConnected == false &&
            headsConnected .Count == 0 && tailsConnected .Count == 0 &&
            bRegisteredWithMover)) && bUseWarningColor)
    {
        grfx .DrawLines (penWarn, m_pts .ToArray ());
    }
    else
    {
        grfx .DrawLines (m_pen, m_pts .ToArray ());
    }
    if (!Movable)
    {
        if (bMarkJoints)
        {
            for (int i = 1; i < m_pts .Count - 1; i++)
            {
                Auxi_Drawing .FillCircle (grfx, m_pts [i], 3, clrJoints);
            }
        }
        if (bMarkEnds)
        {
            Auxi_Drawing .FillCircle (grfx, m_pts [0], 3, clrEnds);
```

```
Auxi_Drawing .FillCircle (grfx, m_pts [m_pts .Count - 1], 3,
                            clrEnds);
        }
    }
}
```

In the current example, neither the visualization parameters nor the number of segments in the buses can be changed, but all these things are regulated in later examples.

The use of two additional colors to mark all movable points makes the change of bus configuration much easier, but there are situations when such changes are not needed at all; then a bus can be shown without all the additional marks. When the user is already familiar with how to change buses, these additional marks are also not needed. In the Family Tree application, there is an easy way to switch them ON/OFF, and the user can do it at any moment.

Any new Bus is constructed as an unmovable object; the Bus constructer was covered earlier. The change of movability is discussed later in this section, while in the current example the buses are always unmovable.

A bus is unmovable as a whole object, but all special points (ends and joints) can be moved. Any movement starts with the call of the Press() method of the appropriate class.

```
private void OnMouseDown (object sender, MouseEventArgs e)
{
    ptMouse_Down = e .Location;
    if (mover .Catch (e .Location, e .Button))
    {
        GraphicalObject grobj = mover .CaughtSource;
        int iNode = mover .CaughtNode;
        if (grobj is Bus)
        {
            (grobj as Bus) .Press (e .Location, e .Button, iNode);
        }
        ... ...
```

If some small circular node is pressed with the left button, then there is an absolutely standard reaction—the cursor position is adjusted to the node central point.

```
public void Press (Point ptMouse, MouseButtons catcher, int iNode)
{
    if (catcher == MouseButtons .Left && iNode < m_pts .Count)
    {
        AdjustCursorPosition (m_pts [iNode]);
    }
}
```

The moving of any caught node is described by the Bus .MoveNode() method; in the current case, we are interested only in that part of the method that is applied to unmovable buses.

```
public override bool MoveNode (...)
{
    if (catcher == MouseButtons .Left)
    {
        if (Movable)
        {
            ... ...
        }
        else
        {
            if (iNode < m_pts .Count)
            {
                m_pts [iNode] = ptMouse;
                InformConnections (PositionUpdate .Soft, iNode - 1, iNode);
                bRet = true;
            }
        }
    }
```

It is too early to talk about connections, but you can see from this code that throughout the moving of the circular node, the special point associated with this node always goes with the cursor.

```
                    m_pts [iNode] = ptMouse;
```

The first example allows you to move special points, but nothing else can be done with the buses here. The next example allows you to add new joints to existing buses.

File: Form_FreeBuses_AddingJoints.cs

Menu position: Applications ➤ FamilyTree design step by step ➤ Free buses; adding joints

There are two ways to change bus configuration in this example (Figure 7-16): either to move one of the special points (ends and joints) or to press with the left button inside a segment and, without releasing the button, continue to move the new joint that appears at the pressed point. This way of adding joints was already demonstrated in Form_Polyline.cs, but because it happened so long ago, I want to remind you about this process.

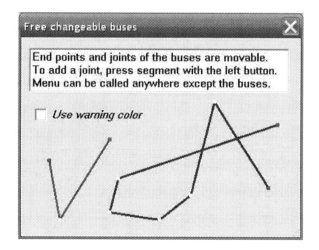

Figure 7-16. *Colored marks show all the special points*

Buses can be used as movable and unmovable. A movable bus is one that can be pressed at any point and moved around the screen without any change of configuration. If the bus is movable, then it is impossible to add new joints by the same press of the left button. A family tree needs both movable and unmovable buses. Some buses can be used only as unmovable (this is explained later); the movability of other buses can be switched ON/OFF, and this is regulated by the user through the menu command. Both buses of the current example are always unmovable, but to keep the code of the OnMouseDown() method similar to all later examples, there is a checking of the bus movability. (I want to stress that in the current example it is redundant.)

The new joint is organized at the moment when a bus segment is pressed, so everything is in the code of the OnMouseDown() method. I think it can be helpful to see some comments before the code.

When an unmovable bus is pressed on a strip node, then there is the following progression of steps:

1. The segment number (iSegment) is easily calculated from the number of the pressed node (iNode).

2. The nearest point on this segment (pt) is calculated by the Bus.NearestPointOnSegment() method.

3. The joint addition will cause the change of the bus cover. After this, the same bus will be caught by another node, so first the bus must be released by the mover.

4. The new joint is organized at the calculated point pt by the Bus.InsertPoint() method. Because the number of joints has changed, the cover is redefined; this is done from inside the InsertPoint() method.

5. The bus is caught again by the mover, but now the cursor is inside the area of the new circular node. All circular nodes precede the strip nodes in the Bus cover, so at the same point the bus is caught not by the strip node but by this circular node.

```
private void OnMouseDown (object sender, MouseEventArgs e)
{
    ptMouse_Down = e .Location;
    if (mover .Catch (e .Location, e .Button))
    {
        GraphicalObject grobj = mover .CaughtSource;
        int iNode = mover .CaughtNode;
        if (grobj is Bus)
        {
            Bus bus = grobj as Bus;
            bus .Press (e .Location, e .Button, iNode);
```

```
if (e .Button == MouseButtons .Left &&
    mover .CaughtNodeShape == NodeShape .Strip && !bus
    .Movable)
{
    int iSegment = iNode - bus .PointsNumber;
    PointF pt = bus .NearestPointOnSegment (e.Location,
    iSegment);
    mover .Release ();
    bus .InsertPoint (iSegment + 1, pt);
    mover .Catch (e .Location, e .Button);
    Invalidate ();
}
}
... ...
```

In this way, a new joint is added to an unmovable bus. The next example demonstrates reactions when pressing movable and unmovable buses.

File: Form_FreeBuses_ChangingMovability.cs

Menu position: Applications ➤ FamilyTree design step by step ➤ Free buses; changing movability

Figure 7-17 is a slightly changed Figure 7-13 with additional marks for buses of different types. Even such a simple tree of only several people demonstrates buses that are used for different types of connections; in Figure 7-17, they are marked with different letters. Buses in a family tree are used to connect different elements, so buses with free ends are an exception.

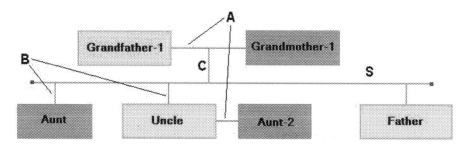

Figure 7-17. *This small tree has only one bus with its ends not placed on other elements. This bus is marked with the letter S (for special)*

Case **A**	In the current case, it is a bus between spouses, but in general this type of bus is used between two people. Its ends must be always connected to rectangles representing these people, so this bus cannot be moved freely to any other location. On the figure these buses are straight. Each of them can be turned into a broken line with several joints, but at any moment it must show a link between those two people.
Case **B**	Short buses of this type connect one long bus with siblings. The rectangles for siblings can be arbitrarily placed on the screen; the bus to any of them can be much longer and can be turned into a broken line, but two ends of each bus are connected to some objects (one to a bus, another to rectangle), so such a bus cannot be moved freely around the screen.
Case **C**	A bus of this type is used as a connection between two buses, so both of its ends are also placed on other elements, and this bus cannot be moved freely.
Case **S**	This is the only bus with the ends not fixed on other objects; the letter *S* for this bus is from the word *special*. The ends of this bus are not fixed, so this bus can be moved around without changing its view. This is the bus to which the siblings are connected; when you move this bus, all connections move with it. In Figure 7-17 this bus is placed at the same distance from rectangles belonging to two generations (between parents and their children). If anyone prefers to move this bus closer to the rectangles of one generation or another, it can be done without destroying the family tree. This would be a good feature of design, but then there is a question of the way to do it because up until now the mouse press on any bus allowed you only to add the new joint and to move this joint.

In all the examples of this book, the forward movement of a whole object or any part of an object is done with the left button, and I am not going to break this rule. In the previous example of Form_FreeBuses_AddingJoints.cs, the left button press at any inner point of a segment adds a joint at the pressed point and starts the process of moving this new joint. Yet, we have a situation when, depending on our wishes, a left button press must start either the adding and moving of the new joint or the moving of the whole bus without any change in its configuration. The computer cannot read the user's mind to determine what type of action this user plans to do at one moment or another, so some preliminary action of the user must determine it. This preliminary action is the change of the bus movability.

```
public override void DefineCover ()
{
    ... ...
    for (int i = 0; i < nCircles; i++)
    {
        nodes [i] = new CoverNode (i, m_pts [i], rad);
    }
    for (int i = 0; i < nStrips; i++)
    {
        nodes [nCircles + i] = new CoverNode (nCircles + i, m_pts [i],
                                    m_pts [i + 1], rad, Behaviour
                                    .Frozen);
    }
    ... ...
```

The results of such declaration were demonstrated in the previous example.

- You can press any circular node (any joint or end point) and move it around the screen.

- You can press any strip node because the mover feels all the frozen nodes, but you cannot move it. Instead, the new joint is organized at the pressed point, and, as any other joint, it is movable; this was already explained in the previous example. This adding of a new joint is done inside the OnMouseDown() method but only if the pressed bus is unmovable (look at the earlier code three pages back).

What happens if the bus is turned from unmovable into movable? The switch of the bus movability does not change the number, shape, or order of nodes in the cover, but it changes the behavior of the strip nodes. For the movable bus, there is a special addition at the end of the Bus.DefineCover() method.

```
public override void DefineCover ()
{
    ... ...
    if (Movable)
    {
        cover .SetBehaviour (NodeShape .Strip, Behaviour .Moveable);
```

```
        cover .SetCursor (Cursors .SizeAll);
    }
}
```

For a movable bus, it doesn't matter at all at which node and at what point the bus is pressed with the left button because the MoveNode() method simply calls the Move() method.

```
public override bool MoveNode (...)
{
    bool bRet = false;
    if (catcher == MouseButtons .Left)
    {
        if (Movable)
        {
            Move (dx, dy);
            ... ...
```

The Move() method changes all the special points in an identical way; the whole bus is moved without changing its configuration.

```
public override void Move (int dx, int dy)
{
    SizeF size = new SizeF (dx, dy);
    for (int i = 0; i < m_pts .Count; i++)
    {
        m_pts [i] += size;
    }
}
```

In the current example (Figure 7-18), the bus movability is changed through a single command of the small context menu.

```
private void Click_miMovable (object sender, EventArgs e)
{
    busPressed .Movable = !busPressed .Movable;
    Invalidate ();
}
```

The reaction on the left button press is absolutely different for movable and unmovable buses, and it would be confusing for users if the movable and unmovable buses looked identical. To avoid such confusion, the view of the bus slightly depends on its movability. For the nonmovable bus, its joints and end points can be shown with special marks (Figure 7-19a); this makes the pressing of the special points easier. There are no special marks on movable buses (Figure 7-19b); the whole bus is painted with one color. The absence of visible special points signals that there are no points to change the configuration, so the reaction on pressing at any point is the same.

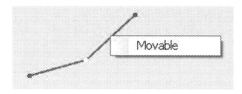

Figure 7-19a. *Menu on unmovable bus*

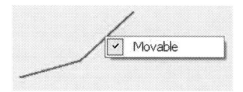

Figure 7-19b. *Menu on movable bus*

The Bus.Draw() method was shown several pages back, while the bus movability was not discussed yet, so here is the part of the method to draw all the special points. If these marks appear, then they are drawn after the drawing of the bus line, and the colors of special marks are the same regardless of whether the bus is shown in its normal color or a warning color.

```
public void Draw (Graphics grfx)
{
    ... ...
    if (!Movable)
    {
        if (bMarkJoints)
        {
            ... ...
        }
```

```
        if (bMarkEnds)
        {
            ... ...
        }
    }
}
```

In the real Family Tree application, more changes in view and the configuration of buses can be needed; these possible changes are demonstrated in the next example.

File: Form_FreeBuses_AllChanges.cs

Menu position: Applications ➤ FamilyTree design step by step ➤ Free buses; all changes

The new example has the same view as the previous one. The main difference is in the availability of all the possible bus changes through the commands of two menus that can be called on different parts of buses. You see these menus when you press on joints or on segments, but at any moment in the working program you can see only one menu. There is no way to see them simultaneously, so Figure 7-20 is a bit artificial, but I think that this view makes all the possibilities more obvious. As usual, the menu to be called is determined in the OnMouseUp() method of the form. When different menus have to be called on different parts of the same object, then the menu selection can be based on the node number and shape; both variants are used in the current example. Throughout this process the number of the pressed special point (iPressedPoint) or segment (iPressedSegment) is determined; these numbers are needed for some of the menu commands.

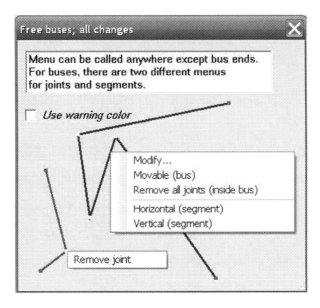

Figure 7-20. *Different menus for segments and joints*

```
private void OnMouseUp (object sender,
                       MouseEventArgs e)
{
    int iWasObject, iWasNode;
    NodeShape shapeNode;
    ptMouse_Up = e .Location;
    double fDist = Auxi_Geometry .Distance (ptMouse_Down, ptMouse_Up);
    if (mover .Release (out iWasObject, out iWasNode, out shapeNode))
    {
        GraphicalObject grobj = mover .ReleasedSource;
        if (e .Button == MouseButtons .Left)
        {
            ... ...
        }
        else if (e .Button == MouseButtons .Right && fDist <= 3)
        {
            if (grobj is Bus)
            {
                int nPoints = busPressed .PointsNumber;
```

```
if (shapeNode == NodeShape .Strip)
{
    iPressedSegment = iWasNode - nPoints;
    ContextMenuStrip = menuOnSegment;
}
else
{
    if (0 < iWasNode && iWasNode < nPoints - 1)
    {
        iPressedPoint = iWasNode;
        ContextMenuStrip = menuOnJoint;
    }
... ...
```

The menu on joints (menuOnJoint) contains a single command to delete the pressed joint; when executed, it allows you to straighten the bus without moving the joints manually. In this example, the removal of the joints is allowed both for movable and nonmovable buses, but there are some doubts about the correctness of applying this command to the movable buses. When the bus is declared movable, then adding new joints by pressing segments with the mouse is impossible; the individual movement of the existing special points is also impossible because a bus can be moved by any point. Thus, two features of a bus—the movability and the possibility of its reconfiguring—to some extent are associated with each other, and there can be different views on the level of their correlation.

- If you look at the change of the bus movability only as the chance to move the whole object, then the possibility to erase the joints of such bus is correct.

- If you think that for movable buses all possibilities of changing their configuration must be blocked, then this command for movable buses must be disabled.

If you decide to block the change of configuration for movable buses, the code must be changed in two different places because the menu on a joint allows you to delete only the pressed joint, while the menu on a segment allows you to delete all joints of the pressed bus.

The menu that is called on segments has several commands (it's the bigger menu in Figure 7-20).

Modify	Calls an additional tuning form to modify the view of the pressed bus. This Form_Tuning_Bus.cs (Figure 7-21) allows you to do the following: To change the color, width, and style (DashStyle) of the bus To regulate the appearance of special marks at the end points and joints To change colors of special marks To regulate the use of warning color
Movable (bus)	Allows you to switch the movability of the pressed bus. The change of movability slightly changes the view of the bus as was explained in the previous example.
Remove all joints (inside bus)	Erases all joints and leaves the bus consisting of a single segment between the end points.
Horizontal (segment)	Turns the pressed segment into a horizontal line.
Vertical (segment)	Turns the pressed segment into a vertical line.

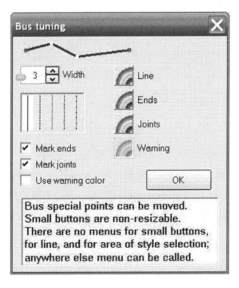

Figure 7-21. *Form for bus tuning*

Two last commands work in a similar way and have similar limitations of their use.

- To change a segment into strictly horizontal or vertical, one end of a segment must be moved. Both ends of a bus look similar, and it is impossible to determine visually from which of them the order of points starts, but all special points are placed in the `List<PointF>` `m_pts` in some order, and these commands move the point with the bigger number. This is correct for any segment except the last one for which the point with the lesser number is moved.

- In the current preliminary example, we deal with free buses. Later the same commands will be used for segments in real trees where buses are connected to some objects. These commands must not affect the points of connection; for this reason, the logic of applying these commands to the last segment of any bus is different. This also means that these two commands cannot be used on a bus consisting of a single segment.

- If the pressed segment is nearly horizontal and you order to turn it into a vertical line, then its end points get the same X coordinate, and the new segment will be very short. If you apply the same command to the horizontal segment, it will turn into a single point and disappear from view. To avoid such situations, these commands are allowed only for segments that will turn into a new segment with the length of not less than 10 pixels.

Up until now we were looking at the free buses that were not connected to anything. In a real family tree, we do not have absolutely free buses; Figure 7-10 shows that buses are either connected to each other or can be used as the links between the rectangles representing people. We will discuss those special rectangles a bit later, and now let's consider the cases of connected buses.

Connected Buses

Buses are not connected to each other by the arbitrary points. On the contrary, there is only one way to organize any bus connection, and there are strict rules on how this connection works. The only way to organize a connection between two buses is to move the end point of one bus and to fix it in some way on another bus. From this moment, the end point of the first bus can be moved only along the second bus using it as a rail. It does not matter whether the second bus is a straight or a broken line; the connected end of the first bus can move along the full length of the second bus between its end points.

An element of the BusConnection class connects two buses.

```
public class BusConnection : GraphicalObject
{
    PointF ptCon;              // connection point
    int m_radius;              // node radius
    Bus m_busOfEnd;            // bus connected by its end
    EndType end_type;          // type of end point
    Bus m_busRail;             // bus to which the end point is connected
                               //   (rail)
    int iSegment;              // rail segment
    double coefOnSegment;      // positioning coefficient on this segment
```

An object of the BusConnection class is organized at the end point of the bus that is going to be connected to another bus. To organize a new connection, some information about both buses is needed. This information includes the connection point (ptCon), the radius of the sensitive area around the connection point (m_radius), the bus that is connected by its end (m_busOfEnd), the additional value that specifies the connected end (end_type), and the bus to which the first one is connected and along which the connected end can be moved (m_busRail).

```
public BusConnection (Form frm, Mover mvr, PointF pt, int rad, Bus bus_End,
                      EndType endType, Bus bus_Rail)
{
    ... ...
    m_radius = Math .Max (Math .Abs (rad), 3);
    m_busOfEnd = bus_End;
    end_type = endType;
    m_busRail = bus_Rail;
    ... ...
    ptCon = Auxi_Geometry .Polyline_NearestPoint (pt, m_busRail .Points,
                                      out dist, out iSegment, out
                                      coefOnSegment);
}
```

Visually, two ends of any bus are indistinguishable from each other, but any bus is a sequence of points that are linked by segments in a strict order. Each Bus object keeps its special points as a List, and the points are linked according to their order in this List. The first point in the List is the bus head; the last one is the bus tail.

```
public enum EndType { Head, Tail };
```

When a bus connection is organized, the suggested connection point is passed as a parameter (pt). It can be an accurately calculated point, not so accurately calculated, or even an arbitrary point. The real point of connection (ptCon) is calculated as the point of the bus closest to the suggested one (pt). The Auxi_Geometry.Polyline_ NearestPoint() method returns not only the exact point on which the connection will be organized (ptCon), but also the number of bus segment to which this point belongs (iSegment) and the positioning coefficient of the calculated point on this segment (coefOnSegment). All special points of a bus are numbered starting from zero at the head and increasing to the tail, so the end points of each segment have two consecutive numbers. The positioning coefficient along the segment gets some value from the [0, 1] range where 0 is associated with the segment end with a lesser number and 1 with another end.

The bus connection geometry is represented by a single point, so the cover of this object is extremely simple and obvious: the cover consists of a single small circular node.

```
public override void DefineCover ()
{
    cover = new Cover (new CoverNode (0, ptCon, m_radius));
}
```

The BusConnection class has one nearly unique feature: these objects are very useful, but they are invisible. There are no parameters of visibility, and there is no Draw() method. All my work is aimed at moving the screen objects, so it is all about changing the positions and sizes of the objects that are shown on a screen. The mentioned feature is nearly unique, and up to now there was only one class with such a feature: while discussing the use of rectangular areas for plotting, I explained the use of the invisible elements in the corners of the plotting area.

We already have a set of four small examples to look at the free buses; now you are going to see a similar set of four examples to explore all the features of bus connections.

File: `Form_ConnectedBuses_Two.cs`

Menu position: Applications ➤ FamilyTree design step by step ➤ Two connected buses

The name of this example tells us that there are two buses in this form. Let's check step-by-step the design of the connection between buses. For this and several following examples, I prefer such a view of the buses that is good for my explanations. At the same time, I don't want the strict determination of the bus points because the discussed mechanism of connection works regardless of those points, so the points are calculated quasirandomly. For this, the full area of the example (form) is divided into rows and columns by the `SubRects()` method.

```
void SubRects (int nRows, int nCols)
```

The numbering of cells (rectangles) starts from the top-left corner, goes to the right along the upper row, then goes from left to right along the next row, and so on, until the bottom-right corner. A random point inside any cell is obtained from the `RandomPointInSubrect()` method.

```
PointF RandomPointInSubrect (int iRect)
```

To organize a quasirandom bus positioning, you need to declare a set of cell numbers in which the points of this bus must be positioned.

```
private List<PointF> Points_QuaziRandom (int [] nums)
{
    List<PointF> points = new List<PointF> ();
    for (int i = 0; i < nums .Length; i++)
    {
        points .Add (RandomPointInSubrect (nums [i]));
    }
    return (points);
}
```

Now we can go on with our example. First, the green bus is organized (`busGreen`) in the upper quarter of the form. Then the blue bus (`busBlue`) is placed somewhere in the middle of the form and goes from top to bottom (Figure 7-22).

348

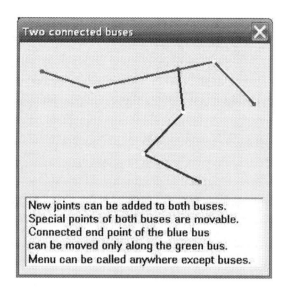

Figure 7-22. *Two connected buses*

```
public DefaultView ()
{
    ... ...
    SubRects (4, 5);
    busGreen = new Bus (this, mover,
                       Points_QuaziRandom (new int [] { 0, 1, 3, 4 }),
                       new Pen (Color .Green, 3));
    busBlue = new Bus (this, mover,
                       Points_QuaziRandom (new int [] { 2, 7, 12, 18 }),
                       new Pen (Color .Blue, 3));
```

The blue bus must be connected to the green by its head, which is points [0], so some correction of this point is needed. The nearest point to it on the green bus is calculated (pt), and the starting point for the blue bus gets this value.

```
    PointF pt = Auxi_Geometry .Polyline_NearestPoint (busBlue .Points [0],
                                                      busGreen .Points);
    busBlue .ChangePoint (0, pt);
```

The head point of the blue bus is now positioned on the green bus, but two buses do not know anything about each other. If nothing else is done, then they behave like absolutely independent objects; such an example was demonstrated several pages back.

To have a real connection, a BusConnection object is organized at the head point of the blue bus, and the green bus receives information about this connection by the Bus. AddConnection() method.

```
con = new BusConnection (this, mover, pt, busBlue, EndType.Head,
busGreen);
busGreen .AddConnection (con);
... ...
```

The end point of the blue bus is positioned exactly on the green bus. There is a visual connection between buses; when the connection point is pressed with a mouse cursor, then the move of this point is expected. The mover has no vision and selects an object for moving according to its order in the queue, so this BusConnection object must be registered in the mover queue ahead of both buses.

```
private void RenewMover ()
{
    mover .Clear ();
    busGreen .IntoMover (mover, 0);
    busBlue .IntoMover (mover, 0);
    con .IntoMover (mover, 0);
    ... ...
```

Now let's look at the details of how this connection works.

The BusConnection object is ahead of buses in the mover queue, so when the point of the connection is pressed with the left button, then not any bus is pressed and caught, but this BusConnection object is. When this happens, the BusConnection.Press() method is called.

```
private void OnMouseDown (object sender, MouseEventArgs e)
{
    ptMouse_Down = e .Location;
    if (mover .Catch (e .Location, e .Button))
    {
        GraphicalObject grobj = mover .CaughtSource;
        int iNode = mover .CaughtNode;
        if (grobj is BusConnection)
        {
```

```
        (grobj as BusConnection) .Press (e .Location, e .Button,
        iNode);
    }
    ... ...
```

Three parameters are used in this Press() method only for uniformity. For a cover consisting of a single small circular node, the pressed point and the number of the pressed node are redundant. When a BusConnection element is pressed by the left button, then the mouse cursor position is adjusted to the central point in a standard way.

```
public void Press (Point ptMouse, MouseButtons catcher, int iNode)
{
    if (catcher == MouseButtons .Left)
    {
        AdjustCursorPosition (ptCon);
    }
}
```

Now the BusConnection object is caught by the mover, so further movement of the caught object is described by the BusConnection.MoveNode() method.

```
public override bool MoveNode (...)
{
    bool bRet = false;
    if (catcher == MouseButtons .Left)
    {
        Location = ptMouse;
        AdjustCursorPosition (ptCon);
    }
    return (bRet);
}
```

Visually it looks as if the pressed mouse moves only along the green bus and at any moment the connection point goes with the mouse cursor. In reality, it works vice versa: the mouse cursor goes to some point (ptMouse) that, with very high probability, is somewhere apart from the green bus, but the connection keeps itself straight on the green bus and returns the cursor to the point of connection. Keeping the connection on the bus is done with a simple use of the Location property.

```
          Location = ptMouse;
```
Thus, we have to look inside the BusConnection.Location property.

```
    public PointF Location
    {
        get { return (ptCon); }
        set
        {
            ptCon = Auxi_Geometry .Polyline_NearestPoint (value, m_busRail
                                      .Points,
                                          out dist, out iSegment, out coefOnSegment);
            DefineCover ();
            if (end_type == EndType .Head)
            {
                m_busOfEnd .HeadPoint = ptCon;
            }
            else
            {
                m_busOfEnd .TailPoint = ptCon;
            }
        }
    }
```

The cursor is moved to some new point, and this point (value) is used to calculate the nearest point on the bus (ptCon). The connected end of the blue bus is now moved to this point. Two ends of any bus—head and tail—are visually indistinguishable, but the end_type field of the BusConnection object specifies the covered end, so there is no problem with moving the correct end of the blue bus to the new point of the bus connection. When the work of the BusConnection.Location property is done, the MoveNode() method orders the adjustment of the cursor position to the new point of the connection with the usual help of the AdjustCursorPosition() method.

The new position of the connection point is determined by the Auxi_Geometry. Polyline_NearestPoint() method, which uses a set of special bus points. In this way, the point of connection is moved only along the green bus, and the connected end of the blue bus moves with this point. This works perfectly while the set of special points of the green bus is fixed, but what happens when in one way or another the green bus configuration is changed? End points and joints of the green bus can be moved at any moment. How does the end of the blue bus keep its connection to the green bus throughout these changes?

I have already mentioned that after the connection at the end of the blue bus was organized, the information about this connection was passed to the bus with which it was connected—the green one.

```
busGreen .AddConnection (con);
```

Any bus keeps track of all its "side" connections. There are two separate Lists for connections by the heads and tails of the other buses.

```
public class Bus : GraphicalObject
{
    List<BusConnection> headsConnected = new List<BusConnection> ();
    List<BusConnection> tailsConnected = new List<BusConnection> ();
```

The Bus.AddConnection() method adds a new element to the appropriate List.

```
    public void AddConnection (BusConnection cnct)
    {
        if (cnct .ConnectionType == EndType .Head)
        {
            headsConnected .Add (cnct);
        }
        else
        {
            tailsConnected .Add (cnct);
        }
    }
}
```

When the green bus is organized, its four points are defined from left to right; their numbers in the List of points are shown in Figure 7-23. The green bus consists of three segments; the blue bus is connected at segment 1 between points 1 and 2. Now let's press and move some special point of the green bus. When any node of the bus is pressed and moved, then the Bus.MoveNode() method is called. Right now we are interested only in that part of the method that is responsible for moving special points. All the special points are covered by circular nodes that are the first in the bus cover, so the number of the moved circular node is equal to the number of the corresponding special point. I want to remind you that special points can be moved only if the bus itself is unmovable.

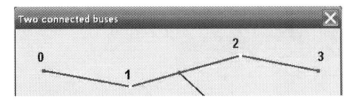

Figure 7-23. *The points of the green bus are numbered from left to right*

```
public override bool MoveNode (...)
{
    bool bRet = false;
    if (catcher == MouseButtons .Left)
    {
        if (Movable)
        {
            ... ...
        }
        else
        {
            if (iNode < m_pts .Count)
            {
                m_pts [iNode] = ptMouse;
                InformConnections (PositionUpdate .Soft, iNode - 1, iNode);
                bRet = true;
            }
        }
        ... ...
```

When any bus is moved or reconfigured, some or all of the connections on this bus must update their positions. Two different types of updating are described by the PositionUpdate enumeration.

```
public enum PositionUpdate { Soft, Hard };
```

- Imagine the situation (it is real, but we did not look at such case yet) when the bus is moved without any change of its configuration and all the connections must retain their relative positions. This means that each connection is still positioned on the same segment and with the same positioning coefficient along the segment. Thus, only the absolute screen coordinates of the connection are changed because the bus has moved; such a change of position is described as `PositionUpdate.Soft`.

- Another situation happens, for example, when the command is given to delete all the joints of a bus and to transform this bus into a straight line. As a result, all the connections have to be positioned on this new bus, and there is no question of keeping the connection on the same segment with the same positioning coefficient. Both values must be recalculated, and this situation is described as `PositionUpdate.Hard`.

When the whole bus is moved, then all its connections must be relocated. When the end point is moved, then only one segment is affected. When any joint is moved, then only the segments on both sides of this joint are changed, and only the connections on these segments must be relocated; all other connections beyond the neighboring joints are not disturbed at all. The type of updating and the range of the affected segments are sent to the `InformConnections()` method.

```
public void InformConnections (PositionUpdate updateType,
                               int iSeg_0, int iSeg_1)
{
    foreach (BusConnection connection in headsConnected)
    {
        connection .RailChanged (updateType, iSeg_0, iSeg_1);
    }
    foreach (BusConnection connection in tailsConnected)
    {
        connection .RailChanged (updateType, iSeg_0, iSeg_1);
    }
}
```

Parameters that are passed to the `Bus.InformConnections()` method include the type of adjustment (`updateType`) and the range of the affected segments (from `iSeg_0` to `iSeg_1`). The same set of parameters is used while applying the `BusConnection.RailChanged()` method to each of the connections. This method has to calculate the new position of connection in reaction to the change of the bus on which it is positioned; any calculation is needed only if the particular connection is situated on a segment inside the specified range. If the connection has to be moved, then its new position (ptNew) depends on the type of update.

- For the PositionUpdate.Soft, the segment number (iSegment) and the positioning coefficient on this segment (coefOnSegment) retain their values; the new point is calculated by using these unchanged values.

- For the PositionUpdate.Hard, the new position is calculated by finding the nearest point on the whole bus; for this calculation, only the bus points are needed. Throughout this process, the new segment number and the positioning coefficient on this segment are also calculated.

```
public void RailChanged (PositionUpdate updateType, int iSeg_0, int
iSeg_1)
{
    if (iSeg_0 <= iSegment && iSegment <= iSeg_1)
    {
        PointF ptNew;
        if (updateType == PositionUpdate .Soft)
        {
            ptNew = Auxi_Geometry .PointOnLine (m_busRail .Points
                                    [iSegment], m_busRail .Points
                                    [iSegment + 1], coefOnSegment);
        }
        else
        {
            ptNew = Auxi_Geometry .Polyline_NearestPoint (ptCon,
                    m_busRail .Points, out dist, out iSegment,
                    out coefOnSegment);
        }
        Location = ptNew;
    }
}
```

The calculated position (ptNew) is passed to the BusConnection.Location property where two things happen: the connection is relocated to this new position, and then this value is sent to the HeadPoint or TailPoint property of the connected bus; the exact property depends on whether that bus is connected by the head or by the tail. (The code of the BusConnection.Location property was shown several pages back.)

In our case, the blue bus is connected by the head to the green bus, so the moved connection sends the new point value to the Bus.HeadPoint property of the connected bus, and the head point of that bus is changed.

```
public PointF HeadPoint
{
    get { return (m_pts [0]); }
    set { ChangePoint (0, value); }
}
```

Instead of the direct change of m_pts[0], you see the call of the Bus.ChangePoint() method because the change of the head point of the connected bus may be not enough. If there are some connections on that second bus (suppose that other buses are connected to the blue one), then the Bus.ChangePoint() method not only relocates the first point of the bus but also disturbs all its connections; eventually this disturbance will die somewhere, but on the way all the involved connections and bus ends will take their new positions.

```
public void ChangePoint (int iPoint, PointF pt)
{
    if (0 <= iPoint && iPoint < m_pts .Count)
    {
        m_pts .RemoveAt (iPoint);
        m_pts .Insert (iPoint, pt);
        DefineCover ();
        InformConnections (PositionUpdate .Soft, iPoint - 1, iPoint);
    }
}
```

Let's look at a bus not as a collection of special points and straight segments that link these points (Figure 7-18), but as a set of nodes. They are invisible, but it is easy to imagine their geometry. Each segment in Figure 7-18 is an axis of a strip node, and each special point is the center of a circular node, so the combined area of all nodes is identical to the line view but only wider than we see in this figure. Though all special points are important for the bus work, the combined area of all their circular nodes represents a negligible part of the cover area. It would make sense to consider the movability of the bus as the movability of its segments, and it really works this way. At the same time, the movability of special points is always opposite to the movability of segments.

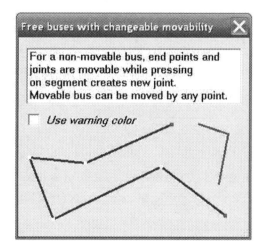

Figure 7-18. *The bus movability can be changed through menu command. The end points and joints are shown only for unmovable buses*

Any bus is initialized as unmovable.

```
public Bus (Form frm, Mover mvr, List<PointF> points, Pen pen)
{
    ... ...
    Movable = false;
```

In accordance with this declaration of bus immovability, the strip nodes must be immovable, and circular nodes must be movable. By default, all nodes are movable, so circular nodes do not need any change on initiation, while strip nodes have to be immobilized with an additional parameter that specifies their behavior.

Now we have the full picture of what happens when one or another special point of the green bus is caught and moved. There can be different consequences for connections positioned next to or far away from the moved special point. In order not to jump back and forth through the text, I'll duplicate here Figure 7-23, which shows the numbers for special points of the green bus. Now let's look at the details of two cases when points 1 and 3 are moved.

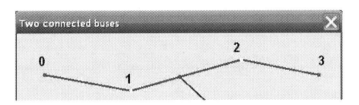

When the second from the left point (number 1) of the green bus is moved, then the following happens:

1. The mouse is moved somewhere (ptMouse). By the Bus. MoveNode() method, the caught joint (iNode == 1) is moved to the same point as the mouse. All connections of the green bus are informed that two segments of the bus have changed.

    ```
    m_pts [1] = ptMouse;
        InformConnections (PositionUpdate .Soft, 0, 1);
    ```

2. The green bus has only one connection, and for this the BusConnection.RailChanged() method is called with the same parameters.

    ```
    connection .RailChanged (PositionUpdate .Soft, 0, 1);
    ```

3. Our connection happens to be inside the specified range of segments (iSegment == 1), so the new position for the connection is calculated using the soft update, and then this new position is passed to the BusConnection.Location property.

    ```
    ptNew = Auxi_Geometry .PointOnLine (busRail .Points [1],
                                        busRail .Points [2],
                                        coefOnSegment);
    Location = ptNew;
    ```

4. The BusConnection.Location property changes the real location of the connection point and sends this new location to the blue bus to be used in the Bus.HeadPoint property.

    ```
    ptCon = Auxi_Geometry .Polyline_NearestPoint (value, busRail
                          .Points, out dist, out iSegment, out
                          coefOnSegment);


    m_busOfEnd .HeadPoint = ptCon;
    ```

5. The Bus.HeadPoint property calls the Bus.ChangePoint() method to change the position of the first point.

    ```
    set { ChangePoint (0, value); }
    ```

6. The Bus.ChangePoint() method changes the position of the head point of the blue bus, and on this the disturbance is over because there are no connections on the blue bus.

When the right point (number 3) of the green bus is moved, then the chain of events is shorter.

1. The mouse is moved somewhere (ptMouse). By the Bus. MoveNode() method, the caught point of the bus (iNode == 3) is moved to the same point as the mouse. All connections of the green bus are informed that two segments of the bus have changed.

    ```
    pts [3] = ptMouse;
    InformConnections (PositionUpdate .Soft, 2, 3);
    ```

2. The green bus has only one connection, and for this, the BusConnection.RailChanged() method is called with the same parameters.

    ```
    connection .RailChanged (PositionUpdate .Soft, 2, 3);
    ```

3. The connection on the green bus is outside the specified range (iSegment == 1), so nothing has to be done. In Figure 7-23, the movement of the right point of the green bus has no effect on the shown connection.

We already saw that whenever an end point or any joint of a bus is moved, the Bus. InformConnections() method must be called. The next examples will demonstrate several situations when this method must be called, and there is some simple logic to determine the set of needed parameters for this call.

- If some special point is moved by a mouse, then the relative position of any connection on that bus is not changed; this means using the PositionUpdate.Soft parameter. As a result of the mentioned movement, not more than two consecutive segments are affected, so two consecutive numbers represent the range of changing segments. For an end point, only one segment is changed, but for the uniformity of the code, the range of segments is still represented by two consecutive numbers. One of the mentioned segments does not exist, but this is not a problem at all as no connection can be positioned on a nonexistent segment, so no action will be required (and done) for this nonexistent segment.

- If the number of joints is changed, then it is always the PositionUpdate.Hard parameter, and all segments must be included in the range of affected segments.

One of the cases that fall into the second variant is the addition of a new joint when any segment of the unmovable bus is pressed with the left button; in this case, the call to the Bus.InformConnections() method is included in the OnMouseDown() method.

```
private void OnMouseDown (object sender, MouseEventArgs e)
{
    ptMouse_Down = e .Location;
    if (mover .Catch (e .Location, e .Button))
    {
        GraphicalObject grobj = mover .CaughtSource;
        int iNode = mover .CaughtNode;
        ... ...
        else if (grobj is Bus)
        {
            Bus bus = grobj as Bus;
            bus .Press (e .Location, e .Button, iNode);
```

```
if (e .Button == MouseButtons .Left &&
    mover .CaughtNodeShape == NodeShape .Strip && !bus
    .Movable)
{
    ... ...
    bus .InformConnections (PositionUpdate .Hard,
                          0, bus .PointsNumber - 1);
    ... ...
```

File: Form_ConnectedBuses_Three.cs

Menu position: Applications ➤ FamilyTree design step by step ➤
Three connected buses

In the next example, there are three buses, and one of them is connected to others
on both ends (Figure 7-24). This example allows you to check the correctness of work for
connections on both ends of a bus, while everything else is nearly the same.

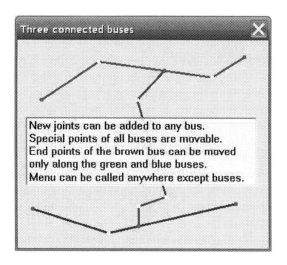

Figure 7-24. *Three connected buses*

Beginning from this example and later until the development of the real Family Tree
application, there are going to be lots of bus connections. In some cases, only one end
of a bus is connected to something; in other cases, a bus is connected by both ends. The
ConnectedBus() method can be useful in any situation. This method constructs a new bus
with its ends connected to one or two other buses. Not only is a new bus organized, but the
new connections (one or two) are included in the existing List of bus connections.

I mentioned one or two new connections, because this method can be used when a new bus is connected by both ends or by only one end. This method could be demonstrated in the previous example, but I decided to postpone its use until this one.

The buses of this example are calculated in a quasirandom way: the green bus (busFrom) appears in the upper quarter of the form, the blue one (busTo) appears in the lower quarter, and then the brown bus (busLink) connects them somewhere in the middle.

```
List<BusConnection> connections = new List<BusConnection> ();
public DefaultView ()
{
    ... ...
    busFrom = new Bus (this, mover,
                        Points_QuaziRandom (new int [] { 0, 1, 3, 4 }),
                        new Pen (Color .Green, 3));
    busTo = new Bus (this, mover,
                        Points_QuaziRandom (new int [] { 15, 17, 19 }),
                        new Pen (Color .Blue, 3));
    busLink = ConnectedBus (this, mover, new Pen (Color .Brown, 3),
                            busFrom, busTo,
                            Points_QuaziRandom (new int [] { 2, 7,
                            13, 18 }),
                            out connections);
    ... ...
```

The ConnectedBus() method gets the List of proposed points, but the first and last ones are adjusted to the geometry of those buses on which the new connections must reside. Both buses to which two ends of the busLink must be connected already exist prior to the call of the ConnectedBus() method. A family tree is often constructed by adding one new element at a time, so it is normal to connect the new bus by one end while another end will be used later. If this method is used to organize a one-end connection, then instead of the bus for another end, the null parameter is used.

```
public Bus ConnectedBus (Form frm, Mover mvr, Pen pn,
                          Bus busHeadConnected, Bus busTailConnected,
                          List<PointF> points, out List<BusConnection>
                          cons)
```

```
{
    List<BusConnection> newcons = new List<BusConnection> ();
    int iLast = points .Count - 1;
    if (busHeadConnected != null)
    {
        points [0] = Auxi_Geometry .Polyline_NearestPoint (points [0],
                                                busHeadConnected
                                                .Points);
    }
    if (busTailConnected != null)
    {
        points [iLast] = Auxi_Geometry .Polyline_NearestPoint (points
                                    [iLast], busTailConnected .Points);
    }
    Bus bs = new Bus (frm, mvr, points, pn);
    if (busHeadConnected != null)
    {
        BusConnection conHead = new BusConnection (frm, mvr, points [0],
                        Math .Max (busHeadConnected .NodeRadius, bs
                        .NodeRadius), bs, EndType .Head, busHeadConnected);

        busHeadConnected .AddConnection (conHead);
        newcons .Add (conHead);
    }
    if (busTailConnected != null)
    {
        BusConnection conTail = new BusConnection (frm, mvr, points [iLast],
                            Math .Max (busTailConnected .NodeRadius,
                            bs .NodeRadius), bs, EndType .Tail,
                                    busTailConnected);
```

```
                busTailConnected .AddConnection (conTail);
                newcons .Add (conTail);
        }
        cons = newcons;
        return (bs);
    }
```

You can test one more interesting thing with the buses. Reconfigure one bus, for example, the green one, in such a way that it will turn into a closed loop. This is easy to do as all special points are movable, and any number of new joints can be added. At the end of all the changes, move one end point of the green bus on top of another. If you turn the green bus into a closed loop, then the connected end point of the brown bus can move without problems around such a loop. You can even put two end points of the green bus somewhere close to each other, and the existence of a small gap is not a problem: the movable end point of the brown bus can easily cross a small gap in the green bus. If the green bus is reconfigured in such a way as to cross itself, then the end point of the brown bus can jump from one segment to another. You can reconfigure the bus that is used as the rail in such a way that its different segments are positioned not far from each other; the end of another bus that is moved along this rail can easily cross the gap and move from one segment to another. This type of movement not only along the track but even across some gap can be a problem in other applications with a movement along the tracks, so the problem and its solution are discussed in my other book [2] (for example, see Form_SpotOnCommentedWay.cs). For the Family Tree application, there is no need to add any special checking to prevent such jumps from one segment of the bus to another.

I cannot imagine a situation when anyone would need to change the bus of a family tree in such a way that it would cross itself, but the case of a bus in a form of a closed loop is different. The bus in a form of a closed loop is not only a funny exercise. A bit later you will see that it is a useful element.

File: Form_ConnectedBuses_ChangingMovability.cs

Menu position: Applications ➤ FamilyTree design step by step ➤ Connected buses; changing movability

In the next example, there are the same three buses connected in the same way, but I added a small menu containing one command to change the movability of the pressed bus. This command can be applied not to every bus, so it is allowed for the green and blue buses but not for the brown one. Certainly, this exclusion is not based on the bus color. It was already explained that only a bus with free ends can be declared movable, so the change of movability is not allowed for the brown bus.

At the moment of initialization, all three buses are nonmovable, and when you press with the left button any segment of any bus, then the new joint appears under the cursor. You continue to move this new joint, and if the pressed bus is green or blue, then the connected point of the brown bus moves only if it happens to be on the neighboring segment of this joint.

Now call the context menu on the green bus and turn this bus into movable. The view of the green bus will change a bit to indicate the movability of the bus; this disappearance of colored marks for all special points of the movable bus (Figure 7-25) was already demonstrated in a similar example with free buses.

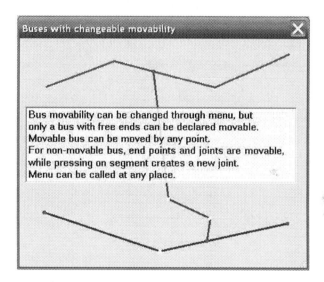

Figure 7-25. *Two buses (blue and brown) are unmovable, while the green bus is movable*

When the bus movability is switched, not only does the bus view change, but its cover is also changed. The number, order, and shape of all nodes do not change, but the behavior of the strip nodes changes.

```
public override void DefineCover ()
{
    ... ...
```

```
    if (Movable)
    {
        cover .SetBehaviour (NodeShape .Strip, Behaviour .Moveable);
        cover .SetCursor (Cursors .SizeAll);
    }
}
```

A movable bus has no marks on special points, and any bus point can be used to start exactly the same movement of the whole bus. In several classes throughout this book I have already demonstrated that if circular nodes are not needed in some situations, then they are simply squeezed to a size of zero. Why is this not done in the Bus class? There are situations when these circular nodes must be excluded from the process of moving, but some menu must be called on them. To be detected by mover, the nodes must have a non-zero size.

When the movable bus is pressed with the left button, then the MoveNode() method simply calls the Move() method. This was already mentioned throughout the discussion of the free buses, but it was too early to mention one more command inside the MoveNode() method.

```
    public override bool MoveNode (...)
    {
        bool bRet = false;
        if (catcher == MouseButtons .Left)
        {
            if (Movable)
            {
                Move (dx, dy);
                InformConnections (PositionUpdate .Soft, 0, pts .Count - 1);
            }
            ... ...
```

When the green bus of the current example is turned into movable and then moved, all its connections must be informed about the change of the bus. The configuration of the green bus is not changed throughout the movement; all its segments have the same length, so all possible connections to the bus must retain their positions. It is the classical variant of the PositionUpdate.Soft update type that must include all the segments, and you see exactly this type of the InformConnections() method called from inside the MoveNode() method.

File: `Form_ConnectedBuses_AllChanges.cs`

Menu position: Applications ➤ FamilyTree design step by step ➤
Connected buses; all changes

This example demonstrates all possible changes that can be applied to connected buses; these changes are the same as were demonstrated for free buses in `Form_FreeBuses_AllChanges.cs` (Figure 7-20). Three menus can be used in this example; two of them are called on the bus segments and joints (Figure 7-26).

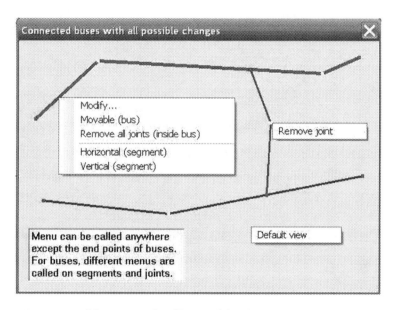

Figure 7-26. *Connected buses with all possible changes*

I think that the buses to be used in the Family Tree application are now developed and tested. It is time to look at other important elements of any family tree—specifically at rectangles that represent people.

People in a Family Tree

Any person in a family tree is represented by an object of the `Person` class. On the screen, this object is shown as a rectangular area with some information (Figure 7-27). The rectangle is movable and resizable (did you expect anything else?); information about a person is organized with the help of three comments associated with this rectangle.

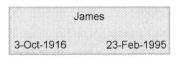

Figure 7-27. *Standard view of a Person object*

```
public class Person : GraphicalObject
{
    PointF [] ptsCorner;
    SolidBrush m_brush;
    Pen penBorder = new Pen (Color .DarkGray);
    CommentToRect cmntName, cmntBirth, cmntDeath;
    Bus busOnBorder;
    static int minSide = 20;
```

One comment—cmntName—is used to show a person's name. The text of this comment cannot be empty. Even if you do not know the person's name, you can call him Unknown or anything else, but you cannot organize a Person object without this comment. Two other comments are not mandatory. If a person is alive, the information about his death is rarely known, so in this case the cmntDeath is not needed. It is not unusual to not know the date of birth for a relative several generations back. It is possible to put some date (for example, a year) with a question mark or simply omit this cmntBirth. While starting the discussion of the Family Tree program, I used Figures 7-10–7-14 on which each Person object contained only the cmntName part, but two other comments were empty.

The name, birth, and death data are only the standard pieces of information that are used in this and other similar programs. These three fields are only strings, and the user can put any needed text there.

An object of the Person class can be moved by any inner point and resized by any border point. Objects of this class use the same type of cover that was demonstrated for several other classes of rectangles (for example, see Figure 5-3), so there are four circular nodes on corners, four strip nodes along the sides, and one rectangular node for the whole object area. The cover of a Person object is based on four corner points of the rectangle; the numbering of points in the ptsCorner[] array starts from the top-left corner and goes clockwise. Person objects are always resizable in all directions, and the cover nodes are never squeezed. Strip nodes on the sides have a default width of six pixels, while circular nodes are slightly enlarged from the default size.

```
public override void DefineCover ()
{
    float rCorner = 4;
    CoverNode [] nodes = new CoverNode [] {
            new CoverNode (0, ptsCorner [0], rCorner, Cursors .SizeNWSE),
            new CoverNode (1, ptsCorner [1], rCorner, Cursors .SizeNESW),
            new CoverNode (2, ptsCorner [2], rCorner, Cursors .SizeNWSE),
            new CoverNode (3, ptsCorner [3], rCorner, Cursors .SizeNESW),
            new CoverNode (4, ptsCorner [0], ptsCorner [3], Cursors
            .SizeWE),
            new CoverNode (5, ptsCorner [1], ptsCorner [2], Cursors
            .SizeWE),
            new CoverNode (6, ptsCorner [0], ptsCorner [1], Cursors
            .SizeNS),
            new CoverNode (7, ptsCorner [3], ptsCorner [2], Cursors
            .SizeNS),
            new CoverNode (8, ptsCorner) };
    cover = new Cover (nodes);
}
```

This is a classical complex object with its parts involved in individual, related, and synchronous movements.

- A rectangle is a dominant element; when it is moved, all the associated comments move synchronously.

- When the rectangle is resized, its associated comments retain their relative positions.

- Any comment can be moved and rotated individually.

Like any complex object, a Person object has to be registered in the mover queue by the Person.IntoMover() method. Comments have to be visible and accessible regardless of their relative position to the rectangle, so they must be registered ahead of the rectangle.

```
new public void IntoMover (Mover mv, int iPos)
{
    mv .Insert (iPos, this);
    mv .Insert (iPos, cmntName);
```

```
    if (BirthInfoToShow)
    {
        mv .Insert (iPos, cmntBirth);
    }
    if (DeathInfoToShow)
    {
        mv .Insert (iPos, cmntDeath);
    }
}
```

Drawing of the parts is always done in the opposite order to their placement in the mover queue, so first we have to draw a rectangle and after that draw all the comments that have to be shown.

```
public void Draw (Graphics grfx)
{
    grfx .FillRectangle (m_brush, Area);
    grfx .DrawRectangle (penBorder, Rectangle .Round (Area));
    cmntName .Draw (grfx);
    if (BirthInfoToShow)
    {
        cmntBirth .Draw (grfx);
    }
    if (DeathInfoToShow)
    {
        cmntDeath .Draw (grfx);
    }
}
```

File: Form_Person.cs

Menu position: Applications ➤ FamilyTree design step by step ➤ Person

This example contains a single Person object and demonstrates its tuning (Figure 7-28). Class Person has several constructors; the current example uses a constructor with the whole set of parameters.

```
private void DefaultPerson (PointF pt)
{
    m_person = new Person (this, mover, new RectangleF (pt .X, pt .Y,
                    210, 60),
                    Color .Cyan, "James", "3-Oct-1916", "23-Feb-
                    1995");
}
```

A Person object organized by this DefaultPerson() method has a view as shown in Figure 7-27. The cyan color of the rectangle is determined by one of the parameters on initialization, while all three comments appear as horizontal strings and with the same font and color. All further transformations, which can be seen in Figure 7-28, were made with the help of a tuning form.

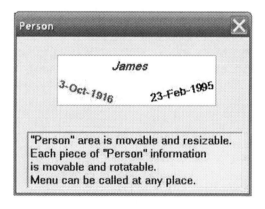

Figure 7-28. *Form_Person.cs contains one Person object*

In any user-driven application, all the visibility parameters are decided by the user. If there is an object on the screen, then there must be an easy way to change its view. A special tuning form for Person objects can be opened through the menu command. Usually each class of objects has its own menu and its own tuning form; the opening of the needed menu or tuning form is easily decided by the class of the clicked object. When any free spot inside a Person object is pressed, the mover informs that the mouse press really touched the Person object, and then its menu (and eventually the tuning form) can be called. When any comment of a Person object is pressed, the mover detects the pressing of the CommentToRect object. For any comment, only the font and color can be changed. The real Family Tree application, to which we'll come to later, provides different reactions for pressing comments or empty spots inside the Person area. However, a tuning form for `Person` objects (Figure 7-29) includes the tuning of all three comments, so in this and a couple of other auxiliary examples there is an identical reaction when clicking with the right button in an empty spot inside the `Person` area or any of its comments.

```
private void OnMouseUp (object sender, MouseEventArgs e)
{
    ptMouse_Up = e .Location;
    double fDist = Auxi_Geometry .Distance (ptMouse_Down, ptMouse_Up);
    if (mover .Release ())
    {
        GraphicalObject grobj = mover .ReleasedSource;
        if (e .Button == MouseButtons .Right && fDist <= 3)
        {
            if (grobj is Person || grobj is CommentToRect)
            {
                ContextMenuStrip = menuOnPerson;
            }
            ... ...
```

The tuning form (Figure 7-29) allows you to change the background color of the rectangle and to modify all three comments. The font and color of each comment can be set individually. There are no strict rules on how the birth and death information must be shown; these are only the strings, and you can type anything there. In this way, the tuning form works in the Family Tree application, but there is one limitation in the case of the current example. I don't want to allow the change of information for this particular `Person` object, so the last parameter of the tuning form initialization blocks the editing of all three comments. The view of three text boxes makes it obvious that the editing is prohibited.

```
private void Click_miModify_Person (object sender, EventArgs e)
{
    Form_Tuning_Person frm = new Form_Tuning_Person (
                                PointToScreen (ptMouse_Up), m_person,
                            false);
    ... ...
```

In the previous examples, we did a lot of things with the Bus objects, and we saw how they can be moved and changed. With the help of the BusConnection objects, buses can be organized into a system of connected buses that will be used in the Family Tree application. We have the Person class, which allows you to show information about any person in the family tree. Now we have to find out how Bus and Person objects can work together.

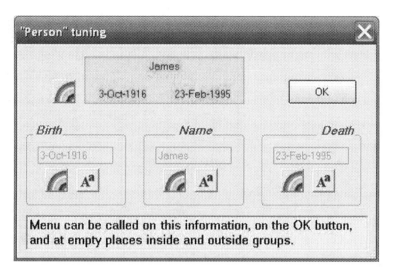

Figure 7-29. *The tuning form for Person objects*

In the Person class, there is an interesting field that has not been mentioned yet.

```
Bus busOnBorder;
```

The code of the Bus.IntoMover() method is shown several pages back. The busOnBorder is not mentioned there, so the mover doesn't know anything about this element. If an element is not registered with the mover, then this element is unmovable. The same bus is not mentioned in the Bus.Draw() method, which is also shown several pages back, so this bus is invisible. What is the purpose of the unmovable and invisible bus, and where is it used at all?

When any Person object is initialized, its busOnBorder field is also initialized; the points of the new bus are prepared by the Auxi_Geometry.ClosedPolyline() method.

```
public Person (Form frm, Mover mvr, RectangleF rect, Color clrRect ,
Font fnt, string strName, string strBirth, string strDeath)
{
    ... ...
    float w = Math .Max (minSide, rect .Width);
    float h = Math .Max (minSide, rect .Height);
    ptsCorner = new PointF [4] {rect .Location,
                                new PointF (rect .X + w, rect .Y),
                                new PointF (rect .X + w, rect .Y + h),
                            new PointF (rect .X, rect .Y + h) };
    busOnBorder = new Bus (m_form, null,
                        Auxi_Geometry .ClosedPolyline (ptsCorner),
                        penBorder);
    busOnBorder .RegisteredWithMover = false;
    ... ...
```

Thus, the busOnBorder is organized as a closed loop, and this invisible bus stretches along the border of the rectangle. The most remarkable feature of this bus initialization is the value that is passed to the RegisteredWithMover property.

```
    busOnBorder .RegisteredWithMover = false;
```

The name of this property and the passed value makes it obvious that this bus is not going to be registered with the mover. The next example shows the role of this unmovable and invisible bus in the design of the family tree.

File: Form_PersonPlusBus.cs

Menu position: Applications ➤ FamilyTree design step by step ➤ Person with connected bus

There is again only one Person object in the new example, but there is also one bus in view (Figure 7-30). This bus has one of its end points on the border of the Person object; if you press this point with the left button and try to move it anywhere, you will immediately find out that it will move only along the rectangle border and nowhere else. Does it look familiar to you? Does it look like moving the end of the bus along another bus with which it is connected?

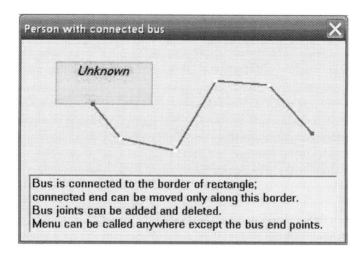

Figure 7-30. *Person object with connected bus*

Yes, this is exactly what happens when a bus is connected to a `Person` object: in reality, this bus is connected to another one—an invisible `busOnBorder` that goes along the border of rectangle. It does not matter at all that one of two involved buses is invisible; the connection between a bus and a `Person` object is organized in the same way as between the buses, for example, in `Form_ConnectedBuses_Two.cs`.

Though the set of elements in the current example is minimal—one `Person` object and one visible bus—this is the first example in which we have three `List`s for three types of elements on which the real Family Tree application is designed. In the following examples, regardless of the number of elements used, you will see exactly the same three `List`s.

```
public partial class Form_PersonPlusBus : Form
{
    List<Person> people = new List<Person> ();
    List<Bus> buses = new List<Bus> ();
    List<BusConnection> connections = new List<BusConnection> ();
```

When `Form_PersonPlusBus.cs` starts, all three lists are cleared, and then the `Person` object is designed.

```
private void DefaultView ()
{
    people .Clear ();
    buses .Clear ();
```

```
connections .Clear ();
Person person = new Person (this, mover, new RectangleF (100, 50,
140, 60), Color .Cyan, "Unknown");
AddPerson (person);
... ...
```

When any new object of the Person, Bus, or BusConnection class is organized, it is added to the end of the appropriate List. In the case of a new Person object, two lists are increased.

```
private void AddPerson (Person prsn)
{
    ... ...
    people .Add (prsn);
    AddBus (prsn .Bus);
}
private void AddBus (Bus busNew)
{
    ... ...
    buses .Add (busNew);
}
```

With the Person object already organized, now is the time to organize a bus, which you can see in Figure 7-30. Among other parameters, the Bus constructor gets a List of points. The bus in this example is going to be not a free bus but a bus that is connected to the invisible bus on the border of the Person object. With very high probability the proposed position for the end point of the new bus must be adjusted, and then the BusConnection object must be organized at the calculated point. All these things are done in the BusFromPerson() method that returns the new bus directly and the new connection—through the parameter.

```
private void DefaultView ()
{
    ... ...
    List<PointF> points = new List<PointF> ();
    points .Add (new PointF (220, 130));
    points .Add (new PointF (270, 170));
```

```
    points .Add (new PointF (410, 90));
    BusConnection con;
    Bus bus = BusFromPerson (this, mover, new Pen (Color .Blue, 3),
    person, points, out con);
    AddBus (bus);
    AddConnection (con);
    ... ...
private Bus BusFromPerson (Form frm, Mover mvr, Pen pn, Person person,
                          List<PointF> points, out BusConnection con)
{
    Bus busFrom = person .Bus;
    points [0] = Auxi_Geometry .Polyline_NearestPoint (points [0],
                                                busFrom .Points);
    Bus bs = new Bus (frm, mvr, points, pn);
    con = new BusConnection (frm, mvr, points [0], bs, EndType .Head,
    busFrom);
    busFrom .AddConnection (con);
    return (bs);
}
```

All new elements are included into the appropriate lists, and we obtain such lists:

• List<Person> people	Contains one element
• List<Bus> buses	Contains two elements; one of them is shown in Figure 7-30, while another is invisible and goes along the border of the Person object
• List<BusConnection> connections	Contains one element

The mover can work with elements of all three mentioned classes, so all of them must be registered with the mover but registered in the correct order: BusConnection elements must precede all the Bus elements, and Bus elements must precede all the Person elements.

The RenewMover() method from this example will be the same for a couple more examples and for the real Family Tree application.

```
private void RenewMover ()
{
    mover .Clear ();
    foreach (Person person in people)
    {
        person .IntoMover (mover, 0);
    }
    foreach (Bus bus in buses)
    {
        bus .IntoMover (mover, 0);
    }
    foreach (BusConnection con in connections)
    {
        con .IntoMover (mover, 0);
    }
    ... ...
```

We have two buses in Form_PersonPlusBus.cs: one is perfectly visible in Figure 7-30, while another one is invisible and goes along the border of the Person object. Both buses are included into the List of buses, and the code of the RenewMover() method shows that for each bus from the List the Bus.IntoMover() method is called. At the same time, I already mentioned that in no case the invisible busOnBorder should be registered with the mover. How is it done?

When any Person object is initialized, one parameter of its busOnBorder gets a special value.

```
busOnBorder .RegisteredWithMover = false;
```

When the Bus.IntoMover() method is called, it checks this value and registers only the bus with the appropriate value of this field.

```
new public void IntoMover (Mover mv, int iPos)
{
    if (iPos < 0 || mv .Count < iPos || !bRegisteredWithMover)
```

```
        {
            return;
        }
        mv .Insert (iPos, this);
    }
```

Thus, though we have two buses in the List of buses, only one of them—the visible one—is registered with the mover. Because the invisible bus on the border of the Person object is not registered with the mover, the mover does not know about this bus and cannot do anything with it. Thus, it is impossible to add any joint to this bus or move it with a mouse (!) anywhere outside of its place on the border of the associated rectangle.

It is impossible to move the busOnBorder with a mouse, but what happens when a Person object is moved or resized? Several pages back I already mentioned that any Person object is a complex object with standard rules of relation between the dominant element (rectangle) and its subordinate comments. At that moment the invisible bus on the border was not even mentioned, but it is another subordinate element, and it has to obey the same rules. When the rectangle is moved or resized, which is done by the Person.Move() and Person.MoveNode() methods, all the subordinate elements must be informed about the changes. This is done with the Person.InformRelatedElements() method.

```
    private void InformRelatedElements ()
    {
        cmntName .ParentRect = Area;
        cmntBirth .ParentRect = Area;
        cmntDeath .ParentRect = Area;
        busOnBorder .Points = Auxi_Geometry .ClosedPolyline (ptsCorner);
    }
```

As you see from this code, the busOnBorder element always stretches along the area border regardless of its change. We already discussed in the previous examples how a connection point always stays on the bus regardless of its change. Exactly the same mechanism works when a visible bus is connected to an invisible one, so throughout any change of the rectangular area the connection point retains its position on the border, so visually the bus is always connected to the border of the rectangle.

One more remark about Form_PersonPlusBus.cs. The connected bus is initialized as the blue one, as shown here:

```
private void DefaultView ()
{
    ... ...
    Bus bus = BusFromPerson (this, mover, new Pen (Color .Blue, 3),
    person, points, out con);
```

However, it appears as magenta (Figure 7-30), and there is no line of code in Form_PersonPlusBus.cs to change the color. What is responsible for this change of color?

The bus in Figure 7-30 is connected to a Person object by one end while its other end is free. For a real family tree, this is not a normal situation; you cannot imagine a bus that connects something with nothing; that is absurd. If this happens in a real family tree, it is an unfinished construction, and the user must be informed about this unusual situation. The best way to attract a user's attention to something unusual is to change the color of an element; it will be a signal that some action is needed from the user. For this reason, there is a special penWarn field in the Bus object. By default, this pen for a bus in this unusual situation has the magenta color.

```
        Pen penWarn = new Pen (Color .Magenta, 2);
```

There are situations when the bus, instead of its real color, is painted with this special pen.

```
public void Draw (Graphics grfx)
{
    if (((bHeadConnected != bTailConnected) ||
        (bHeadConnected == false && bTailConnected == false &&
        headsConnected .Count == 0 && tailsConnected .Count == 0 &&
        bRegisteredWithMover)) && bUseWarningColor)
    {
        grfx .DrawLines (penWarn, pts .ToArray ());
    }
    else
```

```
    {
        grfx .DrawLines (m_pen, pts .ToArray ());
    }
    ... ...
```

The use of this special warning color is easily regulated by the Bus.UseWarningColor property. In the first example with the connected buses, I wanted both buses to have their natural (declared) colors, so the warning by color for the blue bus was switched OFF.

```
public Form_ConnectedBuses_Two ()
{
    ... ...
    busBlue = new Bus (...);
    ... ...
    busBlue .UseWarningColor = false;
    ... ...
```

File: Form_Spouses.cs

Menu position: Applications ➤ FamilyTree design step by step ➤ Spouses

This example takes us closer to our goal of family tree design and represents a simple tree consisting of three Person objects and two buses between them (Figure 7-31). Regardless of the tree complexity, it is enough to have three Lists for three classes, and all work with these Lists can be checked and demonstrated even with such a simple family tree.

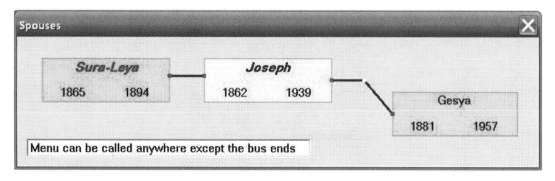

Figure 7-31. *A primitive family tree*

```
List<Person> people = new List<Person> ();
List<Bus> buses = new List<Bus> ();
List<BusConnection> connections = new List<BusConnection> ();
```

For such a small tree, it is easier first to organize all the needed Person objects and then connect them with the buses.

```
private void DefaultView ()
{
    ... ...
    people .Clear ();
    buses .Clear ();
    connections .Clear ();
    float w = 180;
    float h = 60;
    Person prsnWife_1 = new Person (this, mover, new RectangleF
    (80, 60, w, h), Color .Cyan, fntSelected, "Sura-Leya", "1865", "1894");
    Person prsnHusband = new Person (this, mover,
                                new RectangleF (320, 60, w, h),
                                Color .Yellow,
                                    fntSelected, "Joseph", "1862", "1939");
    Person prsnWife_2 = new Person (this, mover,
                                new RectangleF (600, 100, w, h), Color
                                .Cyan, fntSelected, "Gesya", "1881",
                                "1957");

    AddPerson (prsnWife_1);
    AddPerson (prsnHusband);
    AddPerson (prsnWife_2);
    ... ...
```

A direct connection between two Person objects is used often in the design of family trees, so a special method LinkPeople() can be useful in such cases.

```
Bus bus = LinkPeople (this, mover, new Pen (Color .Blue, 3),
                      prsnWife_1, Side .E, 0.4, prsnHusband, Side
                      .W, 0.4);
AddBus (bus);
bus = LinkPeople (this, mover, new Pen (Color .Blue, 3),
                  prsnHusband, Side .E, 0.5, prsnWife_2, Side .W, 0.5);
AddBus (bus);
... ...
```

A bus prepared by the LinkPeople() method consists of a single segment, so Figure 7-31 shows not the default view; the second bus was pressed with a mouse, and the new joint was moved to the new position.

The LinkPeople() method prepares not only a straight bus between two Person objects but also two new BusConnection elements at the ends of the new bus that have to be placed on the sides of rectangles. The initial position of each connection point is determined by the side of rectangle and by the positioning coefficient along this side. This coefficient takes a value from the [0, 1] range. For horizontal sides, it increases from left to right; for vertical sides, it increases from top to bottom.

```
private Bus LinkPeople (Form frm, Mover mvr, Pen pn,
                        Person personFrom, Side side_From, double coef_
                        From,
                        Person personTo, Side side_To, double coef_To)
{
    Bus busFrom = personFrom .Bus;
    PointF ptA = Auxi_Geometry .PointOnRectangleBorder (personFrom .Area,
                                                        side_From,
                                                        coef_From);
    ptA = Auxi_Geometry .Polyline_NearestPoint (ptA, busFrom .Points);
    Bus busTo = personTo .Bus;
    PointF ptB = Auxi_Geometry .PointOnRectangleBorder (personTo .Area,
                                                        side_To,
                                                        coef_To);
    ptB = Auxi_Geometry .Polyline_NearestPoint (ptB, busTo .Points);
    Bus bs = new Bus (frm, mvr, ptA, ptB, pn);
    List<BusConnection> conecs = new List<BusConnection> ();
```

```
        conecs .Add (new BusConnection (frm, mvr, ptA, bs, EndType.Head,
        busFrom));
        conecs .Add (new BusConnection (frm, mvr, ptB, bs, EndType .Tail,
        busTo));
        busFrom .AddConnection (conecs [0]);
        busTo .AddConnection (conecs [1]);
        connections .AddRange (conecs);
        return (bs);
    }
```

There is no bus tuning in this example, while the tuning of Person objects is done with the help of the tuning form that was already demonstrated (Figure 7-29). Tuning is started through the menu command; the same menu is called regardless of whether an empty spot inside the Person object was pressed or one of its comments, but in any case, the Person object has to be identified. When an empty spot is pressed, then it means the direct pressing of the Person object (personPressed). When a comment is pressed, then it means pressing some CommentToRect object. This comment is a subordinate of some Person object, so comment keeps the ID of its dominant object. A quick search through all the Person objects returns the needed one.

```
    private void OnMouseUp (object sender, MouseEventArgs e)
    {
        ... ...
        if (mover .Release (out iWasObject, out iWasNode, out shapeNode))
        {
            GraphicalObject grobj = mover .ReleasedSource;
            if (e .Button == MouseButtons .Right && fDist <= 3)
            {
                ... ...
                else if (grobj is CommentToRect)
                {
                    long idPerson = grobj .ParentID;
                    foreach (Person prsn in people)
                    {
                        if (prsn .ID == idPerson)
```

```
        {
            personPressed = prsn;
            break;
        }
    }
    ContextMenuStrip = menuOnPerson;
... ...
```

The procedures to save and restore the family tree do not depend on the size of a tree, and they are explained with the next example.

File: Form_TwoGenerations.cs

Menu position: Applications ➤ FamilyTree design step by step ➤ Two generations

This is the last preliminary example before the design of a full-size Family Tree application. In reality, this is not an example to demonstrate one or another feature but a real, though small, family tree with only one limitation: after this small family tree is constructed, there are no commands to add new people into it. Figure 7-32 shows that there are only four people from two generations.

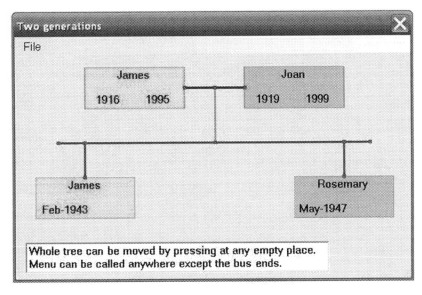

Figure 7-32. *A small family tree for two generations*

Though this family tree is small, it represents all possible types of buses. The classification of buses can be based on their connections to different objects. For a better explanation, I use different colors for the buses of different types. In Figure 7-17 the same four types of buses were marked with the letters *A*, *B*, *C*, and *S*. In the current example, this marking by letters is not used, but the order of definitions in the new explanation is the same as in the old one.

- *Bus between two Person objects*: In Figure 7-32, it is a blue one. Visually it is a bus between two people, but in reality, this bus is connected to the invisible buses on the borders of these `Person` objects.

- *Bus between a bus and a Person object*: In Figure 7-32, there are two green buses of this type. In reality, each of them is between two buses, but one of them is invisible.

- *Bus between two buses*: In Figure 7-32, it is a gray one.

- *Bus without connections at the ends*: In Figure 7-32, it is a brown one.

Any family tree, even such simple one, can be constructed in different ways. The design of this tree starts with two `Person` objects that represent the parents with the bus between them; this bus is constructed with the help of the `LinkPeople()` method, which was used in the previous example.

```
private void DefaultView ()
{
    float w = 150;
    float h = 60;
    Person father = new Person (this, mover, new RectangleF (140, 60, w, h),
                              Color .Cyan, fntSelected,
                              "James", "1916", "1995");
    AddPerson (father);
    Person mother = new Person (this, mover, new RectangleF (380, 60, w, h),
                              Color .LightPink, fntSelected,
                              "Joan", "1919", "1999");
    AddPerson (mother);
    Bus busParents = LinkPeople (this, mover, new Pen (Color .Blue, 3),
```

```
                    father, Side .E, 0.5, mother,
                    Side .W, 0.5);
AddBus (busParents);
... ...
```

At the next step, two more `Person` objects are designed; they represent children. A bus above them (the brown one) is initialized, but all links to this bus will be added a bit later.

```
float cyChildren = father .Bottom + 100;
Person son = new Person (this, mover,
                new RectangleF (father .Left - w / 2,
                cyChildren, w, h),
                    Color .Cyan, fntSelected, "James",
                    "Feb-1943", "");
Person daughter = new Person (this, mover,
                new RectangleF (mother .Right - w / 2, son .Top,
                             w, h),
                        Color .LightPink, fntSelected,
                        "Rosemary",
                        "May-1947", "");
AddPerson (son);
AddPerson (daughter);
float cyAbove = (father .Bottom + son .Top) / 2;
float cxL = Auxi_Geometry .Middle (son .Area) .X;
float cxR = Auxi_Geometry .Middle (daughter .Area) .X;
Bus busAbove = new Bus (this, mover, new PointF (cxL - 40, cyAbove),
                                new PointF (cxR + 40, cyAbove),
                        new Pen (Color .Brown, 3));
AddBus (busAbove);
```

Now it is time to connect "children" with the bus above them (the brown bus). Each green bus is organized by the `LinkBusPerson()` method. Even from the name of the method it is obvious that the new bus works as a link between the existing bus and the `Person` object.

```
AddBus (LinkBusPerson (this, mover, new Pen (Color .Green, 3),
        busAbove, new PointF (cxL, cyAbove), son, Side .N, 0.5));
AddBus (LinkBusPerson (this, mover, new Pen (Color .Green, 3),
        busAbove, new PointF (cxR, cyAbove), daughter,
        Side .N, 0.5));
```

The new bus is connected by the head to the existing bus (in this case, brown). The point of the connection on the existing bus is passed as a parameter (ptFrom), but this is only a preferable point, while the real point is calculated inside the method. By the tail the new bus is connected to the Person object; the point of connection (ptTo) is described by the side of the rectangle and the positioning coefficient along this side; this is done in the same way as in the LinkPeople() method.

```
private Bus LinkBusPerson (Form frm, Mover mvr, Pen pn,
                           Bus busFrom, PointF ptFrom,
                           Person personTo, Side side_To, double coef_To)
{
    ptFrom = Auxi_Geometry .Polyline_NearestPoint (ptFrom, busFrom
    .Points);
    Bus busTo = personTo .Bus;
    PointF ptTo = Auxi_Geometry .PointOnRectangleBorder (personTo .Area,
                                                 side_To, coef_To);
    ptTo = Auxi_Geometry .Polyline_NearestPoint (ptTo, busTo .Points);
    Bus bs = new Bus (frm, mvr, ptFrom, ptTo, pn);
    List<BusConnection> conecs = new List<BusConnection> ();
    conecs .Add (new BusConnection (frm, mvr, ptFrom, bs, EndType .Head,
                                 busFrom));
    conecs .Add (new BusConnection (frm, mvr, ptTo, bs, EndType .Tail,
    busTo));
    busFrom .AddConnection (conecs [0]);
    busTo .AddConnection (conecs [1]);
    connections .AddRange (conecs);
    return (bs);
}
```

The last step in design of this small family tree is the construction of the link between two generations—the gray bus.

```
private void DefaultView ()
{
    ... ...
    PointF pt = Auxi_Geometry .Middle (busParents .HeadPoint,
                                       busParents .TailPoint);
    AddBus (LinkBusBus (this, mover, new Pen (Color .DarkGray, 3),
            busParents, pt, busAbove, new PointF (pt .X, busAbove
            .TailPoint .Y)));
    ... ...
```

The link between two buses is organized by the LinkBusBus() method. Two points that are passed as parameters to this method are again the preferable locations, while the real points of connections are calculated inside the method.

```
private Bus LinkBusBus (Form frm, Mover mvr, Pen pn,
                        Bus busFrom, PointF ptFrom, Bus busTo,
                        PointF ptTo)
{
    ptFrom = Auxi_Geometry .Polyline_NearestPoint (ptFrom, busFrom .Points);
    ptTo = Auxi_Geometry .Polyline_NearestPoint (ptTo, busTo .Points);
    Bus bs = new Bus (frm, mvr, ptFrom, ptTo, pn);
    List<BusConnection> conecs = new List<BusConnection> ();
    conecs .Add (new BusConnection (frm, mvr, ptFrom, bs, EndType .Head,
                                    busFrom));
    conecs .Add (new BusConnection (frm, mvr, ptTo, bs, EndType .Tail,
    busTo));
    busFrom .AddConnection (conecs [0]);
    busTo .AddConnection (conecs [1]);
    connections .AddRange (conecs);
    return (bs);
}
```

When the design of this small family tree is over, there are the following collections of elements:

• List<Person> people	Contains four elements.
• List<Bus> buses	Contains nine elements. Five of them are shown in Figure 7-32 in different colors, while four other buses are invisible and go along the borders of the Person objects.
• List<BusConnection> connections	Contains eight elements. All of them are shown in Figure 7-32 as small red spots.

Once again the order of elements in the mover queue is defined by the RenewMover() method.

```
private void RenewMover ()
{
    mover .Clear ();
    foreach (Person person in people)
    {
        person .IntoMover (mover, 0);
    }
    foreach (Bus bus in buses)
    {
        bus .IntoMover (mover, 0);
    }
    foreach (BusConnection con in connections)
    {
        con .IntoMover (mover, 0);
    }
    ... ...
```

As shown in the previous code, first comes all the BusConnection elements, then all Bus elements, and at the end all the Person elements. The BusConnection elements must be at the head of the queue; otherwise, something else can close the connection points from the mover, and it will be impossible to move the connection points. The order of Bus and Person objects is not so important and can be changed. The order of elements in the mover queue correlates with the order of their drawing, so all depends on what you prefer to see in the situation when a bus goes across the rectangle of a `Person` object. If you prefer to see a bus over any `Person` object and you want to have an opportunity to press the bus and move it aside, then the coded order of elements is correct. If you prefer the buses to go beneath the `Person` objects, then you have to change both the `RenewMover()` and `OnPaint()` methods.

The brown bus in Figure 7-32 is the only bus in this family tree that can be declared movable (via the command of its context menu) because it is the only bus with both ends free. If you declare the brown bus movable, then you can move it, for example, closer to the `Person` objects above or below, and throughout this movement all the points of connection on this bus (there are three of them) will retain their relative positions.

Two new features appear in this example. They are not needed too much in this small tree, but they will be helpful in the really big family trees.

The first feature is the saving of the family tree in a binary file and the restoration of the tree from this file; this is done through the commands of a small File menu.

The second new feature is the ability to move the whole family tree around the screen. This feature is not needed at all for such a small tree, but in a really big family tree it is useful. First, there is no rule that regulates the order of construction of your real tree. You can start from the farthest known ancestor and go down from generation to generation, or you can put yourself in the middle of the screen and start adding relatives and the links to them in all directions. In any case, the chances are high that even the biggest screen will be not enough, and you will need to scroll it. This is done by a simple press of the left button at any empty place and by moving it in the direction you need. The instrument is simple.

There is a Boolean field to inform you whether the whole family tree is currently being moved or not.

```
bool bMoveAll = false;
```

When the left button is pressed at any empty place, the value of this field is changed, and the current position of the mouse is remembered (`ptMouse_prev`).

```
private void OnMouseDown (object sender, MouseEventArgs e)
{
    ptMouse_Down = e .Location;
    if (mover .Catch (e .Location, e .Button))
    {
        ... ...
    }
```

```
    else
    {
        if (e .Button == MouseButtons .Left)
        {
            bMoveAll = true;
            ptMouse_prev = e .Location;
        }
    }
    ... ...
```

When no object is caught by the mover but this Boolean parameter bMoveAll signals that everything is under move, then the distance between the current mouse position and the previous one is calculated; this pair of values (dx, dy) is used for the synchronous movement of all the elements.

```
private void OnMouseMove (object sender, MouseEventArgs e)
{
    if (mover .Move (e .Location))
    {
        Invalidate ();
    }
    else
    {
        if (bMoveAll)
        {
            if (ptMouse_prev != e .Location)
            {
                int dx = e .X - ptMouse_prev .X;
                int dy = e .Y - ptMouse_prev .Y;
                foreach (Person person in people)
                {
                    person .Move (dx, dy);
                }
                foreach (Bus bus in buses)
                {
                    bus .Move (dx, dy);
                }
```

```
            foreach (BusConnection con in connections)
            {
                con .Move (dx, dy);
            }
            ptMouse_prev = e .Location;
            Invalidate ();
        }
    }
    ... ...
```

When the mouse is released without releasing any object, the value of this bMoveAll field is changed to false.

```
private void OnMouseUp (object sender, MouseEventArgs e)
{
    ... ...
    if (mover .Release (out iWasObject, out iWasNode, out shapeNode))
    {
        ... ...
    }
    else
    {
        bMoveAll = false;
        ... ...
```

All Pieces Together

File: Form_FamilyTree.cs

Menu position: Applications ➤ Family Tree

Now is the time to put everything together, to add some commands to simplify the design of real family trees, and finally to develop a Family Tree application. This application is not going to use any new classes that were not discussed in the preliminary examples. A tree of any complexity can be constructed with Person, Bus, and BusConnection objects. How these three classes work was already discussed in detail, and in the Family Tree application you will find a lot of familiar things. There are going to be new things that were not used yet, but the novelty is not in the details. The main difference of this program is in the process to design the family tree.

While starting any of the preliminary examples, you will immediately see something. There can be a bus or several buses, a `Person` object, or several objects with some connections, but there is always something in view, and the main purpose of all those small examples is the demonstration and explanation of later work with the already existing objects. When you start the Family Tree application, there is nothing except a rectangle with some short information. You can squeeze this information to a tiny size and leave it somewhere in the corner. The form area is empty! Nobody knows beforehand what kind of family tree a particular user is going to construct, and nobody, except this user, knows from what part of the family tree he wants to start.

Suppose that you decide to draw your family tree in a standard (old) way. There is no standard order of drawing. You can start from the oldest known ancestor and then move from generation to generation. You can start from your parents and move in both directions. You can start from the youngest generation and move backward in time. Each person is usually represented by an oval or rectangle with a name inside. The known dates (or only years) of birth and death (the last one if it already happened) are placed next to the name, while the frame of this small area makes it obvious that the name and dates belong to the same person.

Relations between people are shown by a proper positioning of those frames and lots of lines. Usually the timeline goes from the top to bottom. Spouses are usually placed side by side, and their rectangles are connected with a short line. Children are usually placed at one level below the parents. The eldest sibling takes a position on the left end of row (this is correct for the countries in which writing is done from left to right). To demonstrate the relation between generations, children are connected with a line between their parents, but the link to the succeeding generation can be shown in different ways. It is possible that you draw a new line from the parents' line somewhere down and then add a rectangle with a name to the lower end of this line. If you know that a couple had three kids, then chances are high that first you will draw three rectangles side by side and then connect each of them to the line on the upper level. This is not a rule, but the whole drawing will be more accurate if you do it this way. It also means that your drawing can consist of several pieces that are united into a single family tree by adding some lines.

Occasionally you will find out that you missed some part, and there is no place for new rectangles at their right place; then you draw them somewhere aside and use a broken line to show the relation. The same thing might happen when you decide to draw some side branch of your family tree.

One sheet of paper will be not enough. You take another sheet and make special marks to show how these sheets have to be placed in relation to one another. Lines of relations between people will go from one sheet to another and around those rectangles that happen to be in the way.

I mentioned the normal way of drawing a family tree on sheets of paper, but if you want to produce some program for the same purpose, then this program has to provide the same level of flexibility in drawing a family tree on the screen. There are going to be some limitations, but their effects must be minimized.

Elements of three classes are used to construct any family tree; all these elements are included into three Lists.

```
List<Person> m_people = new List<Person> ();
List<Bus> m_buses = new List<Bus> ();
List<BusConnection> m_connections = new List<BusConnection> ();
```

The Bus and BusConnection objects are added to the appropriate lists in a similar way. Each object has a unique ID, so there is a simple check by this ID to prevent the double inclusion of the same object.

```
private void AddBus (Bus busNew)
{
    foreach (Bus bus in m_buses)
    {
        if (busNew .ID == bus .ID)
        {
            return;
        }
    }
    m_buses .Add (busNew);
}
private void AddConnection (BusConnection conNew)
{
    foreach (BusConnection con in m_connections)
    {
        if (conNew .ID == con .ID)
        {
```

```
            return;
        }
    }
    m_connections .Add (conNew);
}
```

Adding a Person object is done in a similar way, but more actions are needed. Each Person object contains an invisible bus, so two elements are checked for the uniqueness of the ID and then two Lists are increased.

```
private void AddPerson (Person prsn)
{
    long idPerson = prsn .ID;
    long idBus = prsn .Bus .ID;
    foreach (Person person in m_people)
    {
        if (idPerson == person .ID)
        {
            MessageBox .Show (...);
            return;
        }
    }
    foreach (Bus bus in m_buses)
    {
        if (idBus == bus .ID)
        {
            MessageBox .Show (...);
            return;
        }
    }
    m_people .Add (prsn);
    m_buses .Add (prsn .Bus);
}
```

Users of the Family Tree program don't know anything about buses or connections; they'd rather think about the constructed tree in terms of children, parents, and spouses, but any command to add a single relative or a group of relatives can be easily traced to these `AddBus()`, `AddConnection()`, and `AddPerson()` methods. These methods are used to collect the data that provides the functionality of the program; the user deals with the representation of the same data on the screen, and not all the data elements are visualized.

- All `Person` objects are visible.

- `Bus` objects are divided between visible and invisible. Buses that represent relations between people in a family tree are visible. Each `Person` object has an invisible bus as its subordinate element.

- All `BusConnection` objects are invisible.

Elements appear on the screen as a result of using many different commands. All screen elements can be modified, but at first appearance any new element gets a standard view. This standard view can be also set by the user, but initially the program defines two standards in such a way.

```
public Form_FamilyTree ()
{
    ... ...
    busStandard = new Bus (this, mover, ..., new Pen (Color .DarkGray, 2));
    personStandard = new Person (this, mover, new RectangleF (0, 0,
                        140, 50), Color .Cyan, "Name", "birth", "death");
    ... ...
```

Later in the chapter the commands are discussed and illustrated with some figures; elements on these figures are mostly shown in their mentioned standard views.

When a family tree is under construction and new elements have to be added to the already existing ones, then a menu is called on some existing element to which the new part must be linked. It is also possible to design a new unrelated part and later link it to the existing family tree.

Designing a new family tree starts with the menu at an empty place (Figure 7-33). Commands of this menu are divided into three groups. All commands that put on the screen some new element are included in the first group; one of these commands has a submenu. The menu is opened at the place where the right button was clicked; new elements born by one or another command are anchored to the same point. Commands in the second group allow you to change some visualizing parameters for all buses of the existing family tree. The view of any bus or Person element can be changed by calling a special tuning form through the menu on this element. The user can simplify his work by setting the preferable visualizing parameters for all future elements; all new elements will be constructed according to these settings. I'll write about these settings closer to the end of this section; now let's look at the reaction on the commands from the menu shown in Figure 7-33.

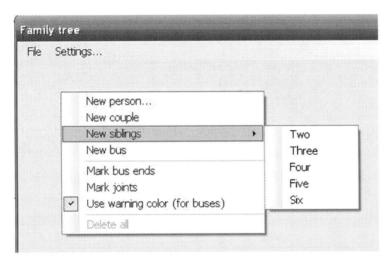

Figure 7-33. *To start the tree construction, call the menu at an empty place*

New person	A new Person object appears on the screen; its top-left corner is placed at the point of the mouse press. The user needs to define at least the name of this person and has to decide whether some additional information about the birth and death has to appear. For this reason, an auxiliary tuning form is automatically called for this new object (Figure 7-34). There can be a lot of Person objects in view, so the initial positioning of the tuning form helps to inform the user about the currently modified element.

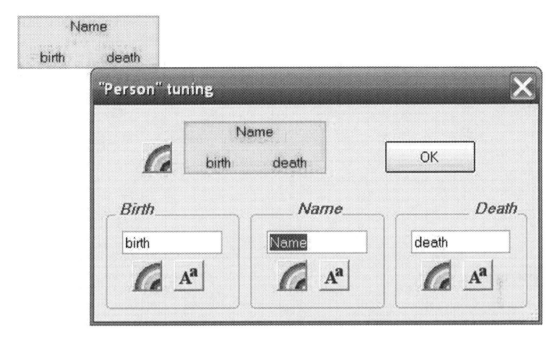

Figure 7-34. *A new Person object with a tuning form*

```
private void Click_miNewPerson (object sender, EventArgs e)
{
    Person person = new Person (this, mover, ptMouse_Up,
    m_personStandard);
    AddPerson (person);
    RenewMover ();
    ModifyPerson (person, Auxi_Geometry .LocationByCoefficients
    (person .Area, 0.5, 0.95));
}
```

New couple   A new couple is represented by a pair of Person objects positioned not far from each other and connected by a short straight bus (Figure 7-35). The top-left corner of the left element is placed at the point of the mouse press. Both new elements are identical and have the standard view. The user can decide which one he wants to modify first and call the tuning form through the menu on an element.

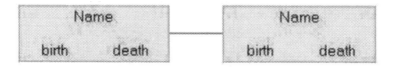

Figure 7-35. *A new couple on the screen*

```
private void Click_miNewCouple (object sender, EventArgs e)
{
    NewCouple (ptMouse_Up);
    RenewMover ();
}
```

The NewCouple() method produces two Person objects that are linked with each other by a short bus; this bus is organized by the LinkPersonPerson() method.

```
private Bus NewCouple (PointF ptLT)
{
    Person personL = new Person (this, mover, ptLT, personStandard);
    AddPerson (personL);
    Person personR = new Person (this, mover,
                        new PointF (personL .Right + m_nDistSpouses,
                        ptLT .Y), personStandard);
    AddPerson (personR);
    Bus link = LinkPersonPerson (this, mover, busStandard, personL,
    Side .E, 0.5, personR, Side .W, 0.5);
    return (link);
}
```

There are several situations when this pair of objects has to be organized and linked to an already existing element; one such case is demonstrated in Figure 7-39. Because a link from the new couple to the existing family tree is often organized from this short bus between two new Person elements, the NewCouple() method returns this bus.

Visually, the bus is between two Person objects, but in reality it is a bus between the invisible buses of these Person objects, so the LinkPersonPerson() method is only a wrapper around the LinkBusBus() method.

```
private Bus LinkPersonPerson (Form frm, Mover mvr, Bus busSample,
                             Person personFrom, Side side_From, double
                             coef_From,
                             Person personTo, Side side_To, double coef_To)
{
    Bus busFrom = personFrom .Bus;
    PointF ptFrom = Auxi_Geometry .PointOnRectangleBorder (personFrom
    .Area, side_From, coef_From);

    Bus busTo = personTo .Bus;
    PointF ptTo = Auxi_Geometry .PointOnRectangleBorder (personTo .Area,
                                              side_To, coef_To);
    return (LinkBusBus (frm, mvr, busSample, busFrom, ptFrom, busTo,
    ptTo));
}
```

A nearly identical LinkBusBus() method was already used in the previous example, and its code was shown 12 pages back. There is one difference in the parameters of two methods: in the previous one, a pen for a new bus was among the parameters, while the current variant uses a bus sample.

```
private Bus LinkBusBus (Form frm, Mover mvr, Bus busSample,
                        Bus busFrom, PointF ptFrom, Bus busTo, PointF ptTo)
{
    ptFrom = Auxi_Geometry .Polyline_NearestPoint (ptFrom, busFrom
    .Points);
    ptTo = Auxi_Geometry .Polyline_NearestPoint (ptTo, busTo .Points);
    Bus bs = new Bus (frm, mvr, ptFrom, ptTo, busSample);
    BusConnection conFrom = new BusConnection (frm, mvr, ptFrom, bs,
                                         EndType .Head, busFrom);
    BusConnection conTo = new BusConnection (frm, mvr, ptTo, bs,
                                         EndType .Tail, busTo);
    busFrom .AddConnection (conFrom);
    busTo .AddConnection (conTo);
    m_connections .Add (conFrom);
    m_connections .Add (conTo);
```

```
        AddBus (bs);
        return (bs);
    }
```

In the situation with the "New couple" command, the LinkPersonPerson() method is used as a wrapper around the LinkBusBus() method. Later you'll see commands that allow you to set a new bus between an existing bus and a Person object. Depending on the head position of the new bus, the LinkBusPerson() and LinkPersonBus() methods are used; both are wrappers around the LinkBusBus() method.

New siblings   This menu command has a submenu that allows you to put on the screen between two and six siblings; Figure 7-36 shows a variant of four siblings. If there must be more than six siblings, then the best way is to use this command to put six siblings on the screen and then to add more with the command from another menu; I'll write about it later in this section. The returned value of the NewSiblings() method is the bus above the siblings (busAbove). The turning point of the long bus above the left element is the point of the mouse press.

Figure 7-36. *Four siblings*

In the previous example Form_TwoGenerations.cs (Figure 7-32), I already explained the procedure to add several siblings. There were only two siblings in that example, but this is not important at all. The main difference can be seen by comparing the two figures. Though the difference between two figures is not big in size—only two small spots disappeared—their disappearance highlights some significant change in the construction of such a group of elements. In the older version, a long horizontal bus of a single segment was organized; then all siblings were connected to this bus in an identical way with the short buses.

I purposely use Figure 7-36 with more than two siblings to demonstrate that in the new variant not all siblings are connected in an identical way; there is an obvious difference in the connection of inner siblings and the two end siblings. Throughout the design of a big family tree, I began to feel some inconvenience in using the old variant for further work with a tree, so I changed the procedure of including siblings into the family tree.

The NewSiblings() method is used for a number of siblings between two and six. First, a long bus consisting of three segments is constructed, so the long line with two short orthogonal segments at the ends are the parts of the same bus (busAbove).

```
private Bus NewSiblings (PointF ptL_busAbove, int nSiblings)
{
    nSiblings = Math .Min (Math .Max (2, nSiblings), 6);
    float cyLineAbove = ptL_busAbove .Y;
    float cySiblings = cyLineAbove + m_nDistGenerations / 2;
    float lenLineAbove =
                (nSiblings - 1) * (m_personStandard .Width +
                m_nDistSiblings);
    PointF ptL_above = ptL_busAbove;
    PointF ptR_above = new PointF (ptL_above .X + lenLineAbove,
    cyLineAbove);
    List<PointF> pts = new List<PointF> ();
    pts .Add (new PointF (ptL_above .X, cySiblings));
    pts .Add (ptL_above);
    pts .Add (ptR_above);
    pts .Add (new PointF (ptR_above .X, cySiblings));
    Bus busAbove = new Bus (this, mover, pts, m_busStandard);
    AddBus (busAbove);
    ... ...
```

Then two siblings—the first (childFirst) and the last (childLast)—are connected at the ends of this bus.

```
    float cxM_person;
    PointF ptOnBus;
    Person childFirst = new Person (this, mover,
        new PointF (ptL_above .X - m_personStandard .Width / 2,
        cySiblings), m_personStandard);
    childFirst .Name_Comment .Text = "Sibling-1";
    AddPerson (childFirst);
```

```
Person childLast = new Person (this, mover,
        new PointF (ptR_above .X - m_personStandard .Width / 2,
        cySiblings), m_personStandard);
childLast .Name_Comment .Text = "Sibling-" + nSiblings .ToString ();
AddPerson (childLast);
LinkBusBus_broken_bus (this, mover, m_busStandard,
                            childFirst .Bus, busAbove .HeadPoint,
                            childLast .Bus, busAbove .TailPoint, busAbove);
```

If there are more than two siblings, then they are connected to the long bus in a standard (old) way with much shorter buses. There is no problem with their positioning without overlap because the length of the long bus was initially calculated for the needed number of siblings.

```
for (int i = 2; i < nSiblings; i++)
{
    cxM_person = ptL_above .X + Convert .ToSingle (
                        lenLineAbove * ((i - 1) * 1.0 /
                        (nSiblings - 1)));
    Person child = new Person (this, mover,
        new PointF (cxM_person - m_personStandard .Width / 2,
        cySiblings), m_personStandard);
    child .Name_Comment .Text = "Sibling-" + i .ToString ();
    AddPerson (child);
    ptOnBus = new PointF (cxM_person, cyLineAbove);
    LinkBusPerson (this, mover, m_busStandard, busAbove, ptOnBus,
                    child, Side .N, 0.5);
}
RenewMover ();
return (busAbove);
}
```

| New bus | This is a simple but interesting command that produces such a small object on the screen that no figure is needed to illustrate it. This new object is a short bus with two free ends. |

Chances are high that the length of the new bus will be only 20 pixels, though circumstances, or really other objects, may force it to become longer. This length (and angle) uncertainty is caused by the requirement of both ends to be free. The code of the Click_miNewBus() method shows that no connection is organized, so regardless of the length and position of the end points, the new bus is not connected to any object, but I would like the new bus to be visually free, and this can cause some problem. The menu with the "New bus" command is called at an empty place, and the head of the new bus is placed at the same point, so this end point is definitely free. Nobody can forecast the positioning of all other elements when this command is used, but I would like the other end of the new bus to be positioned also at a free place, so the search of a suitable point for another end is done by the AnotherEndOfNewBus() method.

```
private void Click_miNewBus (object sender, EventArgs e)
{
    Bus bus = new Bus (this, mover, ptMouse_Up,
                    AnotherEndOfNewBus (ptMouse_Up), m_busStandard);
    AddBus (bus);
    RenewMover ();
}
```

At the beginning of the book in Chapter 1 I mentioned that the mover can check the existence of objects not only at the point of cursor but at any point of the form in which this mover works. Such checking is needed rarely enough, and it wasn't used in all other examples, but in the Family Tree application this checking is useful in a couple of cases, and a free positioning of the end point of a new bus is one of them.

The method starts with an attempt to design a vertical bus of minimal length and uses the Mover.PointInfoAll() method to check the existence of any object at the proposed end point. If the point is occupied, then another point around the circle of the same radius is checked. If all positions on a circle of this radius are occupied, then the radius is increased, and the same check is repeated. Eventually some free point is found, and the new bus is organized.

There can be another solution for the same problem. For example, a free bus can be organized as unusually wide, so its view would get the attention even if another end is placed on some object, but I preferred to install the search for a free place.

The new bus is short and is not connected to anything, but this free bus allows you to organize any needed link in the family tree; this can be a link between two buses, between two Person objects, or between a bus and a person. To do this, you press the end point of the bus, move it on top of the object with which you want to connect it, and release the end bus there. Because the last action is the release of an object, for the result we have to look at the code of the OnMouseUp() method. I am going to interrupt the following piece of code with some helpful explanations.

The released end of the bus can be connected either to a visible bus or to an invisible bus on the border of a Person object; in the second case, it looks like a connection to the person. The code for these two cases differs only in some tiny details, so it is enough to look at the case of a bus released over a bus. The number (iWasNode) and shape (shapeNode) of the released node are needed for further analysis, so the appropriate version of the Mover.Release() method is used.

```
private void OnMouseUp (object sender, MouseEventArgs e)
{
    ptMouse_Up = e .Location;
    double dist = Auxi_Geometry .Distance (ptMouse_Down, ptMouse_Up);
    int iWasObject, iWasNode;
    NodeShape shapeNode;
    if (mover .Release (out iWasObject, out iWasNode, out shapeNode))
    {
        GraphicalObject grobj = mover .ReleasedSource;
        long id = grobj .ID;
        if (e .Button == MouseButtons .Left)
        {
```

The released element has to be a circular node of an unmovable bus.

```
            if (grobj is Bus && shapeNode == NodeShape .Circle && !grobj
            .Movable)
            {
```

The bus can be connected only by the head or by the tail. Circular nodes are the first in the bus cover, and those nodes are numbered from head to tail; the node at the head has the number 0. The type of the released bus end (end_type) is also determined from the node number.

```
if (iWasNode == 0 || iWasNode == busPressed .TailPointNumber)
{
        EndType end_type = (iWasNode == 0) ? EndType .Head
                                           : EndType .Tail;
```

The connection of the released bus to some object depends on the situation with those objects at the point of release. The full information about objects at any point can be obtained from the mover through the Mover.PointInfoAll() method. This method returns a List of objects that can be found at the specified point; the order of objects in this List is the same as their order in the mover queue.

```
List<MoverPointInfo> infoAll = mover.PointInfoAll
(ptMouse_Up);
for (int j = 0; j < infoAll .Count; j++)
{
    MoverPointInfo info = infoAll [j];
    GraphicalObject objFound = mover [info .ObjectNum]
    .Source;
```

The bus is released over some object (objFound). Connection of the bus to itself makes no sense. I do not think that anyone would really need to organize such a connection, but there are always people who like to check any application for unthinkable situations, and there is also a possibility of accidental release of an object at the wrong place.

```
if (id != objFound.ID)           // bus cannot be
                                    connected to
                                    itself

    {
```

There are two situations when the released bus must be connected to an object underneath: it can be another bus, or it can be a Person object. In the second case, the connection is organized with the invisible bus under the border of the rectangular object. These two cases differ only in some small details, so it is enough to look into the details of one of them; let's consider a case of a bus released over another visible bus. We need to check and avoid the situation when we try to connect the released bus end to the same bus to which its other end is already connected. Also prohibited is the connection of two buses to each other, so the case of two buses creating a loop is prohibited.

```
if (objFound is Bus)
{
    Bus busFound = objFound as Bus;
    if ((iWasNode == 0 && busPressed
    .TailConnected &&
        busPressed .ID_OnTail == busFound .ID) ||
        (iWasNode == busPressed
        .TailPointNumber &&
        busPressed .HeadConnected &&
        busPressed .ID_OnHead == busFound .ID) ||
        id == busFound .ID_OnHead ||
        id == busFound .ID_OnTail)
    {
        // two ends cannot be connected to the
            same bus
        // two buses cannot be connected to
            each other
    }
    else
    {
```

It looks like we successfully avoided all traps, and the released end of the bus can be connected to another bus found at the point of release. This action requires a bit of calculation and the change of several parameters of two objects.

- The exact point of connection is calculated (ptOnBus).

- The released end of the bus (head or tail) must take this calculated position.

- The new connection (con) is organized at the calculated point.

- It is a new connection to the found bus. Each bus keeps information about all connections, so the information in the found bus must be updated with the Bus.AddConnection() method.

- The new connection is included in the full List of connections.

- A new movable object appears on the screen, so the mover queue must be renewed.

```
PointF ptOnBus =
    Auxi_Geometry .Polyline_
    NearestPoint (
                ptMouse_Up, busFound
                .Points);
if (end_type == EndType .Head)
{
    busPressed .HeadPoint = ptOnBus;
}
else
{
    busPressed .TailPoint = ptOnBus;
}
BusConnection con = new BusConnection
(this, mover, ptOnBus, busPressed,
                end_type, busFound);
busFound .AddConnection (con);
m_connections .Add (con);
RenewMover ();
        }
        break;
    }
    else if (objFound is Person)
    ... ...
```

The Family Tree application provides different commands to design trees. These commands are named in such a way as to make them easier to understand from the point of human relations (new couple or new siblings), but in reality there is no information inside the organized elements about those declared relations and no traces of the commands by which the elements were constructed. There are only `Bus`, `Person`, and `BusConnection` elements linked with each other in different ways. The same tree can be constructed in many different ways, and the order of elements in three lists (`m_people`, `m_buses`, and `m_connections`) can be different. It does not matter at all whether you prefer to use the commands that put on the screen groups of connected elements or to use other commands that add one bus or one person at a time.

For example, a "New couple" command that was discussed several pages back can be substituted with the following sequence of commands and actions:

1. Use the "New person" command at one point and then the same command somewhere slightly aside; two independent `Person` objects will appear on the screen.

2. Use the "New bus" command to put a new bus on the screen; on initialization, this bus is not connected to anything.

3. Move one end of the new bus and drop it somewhere inside one `Person` object; the bus will be connected to this object (visually to the border of this object).

4. Move another end of the bus and drop it inside the second `Person` object; this end of the bus will be connected to the border of this object.

This sequence is much longer than a single "New couple" command, but for the work of the designed tree it doesn't matter.

What to do if you need to disconnect a bus? Call the menu at the point of connection and select the only command on this menu—"Delete connection" (Figure 7-37a). The bus will be disconnected, and in most cases its end point will be moved aside to organize a visual gap between two elements. The end point is not moved aside, and the gap is not organized if the decrease of the bus length will make it too small. Regardless of whether the gap is organized or not, the bus will be disconnected. The bus with a free end is an abnormal situation, so the warning color is used to draw the bus after disconnection (Figure 7-37b).

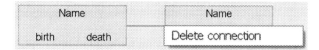

Figure 7-37a. *The menu on connection has only one command*

Figure 7-37b. *After disconnection, there is a gap between two objects, and the warning color is used for a bus*

Several menus can be called on elements of the family tree. Some of these menus are small with only one or two commands, but menus on Person objects and on bus segments are really big with commands to change the existing family tree and to add new parts.

The menu on bus segments (Figure 7-38) can be called on any bus, and it does not matter at all whether this bus is connected to anything or absolutely free. As always, the menu is called at the point where the bus is pressed. If the selected command of the menu brings new elements on the screen, then this new part will be connected to the pressed bus at the same point. On the four following figures for the commands that put new elements on the screen, the pressed bus is shown with a wide blue line.

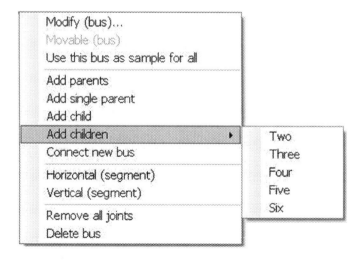

Figure 7-38. *Menu on bus segments*

Modify (bus)	This command opens the auxiliary form (Figure 7-21), which allows you to change the view of the pressed bus.
Movable (bus)	This command allows you to change the movability of the pressed bus, but this command can be applied only to a bus with both free ends. It is an extremely rare and strange situation for a real family tree, but it is possible, so I decided to keep this command in the menu.
Use this bus as sample for all	Suppose that you have spent some time constructing the family tree and then decide to change the view of all the buses. You can change the view of any bus individually by using its tuning form, but it would take too long to repeat this procedure for every bus in a big tree. Instead, you can change the view of one bus to whatever you prefer and then use this command; all buses will change their view according to this sample.
Add parents	A pair of Person objects with a bus between them represents a couple; the bus between the parents is linked with the pressed bus (Figure 7-39). The pair of new Person elements is identical to the pair in Figure 7-35; the only difference in result is the link between this pair and the pressed bus.

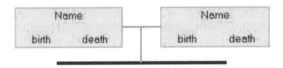

Figure 7-39. *The result of the "Add parents" command*

Add single parent	If there is information about one parent or the user wants to include in the family tree only one person of a couple, then the user can use the "Add single parent" command. Because only one new Person object appears on the screen (Figure 7-40) and this new object needs at least some change of information, then an auxiliary form for tuning Person objects is automatically called on this new object.

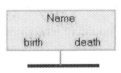

Figure 7-40. *Adding a single parent*

(*continued*)

Add child	This command is similar to the previous one, but the new Person object appears below the pressed bus (Figure 7-41). There are two standard cases for using this command: it is the case of a single child of some couple, or it can be the case of more than six siblings. The screen elements for six siblings can be organized with a single command; more siblings can be added by using this command on the bus above the siblings.

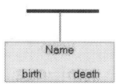

Figure 7-41. *Adding a single child*

Add children	There is a submenu to put on the screen between two and six siblings; Figure 7-42 shows the variant of two siblings. If there must be more than six siblings, you can put six of them using one command and then apply to the bus above the siblings the "Add child" command as many times as you need.
	I already explained the sequence of steps to add several siblings. Everything starts with a bus designed as a broken line of three segments; then the first and last siblings are connected to the ends of this bus. For better understanding, the joints in Figure 7-42 are marked in a special way.

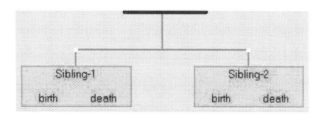

Figure 7-42. *The result of "Add children": two siblings*

Connect new bus	The new short bus is connected to the pressed bus; the second end of the new bus is free. You can reconfigure the new bus, move its free end, and connect it to any object (bus or person) you need.

A family tree can be constructed by linking a group of new elements not only to a bus but also to any Person object; this is done through the commands of the menu that can be called on such an object (Figure 7-43). As you can see from the list of available commands for adding new elements, these commands are similar to the commands of the menu for empty places (Figure 7-33) and the commands of the menu for bus segments (Figure 7-38).

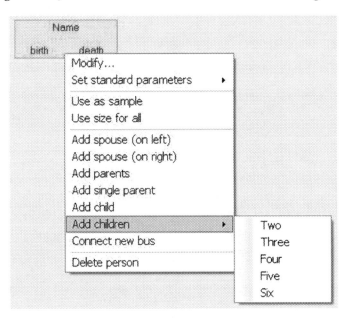

Figure 7-43. *Menu on a Person object*

The first command of the menu on a Person object calls its tuning form, which was already demonstrated 40 pages back (see Figure 7-29), but in the case of the real Family Tree application, the user needs to edit all the pieces of information, so all three text boxes allow such editing (Figure 7-44).

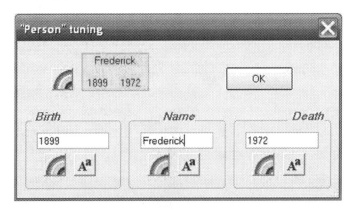

Figure 7-44. *Tuning form for Person objects*

414

If you clear the information from the text boxes for birth and death, then those comments will not appear in the `Person` object. If you try to do the same with the text box for a name, then the word *Unknown* will appear instead of the name. This tuning form allows you to change the font and color individually for each comment, though I think that users would need a more standard view of elements in a big family tree. I assume that this tuning form would be used to change only the text of comments. With such a preferable use of this tuning form, those six small buttons inside the groups become redundant, so their appearance is regulated through commands of the menu at empty places.

The main part of the menu on `Person` objects contains six different commands to add some relatives to the pressed person; four of these commands add one new `Person` object. I want to stress again that commands in the menu are formulated in terms of relation between the existing person and the new person, but these relations are not stored anywhere inside the family tree. There are only elements of `Bus`, `Person`, and `BusConnection` classes.

Figure 7-45 demonstrates the results of using those four commands that add one `Person` object. This object appears on the screen together with the tuning form; this happens exactly as shown in Figure 7-34. In all versions of Figure 7-45, the yellow rectangle represents the already existing `Person` object on which the menu is called; the cyan rectangle appears as the result of using one or another command. As you see, four different commands place the new rectangle at one or another side of the existing rectangle, and this is the only difference between the four commands.

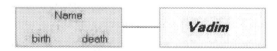

Figure 7-45a. *Command "Add spouse" (on left)*

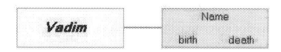

Figure 7-45b. *Command "Add spouse" (on right)*

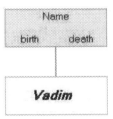

Figure 7-45c. *Command "Add single parent"*

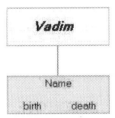

Figure 7-45d. *Command "Add child"*

One variant can be transformed into another variant in these three simple movements:

- Move the cyan rectangle to another side of the yellow rectangle.

- Move the end of the bus on the yellow rectangle to the same side where the cyan rectangle is placed now.

- Move the end of the bus on the cyan rectangle in such a way that the bus will demonstrate the shortest line between two rectangles.

Several other commands need some remarks.

Connect new bus	This menu is called somewhere inside the rectangle. After this command, the new bus is connected to the border point that is nearest to the calling point of menu. If needed, the new connection can be easily moved around the border.
Set standard parameters	This command has a submenu with variants to change some or all of the visibility parameters. I already mentioned the existence of Bus and Person elements that keep standard views and also mentioned that the user can change these views.

In the main menu of the Family Tree application, there is the Settings item; if you click this menu command, Form_FamilyTree_NewElemParams.cs is opened (Figure 7-46).

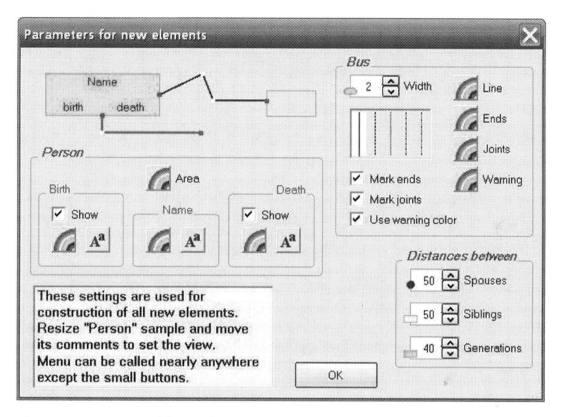

Figure 7-46. *A special form allows you to set parameters that are used for the design of all new elements*

The Bus group allows you to set the parameters of all new buses, so elements of this group are the same as shown in the tuning form for buses (Figure 7-21).

The Distances group allows you to define the standard distances between several Person objects that are added to the family tree by different menu commands. The regulated values are horizontal spaces between rectangles for spouses and siblings and vertical space between parents and children.

Elements of the Person group allow you to set all fonts and colors for future Person objects. There is a Person object in the top-left corner of this form. The needed sizes are set by resizing this sample; positioning coefficients for all three comments (name, birth, and death) are set by moving the comments.

I want to stress that all changes in this auxiliary form have no immediate effect when you close this form and return to the main form of the Family Tree application. These settings are used when you begin to add new elements to the family tree. You can spread these settings on the existing family tree, but because there is a possibility that such an operation can destroy the carefully prepared view of a big tree and thus can be harmful, I purposely included some intermediate steps in this operation of changing the whole view.

First, you call the menu on some `Person` object and use the submenu to the command Set standard parameters. I recommend doing this not for one but for several `Person` objects and maybe with different commands from the submenu. If you like the result and want to make a global change, then call the menu on the same `Person` object and use the command Use as a sample.

Changing the buses cannot produce a catastrophic result, but it is better to make the global changes also in two steps. First, call the menu on some bus and use the Modify (bus) command. If you like the result, then call the same menu and use this bus as a sample for all others.

Let's return to the main family tree. There are two useful commands in the main menu of `Form_FamilyTree.cs`. The File ➤ Save As command allows you to save the tree in a binary file, while the File ➤ Open command allows you to restore a family tree from a file.

A real family tree can be big, and chances are high that you will need more space for it than you have on the screen. The whole tree can be easily scrolled in any way you want; simply press the left button at any empty place and start moving it. This scrolling of the whole family tree was already explained in the previous example.

Do not be afraid to do anything and to make any mistakes in the design because several rules are implemented in this Family Tree application.

- No user's action is fatal for the design of a family tree. If you have placed a wrong element, you can delete it by using a command in the context menu; if you placed a wrong combination of elements, you can use the Delete command for each of these elements. If the bus is connected to the wrong element, simply disconnect it (via the command in the menu at the place of the wrong connection) and continue with your design.

- There are a few restrictions on the design: a bus cannot be connected to itself; both bus ends cannot be connected to the same bus; two buses cannot organize a loop by connections to each other. Everything else is allowed.

- By playing with the visibility parameters, you can add personal information that may be important from your point of view, but that is not going to be mentioned in any system of standard commands. For example, if you want to highlight the link between spouses by two buses, you can do this. Nobody is going to catch you on such an attempt and not allow you to organize two parallel buses between the same two Person objects. Or you can mark in the buses different ways for religious and civil marriages.

- Not only can the visual parameters of elements be changed, but even some standard family links can be shown differently from what is proposed by the previously described system of commands. Figure 7-47a shows the result of using two commands that were discussed several pages back: first the couple was set; then another command on a bus between them added three children. The same family of parents with three kids can be represented in a different way (Figure 7-47b). The first command is the same; then a command to add a single child is applied three times to the upper bus.

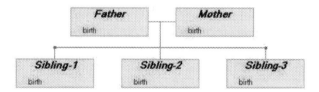

Figure 7-47a. *This view is a result of using two standard commands*

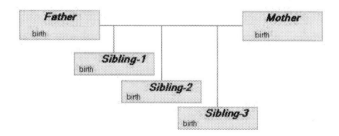

Figure 7-47b. *Rectangles for parents appear as a result of a standard command, while children are added one by one by calling a command on the upper bus*

This is a standard user-driven application. It is your application, you are the boss, and you can organize the view exactly as you want.

Function Viewer: A Glimpse at Scientific Applications

You are going to see a few short pieces of code in the description of this example because all the elements and how they work were already discussed. The main thing to be demonstrated in this section is the overall design of a relatively complex application with unpredictable user actions and requests. All scientific applications must be developed according to one simple rule: "The user can do everything." As a developer, I have to provide a program according to this rule. It might look to many readers that the development of applications that allow the user to do everything puts a huge overwhelming burden on programmers, so I want to show that this is not correct. The designer doesn't need to respond to all imaginable and unimaginable situations, but rather develop a program on the basis of elements that are fully controlled by users.

In 2001–2004 I was involved in the development of a huge engineering program that was successfully sold all around the world. The program was designed for the analysis of big electricity networks and included dozens of dialogs that allowed skillful users to play with hundreds of parameters in order to analyze different scenarios and situations. As is usual for such programs, the results of many calculations had to be shown not only in the form of some numbers and filled tables but also as graphs. (People understand and estimate data much better when it is shown in graphical form.) In the middle of 2004 we— the developers of that program—were discussing the ideas for the new version of the program. One of the ideas was to increase the graphical presentation of results and to give users some control over this presentation, for example, letting users decide about the number of shown plotting areas.

The program was designed in a classical way. At that time, nobody was talking about the movability of the screen objects. The whole application was a classic example of an adaptive interface, so all the scenarios of future work had to be thought out and put into code. I was thinking about an easy instrument (for users) to declare the needed number of plots and their positions. As was the standard practice at that time, all dialogs were designed on the basis of ordinary controls. Regardless of the variants I tried, the mechanism of declaring plot positions and sizes did not look elegant, but at least it worked, and I hoped to think of something better in the process. Yet, there was a small problem for which I did not see even a close to good solution.

In scientific articles you often see a plotting area with several graphs shown with lines of different colors and styles. The difference in graphs is caused by the change of some parameter, so graphs need comments that inform about the associated parameters. When the author of an article prepares such a figure for publication, the graphs to be shown are already known, and it is not a problem to select the best place for comments near the lines, so in a scientific magazine the whole figure always looks good.

When you develop an application that has to demonstrate such plotting areas, you do not know beforehand the view of the graphs that will appear inside, so you have to place the needed comments not inside the plotting area but somewhere nearby. Can you reserve for them someplace below the plotting area or at the side? Well, you can, but:

- Comments will occupy a lot of very valuable screen space.

- Comments will be far away from the lines and thus make it difficult to associate the lines with the comments (especially when you have many graphs in the same area).

- There is also a problem of scales positioned around the plotting area. There can be multiple scales with their own comments, so there will be all imaginable and unpredictable conflicts between positions of scales and different comments.

- In the case of several plots in a view, the problems increase much faster than a linear function.

To summarize all these requests, the interface that is already complicated by several controls used to place all the needed plotting areas on the screen has to be complicated much more with an additional instrument to place all the needed comments. Even if it is all organized in one way or another, it looks awkward (to say it in the most polite way). Users of such programs are highly qualified specialists who try to solve very serious engineering/scientific problems, and they do not need to spend their time fighting with some stupid interface design. This problem of a quick, accurate, and easy way to place the needed comments at an arbitrary place on the plotting areas with unknown graphs might not look like a first-degree problem when you design a huge and very complicated scientific application, so many people think that it can be solved in one way or another, but this problem has no solution under the standard design. And this is not the only problem of this type in scientific applications.

In 2006–2007 I designed an algorithm for the screen objects' movability, and the main reason for working on such algorithm was its need for engineering/scientific programs. At the beginning of 2008, when my algorithm was ready to be used in real scientific programs, I started to work in the Department of Mathematical Modelling at the Heat and Mass Transfer Institute. Scientists from this and other departments were highly qualified specialists in the area of thermodynamics, and many of them were also good programmers, so they were aware of the interface limitations. They put in front of me a list of tasks that had to be developed into the working programs, but that were impossible to implement in the realm of standard design. The tasks were different, but they had one common feature: each one had to deal with the uncertainty of data that came from experiments and calculations. This unpredictability of the first stage made further work under the standard interface nearly impossible. If you try to design a program to deal with all the possible variants, then the standard interface becomes so clumsy that it is impossible to use such a program. Each program required manual work with the screen elements, and that perfectly matched with the ideas and possibilities of user-driven applications. One by one I designed the programs for those tasks, and in each case users got even more than they expected (or requested) at the beginning. Those programs were helpful in research work, and I got a question about the possibility of redesigning all the older programs into user-driven applications.

Usually engineering and scientific programs are big and complex. Each one has a lot of special features and details that require a lengthy explanation and are of high interest for specialists of a particular area but make no sense for people outside this area. At the same time, those programs have many similarities in design, so throughout the years I was designing applications for areas of knowledge that were far away from each other. A demonstration of any such program requires explanations on the problems and specifics of particular area, and this is far from what I want to discuss in this book. That is why I prefer to demonstrate an example that contains all the features of scientific applications but can be easily understood by any reader. I want to demonstrate and discuss a Function Viewer, which is a program that allows you to type in the expressions for Y(x) functions or parametric functions of the {X(p), Y(p)} type and to play with these functions. The program can be helpful for teaching math in school, and at the same time it demonstrates a lot of things that can be used in the design of complex and specialized scientific applications.

File: `Form_FunctionViewer.cs`

Menu position: Applications ➤ Function Viewer

There is no novelty in the main instrument on which this Function Viewer is based. You can find several programs that allow you to transform a math expression into graph; all these programs are based on the same math instrument. In the 1920s, the Polish mathematician Jan Lucasiewicz invented the notation in which all brackets were omitted and the operator came before operands; in honor of the author, this notation was called Polish notation. In the late 1950s, the Australian computer scientist Charles Hamblin changed the order of operands and operators and thus invented the reverse Polish notation. Any interpreter of math expressions is based now on using such a notation. In some books published 30 and more years ago, you can find the explanation of such interpreters, with the pictures demonstrating the turning of cars at a railroad station. Each car contains some element of the original expression, and depending on the order of elements, a car can move straight through the station or can turn for some time into the dead-end only to be taken out of there at the right moment. In this way, the order of elements from the original expression is changed, and in the output you get the same expression in the form of reverse Polish notation. Writing such an interpreter is a standard exercise for those who take courses in programming and have just learned about queues and stacks, so I am not going into the details of coding such an interpreter, but I am going to use the `FunctionInterpreter` class, which is included into `MoveGraphLibrary.dll`.

This class has only a few methods, but it is enough for its use. Interpretation always starts with an analysis of some string that has to be transformed into a `List` of elements of the `Elem` class, so the first method to be used is the `FunctionInterpreter.Analyse()` method.

```
bool Analyse (string strIn, ref List<Elem> elems, out int iError,
                                              out int kErrPlace)
```

The original function text can include different elements.

- Names of standard functions: { sin, cos, tg, sh, ch, th, ln, lg, exp, sqrt, mod, arcsin, arccos, arctg }.

- Binary operations: { +, -, *, /, ^ }. The symbol ^ is used for the degree function.

- Unary operation: –

- Brackets: (and)

- Variables: { x, p, r, X, P, R }

- Numbers.

If there is any mistake in the text of a function, then the type of error and its place are returned. If the text is correct, then it is transformed into a special view—a collection of elements List<Elem>; this List can be used for calculations. The calculation is done by another method of the FunctionInterpreter class.

```
bool Calculate (List<Elem> PolishForm, double fArg, ref double fVal)
```

The Boolean value returned by this method only signals whether the calculation is correct; the result of calculation is obtained via one of the parameters (fVal).

While there is no novelty in the main idea of the Function Viewer, it is absolutely a new way of using such program. The developer has to provide an error-free interpreter and to unite it with a nearly limitless instrument for function demonstration. Only the user has to decide about the functions to look at and about all the parameters of visibility. I compare this Function Viewer to similar pieces of the old scientific programs that I designed years ago and the problems that I mentioned earlier without solutions simply vanished.

There is no clumsy instrument to set the number of the new plots, their places, and their sizes. Neither is there a good instrument to set all these things. Such an instrument is not needed anymore. At any moment, the user adds or deletes the plotting areas, creates areas for one or several graphs, moves and resizes the plotting areas, and easily changes all imaginable visibility parameters. The user is not obliged to do this; he can do it whenever he wants and in the way he wants. The developer is not interfering in any of these actions; the developer only provides an easy-to-use instrument for doing all these things.

Years ago, there was a problem of comments positioning that had no solution; now you don't think about some solution because there is no problem. The user decides about the text of comments to appear and about the disappearance of the comments. The comments can be moved, rotated, hidden, unveiled, and changed at any moment, so the user easily decides about the needed comment(s) for any graph.

All changes are saved and restored; the user can organize different variants and easily switch between them.

This is not the first variant of the Function Viewer that I have demonstrated throughout the years; it is included as one of the examples in my big book [2].[2] Though the current version has a strong resemblance to the older variant, this new version uses different classes for plotting and has some different features.

---

[2]Previous versions of the same program were called Function Analyzer, but I think that Function Viewer is more correct name for this program.

Scientific and engineering applications might have special plotting requests that depend on particular area, but at the same time the plotting used in many areas have a lot of common features. In the majority of cases, scientists deal with the Y(x) functions that are demonstrated by plotting in the rectangular area with two orthogonal scales. As a rule, these are linear scales, though in some areas the logarithmic scales are also popular. In the majority of cases, it is enough to have one horizontal and one vertical scale, but there are situations when for better visual comparison several graphs in the same area have to be shown in absolutely different ranges, and then several different scales are required. The older Plot class allows you to work with multiple scales, while the current version of the Plot_Adh class uses one scale for each direction.

```
public class Plot_Adh : GraphicalObject
{
    Scale_Numbers scaleHor, scaleVer;
    List<CommentToRect> m_comments = new List<CommentToRect> ();
```

The Plot_Adh class uses the familiar classes of comments and scales; these scales were demonstrated in Chapter 6 while we discussed the bar charts, their scales, and their tuning (Figures 6-4–6-7). The tuning of the main area for the Plot_Adh class is done in a special form (Figure 7-48), which includes several familiar parts and elements that were already demonstrated with the tuning of the bar chart area (see Figure 6-8).

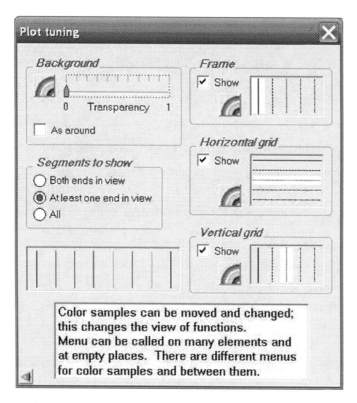

Figure 7-48. *Auxiliary form for tuning plotting areas*

- The background is often set the same as the surrounding form (or page of TabControl) though it is easy to select any needed background color and its transparency.

- The frame of the plotting area and grids of both directions are tuned independently but in a similar way. Each of them can be shown or not; if shown, then the line color and style can be selected. The positions of the grid lines are determined by the positions of the numbers (and ticks) on the scales, but the appearance of ticks and grids are independent, and they are regulated in different tuning forms for scales and main area.

- The selection of colors is also similar to color selection for the bar charts. A rectangular area includes the samples of colors. The colors to be used are selected starting from the left one, so it is possible to change the view of functions by changing the order of these samples (press and move the sample to another place), by changing the samples (call the menu on the one you want to change), or by adding more samples (call the menu at an empty place in the samples area).

Any graph is shown as a sequence of segments that connect the calculated points. End points of segments can be either inside the plotting area or outside; the group "Segments to show" allows you to select the segments to be shown. Usually, the functions to be shown are smooth enough, and the selection in this group does not change the view of the graph. For the Y(x) function, the value is calculated for each horizontal pixel inside the plotting area, and the resulting line is the sequence of segments between each pair of following values. The difference between variants becomes obvious when the graph line is nearly vertical with the huge difference in values for neighboring horizontal points. The worst situation happens in the case of vertical asymptotes. In such a case, it is much better to select the first position (both ends in view), while the last one (all) can show vertical lines at the places of asymptotes.

For a better understanding of the Function Viewer, let's use it for some simple enough task that would not require a lot of explanations on its math side. Suppose that you want to discuss with somebody the features of polynomial functions and the change of such functions depending on the polynomial degree. For this discussion, you need to prepare several functions and select different views of them for a better demonstration.

When you start the Function Viewer for the first time, you see only a group with an empty list of functions and all the disabled buttons (Figure 7-49). Function Viewer allows you to deal with functions of two types. Polynomial functions belong to the Y(x) type, so the corresponding command of the main menu opens the needed auxiliary form (Figure 7-50).

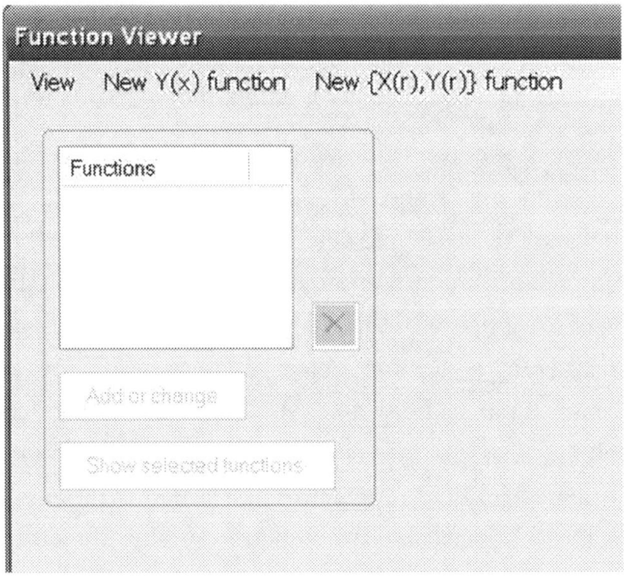

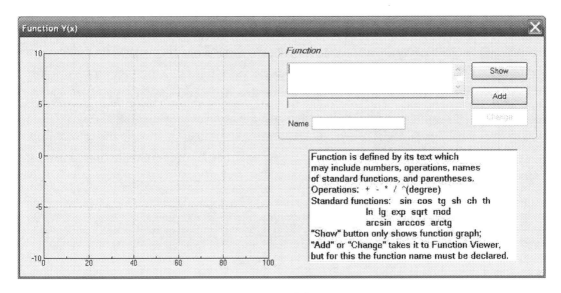

Figure 7-49. *At the beginning, there are neither functions nor plots*

Figure 7-50. *An auxiliary form to define Y(x) functions*

For many years descriptions to my programs often included phrases like "on the left you see...." For user-driven applications such words in explanation become confusing because users can change the program view in any possible way, and the view of a working program may have nothing common with the original view that was carefully thought out and prepared by a designer. Form_FuncYx.cs has a plotting area, the group for the function definition, and information. Information can be read once and not needed anymore, so it can be squeezed to a tiny size. All elements can be moved and resized, so each user can organize in seconds the view he prefers.

The majority of elements in this form are graphical objects that were already discussed in the previous chapters. There are also two ordinary controls that, as all other elements, are also movable and resizable. Moving and resizing of ordinary controls will be discussed in Appendix A, so here I want to mention them only briefly.

All elements must be moveable and resizable. In general, graphical elements are resized by border and moved by any inner point. This is impossible for ordinary controls because any click inside their area triggers some action that is predefined and expected by users. Thus, for controls, both moving and resizing are started at the border. Resizing is started at the corners and at the middle parts of the sides; moving is started at all other border parts.

While designing any form, I try to organize it in the best possible way for real work, but this is only my opinion about the "best possible." Every user is invited to organize his own view. Users are not only invited to change the view in the way they want, but my main effort is to make this process of changing as simple as possible for users.

For paper illustration, I change the program view in such a way that it will match with the paper format; occasionally I have to think about the positioning of several neighboring figures inside the paper text. Thus, on entering Form_FuncYx.cs you are going to see not the same view as shown in Figure 7-50, but I guarantee that the elements will do exactly what they have to do regardless of the way you change them.

When user opens Form_FuncYx.cs for the first time, the function to be defined is unpredictable, and the best ranges to show this function are unknown, so the scales are organized in such a way.

```
private void DefaultView ()
{
    plot = new Plot_Adh (this, mover, new Rectangle (50, 30, 400, 280),
                         Side .S, 0, 100, GridOrigin .ByStep, 20,
                         Side .W, 10, -10, GridOrigin .ByStep, 5);
    ... ...
```

For any Y(x) function, you need to define the function expression; you also need to give this function a unique name by which to distinguish it from others. The function expression and name are typed inside two controls that are included in the Function group. Like all ordinary controls, these two elements are moved and resized by their borders; all other elements are moved by inner points and resized by borders.

We start our investigation of polynomial functions with the first-degree function and enter the text of a simple function x-3. To see its graph, click the Show button. The end values for horizontal and vertical scales were set at the plot area initialization. For our current function, the default range [0, 100] for the X scale does not fit very well, so it is better to change it. Tuning forms for horizontal and vertical scales of the Scale_Numbers class were already discussed (Figures 6-4 and 6-5). By using tuning forms for horizontal and vertical scales, we can obtain a better view for our function (Figure 7-51). Throughout the preparation of the function in an auxiliary form, not only the scale ranges but a lot of other parameters can be set. As usual, whenever you need to change some object, you call the menu on this object; there will be either commands to change a specific parameter or commands to call a tuning form.

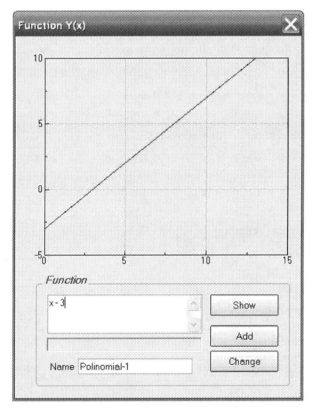

Figure 7-51. *The Form_FuncYx.cs after some scale tuning*

The name of a function must be declared. The name is only text, so there is a wide area for your imagination.

When everything is ready, we can click the Add button and return this prepared function to the main form of the Function Viewer. The name of the function appears in the list, while the function itself is shown in the new plotting area (Figure 7-52) by the NewPlotForSingleFunction() method.

```
private void Click_miNewFunc_Yx (object sender, EventArgs e)
{
    Form_FuncYx form = new Form_FuncYx (m_functions, -1);
    form .ShowDialog ();
    if (form .FunctionReady)
    {
        ... ...
        NewPlotForSingleFunction (iNew);
    }
}
```

There is a big difference between the appearance of a function in the auxiliary form (Figure 7-51) and in the Function Viewer. In the auxiliary form, there is always only one plotting area. When we prepare the first function of our example, we have a single plotting area in the main form; later we'll have more and more plotting areas, and each new one will appear on top of the already existing plots. There is no sense even in trying to place the new plot at some empty place, and it simply appears on top of whatever is already shown. The size of the new plotting area depends on the size of the form, while the position of each new plot is slightly changed from the previous one.

The most crucial parameters, such as scale range, are copied from the auxiliary form while others get the default values. Two comments show the name of the function and its expression.

```
private void NewPlotForSingleFunction (int iFunc)
{
    RectangleF rc = NewArea ();
    Function_Origin func = m_functions [iFunc];
    Plot_Adh plot = new Plot_Adh (this, mover, rc, Side .S, ..., Side
    .W, ...);
    plot .AddFunction (func);
```

· · ·   · · ·

The user can move, resize, and modify the new plot in any possible way either immediately after its appearance in the main form or at any moment later. For further discussion of polynomial functions, I prefer first to prepare all the needed functions and then organize a good view for all the plots.

When any function in the list is selected, several buttons of the group become enabled (Figure 7-52). To prepare a second-degree polynomial, I can repeat the previously described procedure, but I want to use the existing first-degree function as some part of the next one, and in such cases it is easier to select in the list the name of the existing function and click this button: | Add or change |. The same Form_FuncYx.cs is opened, but a bit less effort is needed to prepare the new function Y = (x-3)(x-1) compared to the previous one. The new function also looks better if shown in a slightly different X range, so I use the tuning form for horizontal scale.

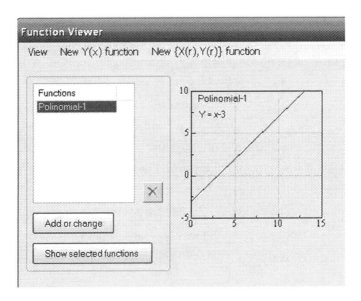

Figure 7-52. *Function Viewer with the first polynomial function*

Because some function was used as a source for entering the auxiliary form, then the Change button in this form is also enabled (Figure 7-53). I do not want to change the first function but to organize the new one, so I type a different name and then return to the main form by clicking the Add button.

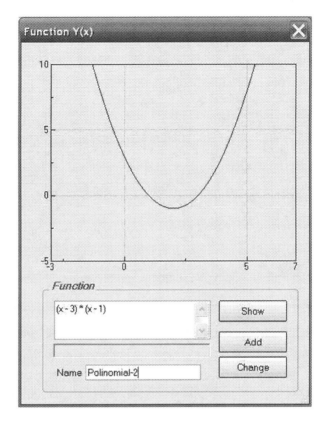

Figure 7-53. *Preparation of the second-degree polynomial function*

The list of functions in `Form_Functions.cs` gets the new line, and the new plotting area with the second function is organized. When a new plotting area with a function is organized, it automatically gets two new comments with the name of a function and its expression. Any comment can be changed, hidden, or deleted. I don't need the names of new functions in their personal plotting areas, so I leave there a comment with an expression but hide the name.

I want to demonstrate the polynomials up to the fifth degree, so I continue the same process several more times and get five different plotting areas with one graph in each (Figure 7-54). These plots can be helpful for some explanations, but this view is not the best for the comparison of polynomials and for a discussion of changes that depend on a polynomial degree. It would be nice to have all of them in the same plotting area, so I select in the list all the needed functions and click this button: Show selected functions . One more plotting area appears on the screen; in this area, five graphs are shown. Now I have all the plots that I need but not in a good view. After some additional tuning, I get the needed view (Figure 7-55).

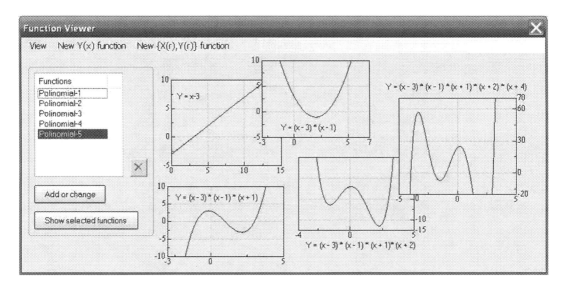

Figure 7-54. *Five polynomials are prepared*

While preparing Figure 7-55, I had to make some tuning of each plotting area, but the changes were minimal. In the area with all graphs together, I did not like the color of one of them, so I had to change that color. Then I decided it would be nice to have each function be shown with the same color in the big plotting area and in the small one, so for small areas I had to open their tuning forms and to move different color samples to the leading positions.

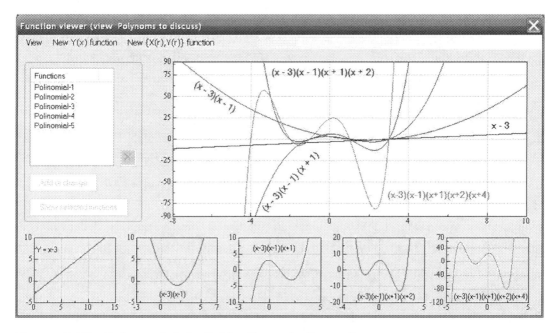

Figure 7-55. *Polynomials individually and all together*

The tuning forms for the Scale_Numbers and Plot_Adh objects are the same regardless of the programs in which they are used. These tuning forms are usually called either by double-click, through a menu, or both. The plotting areas are extremely valuable objects of the engineering/scientific programs, but there are always objects of other classes and, depending on the complexity and novelty of a program, users can see familiar objects and new ones. To make the work with any program much easier, several simple rules are implemented in all of them.

- To do anything with an element, the user calls a menu on this element.

- To do anything with a group or with all the elements of a group, the user calls a menu on this group. (This means to call a menu at any empty place inside the group.)

- To do anything with all the elements in view, the user calls the menu at any empty place in the form.

Applying these few simple rules to any application means one important thing: users do not need to read huge manuals before starting to work on a new application. It is like using a new car: you do not need instructions to find the brake pedal.

With these rules applied to the Function Viewer, there is hardly any inner point at which some menu cannot be called. In this example, the menu cannot be called only on a small button inside the group. (I simply could not think of any needed commands for this button.) Figure 7-56 demonstrates the result of the menu calling at all other points. With all these menus in view, a user's control over the Function Viewer might look too complicated, but in reality it is not. In the working application, you never see more than one menu at a time, and this is exactly the menu you want to see. If you want to change some element, call the menu on this element.

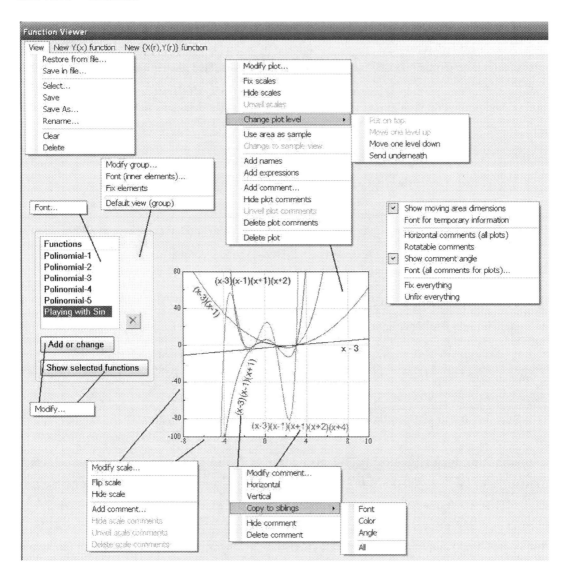

Figure 7-56. *Blue lines show areas that menus are associated with. The right menu can be called at any empty place. Commands to deal with views are included in the main menu*

Up until now I have demonstrated the process of organizing functions of the Y(x) type. The current Function Viewer also allows you to deal with the parametric functions of the {X(p), Y(p)} type, which can be defined in another auxiliary form. To declare such a function, the user has to type two expressions for functions and three values for the range and step of a parameter. Thus, Form_FuncXrYr.cs has more elements, but otherwise it is designed in a familiar way (Figure 7-57).

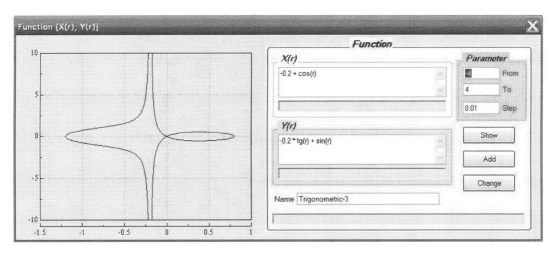

Figure 7-57. *This auxiliary form is used to define the parametric functions of the {X(p), Y(p)} type*

Y(x) functions are much more popular than parametric functions, and the second group was included in the Function Viewer mainly thanks to a special place that one type of these functions holds in my memory. Many years ago, at the time when I was even too young for school, my father—a professor at the Moscow Institute of Telecommunication— took me and my elder brother to the laboratory. To keep the kids busy for some time, our father switched on an oscilloscope and showed us how to play with the Lissajous curves.[3] This new thing was so exciting for two kids that for some time an armistice was declared, and we tried to cooperate in an attempt to get the best curves on a small screen. Decades later, when I decided to add something special to my Function Viewer, I added the ability to play with parametric functions, and the first one to be checked in this part of a program was the Lissajous curve.

---

[3]I remembered that visit throughout the years, but only recently I found evidence in a nearly forgotten part of our family photo archive. One of father's colleagues took a picture on that day many years ago.

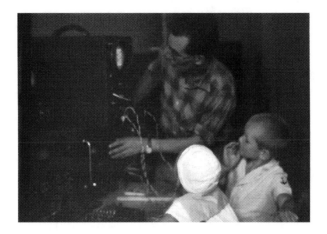

By using two auxiliary forms (Figures 7-51 and 7-57), a lot of needed functions and their variants can be prepared. Tuning forms for plotting areas, scales, and comments allow you to organize different views and to demonstrate those functions in different combinations in many plotting areas. You can prepare any number of plots, but the screen size is limited, so there is always a problem of good demonstration and of saving/restoring the prepared images without losing any of them. For the work on my own computer, I prefer saving/restoring through the Registry. When the number of functions is significant or I need to exchange the results with other people, it is better to save/restore through the binary files. Function Viewer provides this through the commands of its main menu (Figure 7-56, menu in the top-left corner).

Function Viewer is included as an example that demonstrates the main style of developing new engineering and scientific applications. Plotting is an important component of such programs, and I wanted to demonstrate the way to include movable/resizable/tunable plots in the new applications. You can find much more about it in my other book [2].

Each new scientific task requires a new program. If you put too many restrictions on scientists in their research work, do not expect outstanding results. The fewer restrictions they have, the more interesting the outcome of their research. Programs have to help scientists in their work and not limit their attempts to investigate new things.

Years ago, after starting to work with those user-driven applications, scientists from the Department of Mathematical Modelling declared that all the new programs had to be of that type. By the way, they asked a simple question: "Can you add this full user control to all the older programs that we still use?"

Several Illustrations of Geometric Optics

Some scientific experiments, especially in physics, can be expensive, may need a lot of time and effort to prepare, and can be even dangerous. Some of experiments cannot be organized on Earth. The widespread use of computers and the achievements in programming brought to the surface the idea of switching from real experiments to their modeling.

In organizing real experiments, you are free in your decisions about using the equipment and all the involved elements. While working with the modeling program designed by somebody else, you are limited by its designer's view on the proposed model, and you can't go out of this view. You can do only whatever the developer of this model considered to be correct. As a rule, scientists in each particular area are much better specialists in their area than developers of the programs they have to use. This difference in levels of knowledge and understanding causes the paradoxical situation when scientists, in their search for new and unexpected, are limited by the vision of lesser specialists. User-driven applications show the way out of this programming dead-end.

Models of different processes on computers usually try to re-create real processes that scientists would like to see in real life. Real experiments always have some limitations, and models developed in a standard programming technique would be designed with the same limitations. Yet, there are several very well-known examples when equipment in real experiments was accidentally used in an unusual way, and that produced some strange results that ended with a Nobel Prize award or famous inventions (the X-ray discovery in 1895 and microwave oven invention in 1945, to mention the few). If a programming model is designed in a standard way with everything predetermined by its developer, then such a model would never be allowed to see the unexpected results. There is a fundamental question to design of all programming models: "Is it possible at all to develop a program (a model) that allows you to get the results outside the scope of developers' knowledge?"

User-driven applications give a positive answer to this question. This happens because programs of the new type are designed as instruments of research and analysis. They are not pure scientific calculators but rather instruments of research that users can use in any way they want.

Car developers produce cars and guarantee that they will move under reasonable conditions. Car developers don't give you a list of allowed destinations, so you are not limited in your desire to explore the world. The same happens with user-driven applications. A well-designed program is an instrument of research; further results depend only on a user's willingness and ability to do such research. To demonstrate such features of user-driven applications, I'll show several examples from the area of geometric optics.

Geometric optics usually is a small part of a physics courses, and, from my point of view, this is one of the easiest parts of this course. All books on geometric optics have nearly a standard order of explanation. It starts with some words about the straight way of light rays; then the discussion of flat mirrors illustrates the equality of angles of incidence and reflection. Spherical mirrors are discussed with the image's construction. Light propagation from one material into another starts with the index of refraction and Snell's law.[4] Then comes the light dispersion. After that, the images in thin lenses are discussed.

In 2019 I wrote a small book called *Illustrations for Geometric Optics* [3] that includes a program with examples of all these topics. Three examples from this book are included in the current section. The mentioned book is divided into two parts: the first one contains an explanation from the point of view of optics, while the second part is about the programming of all the examples. In the current section, the explanation of geometric optics is reduced to a minimally required level while I try to stress the advantages of new design for the users of the programs. Let's start with the flat mirrors; this example perfectly demonstrates the design of all the examples.

File: `Form_Mirror_Flat_Any.cs`

Menu position: Applications ➤ From Geometric Optics ➤ Flat mirrors

---

[4]There is a controversy about the priority of discovery of this law (or formula), which causes the use of two different names. It is always mentioned as Snell's law in English-speaking countries, while in French-speaking countries it is often called the Descartes' law. Willebrord Snellius (1580–1626) came to the mathematically correct expression in 1621, but it wasn't published during his lifetime, while René Descartes (1596–1650) published it in 1637, and it is widely believed that at that time he didn't know anything about Snell's result.

In this example, the user can deal with an arbitrary number of flat mirrors (Figure 7-58). Mirrors can be placed and rotated individually. The number of mirrors can be easily changed, and these features allow you to organize very strange ray routes. It looks like a funny play, but from the first moment when I decided to design this example, I thought about the famous experiment by Albert Michelson when the light traveled between the Mount Wilson Observatory and Lookout Mountain.

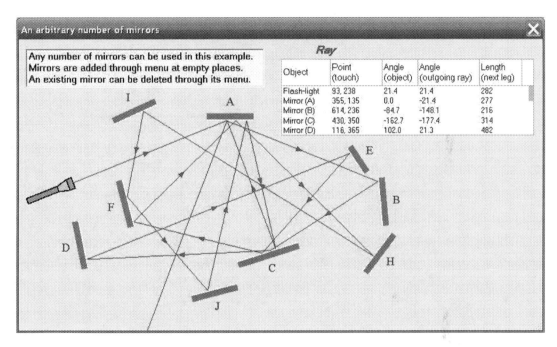

Figure 7-58. *An arbitrary number of mirrors can be used in this example*

Each mirror (of the `Mirror_Flat` class) has a rectangular shape. The cover is designed in a standard way for all rectangles. The user can decide about the allowed resizing for each object, but in general a rectangle can be resized by the sides and corners. The mirror has one reflective side that can be highlighted by using different color. The three other sides absorb the rays.

The light source (class `Flashlight`) is designed in the form of a flashlight. This flashlight is the only nonresizable element in the following examples; I simply couldn't imagine the need of the resizable source of light, though it is easy to organize. In real experiments, it is impossible to place a pair of optical objects (mirrors and flashlight) at the same position, so the same overlapping is prohibited in the current example.

The ray route is calculated in such a way.

- The initial ray point and its angle are obtained from the flashlight.

- The ray can touch any mirror, each mirror has four sides, and each side is a line segment determined by two end points. The reflected ray can touch the flashlight. The border of a flashlight consists of eight straight segments. Thus, for a system of N mirrors, we have 4 * N + 8 segments, which can be intersected by a ray. The nearest point of the intersection is calculated.

- If there is no intersection, then it is the last leg in the route. (In Figure 7-58, the ray is reflected at the middle of mirror A and goes beyond the bottom side of the form.)

- If a ray touches the flashlight or any nonreflective side of any mirror, then the calculation is over.

- If a ray touches the reflective side of a mirror, then the touch point becomes the new source point, the angle of reflection is equal to the angle of incidence, and the calculation starts again.

When the calculation shows that some border is touched by the ray, an optical border (an element of the OpticalBorder class) is organized on this border. This element allows you to deal with absorption, reflection, or refraction. While in the current example only absorption and reflection occur, cases of refraction are used in the following examples.

This example is based on simple elements—rectangles—but even this simplest base allows you to organize absolutely different examples. In nearly every book on geometric optics you can see a reflector in a shape of a right angle with two reflective sides inside the angle. This design perfectly demonstrates the equality between the angle of incidence and the angle of reflection. In the current example, the same reflector can be constructed with two mirrors placed at right angles to each other and with end points of reflective sides placed next to each other. Another interesting design is a polygon with reflective sides looking inside. Leave a small gap through which a ray can be sent inside and see the results.

I mentioned only two possibilities, but a user-driven application sets no limitations on users' imagination.

The speed of light in any material is less than in a vacuum. The ratio of speeds in vacuum (c) and in material (v) is called the *index of refraction* of that material: n = c / v. Because v is always lesser than c, the index of refraction for any material is greater than 1.

The index of refraction slightly depends on the wave length, but for waves from a visual spectrum, it is a tiny difference in the second or even third digit after the point. This tiny difference is the cause of dispersion that is discussed in book [3] but not in the current book. In the following examples, the monochromatic rays are used, so a single index of refraction is used for each material.

When a ray comes to the boundary of two materials, the ray is partly reflected and partly enters another material. The angle of reflection is equal to the angle of incidence, while the angle of refraction can be obtained from Snell's law. $n_1 * \sin \alpha_1 = n_2 * \sin \alpha_2$

n_1 and n_2 indices of refraction in two materials

α_1 angle of incidence

α_2 angle of refraction

Material	Index of Refraction
Air	1.0003
Water	1.33
Glass	1.5
Diamond	2.48

There are two classical examples of refraction that are discussed in each book on geometric optics: the light propagation through a window and the view from the bank of the lake (or river) of somebody staying in the water. These two examples are popular because we see them many times throughout our life.

When a ray goes from optically less dense to optically more dense material, for example, from air into water (Figure 7-59), then $n_1 < n_2$ and this means that $\alpha_1 \blacktriangleright \alpha_2$, so the refracted ray (in the current case, in the water) bends toward the normal. This works in the same way for any angle of incidence.

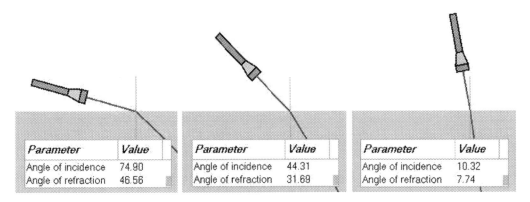

Figure 7-59. *For the ray going from optically less dense to optically more dense material, the refracted ray always bends toward normal*

Now imagine that at the place of the flashlight there are eyes of somebody staying on the bank, and the red line shows the way of the light reflected from the feet of a person staying in the water. Eyes catch the ray and see the feet, but the brain doesn't know anything about the ray bending. The brain thinks that the whole ray is straight, so the brain "sees" feet in the water at the continuation of the upper line. As a result, the legs of the person in the water look shorter than they are in reality, while the view of the body above the water is not distorted.

Snell's law doesn't say anything about the ray direction, so it has to work when a ray goes from optically more dense to optically less dense material. Only now we have the case of $n_1 > n_2$, so we have a different relation between two angles, and with $\alpha_1 < \alpha_2$ the refracted ray bends away from the normal (Figure 7-60a). Let's start from some small angle of incidence and steadily increase it. It is easily done in the current program because you can press the flashlight and rotate it. For some time Snell's law still works; the refracted ray bends more and more from the normal and approaches the surface (Figure 7-60b). In our case the boundary line is horizontal, so it is easy to watch and estimate how the angles change.

The critical angle is the angle at which the Snell's equation still works, but with the Sin $\alpha_2 = 1$. For the water–air boundary, it happens when the angle of incidence is 47.77 degrees. For a bigger angle of incidence, the equation would be correct only with Sin $\alpha_2 > 1$, which is impossible, so there is no refraction but total internal reflection (Figure 7-60c). As usual, the angle of reflection is equal to the angle of incidence.

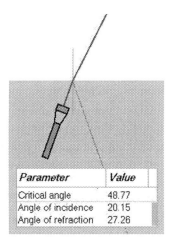

Figure 7-60a. *For an angle of incidence less than critical, there is normal refraction according to Snell's law*

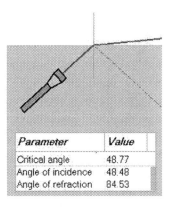

Figure 7-60b. *When the angle of incidence approaches a critical angle, the refracted ray goes nearly along the surface*

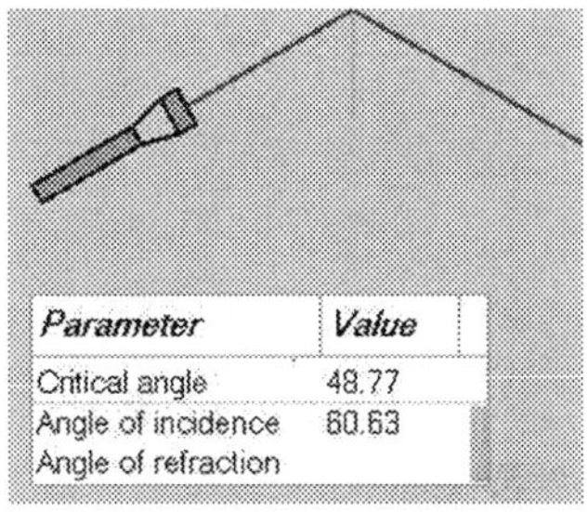

Figure 7-60c. *For an angle of incidence bigger than critical, there is a total internal reflection*

The situation in Figure 7-59 is easy to explain and understand because it happens many times throughout our lifetime, and we are well familiar with the distortion of objects that we see through the water. The situation in Figure 7-60 is easy to explain but not so easy to understand because we don't live under water, and in this case we have to rely only on math but not on our feelings. Let's look at one more familiar situation.

When a ray goes through the window glass (Figure 7-61), refraction happens on both boundaries. At first, the air–glass boundary bends a ray closer to the normal. Then this ray touches the glass–air boundary where the same pair of refraction indices but used in opposite order bends the ray away from the normal. Because the same pair of indices is used on both boundaries but works in opposite directions, the result of the second angle change is the same as the first one but with an opposite sign, so the outcoming ray is parallel to the original one. There is only a side shift on the way; this is perfectly seen in Figure 7-61. This is exactly what happens when we look through any window.

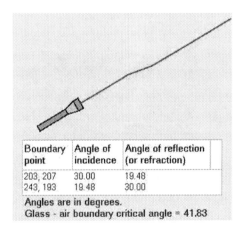

Boundary point	Angle of incidence	Angle of reflection (or refraction)
203, 207	30.00	19.48
243, 193	19.48	30.00

Angles are in degrees.
Glass - air boundary critical angle = 41.83

Figure 7-61. *The refraction on the second boundary sets the outcoming ray parallel to the original*

The two mentioned cases—a view from the bank and a view through the window—are familiar to everyone, so their explanation never causes any excitement. Both cases are included in the next example. Though this example also deals with a familiar situation, I am sure that you will see that there are some absolutely unexpected results.

File: Form_Aquarium.cs

Menu position: Applications ➤ From Geometric Optics ➤ Aquarium

Suppose that you have some kind of a big aquarium (let's say an oceanarium). On one side of the glass wall is the territory for visitors that have a chance to look into the aquarium from different levels. On another side of the wall, the water always fills half of the volume (Figure 7-62). Because I am more interested in the optical effects than in the real construction of such an aquarium, the glass wall is easily moved left and right, and in the same easy way its thickness can be changed inside some reasonable limits. The thickness does not affect the physics of the discussed process but makes the change of the ray route more obvious. The ray source—flashlight—can be placed anywhere in the air and in the water; however, any variant of the flashlight overlapping with the glass is prohibited.

The variant of the ray route in Figure 7-62 is the simplest and represents a sequence of cases from Figures 7-61 and 7-59. There are three cases of ordinary refraction on three boundaries. First the ray touches the vertical side of the glass wall; then there is a refraction on the opposite side of the glass wall. At both points we have air on the outside, so the ray angle after the second refraction is equal to the original angle; ray angles before and after each special point are shown in a list. The third refraction happens on the air–water boundary.

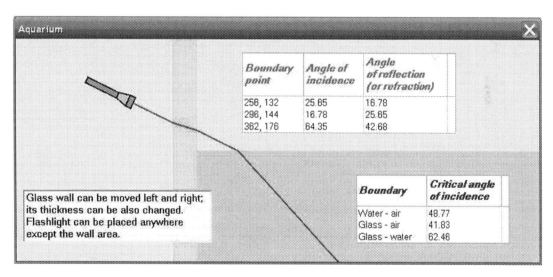

Figure 7-62. *The glass wall goes from bottom to top; water fills half of the volume on the right side*

The easiest way to organize any ray route is to place the flashlight at the point of interest and to rotate it for the needed angle. One of the main laws of optics is the reversibility of light. This means that if another flashlight is placed anywhere on the ray route and aimed in the opposite direction to the ray, then the ray from the second flashlight will come exactly to the source point on the first flashlight. We see objects because the light is reflected from them and comes to our eyes. In the case of our example with an aquarium, it means that if a visitor looks from the point of our source (flashlight) and in the direction of the sent ray, then this visitor sees objects along the ray.

Suppose that parents with small kids are on a visit to the oceanarium; the difference in height is important for further discussion. Family members stay near the glass wall and look for interesting creatures on the other side. A grown-up sees something amazing in front (Figure 7-63a) and tells kids to look there. They try, but in order to see the mentioned creature, they have to look at absolutely different angles (Figure 7-63b). Maybe they will see the same creature, but chances are high that they miss it because of those turns of the ray at both sides of the glass wall. The parent insists that there is really something amazing just in front, so kids, in an attempt to find it, slightly change the angle of their look. Instead of something just near the glass wall, they have a chance to see creatures in the far-away corner at the bottom of the oceanarium (Figure 7-63c doesn't show the full size of the oceanarium because of the page limit, but you can easily prolong the last leg of the ray route). Kids were not even thinking about that far-away part of oceanarium, but they can see it now.

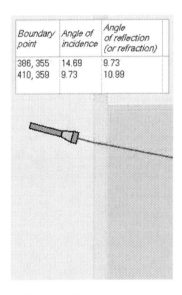

Boundary point	Angle of incidence	Angle of reflection (or refraction)
386, 355	14.69	9.73
410, 359	9.73	10.99

Figure 7-63a. *This ray is nearly straight*

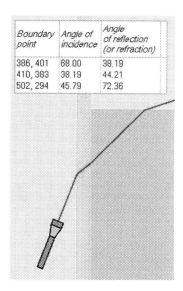

Boundary point	Angle of incidence	Angle of reflection (or refraction)
386, 401	68.00	38.19
410, 383	38.19	44.21
502, 294	45.79	72.36

Figure 7-63b. *It is not easy to reach exactly the same spot in the water with such refraction*

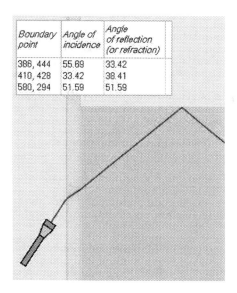

Boundary point	Angle of incidence	Angle of reflection (or refraction)
386, 444	55.69	33.42
410, 428	33.42	38.41
580, 294	51.59	51.59

Figure 7-63c. *This ray reaches places that are somewhere far away from its initial direction*

It is not an artificial situation that I thought out in order to make the text more interesting. Figure 7-63c reminded me of one unsolved problem that puzzled me many years ago. In my childhood, we had an aquarium placed on top of a bookcase. The bookcase was nearly twice as high as I was at that time. To see a fish, I had to look up, and then I could see a fish just behind the glass. If I stood some distance away from the bookcase and looked up at an angle, then occasionally I could see the underwater cave in the farthest corner of the aquarium. I couldn't see it directly because its view was blocked by the upper part of the bookcase. This occasional view of the hidden corner puzzled me, but it was years before I learned about the total internal reflection. Now years later I can easily explain that episode from childhood. Those strange pictures of the hidden aquarium corners were stored somewhere deep inside my memory for many years and came back only when the program showed me the route in Figure 7-63c.

With the help of this program, I am trying to demonstrate that if users get total control over all the screen elements, a small change initiated by the user allows you to move from expected results to unexpected. In science, both types of results can be valuable. Expected results allow you to prove the correctness of suppositions made before the experiment. Unexpected results show that the theory on which experiments are based can be partly or entirely wrong. The same experiment (Figure 7-62) allowed me to see other results that I couldn't make any predictions about before I designed this example.

Can you say what the underwater creatures see when they look from inside the oceanarium? To avoid the discussion of nonhuman minds, let's assume that there are mermaids performing inside or scientists/maintenance workers doing something. Can they see visitors behind the glass wall? I don't think that too many visitors burden themselves with such questions. In our everyday life, if we see somebody, then this somebody can see us. The reversibility of light means that if it is sent in the opposite direction, it goes back by the same route. If we stay near the glass wall and watch different creatures on the other side, then those creatures can see us. The law always works if a creature looks exactly along the ray route in the opposite direction, but what happens if the angle is different?

Figure 7-64 shows route variants when somebody looks from the same place under the water but at different angles to the glass wall. I would say that only the result in Figure 7-64a is expected, while the three others are unexpected. When a creature looks at a relatively small angle of incidence (Figure 7-64a), there is some distortion caused by refraction on two boundaries, but at least something on the outside can be seen. With the bigger angle of incidence, the underwater creature has no chance to see visitors. Figures 7-64b, 7-64c, and 7-64d show variants for the steadily increasing angle of incidence; I wonder how many readers would expect such results. I wasn't thinking about such results, and you would never see them at all if not for the movability and rotatability of a flashlight in the current example.

450

Figure 7-64a. *Two points of ordinary refraction*

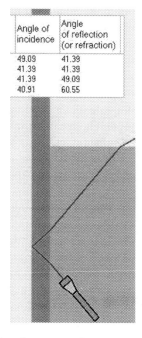

Figure 7-64b. *Three points of ordinary refraction and one point of total internal reflection*

Angle of incidence	Angle of reflection (or refraction)
64.67	52.27
52.27	52.27
52.27	64.67
25.33	34.67

Figure 7-64c. *The same set of refractions and total internal reflection, but the last ray leg bounds to the glass*

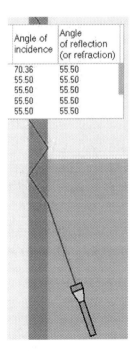

Angle of incidence	Angle of reflection (or refraction)
70.36	55.50
55.50	55.50
55.50	55.50
55.50	55.50
55.50	55.50

Figure 7-64d. *First point of ordinary refraction and then a set of total internal reflections*

452

Good books on physics not only give explanations but also ask readers to answer some questions. With the standard design of a book, users have to make some calculations to answer such questions. This book is accompanied with a program that allows readers to play the role of experimenters.

Suppose that you are visiting the same oceanarium and do not stay close to the glass wall but somewhere on the floor in the far-left corner. (In Figure 7-62 this is the position of the bottom-left corner of the yellow rectangle.) Is it possible from there to see anything above the water at the far right?

- If YES, then where do you have to look?

- If NO, where do you have to move, and where do you have to look from the new position?

From the point of view of programming, this example is at the same level of simplicity as the previous one. Four straight segments describe the boundaries inside the oceanarium; there are also eight standard segments for the border of the flashlight. I never found the ray route that would return to the flashlight, so these eight segments look unnecessary, but I still count them to keep the same method of route calculation. On the four boundaries inside the oceanarium, the refraction or total internal reflection may occur; this depends on each particular boundary and the angle of incidence.

This example perfectly demonstrates the difference between the standard design of programs and user-driven applications. To explain refraction, a program of standard design would demonstrate the cases in Figures 7-59 (middle case), 7-60a , and 7-60c. The new design allows much more. It easily allows you to see the standard cases of a ray going through window glass and of a ray falling down on the water surface. If a student is not interested in physics at all, the student can look at the standard cases and forget about the program. But there are many opportunities for those who want to play with rays and boundaries. There are interesting results that I didn't mention and that I may not even have found. The array of possible results depends on the person's desire and ability to play with the involved elements. So, the more skillful the experimenter, the more interesting the results can be. This is the power of user-driven applications when they are used in science and education.

Let's try one more example.

File: `Form_Prism_RegularPolygon.cs`

Menu position: Applications ➤ From Geometric Optics ➤ Prism (regular polygon)

About 350 years ago Isaac Newton demonstrated his famous experiments with a triangular prism to explain the origin of light. Since then, the picture of a triangular prism with a white ray touching one plane and a set of seven colored rays (or cones) emerging from another plane can be found in every book on geometric optics. To demonstrate that the difference between expected and unexpected is infinitesimal, I can ask a simple question: "Is it possible to see fewer than seven colored cones emerging from the second plane"? (Book [3] with an example of a triangular prism allows you to find an answer.)

Seven colored cones emerging from a triangular prism is a perfect demonstration of light dispersion. Another, even more famous, example of such dispersion is a rainbow. To explain the rainbow phenomenon, the ray propagation through a water droplet is used. A water droplet is circular. A circle can be considered as a regular polygon with the infinitive number of vertices (or planes). Thus, we observe light dispersion in a triangular prism, and we observe dispersion (rainbow) with the help of prisms that have an infinitive number of planes. (To be correct, a rainbow is the result of dispersion on a set of droplets with each colored ray coming from a different droplet.) What happens when the white light comes to a regular polygon with more than three planes? What happens when this number is changed?

A real experiment would require preparing a whole set of prisms, which is not an easy task; modeling on a computer would be much easier. The transformation of the screen's triangular prism into another one with the changeable number of planes was done quickly. I could see the results similar to a triangular prism, so at first such a prism transformation didn't produce any unexpected results. Then I began to watch something absolutely different; after some time I understood that similar results were described in a famous Pollyanna book by Eleanor H. Porter [6].

> *"Pollyanna had not hung up three of the pendants in the sunlit window before she saw a little of what was going to happen. She was so excited then she could scarcely control her shaking fingers enough to hang up the rest. But at last her task was finished, and she stepped back with a low cry of delight.*
>
> *It had become a fairyland--that sumptuous, but dreary bedroom. Everywhere were bits of dancing red and green, violet and orange, gold and blue. The wall, the floor, and the furniture, even to the bed itself, were aflame with shimmering bits of color."*

It is definitely a dispersion of white light into components, but it is a bit strange of a dispersion, not the one we see in a rainbow or with a triangular prism. In a rainbow, we always see seven colors side by side; they never appear separately from each other in different parts of the sky. In the case of an equilateral triangular prism, the colored cones also stay together, and the maximum angle between the red and violet parts of the dispersed light is somewhere around 10 degrees. The light coming out from such a prism would place the colored spots next to each other. The vivid description from the book tells about the colored spots all around the room, so the cause of such a picture must be different; Figure 7-65 shows how it happens. To avoid the mess of all the different colors on one figure, I prepared three different figures for the different light components. The geometry of the involved elements is the same for all three. Now imagine that sunlight touches the pendant in the way it is shown on the figures. The white light is dispersed; then each component will go its own way and will come out at its own angle. As a result, we get different colored spots in absolutely different places.

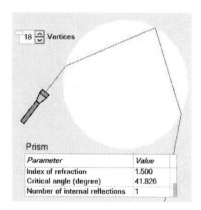

Figure 7-65a. *A red light has a single point of internal reflection and then comes out*

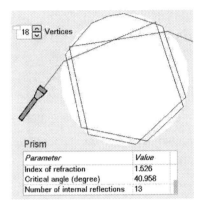

Figure 7-65b. *A blue light comes out after 13 internal reflections*

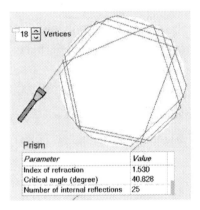

Figure 7-65c. *A violet light makes nearly 4 circles inside and comes out after 25 internal reflections*

Did I expect to see such a result when I designed an example with a regular polygonal prism? Certainly not, though I was aware of gem cutting that has been used for centuries. (We can skip the discussion of my ability to predict the results, but at least I am honest.) Luckily, the program was designed as a user-driven application, so the user (me!) could do whatever he wanted with the involved elements. As usual, this user decided to play with the screen elements and on the way received the results that the designer (also me!) would never think about. It is a perfect answer to the fundamental question of "Is it possible to receive unexpected results from the scientific program?"

Conclusion

This book is not about some algorithm or programming product. It is about the new philosophy of user–program relations and how this change of philosophy triggers the development of programs that allow users to get much more from the applications.

The main idea of user-driven applications is in the passing of control of programs from developers to users. It is unthinkable in the realm of standard design, so the new programs are designed on a new basis—on the movability of each and all of the screen objects. All the demonstrated programs use my algorithm of movability, but I stress all the time that the most valuable result is not the algorithm itself but the consequences of using it. There can be different algorithms of movability, but the results of using any one of them will be absolutely the same.

Since inventing the algorithm of movability and starting to design the programs of the new type, I often think about the analogy of the invention of integrals. Integrals were invented to help in solving a particular problem but turned into an extremely powerful instrument of very wide use. As always, the results of using some powerful instrument depend mostly on the skills of those who use it.

The area of programs is extremely wide. Long gone are the times when computers were used only as calculators. Now the most important is the use of programs in science and engineering where the uncertainty of the tasks and the ways of solving them make the help of predetermined solutions inefficient. Programs have to help and in no way limit the ability of talented researchers to find the solutions to complex problems. Currently used programs in which all the decisions are made by somebody at the stage of the program design has become a less and less effective instrument for researchers. The switch to user-driven applications breaks this wrong practice and raises the efficiency of programs to the level of those who use them.

© Sergey Andreyev 2020

S. Andreyev, *User-Driven Applications for Research and Science*, https://doi.org/10.1007/978-1-4842-6488-1

CONCLUSION

Science is a conservative area and prefers to reject the new ideas as long as possible and even much longer [5], so I have to think about the best way to demonstrate the new ideas to those who really need them. In many universities, programming and engineering faculties often work not too far away from each other. You can teach students a new design, and for practice they can develop programs of the new type for scientific research work. The students will learn the new technique, while scientists will get programs of the new type and estimate their usefulness for their work.

Dr. Sergey Andreyev (andreyev_sergey@yahoo.com)

June 2018

APPENDIX A

Ordinary Controls

Since the development of personal computers, interface design has been based on ordinary controls and is unthinkable without such elements. Yet, throughout all the examples of this book, the appearance of such elements was so rare (the fingers on one hand would be enough to count them) that it is now obvious that ordinary controls have lost their dominant role in design. If you have been using such elements for years, it would be hard to agree with such an abrupt change of the preferable elements. The majority of developers cannot imagine programs without ordinary controls, so this chapter demonstrates the use of them in user-driven applications.

For the last 30+ years, the design of applications has been based on elements of two different types: graphical objects and controls. A graphical object is a product of the skill and imagination of a particular developer. You create a class according to some requirements, and you give this class the needed features plus a set of methods and properties to deal with these features. Controls are also graphical objects but with such features that make them absolutely different from other elements and put them into a class of their own. Usually controls are produced by an author of the operating system in which they are used, and there exists a symbiosis between the operating system and the controls: these elements are designed especially to be used by this system and are treated by the system as a favorite child. The variety of ordinary controls is limited, while the quality of the design and implementation is usually very high, so every developer can easily use these elements for the design of different programs. As a result, *all* developers use the same set of controls. This has advantages and disadvantages. Among the advantages are quality and predetermined behavior, so users know what to expect and how to deal with these elements. In a situation when 10 most often used controls hardly changed at all throughout the last 30 years and nearly all applications are based on this set of controls, users have no problems dealing with elements of the new applications. The biggest disadvantage is the way the operating system deals with all the controls: they are considered as special elements with a higher priority than graphical objects.

© Sergey Andreyev 2020
S. Andreyev, *User-Driven Applications for Research and Science*, https://doi.org/10.1007/978-1-4842-6488-1

This is not considered a disadvantage for the programs with total developer control. When only the developer is allowed to make all the decisions about the application view and behavior, then he puts all the needed elements in the way he considers (and declares!) to be the best. After that, users have only to deal with whatever they are given. Under such a design, there is no question of higher or lower element priority. All elements are fixed at their predetermined places, and it does not matter at all whether a particular element is a control or a graphical one.

For user-driven applications, this special status and higher priority of ordinary controls over all graphical objects is simply inaccessible. Controls are always shown atop all the graphical objects, and the user cannot overrule this decision of the operating system. In the new applications, only the user decides on the program view at any moment, and the use of elements with only partial user control mars the whole idea and the entire work of user-driven applications. The most popular controls are useful and highly demanded elements of design, so the best solution would be to design the graphical analogs of such controls. Such graphical "controls" have all the needed functionality of their classical analogs, but they do not have a special status, so they work in applications at an equal level with other objects. Such graphical controls were already discussed, and their work was demonstrated in many examples.

Years ago when I started my work on the movability of screen elements, ordinary controls were widely used in the design of my applications. It is impossible to use side-by-side movable and unmovable objects because even a single unmovable element among movable produces the same result as placing a big boulder in the middle of a highway. If you have movable and resizable graphical objects, then all the controls that work with them side by side must be also turned into movable and resizable. Thus, from the beginning of my work, there was a demand to incorporate ordinary controls into the same algorithm of movability, though the special status of all controls demanded a special treatment for them even inside the same algorithm.

Controls can be used in applications in different ways. There are solitary elements, there are controls with associated comments, and there are groups of solitary and commented controls. All these cases are demonstrated in the following examples. It is a relatively short appendix; much more on the theme of using ordinary controls can be found in my other book [2].

Before turning to the details of the following examples, let's talk a bit about the features on which the movability and resizability of controls can be organized. Surprisingly, we are going to start with a broader look not at elements inside any program but on a higher level. From time to time the developers of operating systems try to change even the basic view of this level, so let's talk about the classical variant. When a multiwindow operating system is started, the user deals with two types of objects: small icons and bigger rectangles that represent the working programs. Icons are small nonresizable rectangles that can be moved around the screen by any inner point. Originally a big rectangle was called a *dialog*; for the last 15 or more years, the word *form* has been used. A form is resizable by its borders and can be moved by a special thin strip along the upper border, which is called a *title bar*. Movability and resizability are the basic features of all forms, so when you deal with any form, you have no doubt that it can be moved around the screen, and its size can be changed to whatever you prefer. Developers can easily regulate these features, but this is done extremely rarely. (The classic Calculator is one of the programs for which the resizing is forbidden.)

Controls are the objects that are closely related to the forms. The exact chain of inheritance between these classes is changed from time to time, but for our further discussion one thing is important: any control is movable and resizable by default. This is the main difference between turning graphical objects and controls into movable and resizable: for graphical objects, you have to invent everything; for controls, you need only to find the way to use the features that they already have.

Solitary Control

File: `Form_Control_Solitary.cs`

Menu position: Ordinary controls ➤ Solitary

For all the screen objects, the main rule of moving and resizing was simple: move by any inner points and resize by border. Unfortunately, for ordinary controls, this cannot be implemented (in a simple way!). Controls are designed to use their inner area for the mouse clicks with already declared purposes; the reaction on any click inside controls is well known, and I am not going to change it in any way. Thus, the only chance to move and resize controls is to use the vicinity of their borders. Any cover node can be used either for moving or for resizing an object, so the frame around control has to be divided between the areas to start both operations.

Any solitary control is wrapped in a `Control_Solitary` object, and then this `Control_Solitary` element is registered in the mover queue as any other object, so we are talking now about the cover for this class. Moving and resizing of a `Control_Solitary` object are directly translated into the moving and resizing of its inner control.

461

A `Control_Solitary` object is organized in such a way that it frames its inner control. The only question is in organizing a frame with an obvious (or expected) placement of the nodes for resizing, but several applications use the same technique, so the practice is already known. For example, when you change the size of some control in Visual Studio, you resize it by the small squares in the corners or in the middle of the sides. So, the best and expected places for the nodes to resize any control are known, and the other details depend on the purpose of the required resizing.

Figure A-1 demonstrates the view of `Form_Control_Solitary.cs`. This example includes two graphical objects and six controls that are easily detected because the covers are shown for them only.

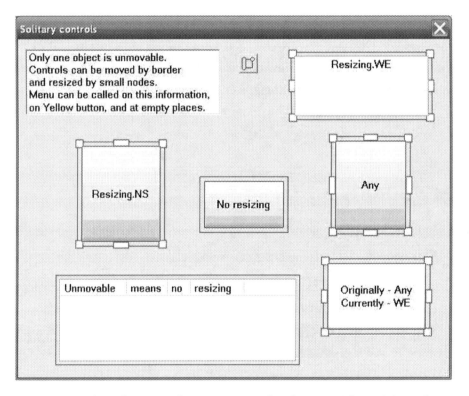

Figure A-1. *Special nodes near the corners and sides provide resizing; the remaining area of the thin frame is used for moving*

One object of the `Control_Solitary` class has a different constructor, it is an unusual one, but I wanted to demonstrate the possibility of such a case. The most commonly used constructor does not mention the needed type of resizing.

```
public Control_Solitary (Form frm, Mover mvr, Control ctrl)
```

However, the text inside the controls (Figure A-1) specifies the different variants of resizability, so it is determined in some other way. Controls have a rectangular shape, and their possible variants of resizing are described by the same enumeration that was used for graphical rectangles.

```
public enum Resizing { None, NS, WE, Any };
```

No resizing	MaximumSize	0, 0
	MinimumSize	0, 0
	Size	129, 75

For the majority of controls (and for each control of this example), the minimum and maximum allowed sizes can be set through their MinimumSize and MaximumSize properties; in this way, the range for resizing a particular control is set. To determine the resizing type of any control, the values of these two properties are compared with the control size.

- If the values of the MinimumSize and MaximumSize properties are not changed from their default values (0, 0) or their values are the same as the size of a control, then this control is nonresizable.

Resizing.NS	MaximumSize	130, 400
	MinimumSize	130, 40
	Size	130, 150

- If the MinimumSize and MaximumSize properties provide a range for one direction only (width or height), then this control is resizable in this direction only. The button on the left can change only its height (the Resizing.NS text); the TextBox control in the top-right corner can change only its width (the Resizing.WE text).

Any	MaximumSize	300, 200
	MinimumSize	28, 28
	Size	115, 139

- If the `MinimumSize` and `MaximumSize` properties provide the ranges for both directions, then this control is fully resizable.

There is one addition in the last case: an additional parameter can be used, and if its value is `false`, then this control becomes unmovable and automatically nonresizable regardless of the size ranges provided by its properties! This is the case of the `ListView` control closer to the bottom-left corner.

```
csUnmovable = new Control_Solitary (this, mover, listviewResizeNotMove,
                                    Resizing .Any, false);
```

Unmovable means no resizing	MaximumSize	600, 300
	MinimumSize	200, 60
	Size	381, 127

According to the values of `MinimumSize` and `MaximumSize` properties, this control has to be fully resizable, but it is forced to be unmovable and, as a consequence, becomes nonresizable.[1]

The sensitive frame around a control is six pixels wide, while special nodes are slightly bigger (nine pixels).

---

[1] Such overruling of movability over resizability is not correct because these two features must be absolutely independent. In all classes of objects demonstrated in the previous examples, these two features were always independent. Unfortunately, when years ago I saw that an unmovable but resizable control could be moved around the screen by a sequence of size changes, I decided to lock that back door but did it in such a strange way. It was definitely a wrong decision, but since then, I never used controls with such a combination of features, so I forgot about that case. Because the `MoveGraphLibrary.dll` has been downloaded by many people around the world, there can be programs that rely on this feature of solitary controls, so I do not want to change it now. However, I want to stress that such an overruling of movability over resizability is definitely a mistake.

The process of making any *solitary control* movable/resizable differs from the same process for graphical objects in several aspects.

1. There is no need to design some new class; simply use one of the `Control_Solitary` constructors, and that is all. The cover is organized automatically, and the mover already knows how to move and resize this object.

2. The resizing ranges are determined by the `MinimumSize` and `MaximumSize` properties of a control and by comparison of these values with the sizes of a control.

3. The `Control_Solitary` objects are registered with the mover in the same way as simple graphical objects by using the `Add()` or `Insert()` method.

```
mover .Add (scWE);
mover .Add (scNS);
mover .Add (scNoResize);
```

Depending on the type of the needed (organized) resizing, the covers in Figure A-1 show a different number of nodes around controls, but this is only on the visualization. A cover for any `Control_Solitary` object consists of nine nodes. The first eight nodes are the small nodes next to the corners and middle points on the sides. If you do not see part of these nodes next to some of the controls in the figure, then it means that in each particular case the unneeded nodes are simply squeezed to a size of zero, but their number did not change. The eight nodes that are used for resizing are numbered from the top-left corner going clockwise, so the node near the top-left corner has the number 0, the node in the middle of the upper side is 1, and so on. The last node in the cover—the node with the number eight—is a big rectangle that is wider than the control itself by six pixels on each side.

There is a `Control_Solitary` constructor that allows you to declare the needed type of resizing.

```
public Control_Solitary (Form frm,

            Mover mvr,

            Control ctrl,              // control

            Resizing resizeForced,     // resize type

            bool bMove)                // declares an object to be movable or not
```

There is one significant limitation on setting the resizing via the `resizeForced` parameter of this constructor: the specified resizing cannot be more general than the resizing estimated in the standard way from comparing the declared size and the values of the `MinimumSize` and `MaximumSize` properties. If the size and two properties allow the full resizing of the control, then you can limit the allowed resizing by passing as a parameter `Resizing.NS`, `Resizing.WE`, or `Resizing.None`. In such a case the control gets the type of resizing that is passed as a parameter. But if the properties of a control allow it to be resized only horizontally (`Resizing.WE`) and you try to change it with the `Resizing.NS` or `Resizing.Any` parameter, this has no effect on the resizing of such a control.

The type of resizing for a control can be set not only at the moment of initialization of its `Control_Solitary` object but later with the help of the `Resizing` property. What can require such a change of resizing for a control in the working application? Consider the case of a fully resizable control. While an application is running, you change the size of this control to whatever you prefer, and after that, you do not want to change its width accidentally. You can change its resizing status to `Resizing.NS`, and there will be no change of the width even if you press the corner node. The pale yellow button in the bottom-right corner in Figure A-1 can be used to check some possibilities. I purposely set a different background color of this button to distinguish it from others; this is the only control in the form on which and around the context menu can be called (Figure A-2). As I already mentioned, an unmovable control cannot be resized, so if you turn this yellow button into unmovable, then the second command of the menu becomes disabled.

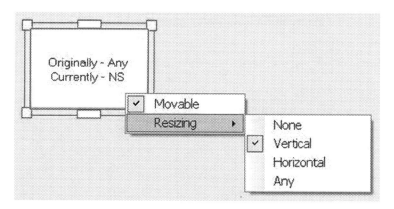

Figure A-2. *The menu on (and around) the yellow button allows you to regulate the movability and the type of resizing*

There is one restriction on the size of the controls that I implemented with the `Control_Solitary` class: controls cannot be reduced to less than 16 pixels. This was done to avoid the accidental disappearance of controls in applications. I do not think that users would appreciate such disappearance. If any control has to be deleted, this must be done in a different way.

There is absolutely nothing special in the movement of controls: press the mouse next to the border and relocate the control. There is nearly nothing special in resizing the majority of controls. For example, you will not find anything strange in resizing the `Panel`, `Button`, or `ListView` object. But you may find something a bit strange in resizing, for example, a `TextBox` object.

The problem is not in the algorithm, which is exactly the same for all controls. The problem is caused by one decision made many years ago by the developers of those controls when they implemented a strict link between the font and size of a control. These parameters have to be absolutely independent, but somebody "too smart" at Microsoft decided to organize a link between them, and the change of font often changes the size of control. Specialists from different branches of engineering know very well that if you organize two independent sources for changing the same parameter, it is often the easiest way to organize a disaster. And the "geniuses" from Microsoft did it on purpose and with sound mind! As one former Russian prime minister once dropped: "We wanted to do the best, but the result was as usual...."

The worst results of that old decision become obvious when you design some really complex forms with lots of different controls inside. You spend a lot of time preparing the best possible view; you add the possibility to change the font (or several fonts) because there are users with very sharp and very poor vision. These people use fonts with significantly different sizes, and you have to think about all the variants. Then, after all possible testing, you give a program to users and watch in astonishment how your perfectly designed forms can change when users apply the fonts they need. I went through this several times, and I never had polite words for those who linked the font and size and proudly hid this link somewhere deep inside the system. Yet, you have to work with what you get, and if you work with Visual Studio, you have to be aware of some of the traps. Usually strange things happen for controls with a single text line; some parameters are stored deep inside their structure and are out of your control when you use such elements in your design.

For example, take the `NumericUpDown` control. You can declare the minimum and maximum width of the control via the `MinimumSize` and `MaximumSize` properties, but the second number in both of them—the height—always has a zero value and cannot be changed. Do not worry about this value: whenever you change the font of the control, its height is adjusted to the font, so you always see one line of text. I would not call adjusting the control size to the size of a font a good decision; I did not ask to change the control size, and I do not like when a system is doing anything by itself without my direct command. But let's agree with this for a moment and decide that this is a normal and expected reaction. Then the different behavior of another but similar control looks at least strange to me.

An ordinary `TextBox` control demonstrates this strange behavior but not always. Suppose that a `TextBox` control is registered with the `Resizing.Any` parameter, so it can be resized by the corners. If the `Multiline` property of this control is set to `true`, then the size can be changed in the range declared by the two size properties `MinimumSize` and `MaximumSize`. As a developer, you set these two values in such a way that allow you to change the height of this text box; after that, users will decide how many lines of text they want to see.

Suppose that you have another resizable `TextBox` control in which a single line of text has to be shown, so its `Multiline` property is set to `false`. When users change the font for such control, its height is not changed at all! It is not adjusted to the size of a font (and I think this is a correct decision), so users can change the height of such a control as they do for `Buttons` or `ListBoxes`. For users to get a chance of changing the height of such a `TextBox`, its two properties have to allow it by providing a wide enough range for the height of the control. So, in the case of such a `TextBox` control, the values for two properties have to be declared in a different way than in the mentioned `NumericUpDown` control. However, visually these two controls with a single line of text are very much alike.

The mentioned things are the only minor negative remarks to an otherwise very important thing: all controls are easily turned into movable and resizable.

Some controls can be used as stand-alone elements, but in many cases they need some kind of comment, and often enough controls with and/or without comments must be united into groups. Let's explore the variants of such "control + comment" pairs, and after that, we'll look at their groups.

Control with Comments

All controls have a rectangular shape, but they differ in size. Comments to those controls also differ in size, so a control can be bigger or smaller than its comment. Depending on the type (class) of control and the relative sizes of two parts, there can be different variants of their preferable positioning. I want to remind you that we are looking at the use of familiar elements inside programs of the new type in which not the designer but the user decides about the positions of all elements, so we are looking at the case of a "control + comment" pair in which the relative positioning can be changed by the user at any moment. There are two general types of relative positioning: there can be a set of predetermined variants among which the user can select, and there can be an arbitrary comment positioning.

Comments with Limited Positioning

The case with the set of predetermined comment positions does not look like a suitable element for a user-driven application. It looks more like a classic case of adaptive interface when the developer provides variants and the user is allowed to select only among these variants. In our case of the "control + comment" pair, there is one feature that can make the use of predetermined positions very attractive.

For a "control + comment" pair, not only must the change of their relative position be provided, but also the synchronous move of the pair must be provided. If an individual move of comment is allowed, then the synchronous move of a pair must be caused by the control move. The previous example with solitary controls demonstrated that resizing and moving of such element are started by pressing different places of the control frame. For relatively big controls, this is easy as it is not a problem to find the places of the control frame by which this control can be moved. For small controls, for example, for small buttons that are often used to call standard dialogs, those places of the frame are small and not easy to detect. Also, the comments of such small controls are often bigger than controls, and it looks really awkward that the synchronous move of a pair can be started only at some places near the smaller element, and it is a problem to find these places. It would be much easier to move such a pair by any point of comment, but it automatically excludes the individual movement of a comment by any point, and in such case the only possibility is to have a set of predetermined comment positions.

File: `Form_Control_FixedComment.cs`

Menu position: Ordinary controls ➤ With fixed comment

The objects in this example (Figure A-3) belong to the `Control_FixedComment` class. A comment can be placed on one of 12 predetermined positions (three on each side of a control). Controls with a set of predetermined comment positions were first designed to be used for a case of "small control with bigger comment," but this size ratio is not a mandatory thing, and the designed class works with all controls. Though the control and its comment are different, there is no individual movement of two halves; they always move together. There is a single cover for both parts, so an object can be registered by the `Mover.Add()` or `Mover.Insert()` method.

The control of this pair is moved and resized in the same way as demonstrated in the solitary controls, so the cover of the `Control_FixedComment` class includes exactly the same nine nodes next to the control border (see the button on the right in Figure A-1). The presence of the comment simply adds two more nodes to those nine.

The comment area is always a rectangle with the sizes determined by the text and used font; the comment area is covered by a single rectangular node with the number nine. You will rarely see text positioned just at the control border because it looks awkward; usually there is some space between a control and its comment. This space can vary, and, as any other parameter, it is regulated by user. It would be strange to have some small nonsensitive area between two sensitive parts of an object, so this space is covered by a node number 10. Thus, the cover of any `Control_FixedComment` object consists of 11 nodes.

The rules of a user-driven application demand full users' control over all elements and their parameters. For `Control_FixedComment` objects, it means that there must be an easy way to change the comment font, color, and position. To change these parameters, you call the menu on comments to be changed, but I want to highlight one detail of this easy process. Usually, the menu selection is determined by the class of the pressed object (one menu for each class). Similar-looking comments were used in the examples in Chapter 2, and there were no questions about calling menu on those comments. What is the problem with calling a menu on a comment fixed somewhere near controls?

I would not call it a real problem, but the current case differs from all those demonstrated earlier because all the text associated with ordinary controls in Figure A-3 do not represent some class of comments. What we see as a comment is in reality a part of some Control_FixedComment object. If a decision about calling a menu is based only on the class of the pressed object, then the same menu would be called on the control frame and on its comment. A menu that is used in the current example contains only the commands to change comments, so there is absolutely no sense in calling this menu at an empty place near the control border. To allow the calling of this menu only on a comment, there must be an additional checking by the node number.

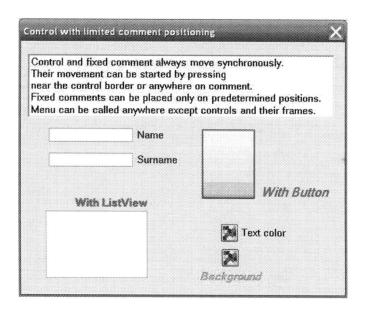

Figure A-3. *A comment has three variants of lining at each control side, so there are 12 different allowed positions*

```
private void OnMouseUp (object sender, MouseEventArgs e)
{
    ... ...
    if (mover .Release (out iObj, out iNode))
    {
        GraphicalObject grobj = mover .ReleasedSource;
```

```
if (e .Button == MouseButtons .Right && fDist <= 3)
{
    if (grobj is Control_FixedComment &&
        iNode == Control_FixedComment .Node_Comment)
    {
        ContextMenuStrip = menuOnComment;
    }
    ... ...
```

A comment position is set in an auxiliary form that also allows you to set the distance between the control and comment.

The current example is a good one to demonstrate the disorder that ordinary controls bring into programs. When an application is designed only on graphical objects, then each of those objects occupies its personal layer. Simple commands give users an easy control over the order of objects and allow you to change it. A complex object may consist of many different parts; throughout the movements one object can block another or only part of it, but for graphical objects it is an unimaginable situation that one element occupies some layer between the parts of another element. Now look at Figure A-4. This is the result of moving the ListView control around the screen.

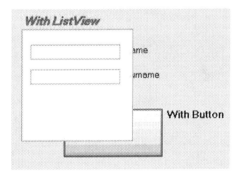

Figure A-4. *Normal mess of controls and their graphical comments*

Some controls can be seen above this list view; others are below. This depends on the order of controls that was set at the design time. Regardless of the order of controls, all comments are below all the controls. Suppose that the list view is released at this moment. Though two TextBox controls are perfectly seen and thus are positioned above the ListView control, these TextBox controls cannot be moved or resized because their sensitive frames are graphical and entirely blocked by the ListView control. In the current situation, the comments of those TextBoxes are partly seen, so two elements can be moved to the side by those visible parts of their comments. Only somewhere at an empty place will those TextBoxes become resizable. This is just a small demonstration of the disorder that ordinary controls bring into the world of movable and resizable graphical objects.

The Control_FixedComment class is easy in design and use, but it has one obvious flaw: the user cannot position comments as he wants but is limited to selecting only among several predetermined positions. Let's look at another class of "control + comment" objects in which the comment can be positioned in an arbitrary way.

Free Comments

File: Form_Control_FreeComment.cs

Menu position: Ordinary controls ➤ With free comment

Before starting to design "control + comment" objects with an arbitrary positioning of comments, let's first formulate the rules of behavior for such objects.

- A control can be moved and resized by different parts of its frame in a standard way that was demonstrated for solitary controls.

- On any moving/resizing of a control, the comment preserves its relative position to the control.

- A comment can be moved and rotated individually (Figure A-5). There are no restrictions on the positioning of a comment in relation to its associated control except one: the comment cannot be totally covered by the associated control because in such a case it becomes inaccessible. To avoid such situations, whenever the comment is released while being totally covered by its associated control, then this comment is forcedly moved outside so that it becomes visible and accessible. I want to underline that this enforced relocation is used only when the comment is blocked by its own associated control and not by any other.

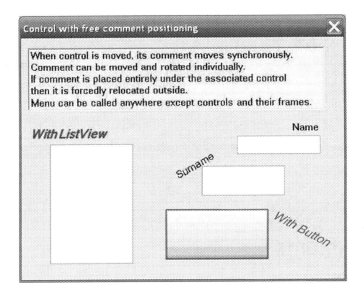

Figure A-5. *A comment can take any relative position except being entirely covered by the associated control*

Controls are rectangular, so a comment belongs to the familiar `Comment_ ToRectangle` class. A comment can be moved individually, but it is also relocated when the size or position of the associated control is changed, so it is a classic example of a complex object. A graphical rectangle with comments was discussed, so we need to look only at the difference that is caused by the dominant element being not a graphical object but an ordinary control.

Move any comment below its control and release it when the comment is entirely out of view. The comment will immediately reappear above the top-left corner of its control. There is nothing about such a relocation in the code of the `OnMouseUp()` method, and you do not need to worry about this situation. The mover is aware of such a possibility, and the correct reaction in such a special case is provided by the library. At the moment when any object is released, the `Mover.Release()` method is called, so the mover checks the class of the released element and can take the needed steps to prevent the disaster.

There are some user actions that can lead to the same disaster; those actions are not related to movement, so the mover does not supervise those actions, and in these cases the developer has to use some pieces of code. One such case happens when a comment is mostly blocked by its control and then through the menu on a comment you decide to decrease the size of its font. As a result of such a font change, the area of the comment will decrease, and the comment will hide under its control. The same entire hiding of comment can occur if, through other commands of the same menu, you turn a comment into horizontal or vertical.

In all three cases, you can change directly one or another parameter of the pressed comment, but such a thing can cause a disaster. The comment does not know that it is used as a subordinate to some control and does not know about the area of this control. On the other side, the control knows about its associated comment; the control knows its own area and knows that a comment cannot be left inside this area. Thus, all changes of a comment that may result in the hiding of the comment are done not through a direct change of comment parameters but through the properties of the parent Control_FreeComment object. Such a property makes the required comment change, but if after that, the comment is placed entirely behind the associated control, then the comment is forcedly relocated to another place where it is not blocked. Such a change of comment parameter is mandatory only when there is a possibility of comment disappearance behind its control; in other cases, a comment parameter can be changed directly. The difference is perfectly seen in the changing of the font and color.

```
private void Click_miFont_Cmnt (object sender, EventArgs e)
{
    FontDialog dlg = new FontDialog ();
    dlg .Font = cmntPressed .Font;
    if (dlg .ShowDialog () == DialogResult .OK)
    {
        ccParent .CommentFont = dlg .Font;
        Invalidate ();
    }
}
private void Click_miColor_Cmnt (object sender, EventArgs e)
{
    ColorDialog dlg = new ColorDialog ();
    dlg .Color = cmntPressed .Color;
    if (dlg .ShowDialog () == DialogResult .OK)
    {
        cmntPressed .Color = dlg .Color;
        Invalidate ();
    }
}
```

The enforced relocation of the comment looks like a good and absolutely needed solution, but I want to remind you about one rule of user-driven applications.

> **Rule 3** *Users' commands on moving and resizing of objects or on changing the parameters of visualization must be implemented exactly as they are; no additions or expanded interpretation by developer are allowed.*

The enforced relocation of a comment is definitely a violation of this rule. Nothing of such kind is needed when applications are constructed of graphical objects only. The whole problem, and it's a serious one because it can cause the fatal disappearance of an element, is born by the use of special objects—ordinary controls—that are out of the users' control and behave according to the rules imposed by the operating system.

Groups with Controls

For the design based on ordinary controls, there are two classes that represent groups. GroupBox is a special class that unites a set of radio buttons to provide a selection among them. On the other hand, Panel can work as a container for different elements and represent a classical type of group. Unfortunately, the Panel class is absolutely unsuitable for user-driven applications, and from the beginning of my work I tried to design more appropriate groups. There were several more or less useful classes that are demonstrated and discussed in my other book [2].

The ElasticGroup class is my best class for the groups that contain ordinary controls. For several years in a row while I continued to use ordinary controls, this was the preferable class of groups in all my programs. This class was designed years ago even before I started to use the adhered mouse technique, so neither for the group class nor for all inner elements this technique is used. Because of such an old design, the classes for solitary and commented controls used inside these groups are slightly different from those that were discussed on the previous pages.

Objects of the ElasticGroup class can include inner elements of several classes.

- SolitaryControl, an old analog of the Control_Solitary class

- CommentedControl, an old analog of the Control_FreeComment class

- CommentedControlLTP, an old analog of the Control_FixedComment class

- DominantControl

- ElasticGroup

This list of classes means that inner element can be a solitary control, a control with a comment, or a group of controls of which one is dominant and others are subordinates, and an element can be a group of the same group class. Especially this recursive definition of the group makes the ElasticGroup class valuable in the design of applications because it allows you to construct complicated groups. I do not see any other types of relations between controls that are not covered by the mentioned cases, so from my point of view, any type of form can be organized with the ElasticGroup objects.[2]

I want to stress that many important features of the ElasticGroup class look identical to the same features of the already discussed Group_ArbitraryElements class, so their presentation in the current section might look a bit strange, but this is a result of contradiction between the order of the design and the order of the explanation in this book. The ElasticGroup class was developed much earlier, and when years later the Group_ArbitraryElements class was designed, it took the best features of its predecessors.

The basic ideas behind the design of the ElasticGroup class are simple.

- Any inner element can be moved and resized individually.

- The group frame is automatically adjusted to the positions and sizes of all inner elements.

- A group can be moved by the frame or any inner point.

```
public class ElasticGroup : GraphicalObject
{
    List<ElasticGroupElement> m_elements = new
    List<ElasticGroupElement> ();
    int [] m_framespaces = new int [4];     // Left, Top, Right, Bottom
    bool bTitleMovable = true;
    RectangleF m_rcFrame;                    // only through calculation
    SolidBrush brushBack;
    bool bShowFrame;
    Pen penFrame;
```

---

[2]I want to emphasize that this is only for the forms that are designed on ordinary controls with and without comments. If there must be some graphical objects inside a group, then the Group_ArbitraryElements class can be used.

The group is relatively simple, so I need to give only short comments to several fields that are shown in this code.

- All inner objects of the group are organized into a List. The particular class of each element is determined by some value from the ElementType_ElasticGroup enumeration.

```
public enum ElementType_ElasticGroup { SolitaryControl, CommentedControl,
                                CommentedControlLTP, Group,
                                DominantControl };
```

- On all four sides, there is some space between inner elements and the frame. On three sides—left, right, and bottom—it is really a space to the frame. At the top, it is the distance between the inner elements and the title. If there is no title in the group, then it is the distance to the frame as on all other sides. The ElasticGroup class has a minimum allowed distance to the frame—six pixels. There is no upper limit for this space in the class itself, so any value can be set via the parameters, but if you change the group view through its standard tuning form, then there is a maximum limit of 20 pixels. I do not think that anyone will need a bigger distance between the inner elements and the frame.

- A group can be used with or without a title. This title can be moved along the upper line of the frame and placed anywhere between the left and right borders of the frame. At any moment the title movability can be changed.

- The group background color can be changed at any moment. Groups can be nested inside each other, and it is possible to spread the same background color on inner groups or to have them different. In many cases, a different color of the nested group improves visibility.

- The frame is not a mandatory element. It is a useful element to make the content of the group more obvious, but a group works in the same way without a frame in view. The title is still movable along the invisible frame, and the distance between the inner elements and invisible frame is changed in the same way as to the visible frame.

There are several examples that can be helpful in the demonstration of the ElasticGroup class; let's start with the simplest one and later turn to more complicated ones with more possibilities.

File: Form_YearsSelection.cs

Menu position: Applications ➤ Selection of years

For many years I used my own program for a family photo archive. This archive includes thousands of pictures that cover the period of more than a century, so there is a flexible mechanism of photo selection. The first version of this program was designed on the basis of ordinary controls even before the invention of the movability algorithm. Later the new achievements in movability were often tested on this program, so I can demonstrate a small piece that is designed as a user-driven application but entirely on controls. Figure A-6 shows a small form for selecting years; two objects of the ElasticGroup class are used here.

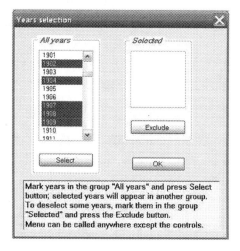

Figure A-6. *Selection of years*

This task deals with the selection of the year, but a similar task is solved in many different applications for the names or objects from one or another area. In general, the task can be formulated in such a way. We have a set of names from which a subset selection must be organized. For the best visual control of the whole process, the set of names and the selected subset are shown as lists. Throughout the process of selection, you may want to select more names or to exclude some of those that were already selected.

`ListView` is an excellent control to demonstrate the full list of names and the selected subset. Selection of the marked names and the removal of the unneeded names can be organized with additional buttons.

The implementation of this task needs only several controls. Information can be read once and then squeezed to a tiny size or moved out of view. After that, there are two similar groups of two elements each and one more button that is pressed when the selection is done. Both groups are identical in design and work, so it is enough to analyze one of them.

```
ctrlsAll = new Control [] { listYearsAll, btnSelect };
```

These two controls—`ListView` and `Button`—can be used as `SolitaryControl` independent objects inside the group, but there is a better solution. One of these elements—a `ListView`—is definitely the main element of the group, while the button is an auxiliary one, so the pair is turned into a `DominantControl` object, and then a group is organized around it. The simplest constructor of the `DominantControl` class needs only an array of controls; the first control is automatically turned into a dominant element, and all others are turned into subordinates. In our case, we have a single subordinate.

```
void DefaultView ()
{
    ... ...
    DominantControl domin = new DominantControl (ctrlsAll);
    groupAll = new ElasticGroup (this, new ElasticGroupElement (domin), 12,
                                "All years");

    ... ...
```

Throughout the discussion of the `Control_FreeComment` class, I purposely drew your attention to the possibility of comment disappearance under the control and to the solution of this problem. When a comment to a control is released, the mover checks the comment position, and if the comment is found to be entirely blocked by its associated control, then the enforced comment relocation is organized into the position that is above the top-left corner of a control.

The `DominantControl` class has a similar problem of fatal disappearance if a subordinate control is released under dominant control, so this class also has to have the solution to this problem. It could be solved in the same way, but in the `DominantControl` class, there can be an arbitrary number of subordinate elements and it would be not good if all of them had the same place for default relocation. Thus, each subordinate element gets its individual place for default relocation; this is the place from which the moving of this subordinate starts. Checking subordinates against their dominant element and the possible relocation of subordinates is done by the `Mover.CheckDominantsSubordinates()` method. In the current example, the possible relocation happens inside one or another group, so groups must be updated.

```
private void OnMouseUp (object sender, MouseEventArgs e)
{
    ... ...
    if (mover .Release ())
    {
        if (e .Button == MouseButtons .Left)
        {
            mover .CheckDominantsSubordinates ();
            groupAll .Update ();
            groupSelected .Update ();
            Invalidate ();
            ... ...
```

The code of this `Form_YearsSelection.cs` example is simple. After all the needed objects are organized and registered in the mover queue, there is hardly any mention of these objects because the mover knows very well how to deal with objects of the `SolitaryControl`, `DominantControl`, `SubordinateControl`, and `ElasticGroup` classes. Much more interesting is to see how the main ideas of user-driven applications are implemented even in such a simple example. In the introduction to this book I mentioned that the developer has to provide the work of an application without crashes, while users decide about what to do and how to do. We can divide a user's control over the application into two parts: general control over action and control over visual parameters.

In the variant shown in Figure A-6, the selected years are moved from the left to right. This means that I prefer to do it this way, but it does not mean at all that everyone has to agree with me. There are people who like to do it in the opposite direction from right to left, and there are users who would like to place two groups in a single column. Never mind, groups can be moved around and placed in any way you prefer. The same things happen to their inner elements: they can be moved, resized, and placed differently in relation to each other.

Visual parameters (fonts, colors, spaces) are regulated either through menu commands or via special tuning forms. A tuning form for `ElasticGroup` objects was designed years ago in parallel with the class itself, and this old form needs some improvement. The class for groups with arbitrary inner elements was designed later, and it has better tuning form, so I still consider the idea of changing the old tuning forms (there are several for different classes) in line with more modern design. Regardless of the outdated style, the tuning form provides everything to change the group view to whatever the user wants.

Now we are back to the year's selection and to its implementation in the user-driven application. I, as a designer, provide the elements for the needed work. Everything else is under the user's control, and only the user decides about all the details and about the whole process of selection.

Let's try another example with an idea that is familiar to everyone. The next example allows you to deal with more elements, but it is for the user to decide about the exact number of them and about everything else at any moment.

File: `Form_PersonalData.cs`

Menu position: Applications ➤ Personal data

Throughout the years nearly everyone has dealt with applications that collect, show, and allow users to change personal data. The processed data can depend on the purpose of each program, but usually there are names, day of birth, contact details, and information about education and work. When you deal with such a program once over several years, the placement of the fields on the screen does not matter too much. Those fields can be positioned in such way that you spend a minimum time on the required actions, or the same fields can be placed in such a strange way that it would require much more time and would make you mad with this program, but at last your task of giving the information will be over. If you have to do it once in several years, the interface is not so important for you. With more or less effort you provide the needed data and can forget about this program for years or forever.

People from HR departments have to work with such programs nearly all the time, and for them the interface of such programs is a crucial thing. Different tasks may require them to deal with different parts of the stored data. If there is an instrument that allows the quick change of the screen view according to the current task and personal preferences of the user, then it is an extremely valuable instrument for such programs.

Figure A-7 shows all the available fields of `Form_PersonalData.cs`. I am going to discuss only the interface of this application, so it is not connected to any database, and no data is going to appear in the shown fields.

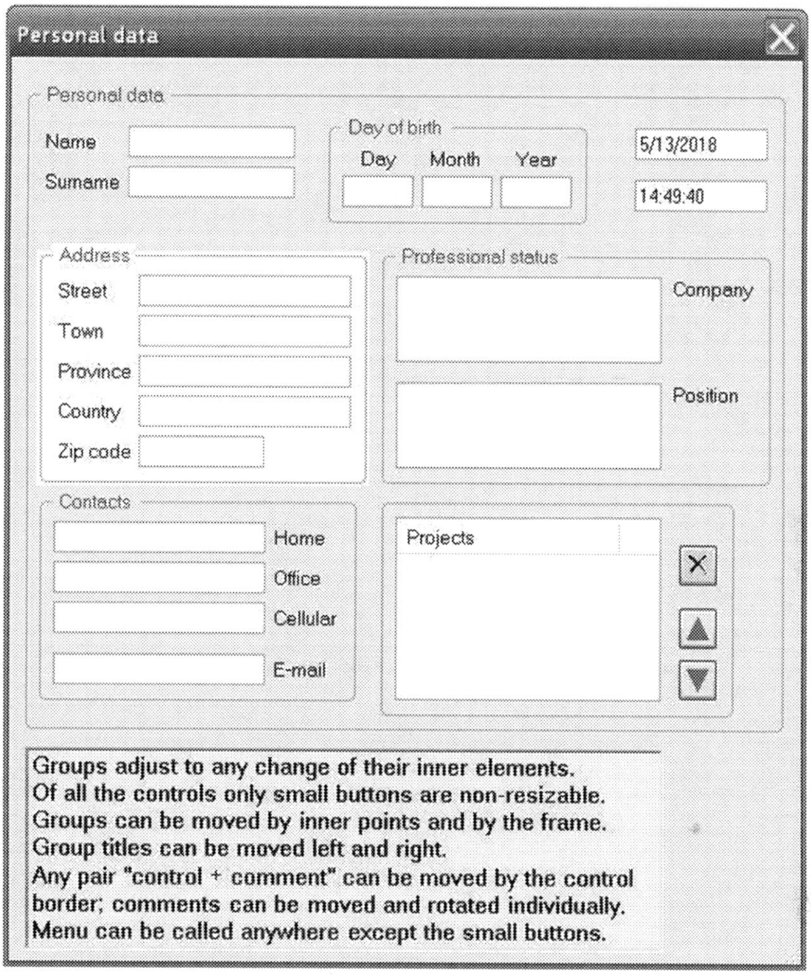

Figure A-7. *Nearly default view of Form_PersonalData.cs*

- Two controls in which the date and time are shown are turned into `SolitaryControl` objects.

```
void DefaultView_groupData (PointF ptLT)
{
    ... ...
    SolitaryControl scDate = new SolitaryControl (textDate);
    SolitaryControl scTime = new SolitaryControl (textTime);
    ... ...
```

483

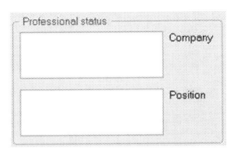

- Nearly each control has its own comment, and such a pair is turned into a CommentedControl object. The group "Professional status" consists of two such elements.

```
void DefaultView_groupProfStatus (PointF ptLT)
{
    ... ...
    CommentedControl ccCompany =
        new CommentedControl (this, textCompany,
                        Side .E, SideAlignment .Top, 6,
                        "Company", fnt);
    CommentedControl ccPosition = new CommentedControl (this,
                            textPosition,
                        Side .E, SideAlignment .Top, 6,
                        "Position", fnt);
    groupProfStatus = new ElasticGroup (this,
                    new CommentedControl [] { ccCompany,
                    ccPosition },
                            "Professional status", fnt);
    ... ...
```

- Group Projects has no title; it includes a big resizable control and three small nonresizable buttons. These buttons are auxiliary elements for the big text box, so it was an obvious thing to turn this set of elements into the DominantControl object.

```
void DefaultView_groupProjects (PointF ptLT)
{
    ... ...
    DominantControl domin = new DominantControl (new Control [] {
                    listProjects, btnDelete, btnMoveUp,
                    btnMoveDown });
    groupProjects = new ElasticGroup (this, domin, "");
    ... ...
```

- All groups belong to the ElasticGroup class, and this is a good
  example to demonstrate the nested groups of this class.

```
void DefaultView_groupData (PointF ptLT)
{
    ... ...
    groupData = new ElasticGroup (this, new ElasticGroupElement [] {
                    new ElasticGroupElement (textDate, Resizing .WE),
                    new ElasticGroupElement (textTime, Resizing .WE),
                    new ElasticGroupElement (ccName),
                    new ElasticGroupElement (ccSurname),
                    new ElasticGroupElement (groupDOB),
                    new ElasticGroupElement (groupAddress),
                    new ElasticGroupElement (groupContacts),
                    new ElasticGroupElement (groupProfStatus),
                    new ElasticGroupElement (groupProjects) },
                        "Personal data");
    ... ...
```

The power of user-driven applications is based on the simplicity of its rules and uniformity of their application. Let's check how these rules work in the current example.

Rule 1 All elements are movable.

All controls, comments, and groups are moved in a standard simple way that was already demonstrated. To move a comment, you press it and move. All controls, except three small buttons, are resizable. Special places along the control border (corners are the best) are used for resizing; the remaining parts of the control border are used for moving. Groups are moved by any inner point.

There are no restrictions on the movement or resizing, but no element is going to disappear as a result of squeezing. If some elements must be hidden, this is done through menu commands.

Rule 2 All parameters of visibility must be easily controlled
by users.

Parameters of all objects are regulated either through an auxiliary tuning form or through the commands of context menus. The ElasticGroup class was developed years ago together with its tuning form (Figure A-8). At that time, the substitution of ordinary controls by their graphical analogs was not among my priorities, so this tuning form uses a lot of controls. I still consider the ability to redesign this tuning form in the way similar to the tuning form of the Group_ArbitraryElements class (Figure 4-2).[3]

---

[3]It is not a problem at all to substitute this old tuning form with a new one, which would be nearly a copy of the tuning form for the Group_ArbitraryElements class (Figure 4-2). There are two reasons why I didn't do it up till now. The minor one is the consistency in dealing with the screen elements in all parts of the same program: if the group includes ordinary controls that you move and resize by the frames, then it is expected to do the tuning in the same way, so the tuning form must also use ordinary controls. Another reason is more important: the last time I used the ElasticGroup class in any design happened years ago. Is there any reason to work on the improvements of the class that I stopped using and have no plans to use anymore? Every time I look at this old tuning form (Figure A-8), my hands are ready to improve it in no time, but the next moment I remember a good old saying "to paint and throw away."

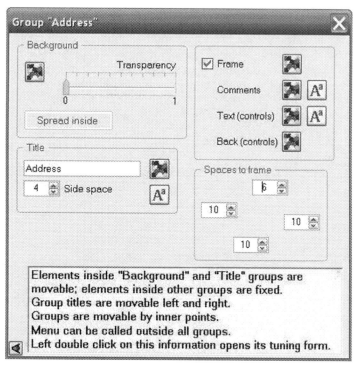

Figure A-8. *Tuning form for ElasticGroup objects*

Comments and all controls with and without comments are regulated via context menus. The general idea of organizing the whole system of menus is simple: you click an object you want to change and get a menu for this object. If there are subordinate elements, then the menu also includes commands for the synchronous change of all the subordinates. Thus, the user decides whether to organize an individual change of an element or a synchronous change for a set of elements. If the moving or resizing of an element does not improve the view, then back moving or resizing can be done in the same easy way. Because everything is easily regulated, the user is not afraid to try different things in order to get the best result. See Figure A-9.

Figure A-9a. *Menu for big group*

Figure A-9b. *Menu on control with comment*

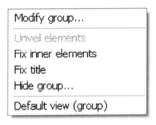

Figure A-9c. *Menu on comment*

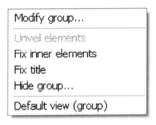

Figure A-9d. *Menu on inner groups*

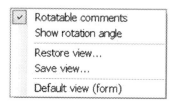

Figure A-9e. *Menu at empty places*

Through menu commands, not only are the visibility parameters regulated but also the movability of them are. This is useful for densely populated groups. For example, inner elements of the Address or Contacts group can be moved and resized until the group gets the needed view; then all inner elements can be fixed with a single command of the group menu (Figure A-9d). After that, there will be no accidental changes of inner elements. If later the user decides to change something inside the group, all elements are unfixed with a single command of the same menu. (For a menu with the fixed elements, there is a different command at the same place.)

Menus in the current example also include commands to hide and unveil elements. The logic of these commands copies the logic of movability commands: an element is hidden through its personal menu (Figure A-9b) but is unveiled through the menu of an upper level (Figure A-9d). There is no mechanism to unveil the hidden elements individually. It is possible to organize such a thing, but I decided that it would be too complicated for such a program, so all hidden elements of the inner group are unveiled simultaneously. See Figure A-10.

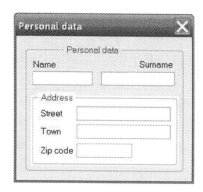

Figure A-10a. *Only the fields with information needed to send the Christmas cards are left in view*

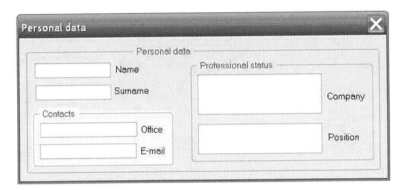

Figure A-10b. *All the fields to organize a professional meeting are left in view while everything unneeded is hidden*

The commands of two levels are used in the same way to hide and unveil inner elements of the big (main) group. Of all those elements, only two with the name and surname are always in view; all other elements can be hidden through the commands of their menus (Figures A-9b and A-9d). To return these hidden elements into view, you have to call the context menu for the big group (Figure A-9a). The same commands can be used to hide the elements of the big group.

In such way the hide/unveil regulation allows you to organize minor view changes (for example, hide the Country control inside the Address group if it is not required at all), but it also allows you to change the overall view of a program in such a way that for an unfamiliar person it is difficult to believe that this is the same application. Figure A-10a shows the view of the same program for the period when Christmas cards have to be sent, while Figure A-10b demonstrates the view that is more suitable for organizing some professional meeting. Preparation of the needed view takes only a couple of seconds; the default view can be reinstalled in an instant via a command of the context menu outside the big group (Figure A-9e). There is nothing common between two views in Figures A-10 and no resemblance of the general view in Figure A-7. Compare all three pictures and keep in mind that the number of variants is infinitive. As a developer of the "Personal data" program, I do not push anyone into using one or another predefined view; I prepare the default view and allow users to transform it in any possible way. The developer has to guarantee that the program is not going to crash throughout all the changes and that data is going to appear in the appropriate fields regardless of their transformations.

Rule 3 Users' commands on moving and resizing of objects or on changing the parameters of visualization must be implemented exactly as they are; no additions or expanded interpretation by developer are allowed.

Applications designed in a standard way are ruled by the developer, so the developer decides what is good and what is not. It is a standard and widely used practice that in such applications a user's commands are corrected by the developer according to his opinion about a good-looking application. In user-driven applications, such a correction is forbidden. It is easy to demonstrate the situations in which the need of some correction is obvious, but do not try to do it behind the curtain. Simply give the user an easy way to make such a correction.

Consider a case of the Contacts group; its default view is shown in Figure A-11a. The default font has the size 8. From my point of view, this is a good-looking group (otherwise I would have designed it differently), but for many users the font size can be too small.

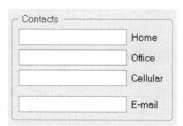

Figure A-11a. *Group default view with the font size 8*

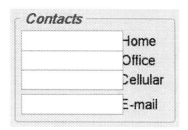

Figure A-11b. *For all elements, the font size is increased to 12*

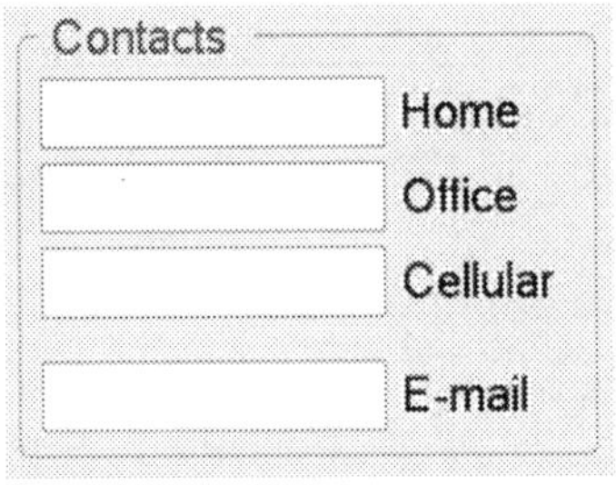

Figure A-11c. *After using the "Default view" command from the Group menu*

Through the menu on the group (Figure A-9d), the user opens its tuning form (Figure A-8) and sets the font to 12 for all the controls, comments, and title. Now the font size is much better for user's work, but the view of the group is not (Figure A-11b). The controls are either too close to each other or even overlap. These are ordinary TextBox controls, so when their font is changed, somebody behind the scenes changes their size. This is the reality of using ordinary controls. Each comment belongs to the CommentToRect class, so it is positioned by its central point; when the comment font is enlarged, the comment simply spreads from its central point on all four sides, and now it is partly blocked by the associated control. (We already discussed that the mover interferes in comment positioning only if the comment is entirely blocked by its associated control. If a comment is blocked only partly, there is no interference.)

It is easy enough to move controls and comments in such a way that they will not overlap and there will be spaces between the elements. A chain of individual movements is one way to change the group view; another is to open the group menu (Figure A-9d) and to use its "Default view (group)" command. This command reinstalls the default view but uses the current set of fonts (Figure A-11c).

The only situation when the developer can (and in this case must) interfere and add something on its own part is the case when the comment disappears under its associated control. For the CommentedControl class, this is already done in the class itself. When you design your own classes that combine an ordinary control with some graphical part, you have to think about such possibilities; these are the only situations when the developer is allowed to add something to the user's action. There is a clear interpretation of the mentioned rule: the developer is not allowed to add anything to improve the view, but he is allowed (and in such case he must interfere) when the user's action accidentally makes some object inaccessible. (Pay attention that the word *accidentally* is important in the previous sentence.)

I would not call Form_PersonalData.cs too complicated because I often work on much more sophisticated applications. The design of the current example is relatively simple; it is based on solitary controls, on controls with comments, and on several groups of such elements. The tuning form for such groups (Figure A-8) allows you to estimate the number of tunable parameters for each group, so the total number of visibility parameters that can be changed in the current example exceeds 100. Plus, there are changeable sizes and positions of all the elements; also, there are parameters to regulate appearance/disappearance of nearly all the elements. Do not forget about the movability regulation. The movability of each object can be regulated individually, but I do not think that this is a correct decision.[4] I think that the movability of all elements inside the group must be the same, so they are either all movable or all fixed; only the movability of the group title is done independently. The same idea of equal movability is realized at the level of the example.

I heard from time to time an objection that the regulation of so many parameters is a huge burden for users, and they do not need it. This is a wrong view on the *possibility of regulation*. The change of all parameters is not mandatory but available. We have the same situation in our houses. We have thousands of items in our houses, and we can move any item at any moment, but we are not doing it all the time. I never heard from anyone a complaint of such type that the possibility of moving at any moment any item in his house was a huge burden for the house owner. Yet, the possibility exists, and we use it whenever we need. Exactly the same thing happens with the change of parameters in user-driven applications: the possibility always exists, but we use it only whenever we want.

Rule 4 All parameters must be saved and restored.

When all parameters in an application are changeable, then there must be an easy way to save all those changes to not lose the results. The current view is saved in the Registry and will be automatically restored at the next call of the same example. There is nothing new in this process; this was done in all the previous examples. The new feature in the current example is the saving and restoration through the files. Two commands from the menu at empty places (Figure A-9e) are used to save the current view and to restore any view that was saved earlier.

---

[4]Similar example in the program for my other book [2] allows an individual regulation of movability for each object. You can compare two examples and make your own decision about the need of such individual regulation of movability.

Rule 5 The previously mentioned rules must be implemented
at all the levels beginning from the main form up to the farthest
corners.

The current example perfectly illustrates this rule. There are two auxiliary forms
that are used to save the view of the current example in a file and to restore it from a file.
Everything in these forms is movable, resizable, and tunable. On closing each form, its
current view is saved; so on the next occasion, the form appears in exactly the same view
that the user prefers.

APPENDIX B

Resources

Bibliography

1. Edsger W. Dijkstra, *A Case against the GO TO Statement,* published as *Go-to statement considered harmful* in Communications of ACM 11, 1968, 3: 147–148

2. S. Andreyev, *World of Movable Objects*, MoveableGraphics project, SourceForge, 2016; `https://sourceforge.net/projects/movegraph/files/`

3. S. Andreyev, *Illustration for Geometric Optics*, MoveableGraphics project, SourceForge, 2019; `https://sourceforge.net/projects/movegraph/files/`

4. C. Perrault, *Cendrillon*, 1697

5. T.S. Kuhn, *The Structure of Scientific Revolutions.* University of Chicago Press, 1970

6. Eleanor H. Porter, *Pollyanna*, L.C. Page, 1913

Programs and Documents

All files are available at `www.sourceforge.net` in the project MoveableGraphics (note that the names of projects are case sensitive). Files are renewed from time to time. As some people strongly oppose using the DOC format, all documents are presented in both the DOC and PDF formats. To run any accompanying application, the `MoveGraphLibrary.dll` file is needed; this file is available by itself but is also included in each project.

© Sergey Andreyev 2020
S. Andreyev, *User-Driven Applications for Research and Science*, https://doi.org/10.1007/978-1-4842-6488-1

`UserDrivenApplications.zip`	This file contains the book *User-Driven Applications* and the entire project of the accompanying program (all code is C#). The algorithm of movability is first shown with examples of simple but widely used screen elements, then complex objects are discussed, and finally real applications are demonstrated.
`ExercisesOnMovability.zip`	This collection of exercises is developed as an addition to the book *User-Driven Applications*.
`GeometricOptics.zip`	This is an application for a geometric optics course. The file contains the whole project (all code is C#) and a description of *Illustration for Geometric Optics*. This small book consists of two parts with an identical order of explanation but with different purposes. The first part contains a normal explanation of the demonstrated examples from the point of view of geometric optics. The second part looks at the application at the programming level.
`MoveGraphLibrary_Classes.zip`	This contains the description of the classes included in `MoveGraphLibrary.dll`.
`MoveGraphLibrary.dll`	This is the library.
`WorldOfMoveableObjects.zip`	This file contains the book *World of Movable Objects* (in DOC format) and the accompanying program (all code is C#). This is the biggest book of this collection. It contains the most detailed explanation and includes many examples that were designed throughout the years of algorithm improvement. This book was not changed at all in the past years. The project is compiled with the latest version of my library, but its innumerous examples were not checked with this library version. I hope that they continue to work.

	Several scientific examples need some additional files that are placed in two subdirectories.
	For the "Data refinement" example, there are three BIN files in ...\DataFiles_for_DataRefinement.
	For the "Simple data viewer of TXT files," there is one TXT file in ...\DataFiles_for_SimpleViewers.
	For the "Simple data viewer of BIN files," there is one BIN file in the same directory.
World_Of_Movable_Objects.pdf	This file contains the book *World of Movable Objects* in PDF format.
OrderOfFormsInBook_Figures.zip	This files contains 17 pages (DOC and PDF variants) of small figures giving an overview of those examples (forms) from the accompanying program that are discussed in the book *World of Movable Objects*. The figures are shown in the same order as they appear in the book.

All these books and programs were prepared in the past ten or so years. Some important examples were changed and improved (I hope) throughout this period, and I think that the best versions appear in the book *User-Driven Applications*. Some versions in the older books were replaced by the new ones; others demonstrate different versions of the same examples.

Occasionally I decide to make some changes at the basic level, and then the previous versions of some forms cannot be restored from the Registry. I try my best to check the new library versions against the older ones saved in the Registry, but it might happen that something was missed throughout such checking, in which case you will need to delete the old key in the Registry.

Index of Forms Used in the Accompanying Application

Form_About

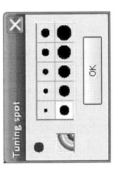

p. 31: Form_Tuning_Spot

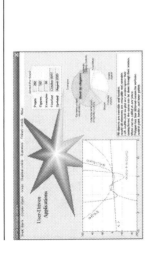

p. XXIV: Form_Main

p. 33: Form_Spot_OnLineAndCircle

p. 24: Form_Spot

p. 40: Form_ElementOnTrack

p. 42: Form_Line_Segment

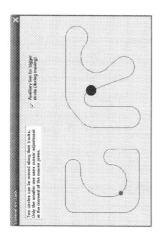

p. 51: Form_Polyline

p. 51: Form_Tuning_Line

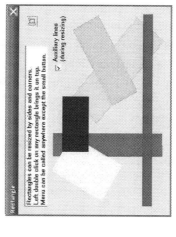

p. 55: Form_Rectangle

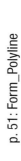

p. 82: Form_Comment

499

p. 89: Form_Ring

p. 107: Form_Polygon_Elastic

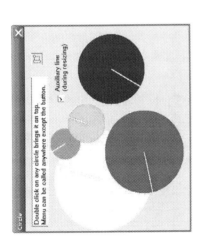

p. 83: Form_Circle

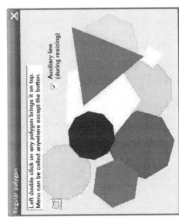

p. 102: Form_Polygon_Regular

Form_AnchorPointSelection

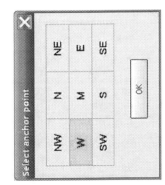

p. 93: Form_Strip

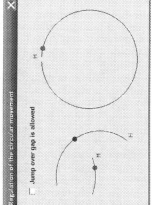

p. 131: Form-Spot_OnArc

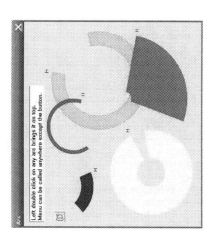

p. 124: Form_Arc

p. 160: Form_Scrolling

p. 149: Form_Rectangle_withComments

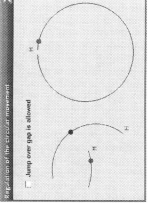

p. 121: Form_NewElasticPolygon

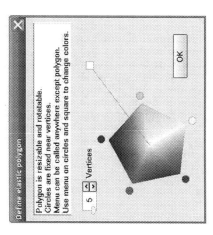

p. 138: Form_FillHoles

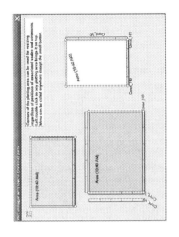

p. 180: Form_PlotAnalogue_Advanced

p. 214: Form_Label

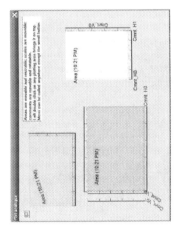

p. 169: Form_PlotAnalogue

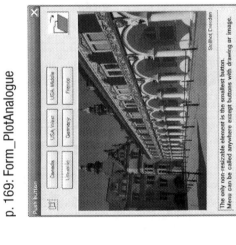

p. 201: Form_Button

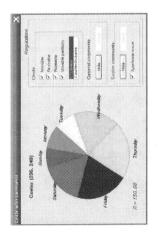

p. 163: Form_Circle_withComments

p. 190: Form_Group_ArbitraryElements

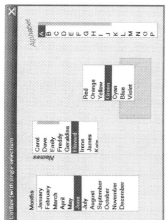

p. 226: Form_ListBox

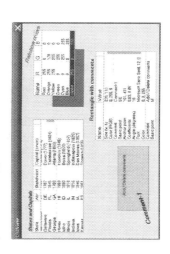

p. 249: Form_ListView

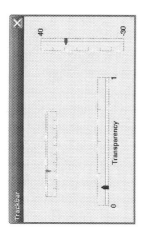

p. 222: Form_Trackbar

p. 243: Form_CheckBox

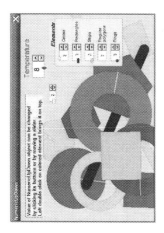

p. 216: Form_NumericUpDown

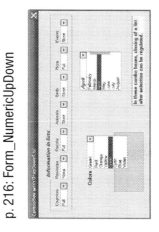

p. 231: Form_ComboBox

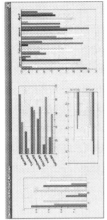

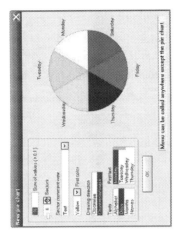

p. 277: Form_BarChart

p. 302: Form_NewPieChart

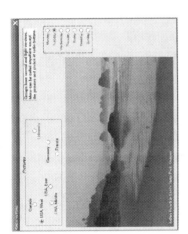

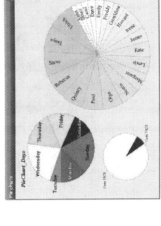

p. 268: Form_RadioButtons

p. 295: Form_PieChart

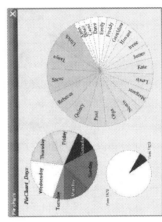

p. 263: Form_RadioBtnsLight

p. 294: Form_NewBarChart

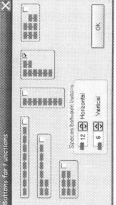

p. 313: Form_BtnPlaces_Functions

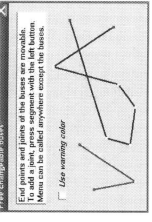

p. 333: Form_FreeBuses_AddingJoints

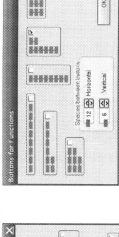

p. 313: Form_BtnPlaces_Numbers

p. 328: Form_FreeBuses

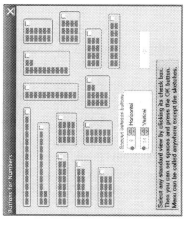

p. 305: Form_Calculator

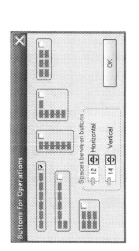

p. 313: Form_BtnPlaces_Operations

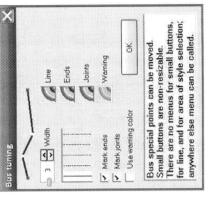

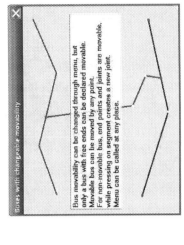

p. 344: Form_Tuning_Bus

p. 365: Form_ConnectedBuses_ChangingMovability

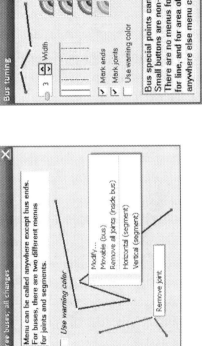

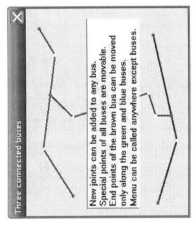

p. 342: Form_FreeBuses_AllChanges

p. 361: Form_ConnectedBuses_Three

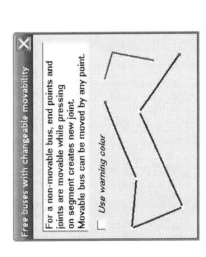

p. 337: Form_FreeBuses_ChangingMovability

p. 349: Form_ConnectedBuses_Two

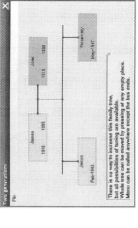

p. 373: Form_Tuning_Person

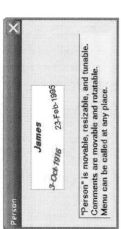

p. 371: Form_Person

p. 381: Form_Spouses

p. 385: Form_TwoGenerations

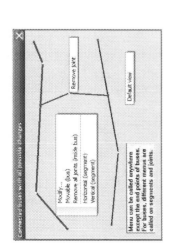

p. 367: Form_ConnectedBuses_AllChanges

p. 375: Form_PersonPlusBus

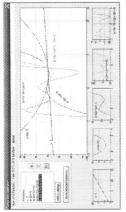

p. 434: Form_FunctionViewer

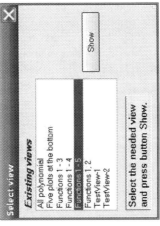

Form_Functions_SelectView

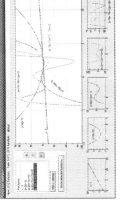

p. 417: Form_FamilyTree_NewElemParams

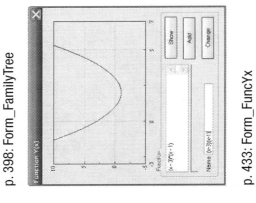

p. 437: Form_FuncXrYr

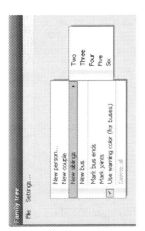

p. 398: Form_FamilyTree

p. 433: Form_FuncYx

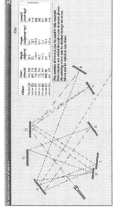

p. 441: Form_Mirror_Flat_Any

p. 456: Form_Prism_RegularPolygon

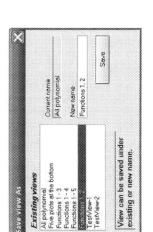

Form_Functions_SaveViewAs

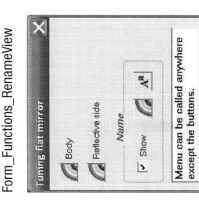

p. 447: Form_Aquarium

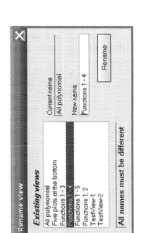

Form_Functions_RenameView

Form_Tuning_Mirror_Simple

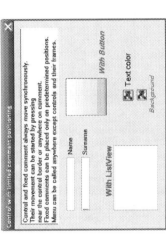

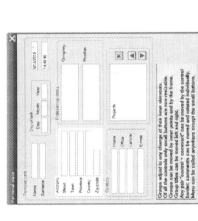

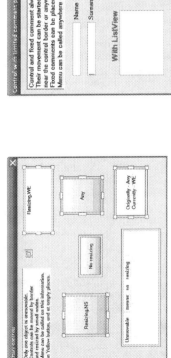

p. 472: Form_Control_FreeComment

p. 469: Form_Control_FixedComment

p. 481: Form_PersonalData

p. 460: Form_Control_Solitary

p. 477: Form_YearsSelection

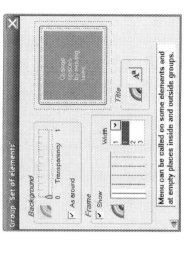

For Group_ArbitraryElements

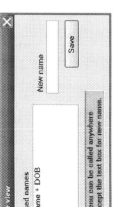

Form_PersonalData_RestoreView

Tuning Forms Provided by the Library

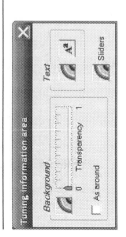

For CheckBox_GR

Form_PersonalData_SaveView

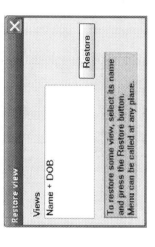

For Info_Resizable

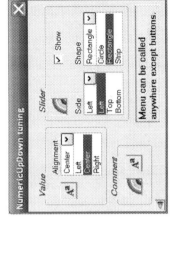

For NumericUpDown_GR

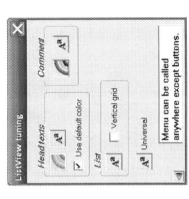

For ListView_GR

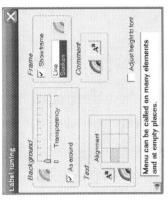

For Label_GR

For ComboBox_DDList

For Button_Text

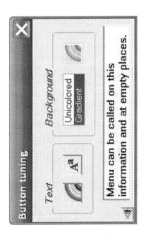

For Trackbar_GR

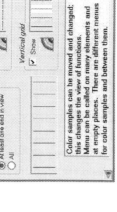

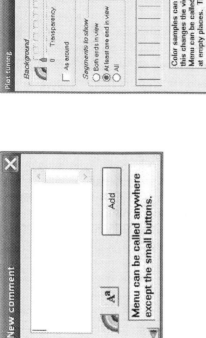

For Plot_Adh

To add or modify comments

For Scale_Texts

For horizontal Scale_Numbers

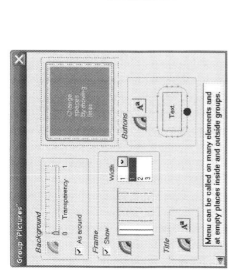

For Group_RadioButtons

For vertical Scale_Numbers

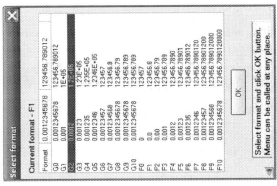

For format selection

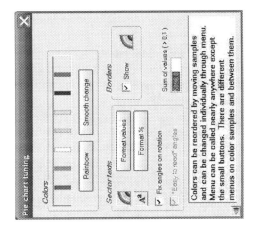

For PieChart_Adh

For BarChart_Adh

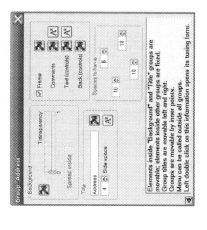

For ElasticGroup

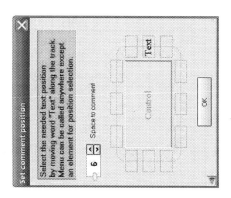

For CommentedControlLTP
and Control_FixedComment

Index

A

AddBus() method, 397
AddConnection() method, 397
AddPerson() method, 397
AdjustCursorPosition()
    method, 59, 60, 261, 262
AnotherEndOfNewBus() method, 405
Arc class
    angles, 124, 127, 128, 131
    border, 125
    cover, 134
    cover variants, 125, 126
    design ideas, 123
    features, 123
    head, 124
    InsideArea, 136
    jump, 136
    MoveNode() method, 136, 137
    NearestPointOnTrail() method, 130
    nodes, 129
    objects, 124
    Press() method, 135
    radius, 129
    rCursor, 129
    Ring_Adh class, 125
    SetTriangles () method, 135
    special areas, 132
    Spot_OnArc class, 131, 133
    spot position, 132
    squeeze, 125
    tail, 124
    tracks, 132
Auxi_Drawing.ShowImage() method, 212
Auxi_Geometry.ClosedPolyline()
    method, 374
Auxi_Geometry.Polyline_NearestPoint()
    method, 352
Auxiliary form, 412, 418, 426–428

B

Bar chart
    Add bar chart, 293
    auxiliary tuning forms, 279
    BarChart_Adh class, 277
    bar colors, 286
    Changeable bars, 290
    check boxes, 284
    colored bars, 277
    definition, 278
    elements, 279
    flip, 289
    flip drawing direction, 291
    flip scale command, 289
    font for temporary information, 293
    group Lines, 282
    group Values, 282
    horizontal Scale_Numbers object, 283
    inner values, 283
    main area, 285, 286

© Sergey Andreyev 2020
S. Andreyev, *User-Driven Applications for Research and Science*, https://doi.org/10.1007/978-1-4842-6488-1

R

Printed in the United States
By Bookmasters